ISBN 978-0-266-65712-5
PIBN 10031851

FB &c Ltd, Dalton House, 60 Windsor Avenue, London, SW19 2RR.
Company number 08720141. Registered in England and Wales.

For support please visit www.forgottenbooks.com

THE

HISTORY OF CIVILIZATION,

FROM THE FALL OF THE ROMAN EMPIRE
TO THE FRENCH REVOLUTION.

BY F. GUIZOT,

AUTHOR OF "HISTORY OF THE ENGLISH REVOLUTION OF 1640."

TRANSLATED BY WILLIAM HAZLITT, ESQ.
Of the Middle Temple, Barrister at-Law.

IN THREE VOLUMES.

VOL. II.

LONDON:
H. G. BOHN, YORK STREET, COVENT GARDEN.
MDCCCLVI.

LONDON:
SAVILL AND EDWARDS, PRINTERS, CHANDOS STREET,
COVENT GARDEN.

CONTENTS.

ELEVENTH LECTURE.

TWELFTH LECTURE.

THIRTEENTH LECTURE.

SEVENTEENTH LECTURE.

EIGHTEENTH LECTURE.

NINETEENTH LECTURE.

TWENTIETH LECTURE.

TWENTY-FIRST LECTURE.

TWENTY-SECOND LECTURE.

TWENTY-THIRD LECTURE.

TWENTY-FOURTH LECTURE.

TWENTY-FIFTH LECTURE.

TWENTY-SIXTH LECTURE.

TWENTY-SEVENTH LECTURE.

TWENTY-EIGHTH LECTURE.

TWENTY-NINTH LECTURE.

THIRTIETH LECTURE.

ILLUSTRATIONS AND HISTORICAL TABLES.

HISTORY

OF

CIVILIZATION IN FRANCE

From the Fall of the Roman Empire.

ELEVENTH LECTURE.

Perpetuity of the Roman law after the fall of the Empire—Of *the History of the Roman Law in the Middle Ages*, by M. de Savigny—Merits and deficiencies of this work—1. Roman law among the Visigoths—*Breviarium Aniani*, collected by command of Alaric—History and contents of this collection—2. Roman law among the Burgundians—*Papiani Responsorum*—History and contents of this law—3. Roman law among the Franks—No new collection—The perpetuity of Roman law proved by various facts—Recapitulation.

You are now acquainted with the state of German and Roman society before the invasion. You know the general result of their first approximation, that is to say, the state of Gaul immediately after the invasion. We have just studied the barbaric laws; that is, the first labour of the German nations to adapt their ancient customs to their new situation. Let us now study Roman legislation at the same epoch, that is to say, that portion of the Roman law and institutions which survived the invasion and continued to rule the Gallic Romans. This is the subject of a German work, for some years past celebrated in the learned world, *The History of the Roman Law in the Middle Ages*, by M. de Savigny. The design of the author is more extended than ours, because he retraces the history of the Roman law, not only in France, but throughout Europe. He has also treated of what concerns

France with more detail than I have been able to give to it here; and, before beginning the subject, I must request your attention a moment while I speak of his work.

The perpetuity of the Roman law, from the fall of the Empire, until the regeneration of sciences and letters, is its fundamental idea. The contrary opinion was long and generally spread; it was believed that Roman law had fallen with the Empire, to be resuscitated in the twelfth century by the discovery of a manuscript of the Pandects, found at Amalfi. This is the error that M. de Savigny has wished to dissipate. His first two volumes are wholly taken up by researches into the traces of the Roman law from the fifth to the twelfth century, and in proving, by recovering its history, that it had never ceased to exist.

The demonstration is convincing, and the end fully attained. Still, the work, considered as a whole, and as an historical production, leaves room for some observations.

Every epoch, every historical matter, if I may so speak, may be considered under three different points of view, and imposes a triple task upon the historian. He can, nay, he should first seek the facts themselves; collect and bring to light, without any aim than that of exactitude, all that has happened. The facts once recovered, it is necessary to know the laws that have governed them; how they were connected; what causes have brought about those incidents which are the life of society, and propel it, by certain ways, towards certain ends.

I wish to mark with clearness and precision the difference of the two studies. Facts, properly so called, external and visible events, are the body of history; the members, bones, muscles, organs, and material elements of the past; their knowledge and description form what may be called historical anatomy. But for society, as for the individual, anatomy is not the only science. Not only do facts subsist, but they are connected with one another; they succeed each other, and are engendered by the action of certain forces, which act under the empire of certain laws. There is, in a word, an organization and a life of societies, as well as of the individual. This organization has also its science, the science of the secret laws which preside over the course of events. This is the physiology of history.

Neither historical physiology nor anatomy are complete and veritable history. You have enumerated the facts, you have followed the internal and general laws which produced them. Do you also know their external and living physiognomy? Have you them before your eyes under individual and animate features? This is absolutely necessary, because these facts, now dead, have lived—the past has been the present; and unless it again become so to you, if the dead are not resuscitated, you know them not; you do not know history. Could the anatomist and physiologist surmise man if they had never seen him living?

The research into facts, the study of their organization, the reproduction of their form and motion, these are history such as truth would have it. We may accept but one or other of these tasks; we may consider the past under such or such a point of view, and propose such or such a design; we may prefer the criticism of facts, or the study of their laws, or the reproduction of the spectacle. These labours may be excellent and honourable; but it must never be forgotten that they are partial and incomplete; that this is not history—that history has a triple problem to resolve; that every great historical work, in order to be placed in its true position, should be considered and judged of under a triple relation.

Under the first, as a research of, and criticism upon, historical material elements, *The History of the Roman Law in the Middle Ages,* is a very remarkable book. Not only has M. de Savigny discovered or re-established many unknown or forgotten facts, but (what is much more rare and difficult) he has assigned to them their true relation. When I say their relation, I do not yet speak of the links which unite them in their development, but merely of their disposition, of the place which they occupy in regard to one another, and of their relative importance. Nothing is so common in history, even with the most exact knowledge of facts, as to assign to them a place other than that which they really occupied, of attributing to them an importance which they did not possess. M. de Savigny has not struck on this rock; his enumeration of facts is learned and equal; and he distributes and compares them with like knowledge and discernment; I repeat, that, in all that belongs to the anatomical study of that portion of the past which forms the subject of his work, he has left scarcely anything to be desired.

As a philosophical history, as a study of the general and progressive organization of facts, I cannot say so much for it. It does not appear to me that M. de Savigny has proposed this task to himself, or that he has even thought of it. Not only has he omitted all attempt to place the particular history upon which he occupied himself in relation with the general history of civilization and of human nature, but even within his own subject, he has troubled himself but little with any systematic concatenation of facts; he has not in the least considered them as causes and effects, in their relation of generation. They present themselves in his work, totally isolated, and having between them no other relation than that of dates, a relation which is no true link, and which gives to facts neither meaning nor value.

Nor do we meet, in any greater degree, with poetical truth; facts do not appear to M. de Savigny under their living physiognomy. It is true, upon such a subject, he had neither characters nor scenes to reproduce; his personages are texts, and his events publications or abrogations of laws. Still these texts and legislative reforms belonged to a society which had its manners and its life; they are associated with events more suited to strike the imagination—to invasions, foundations of states, &c. There is among these a certain dramatic aspect to seize; in this M. de Savigny has failed; his dissertations are not marked with the hue of the spectacle with which they are connected; he does not reproduce the external and individual traits of history any more than its internal and general laws.

And do not suppose that in this there is no other evil than that of a deficiency, and that this absence of philosophical and poetical truth is without influence upon the criticism of the material elements of history. More than once M. de Savigny, from not properly taking hold of the laws and physiognomy of facts, has been led into error regarding the facts themselves; he has not deceived himself as to texts and dates; he has not omitted or incorrectly reported such or such an event; he has committed a species of error for which the English have a word which is wanting in our tongue, *misrepresentation*, that is to say, he has spread a false hue over facts, arising, not from any inaccuracy in particular details, but from want of verity in the aspect of the whole, in the manner in which the mirror reflects the picture. In treating, for example, of the social state of the Germans before the invasion, M. de Savigny speaks in detail of the free men, of their situation and their share in the national institutions;[1] his knowledge of historical documents is extensive and correct, and the facts alleged by him are true; but he has not rightly considered the mobility of situations among the barbarians, nor the secret contest between those two societies, the tribe and the warlike band, which coexisted among the Germans, nor the influence of the latter in altering the individual equality and independence which served as the foundation of the former, nor the vicissitudes and successive transformations to which the condition of the free men was subjected by this influence. Hence arises, in my opinion, a general mistake in the painting of this condition; he has made it too fine, too fixed, and too powerful; he has not, in the least, represented its weakness and approaching fall.

The same fault is seen, although in a less degree, in his history of the Roman law itself, from the fifth to the twelfth century; it is complete and correct, as far as the collection of facts goes; but the facts are all placed there, so to speak, upon the same level; one is not present at their successive modifications, one does not perceive the Roman law transform itself in proportion as the new society is developed. No moral concatenation connects these so learnedly and ingeniously re-established facts. Anatomical dissection, in a word, is the dominant character of the work; internal organization and external life, are alike wanting to it.

Reduced to its true nature, as a criticism of material facts, M. de Savigny's book is original and excellent; it ought to serve as the basis of all studies whose subject is this epoch, because it places beyond all doubt the perpetuity of Roman law from the fifth to the twelfth century, and thus fully resolves the problem which the author proposed to himself.

Now that it is resolved, one is surprised that this problem should ever have been raised, and that the permanence of the Roman law, after the fall of the Empire, should ever have

[1] T. i. pp. 160—195.

been doubted. Not only do the barbaric laws everywhere make mention of the Roman laws, but there is scarcely a single document or act of this epoch which does not, directly or indirectly, attest their daily application. Perhaps the error which M. de Savigny has contested, has not been so general nor so absolute as he appears to suppose, and as it is commonly said to be. It was the *Pandects* which reappeared in the twelfth century; and when people have celebrated the resurrection of the Roman law at this period, it is above all of the legislation of Justinian that they have spoken. On regarding more closely, one will perceive, I think, that the perpetuity of other portions of the Roman law in the west, the Theodosian code, for example, and of all the collections of which it served for the basis, has not been so entirely departed from, as the work of M. de Savigny would give us to believe. But it matters little; more or less extended, the error upon this subject was real, and M. de Savigny, in dissipating it, has given a prodigious progress to knowledge.

I shall now place before you the principal results of his work, but I shall do so in an order contrary to that which we have followed in studying the German laws. We commenced with the most barbarous, in order to finish with those in which the Roman spirit had penetrated the deepest. We shall now, on the contrary, first study the countries where the Roman law preserved the greatest empire, in order to follow it in the various degrees of its diminution of strength.

It follows that the kingdom of the Visigoths is the first upon which we have to occupy ourselves. It was, you will recal to mind, from the year 466 to 484 that king Euric, who resided at Toulouse, for the first time caused the customs of the Goths to be written. In 506, his successor, Alaric II., caused the laws of his Roman subjects to be collected and published under a new form. We read, at the beginning of some of the manuscripts of this collection, the following preface:—

"In this volume are contained the laws or decisions of equity, selected from the Theodosian code and other books, and explained as has been ordered, the lord king Alaric being in the twenty-second year of his reign, the illustrious count Goiaric presiding at this work. Copy of the decree:—Letter of advice to Timothy, Viscount. With the aid of God, occupied with the interests of our people, we have corrected, after mature deliberation, all that seemed iniquitous in the laws, in such manner that, by the labour of the priests and other noblemen, all obscurity in the Roman and in our own ancient laws is dissipated, and a greater clearness is spread over it, to the end that nothing may remain ambiguous, and offer a subject for lengthened controversies for pleaders. All these laws, then, being explained and re-united in a single book by the choice of wise men, the assent of venerable bishops and of our provincial subjects, elected with this view, has confirmed the said collection, to which is appended a clear interpretation. Our Clemency, then, has ordered the subscribed book to be entrusted to count Goiaric, for the decision of affairs, to the end that hereafter all processes may be terminated according to its dispositions, and that it be not allowed to any person to put forward any law or rule of equity, unless contained in the present book, subscribed as we have ordered, by the hand of the honourable man Anianus. It is, therefore, expedient that thou take heed that, in thy jurisdiction, no other law or form be alleged or admitted; if perchance such a thing should happen, it shall be at the peril of thy head or at the expense of thy fortune. We order that this prescript be joined to the book that we send thee, to the end that the rule of our will and the fear of the penalty may restrain all our subjects.

" 'I, Anianus, honourable man, according to the order of the very glorious king Alaric, have subscribed and published this volume of Theodosian laws, decisions of equity, and other books, collected at Aire, the twenty-second year of his reign. We have collated them.

" 'Given the fourth day of the nones of February, the twenty-second year of the reign of king Alaric, at Toulouse.' "

This preface contains all we know concerning the history of the digestion of this code. I have a few explanations to add to it. Goiaric was the count of the palace, charged with the superintendence of its execution throughout the kingdom; Anianus, in quality of referendary, was to subscribe the various copies of it, and send them to the provincial counts; Timothy is one of these counts. The greater part of the manuscripts being but copies made for private purposes, give neither the preface nor any letter. The collection of Alaric contains: 1st, the Theodosian code (sixteen books); 2nd, the books of civil law of the emperor Theodosius, Valentinian, Marcian, Majorian, and Severus; 3rd, the Institutes of Gaïus, the jurisconsult; 4th, five books of Paul, the jurisconsult, entitled *Receptæ Sententiæ;* 5th, the Gregorian code (thirteen titles); 6th, the Hermoginian code (2 titles); 7th, and lastly, a passage from the work of Papinian, entitled *Liber Responsorum.*

The Constitutions and Novels of the emperors are called *Leges ;* the works of the jurisconsults, including the Gregorian and Hermoginian codes, which did not emanate from any official or public power, bear simply the name of *Jus.* This is the distinction between law and jurisprudence.

The whole collection was called *Lex Romana,* and not *Breviarium ;* the latter name was unknown before the sixteenth century.[1] Of the *Breviarium Alaricianum,* there is but one separate edition, published in 1528, at Basle, by Sichard. It has besides this been inserted, sometimes partially and sometimes entire, in the various editions of the Theodosian code.

It is divided into two essential parts: 1st, a text or abstract of the sources of the law which I have just enumerated; 2nd, an interpretation. The *Institutes* of Gaïus is the only work in which the interpretation and the text are fused in one.

The text is merely the reproduction of the original text, it is not always complete; all the imperial constitutions, for example, are not inserted in the *Breviarium ;* but those which it did reproduce are not mutilated. There the ancient law appears in all its purity, independent of the changes which the fall of the Empire must have introduced into it. The *Interpretation,* on the contrary, digested in the time of Alaric by civil or ecclesiastical jurisconsults, whom he had charged with this work, takes cognizance of all these changes; it explains, modifies, and sometimes positively alters the text,

[1] In the preceding lecture it is said that Alaric caused the laws of his Roman subjects to be collected and published under the name of *Breviarium.* This is an oversight.

in order to adapt it to the new state of the government and of society; it is, therefore, for the study of the institutions and Roman laws of this epoch, more important and curious than the text itself. The mere existence of such a work is the most clear and conclusive proof of the perpetuity of Roman law. One need, indeed, scarcely open it. Should we open it, however, we shall everywhere find the trace of the Roman society, of its institutions and magistrates, as well as of its civil legislation. The municipal system occupies an important place in the *Interpretation* of the Breviarium; the curia and its magistrates, the *duumvirs*, the *defensores*, &c., recur at every step, and attest that the Roman municipality still subsisted and acted. And not only did it subsist, but it acquired more importance and independence. At the fall of the Empire, the governors of the Roman provinces, the *præsides*, the *consulares*, the *correctores*, disappeared; in their place we find the barbarian *counts*. But all the attributes of the Roman governors did not pass to the counts; they made a kind of partition of them; some belonged to the counts; and these, in general, were those in which the central power was interested, such as the levying of taxes, men, &c.; the others, those which only concerned the private life of the citizens, passed to the curiæ and the municipal magistrates. I have not cared to enumerate all these changes; but here are some examples drawn from the *Interpretation*.

1st. That which was formerly done by the prætor (*alibi* the president) shall now be executed by the judges of the city.—Interp. Paul, 1, 7, § 2; Int. C. Th. xi. 4, 2.

2nd. Emancipation, which has usually been done before the president, must now be done before the curia.—Gaïus, 1, 6.

3rd. Guardians were nominated at Constantinople by the prefect of the town, ten senators, and the prætor. The *Interpretation* puts in their place "the first of the city with the judge" (probably the duumvir).—Int. C. Th. iii. 17, 3.

4th. Wills must be opened in the curia.—Interp. C. Th. iv. 4, 4.

Cases of this kind are numerous, and do not allow of a doubt, but that, so far from perishing with the Empire, the municipal system acquired after the invasion, at least in Southern Gaul, more extension and liberty.

A second considerable change is also visible. In the ancient Roman municipality, the superior magistrates, the *duumvir*, the quinquennalis, &c., exercised their jurisdiction as a personal right, not by any means by way of delegation, or in quality of representatives of the curia; it was to themselves, not to the municipal body, that the power appertained. The principle of the municipal system was more aristocratical than democratical. Such was the result of the ancient Roman manners, and especially of the primitive amalgamation of the religious and political powers in the superior magistrates.

In the *Breviarium* the aspect of the municipal system changes; it was no longer in its own name, it was in the name and as the delegate of the curiæ that the defensor exercised his power. The jurisdiction belonged to the curia in a body. The principle of its organization became democratical; and already the transformation was in preparation, which was to make of the Roman municipality the corporation of the middle ages.

These are the principal results of M. de Savigny's work, with regard to the permanence of Roman law under the Visigoths. I hardly know whether he has measured its whole extent and all its consequences in the history of modern society, but he has certainly caught glimpses of it; and in general his ideas are as precise as his learning is correct and extensive. Of all German savans who have occupied themselves on this subject, he is certainly the most exempt from all German prejudices, who least allows himself to be carried away by the desire to enlarge upon the power of the ancient German institutions and manners in modern civilization, and who makes the Roman element constitute the better part. Sometimes, however, the prepossession of the national spirit, if I may so express myself, has still deceived him, and of this I will cite a single example. He says at the end of the chapter upon the municipal system under the Visigoths:—

"The text of the *Code* orders that at Rome, in order to pronounce upon a criminal accusation against a senator, five senators be appointed by lot: the *Interpretation* renders this rule general, and requires five of the principal citizens, *of the same rank as the accused*, that is to say, *decurions* or *plebeians*, *according to the condition of the accused himself* .... May we not here conjecture the influence of the German *Scabini?*"[1]

Thus M. de Savigny supposes that, according to the *Interpretation* of the *Breviarium*, the judges drawn by lot, in criminal matters, were, under the Visigoths in the sixth century, to be of the same condition as the accused, that every man was to be judged by his peers; for it is thus that they commonly digest the principle of the institution of the jury, according to German manners. Here is the Latin sentence upon which this induction is founded.

"*Cum pro objecto crimine, aliquis audiendus est, quinque nobilissimi viri judices, de reliquis sibi similibus, missis sortibus eligantur.*"[2]

That is to say:

"If any one be cited to appear on accusation of crime, let five nobles be appointed by lot, from among co-equals, to be judges."

These words, *de reliquis sibi similibus*, evidently signify that the five judges shall be drawn by lot from the same class, and not from the class of the accused. There is, therefore, no trace in it of the idea that the judges must be of the same rank and condition of the accused. The words *nobilissimi viri* might have convinced M. de Savigny, and prevented his error: how, indeed, can they apply to plebeian judges?

Let us pass from the Visigoths to the Burgundians, and see what was the state of the Roman legislation at the same epoch, among the latter.

The preface to their law contains, as you will recollect, this sentence:

"We order that Romans be judged according to Roman laws, as was done by our ancestors, and that they receive in writing the form and tenour of the laws according to which they shall be judged, to the end that no person can excuse himself upon the score of ignorance."

The Burgundian Sigismond, therefore, intended to do in 517, what Alaric, the Visigoth, had done eleven years before, to collect the Roman laws for his Roman subjects.

In 1566, Cujas found in a manuscript a law work which he published under the title of *Papiani Responsum*, or *Liber*

[1] Vol. i. p. 265. [2] Interp. Cod. Th. xi. l. 12.

Responsorum, and which has always since borne that name. It is divided into 47 or 48 titles, and offers the following characteristics:

1st. The order and heading of the titles corresponds almost exactly with those of the barbaric law of the Burgundians; title II. *de homicidiis*, to title II. *de homicidiis;* title III. *de libertatibus*, to title III. *de libertatibus servorum nostrorum*, and so on. M. de Savigny has drawn up a comparative view of the two laws,[1] and the correlativeness is evident.

2nd. We read in title II. of this work, *de homicidiis :*

"And as it is very clear that the Roman law has regulated nothing concerning the value of men killed, our lord has ordered that according to the quality of the slave, the murderer shall pay to his master the following sums, namely:

For an intendant	100 solidi.
For a personal servant	60
For a labourer or swineherd	30
For a good gold-worker	100
For a smith	50
For a carpenter	40

This must be observed according to the order of the king."

The enumeration and the composition, under the corresponding title, are the same in the law of the Burgundians.

3rd. Lastly, two titles of the first supplement of this law (tit. I. and XIX.) are textually borrowed from the *Papiani Responsum*, published by Cujas.

It is evident that this work is no other than the law proclaimed by Sigismond to his Roman subjects, at the time that he published the law of his barbaric subjects.

Whence comes the title of this law? Why is it called *Papiani Responsum?* Is it, in fact, a repetition of a work of Papinianus, often called Papian by the manuscripts? Nothing is less probable. M. de Savigny has very ingeniously resolved this question. He conjectures that Cujas found the manuscript of the Roman law of the Burgundians at the end of a manuscript of the *Breviarium* of Alaric, without marking the separation of the two works; and that the *Breviarium* finishing by a passage of the *Liber Responsorum* of Papinianus, Cujas has inadvertently ascribed this

[1] Vol. ii. pp. 13—16.

passage and given this title to the work following. The examination of many manuscripts confirms this conjecture, and Cujas himself was doubtful of error.

As the *Breviarium* of Alaric preceded the law of the Roman Burgundians by only a few years, some people have supposed the latter to be merely an abstract of it. This is an error. Much more brief and incomplete than the Breviarium, the Papiani Responsum, since it keeps that name, has still, more than once, drawn from the sources of the Roman law, and furnishes upon this point many important indications.

It probably fell into disuse when the kingdom of the Burgundians fell under the yoke of the Franks. Everything indicates that the *Breviarium* of Alaric, more extensive and better satisfying to the various wants of civil life, progressively replaced it, and became the law of the Romans in all the countries of Gaul that the Burgundians, as well as the Visigoths, had possessed.

The Franks remain to be considered. When they had conquered, or almost conquered the whole of Gaul, the *Breviarium*, and, for some time also, the *Papian*, continued in vigour in the countries where they had formerly prevailed. But in the north and north-east of Gaul, in the first settlements of the Franks, the situation was different. We there find nothing of a new Roman code, no attempt to collect and digest the Roman law for the ancient inhabitants. It is certain, however, that it continued to rule them; here are the principal facts which do not admit of a doubt of this.

1st. The Salic and Ripuarian laws continually repeat that the Romans shall be judged according to the Roman law. Many decrees of the Frank kings—among others, a decree of Clotaire I., in 560, and one of Childebert II., in 595, renew this injunction, and borrow from the Roman law some of its provisions. The legislative monuments of the Franks, therefore, attest its perpetuity.

2nd. A different kind of monuments, no less authentic, likewise prove it. Many of you know the formulæ, or models of forms, according to which, from the sixth to the tenth century, the principal acts of civil life, wills, bequests, enfranchisements, sales, &c., were drawn up. The principal collection of formulæ is that published by Marculf the monk, towards the end, as it seems, of the eighth century.

Many men of learning—Mabillon, Bignon, Sirmond, and Lindenbrog—have recovered others of them from old manuscripts. A large number of these formulæ reproduced, in the same terms, the ancient forms of Roman law concerning the enfranchisement of slaves, bequests, testaments, prescriptions, &c., and thus prove that it was still of habitual application.

3rd. All the monuments of this epoch, in the countries occupied by the Franks, are full of the names of the Roman municipal system—duumvirs, advocates, curia, and curial, and present these institutions as always in vigour.

4th. Many civil acts, in fact, exist, testaments, bequests, sales, &c., which passed according to the Roman law in the curia, and were so inscribed upon the registers.

5th. Lastly, the chroniclers of the time often speak of men versed in the knowledge of the Roman law, and who make an attentive study of it. In the sixth century, the Auvergnat Andarchius "was very learned in the works of Virgil, the books of the Theodosian law, and in the art of calculation."[1] At the end of the seventh century, Saint Bonet, bishop of Clermont, "was imbued with the principles of the grammarians, and learned in the decrees of Theodosius."[2] Saint Didier, bishop of Cahors, from 629 to 654, "applied himself," says his life in manuscript, "to the study of the Roman laws."

Of a surety there were then no *erudits;* there was then no Académie des Inscriptions, and people did not study the Roman law for mere curiosity. There can, then, be no reason for doubting that among the Franks, as well as among the Burgundians and Visigoths, it continued in vigour, particularly in the civil legislation and in the municipal system. Those among you who would seek the proofs in detail, the original texts upon which the results which I have just stated are founded, will find a large number of them in the work of M. de Savigny, (vol. i. p. 267—273; vol. ii., p. 100—118,) and still more in the *Histoire du Régime Municipal de France,* published by M. Raynouard—a work replete with curious researches, researches so complete upon certain questions that, in truth, one might almost tax them with superfluity.

You see the fact which I proposed to bring forward is indubitable. Monuments of all kinds show it, doubtless in

[1] Greg. of Tours, l. 4 c. 47. [2] *Acta sanc Juana,* c. 1, No. 3

unequal degrees among different nations, but everywhere real and permanent. Its importance is great, because it proclaimed to Gaul a social state entirely different from that in which it had hitherto lived. It was hardly more than five centuries since it had fallen beneath the power of the Romans, and already scarcely a trace of the ancient Gaulish society remained. Roman civilization had the terrible power of extirpating the national laws, manners, language, and religion—of fully assimilating its conquests to itself. All absolute expressions are exaggerated; still, in considering things in general at the sixth century, we may say, everything in Gaul was Roman. The contrary fact accompanies barbaric conquest: the Germans leave to the conquered population their laws, local institutions, language, and religion. An invincible unity followed in the steps of the Romans: here, on the contrary, diversity was established by the consent and aid of the conquerors. We have seen that the empire of personality and individual independence, the characteristic of modern civilization, was of German origin; we here find its influence; the idea of personality presided in laws as in actions; the individuality of peoples, while subject to the same political domination, was proclaimed like that of man. Centuries must pass before the notion of territory can overcome that of race, before personal legislation can become real, and before a new national unity can result from the slow and laborious fusion of the various elements.

This granted, and the perpetuity of Roman legislation being established, still do not let this word deceive you: there is in it a great deal that is illusory; because it has been seen that the Roman law continued, because the same names and forms have been met with, it has been concluded that the principles, that the spirit of the laws had also remained the same: the Roman law of the tenth century has been spoken of as that of the Empire. This is erroneous language; when Alaric and Sigismond ordered a new collection of the Roman laws for the use of their Roman subjects, they did exactly what had elsewhere been done by Theodoric and Dagobert, in causing the barbaric laws to be digested for their Frank subjects. As the Salic and Ripuarian laws set forth ancient customs, already ill suited to the new state of the German people, so the *Breviarium* of Alaric, and the *Pa-*

piani Responsum collected laws already old, and partly inapplicable. By the fall of the Empire and by the invasion, the whole social order was entirely changed; the relations between men were different, and another system of property commenced; the Roman political institutions could not subsist; facts of all sorts were renewed over the whole face of the land. And what laws were given to this rising society, so disordered and yet so fertile? Two ancient laws: the ancient barbarous customs and the ancient Roman legislation. It is evident that neither could be suitable; both must be modified, must be profoundly metamorphosed, in order to be adapted to the new facts.

When, therefore, we say that at the sixth century the Roman law still lasted, and that the barbarous laws were written; when we find in posterior centuries always the same words, Roman law, and barbaric laws, it must not be supposed that the same laws are spoken of. In perpetuating itself, the Roman law altered; after having been written, the barbaric laws were perverted. Both are among the number of the essential elements of modern society; but as elements entering into a new combination, which will arise after a long fermentation, and in the breast of which they will only appear transformed.

It is this successive transformation that I shall attempt to present to you; historians do not speak of it; unvarying phrases hide it; it is an internal work, a profoundly secret spectacle; and at which one can only arrive by piercing many inclosures and guarding against the illusion caused by the similitude of forms and names.

We now find ourselves at the end of our researches concerning the state of civil society in Gaul from the sixth to the middle of the eighth century. In our next lecture, we shall study the changes which happened in the religious society at the same epoch, that is to say, the state and constitution of the church.

TWELFTH LECTURE.

Object of the lecture—State of the church in Gaul, from the sixth to the middle of the eighth century—Analogy between the primitive state of the religious society and the civil society—The unity of the church or the spiritual society—Two elements or conditions of spiritual society; 1st. Unity of truth, that is to say, of absolute reason; 2nd. Liberty of minds, or individual reason—State of these two ideas in the Christian church from the sixth to the eighth century—She adopts one and rejects the other—Unity of the church in legislation—General councils—Difference between the eastern and the western church as regards the persecution of heretics—Relations of the church with the state, from the sixth to the eighth century: 1st, in the eastern empire; 2nd, in the west, especially in Frankish Gaul—Interference of the temporal power in the affairs of the church—Of the spiritual power in the affairs of the state—Recapitulation.

We re-enter a route over which we have already gone; we again take up a thread which we have once held: we have to occupy ourselves with the history of the Christian church in Gaul, from the completion of the invasion to the fall of the Merovingian kings, that is to say, from the sixth to the middle of the eighth century.

The determination of this epoch is not arbitrary; the accession of the Carlovingian kings marked a crisis in religious society as well as in civil society. It is a date which constitutes an era, and at which it is advisable to pause.

Recal the picture which I have traced of the state of the religious society in Gaul, before the decisive fall of the Roman empire, that is to say, at the end of the fourth and the beginning of the fifth century. We have considered the church under two points of view: 1st, in her external situation, in her relations with the state; 2nd, in her internal constitution, in her social and political organization. Around these two fundamental problems we have seen that all the particular questions, all the facts collect.

This two-fold examination has enabled us to see, in the first five centuries of the church, the germ of all the solutions of the two problems, some example of all the forms, and trials of all the combinations. There is no system, whether in regard to the external relations of the church, or her internal organization, which may not be traced to this epoch, and there find some authority. Independence, obedience, sovereignty, the compromises of the church with the state, presbyterianism or episcopacy, the complete absence of the clergy, or its almost exclusive domination, we have found all these.

We have just examined the state of civil society after the invasion, in the sixth and seventh centuries, and we have arrived at the same result. There, likewise, we have found the germ, the example of all the systems of social organization, and of government: monarchy, aristocracy, and democracy; the assemblies of free men; the patronage of the chief of the land towards his warriors, of the great proprietor towards the inferior proprietor, royalty, absolute and impotent, elective and hereditary, barbarous, imperial, and religious: all the principles, in a word, which have been developed in the life of modern Europe, at that time simultaneously appeared to us.

There is a remarkable similarity in the origin and primitive state of the two societies: wealth and confusion are alike in them; all things are there; none in its place and proportion; order will come with development; in being developed, the various elements will be disengaged and distinguished; each will display its pretensions and its own powers, first in order to combat, and afterwards to become reconciled. Such will be the progressive work of ages and of man.

It is at this work that we have hereafter to be present; we have seen in the cradle of the two societies all the material elements, and all the rational principles of modern civilization; we are about to follow them in their struggles, negotiations, amalgamations, and in all the vicissitudes both of their special and their common destiny. This, properly speaking, is the history of civilization; we have as yet only arrived at the theatre of this history, and named its actors.

You will not be surprised that in entering upon a new era we should first encounter the religious society: it was, as you are aware, the most advanced and the strongest; whether in the Roman municipality, in the palace of the barbarous kings, or in the hierarchy of the conquerors now become proprietors, we have everywhere recognised the presence and influence of the heads of the church. From the fourth to the thirteenth century, it was the church that took the lead in the career of civilization. It is natural, then, that, during this period, every time that we have made a halt, and again moved forward, it should be with her that we recommence.

We shall study her history from the sixth to the eighth century, under the two points of view already indicated; 1st, in her relations with the state; 2ndly, in her peculiar and internal constitution.

But before approaching either of these questions, and the facts which are attached thereto, I must call your attention to a fact which dominates over all, which characterises the Christian church in general, and has, as it were, decided her destiny.

This fact is the unity of the church, the unity of the Christian society, despite all the diversities of time, place, domination, language, or origin.

Singular phenomenon! It was at the very time that the Roman empire fell to pieces and disappeared, that the Christian church rallied, and definitively formed herself. Political unity perished, religious unity arose. I know not how many nations, of various origins, manners, language, and destiny, are thrown upon the scene; all becomes partial and local; every extended idea, every general institution, every great social combination vanishes; and at this very moment the Christian church proclaims the unity of her doctrine, the universality of her right.

This is a glorious and powerful fact, and one which, from the fifth to the thirteenth century, has rendered immense services to humanity. The mere fact of the unity of the church, maintained some tie between countries and nations that everything else tended to separate; under its influence, some general notions, some sentiments of a vast sympathy continued to be developed; and from the very heart of the most frightful political confusion that the world has ever known, arose perhaps the most extensive and the purest idea that has ever rallied mankind, the idea of spiritual society; for that is the philosophical name of the church, the type which she wished to realize.

What sense did men, at this period, attach to these words, and what progress had they already made in this path? What was actually, in minds and in facts, this spiritual society, the object of their ambition and respect? How was it conceived and practised? These questions must be answered in order to know what is meant when we speak of the unity of the church, and what ought to be thought of its principles and results.

A common conviction, that is to say, an identical idea, acknowledged and received as true, is the fundamental basis, the secret tie of human society. One may stop at the most confined and the most simple association, or elevate oneself to the most complicated and extensive; we may examine what passes between three or four barbarians united for a hunting expedition, or in the midst of an assembly convoked to treat of the affairs of a great nation; everywhere, and under all circumstances, it is in the adhesion of individuals to the same thought, that the fact of association essentially consists: so long as they do not comprehend one another, they are mere isolated beings, placed by the side of one another, but not holding together. A similar sentiment and doctrine, whatever may be its nature or object, is the first condition of the social state; it is in the midst of truth only, or in what they take for truth, that men become united, and that society takes birth. And in this sense, a modern philosopher[1] was right in saying that there is no society except between intellects; that society only subsists upon points and within limits, where the union of intellects is accomplished; that where intellects have nothing in common, there is no society; in other words, that intellectual society is the only society, the necessary element, and, as it were, the foundation of all external and visible associations.

Now, the essential element of truth, and precisely what is, in fact, the social tie, *par excellence*, is unity. Truth is one,

[1] M. l'Abbé de Lamennais.

therefore the men who have acknowledged and accepted it are united; a union which has in it nothing accidental nor arbitrary, for truth neither depends upon the accidents of things, nor upon the uncertainties of men; nothing transitory, for truth is eternal; nothing confined, for truth is complete and infinite. As of truth, unity then will be the essential characteristic of the society which shall have truth alone for its object, that is to say, of the purely religious society. There is not, there cannot be, two spiritual societies; it is, from its nature, sole and universal.

Thus did the church take birth: hence that unity which she proclaims as her principle, that universality which has always been her ambition. In degrees more or less evident, and more or less strict, it is the idea which rests at the bottom of all her doctrines, which hovers over all her works. Long before the sixth century, from the very cradle of Christianity, it appears in the writings and acts of its most illustrious interpreters.

But unity of truth in itself is not sufficient for the rise and subsistence of the religious society; it is necessary that it should be evident to minds, and that it should rally them. Union of minds, that is to say, spiritual society, is the consequence of the unity of truth; but so long as this union is not accomplished, the principle wants its consequence, spiritual society does not exist. Now, upon what condition do minds unite themselves in truth? Upon this condition, that they acknowledge and accept its empire: whoever obeys truth without knowing it, from ignorance and not from light, or whoever, having knowledge of the truth, refuses to obey it, is not part of the spiritual society; none form a part of it if they do not see nor wish it; it excludes, on one side, ignorance, and on the other, constraint; it exacts from all its members an intimate and personal adhesion of intellect and liberty.

Now, at the epoch upon which we are occupied, this second principle, this second characteristic of spiritual society, was wanting to the church. It would be unjust to say that it was absolutely unknown to her, and that she believed that spiritual society could exist between men without the consent of their intellect or liberty. Thus put in its simple and naked form, this idea is offensive and necessarily repulsed;

besides, the full and vigorous exercise of reason and will was too recent and still too frequent in the church, for her to fall into so entire an oblivion. She did not affirm that truth had a right to employ constraint; on the contrary, she incessantly repeated that spiritual arms were the only arms of which she could and ought to avail herself. But this principle, if I may so express myself, was only upon the surface of minds, and evaporated from day to day. The idea that truth, one and universal, had a right to pursue by force the consequences of its unity and universality, became from day to day the dominant, active, and efficacious idea. Of the two conditions of spiritual society, the rational unity of doctrine, and the actual unity of minds, the first almost solely occupied the church; the second was incessantly forgotten or violated.

Many centuries were necessary in order to give to it its place and power, that is to say, to bring out the true nature of spiritual society, its complete nature, and the harmony of its elements. It was long the general error to believe that the empire of truth—that is, of universal reason—could be established without the free exercise of individual reason, without respect to its right. Thus they misunderstood spiritual society, even in announcing it; they exposed it to the risk of being but a lying illusion. The employment of force does far more than stain it, it kills it; in order that its unity may be, not only pure, but real, it is necessary that it shine forth in the midst of the development of all intellects and all liberties.

It will be the honour of our times to have penetrated into the essence of spiritual society much further than the world has ever yet done, to have much more completely known and asserted it. We now know that it has two conditions: 1st, the presence of a general and absolute truth, a rule of doctrines and human action; 2nd, the full development of all intellects, in face of this truth, and the free adhesion of souls to its power. Let not one of these conditions ever allow us to forget the other; let not the idea of the liberty of minds weaken in us that of the unity of spiritual society: because individual convictions should be clear and free, let us not be tempted to believe that there is no universal truth which has a right to command; in respecting the reason of each, do not lose sight of the one and sovereign reason.

The history of human society has hitherto passed alternately from one to the other of these dispositions. At certain epochs men have been peculiarly struck with the nature and rights of this universal and absolute truth, the legitimate master to whose reign they aspired: they flattered themselves that at last they had encountered and possessed it, and in their foolish confidence they accorded to it the absolute power which soon and inevitably engendered tyranny. After having long submitted to and respected it, man recognised it; he saw the name and rights of truth usurped by ignorant or perverse force; then he was more irritated with the idols than occupied with God himself; the unity of divine reason, if I may be permitted to use the expression, was no longer the object of his habitual contemplation; he above all thought upon the right of human reason in the relations of men, and often finished by forgetting that, if it is free, the will is not arbitrary; that if there is a right of inquiry for individual reason, it is still subordinate to that general reason which serves for the measure and touchstone of all minds. And even as in the first instance there was tyranny, so in the second there was anarchy, that is to say, the absence of general and powerful belief, the absence of principles in the soul, and of union in society. One may hope that our time is called to avoid each of these sand-banks, for it is, if I may so speak, in possession of the chart which points them both out. The development of civilization must be accomplished hereafter under the simultaneous influence of a two-fold reverence; universal reason will be sought as the supreme law, the final aim; individual reason will be free, and invoked to develop itself as the best means of attaining to universal reason. And if spiritual society be never complete and pure—the imperfection of humanity will not allow it—at least its unity will no longer run the risk of being factitious and fraudulent. You have had a glance at the state of minds concerning this great idea, at the epoch upon which we are occupied: let us pass to the state of facts, and see what practical consequence had already been produced by that unity of the church, of which we have just described the rational characteristics.

It was seen above all in the ecclesiastical legislation, and it was so much the more conspicuous there, from being in contradiction to all that passed elsewhere. We have studied in our last lectures civil legislation from the fifth to the eighth century; and diversity, which gradually increased, has appeared to us its fundamental trait. The tendency of religious society is very different; it aspired to a unity in laws, and attained it. And it is not that she exclusively drew her laws from the primitive monuments of religion, from the sacred books, always and everywhere the same: in proportion as she was developed, new desires were manifested, new laws were necessary, or a new legislator. Who should it be? The east was separated from the west, the west was daily parcelled out into distinct and independent states. Should there be, for the church thus dispersed, many legislators? Shall the councils of Gaul, Spain, or Italy, give them religious laws? No; there shall be an universal and sole legislation for the whole church, superior to all the diversities of national churches and councils, and to all the differences which are necessarily introduced into discipline, worship, and usages. The decrees of the general councils shall everywhere be obligatory and accepted. From the fourth to the eighth century there were six œcumenical or general councils; they were all held in the east, by the bishops of the east, and under the influence of the eastern emperors; there were scarcely any bishops from the west among them.[1] Yet, despite so many causes for misunderstanding and separation, despite the diversity of languages, governments, and manners, and moreover, despite the rivalry of the patriarchs of Rome, Constantinople, and Alexandria, the legislation of the general councils was everywhere adopted; the west and the east

[1] *Table of the General Councils from the Fourth to the Eighth Century.*

Date.	*Place.*	*Present.*	*Eastern.*	*Western.*
325	Nicea	318	315	3
381	Constantinople .	150	149	1
431	Ephesus . . .	68	67	1
451	Chalcedonia . .	353	350	3
553	Constantinople .	164	158	6
680	Constantinople .	56	51	5

alike yielded to it; a few only of the decrees of the fifth council were for a moment contested. So powerful already was the idea of unity in the church; such was the spiritual tie dominating all things!

With regard to the second principle of spiritual society, liberty of minds, some distinction must be made between the east and the west; the state of facts was not the same in them.

In setting forth the state of the church in the fourth and fifth centuries, I have made you acquainted with the disposition of the legislation, and of minds generally, with regard to heresy. The principle of persecution, you will recollect, was neither clearly established, nor constantly dominant; still it gradually prevailed; in spite of the generous protestations of some bishops, in spite of the variety of cases, the laws of Theodosius, the persecution of the Arians, the Donatists, the Pelagians, and the punishment of the Priscillianists, do not admit a doubt of this.

Dating from the sixth century, and in the Empire of the east, the true successor and continuator of the Roman empire, events and ideas followed the same course; the principle of persecution was developed; the history of the Monophysites, and Monothelites, that of many other heresies, and the legislation of Justinian, give proof of this.

In the west, the invasion and all its consequences for some time delayed its progress; almost all intellectual movement came to a stand still. Amidst the incessant confusion of life, what room could be left for contemplation and study? Heresies were rare; the contest continued between the Arians and the orthodox; but we see but few new doctrines arise, and those which attempted to introduce themselves were scarcely anything more than a weak echo of the heresies of the east. Persecution, therefore, so to speak, wanted matter and occasion. Besides, the bishops did not in any way provoke it; more pressing affairs occupied them; the situation of the church was perilous; she not only was under the necessity of occupying herself about her temporal interests, but her safety, her very existence, was in danger; they cared little for minor varieties of opinion. Fifty-four councils were held in Gaul in the sixth century; two only, that of Orange and that of Valencia, in 529, occupied themselves with dogmas; they condemned the heresy of the semi-Pelagians, which the fifth century had bequeathed to them.

Lastly, the barbaric kings, the new masters of the soil, took but little interest, and rarely any part in such debates. The emperors of the east were theologians as well as bishops; they had been born and bred in theology; they had personal and fixed opinions concerning its problems and quarrels. Justinian and Heraclius willingly engaged upon their own account in the suppression of heresy. Unless impelled by some powerful political motive, neither Gondebald, Chilpiric, nor Gontran, troubled themselves in the matter. Numerous actions and words have come down to us of the Burgundian, Gothic, and Frank kings, which prove how little they were disposed to exert their power in such causes. "We cannot command religion," said Theodoric, king of the Ostrogoths; "no one can be forced to believe, in spite of himself."[1] . . . "Since the Deity suffers various religions," said king Theodobat, "we dare not prescribe a single one. We remember having read that God must be sacrificed to willingly, and not under the constraint of a master. Those, therefore, who attempt to do otherwise, evidently oppose themselves to the divine commands."[2]

Doubtless, Cassiodorus here lends to the two Gothic kings the superiority of his reason; but they adopted his language; and in many other cases, whether it be ignorance or good sense, we find the barbaric princes manifesting the same disposition.

In fact, therefore, from the concurrence of various causes, the second condition of spiritual society, liberty of minds, was at this epoch less violated in the west than in the east. It is necessary, however, not to be mistaken in this matter; it was but an accident, the temporary effect of external circumstances; at bottom, the principle was equally overlooked, and the general course of things tended equally to bring about the prevalence of persecution.

You see, that, in spite of some differences, the unity of the church, with all the consequences attached thereto, was everywhere the dominant fact, alike in the west and in

[1] *Cassiod. Variar. Ep.* l. xi. ep. 27. [2] Ibid. l. x. ep. 26.

the east, alike in the social state and in minds generally. That was the principle which, in religious society, presided over opinions, laws, and actions, the point from which they always started, the end to which they incessantly tended. From the fourth century, this idea was, as it were, the star under whose influence religious society was developed in Europe, and which it is necessary to keep always in view in order to follow and to comprehend the vicissitudes of its destiny.

This point agreed upon and the characteristic fact of this epoch being well established, let us enter upon the particular examination of the state of the church, and seek what were: first, her relations with civil society and its government; secondly, her peculiar and internal organization.

I would pray you to recal what I said when speaking of the church in the fifth century: it appeared to us that her relations with the state might be determined into four different systems: 1st, the complete independence of the church; the unnoticed and unknown church, receiving neither law nor support from the state: 2ndly, the sovereignty of the state over the church; religious society governed, if not completely, at least in its principal elements, by the civil power; 3rdly, the sovereignty of the church over the state; the temporal government, if not directly possessed, at least completely dominated by the spiritual power; 4thly, and lastly, the co-existence of the two societies, the two powers, which though separate were allied by certain various and variable conditions, which united without confounding them.

We at the same time recognised that in the fifth century this latter system prevailed; that the Christian church and the Roman empire both existed, as two distinct societies, each having its government and laws, but adopting and mutually sustaining each other. In the midst of their alliance we discovered traces still visible of another principle, of an anterior state, the sovereignty of the state over the church, the intervention and decided preponderance of the emperors in her administration; lastly, but only in the distance, we caught a glimpse of the sovereignty of the church over the state, the domination over the temporal government by the spiritual power.

Such appeared to us, in its whole, the situation of the

Christian church of the fifth century in her relations with the state.

In the sixth century, if we regard the eastern empire, over which it is always necessary to extend our view in order to comprehend properly what happened in the west, and the changes which the barbaric invasion brought about in the course of things, we shall be struck by two simultaneous facts:

1st. The clergy, especially the episcopacy, unceasingly procured from the emperors new favours and privileges. Justinian gave to the bishops: 1st, the civil jurisdiction over monks and nuns, the same as over clerks;[1] 2nd, the inspection of property in cities, and the preponderance in all municipal administration;[2] 3rd, the enfranchisement from paternal power;[3] 4th, he forbad the judges calling them as witnesses, and demanding an oath of them.[4] Herodius granted them the criminal jurisdiction over clerks.[5] The influence and immunities of religious society in civil society were ever increasing.

2nd. The emperors, however, mixed themselves more and more in the affairs of the church; not only in her relations with the state, but in her internal affairs, constitution, and discipline. And not only did they meddle with her government, but they interfered in her creeds; they gave decrees in favour of such or such a dogma, they regulated the faith.

Upon the whole, the authority of the eastern emperors over religious society was more general, active, frequent, despotic, than it had ever been hitherto; despite the progress of her privileges, the situation of the church with regard to the civil power was weak, inferior, and fallen off from what it was in the ancient Empire.

Two contemporaneous texts will prevent your doubting this.

In the middle of the sixth century, the Franks sent an embassy to Constantinople; the clergy of Italy wrote to the Frank envoys to give them, as to the empire of the east, such information as they believed might be beneficial to the success of their mission:

"The Greek bishops," it said to them, "have great and opulent churches, and they cannot bear being suspended two months

[1] *Nov. Justin.* 79, 83; A.D. 539. [2] *Cod. Justin.* i. tit. iv. l. 26.
[3] *Nov.* 81. [4] *Nov.* 123, c. 7.
[5] Gieseler, *Lehrbuch der Kirchengeschichte*, t. i. p. 602.

from the government of ecclesiastical affairs; so, accommodating themselves to the age, and to the will of princes, they consent without contest to all that is demanded of them."[1]

The next is a document which speaks still more emphatically. Maurice, emperor of the east, (582—602,) had interdicted all persons occupied in civil functions from becoming clerks or entering a monastery; he had sent this law to Rome, to pope Gregory the Great, in order that he might spread it in the west. Rome was only held to the Greek empire by a feeble tie; Gregory had not in reality anything to fear from the emperor; he was ardent and proud; the decree of Maurice offended him; he wished to mark his disapprobation, perhaps even attempt some resistance; he thus terminated his letter:

"I, who say these things to my lords, what am I, but dust or an earth-worm? Still, as I think that this law goes against God, the author of all things, I cannot conceal this thought from my lords; and see what Christ answers to it, in saying to you, through me, the last of his servants and yours: 'From secretary I have made thee count of the guards, from count of the guards, Cæsar, from Cæsar, emperor, and not only emperor; but also father of an emperor; I have confided my priests to thy hands and thou withdrawest thy soldiers from my service.' I pray thee, most pious lord, say, to thy servant, what wilt thou answer at the day of judgment to thy God, who will come and say these things to thee?

"As for me, submitting to thy order, I have sent this law to the various countries of the earth, and I have said to my serene lords, in this paper, whereon I have deposited my reflections, that this law goes against that of the all-powerful God; I have therefore fulfilled my duty upon each side; I have rendered obedience to Cæsar, and I have not been silent as to what appeared to me against God."[2]

Of a surety, from such a man, in such a situation, and with such a design, the tone of this letter is singularly mild and modest. Some centuries later, Gregory would have used a very different language towards even the nearest and most redoubtable sovereign. The language which he adopts here, can have no other cause than the habits of subordination and

[1] Mansi. Conc. t. ix. p. 153.

[2] *Greg. M. Epist.*, l. iii. ep. 65, to the emperor Maurice.

dependence of the church towards the eastern emperors, amidst the continual extension of her immunities.

The church of the west, after the invasion and under the barbaric kings, offers a different spectacle. Her new masters mixed themselves in no manner with her dogmas; they left her, in matters of faith, to act and govern herself as she pleased. They interfered almost as little in her discipline, properly so called, in the relations of the clergy among themselves. But in all which concerned the relations between the religious and civil societies, in all that could interest temporal power, the church lost independence and privilege; she was less free, and not treated so well as under the Roman emperors. 1st. You have seen that before the fall of the Empire, the bishops were elected by the clergy and the people. The emperor only interfered in rare cases, in the election for the most considerable towns. It was no longer so in Gaul after the establishment of the barbaric monarchies. The churches were wealthy; the barbaric kings made them a means of recompensing their servants and enriching themselves. In numerous instances, they directly nominated the bishops. The church protested; she claimed the election; she did not always succeed therein; many bishops were retained in the sees where they had been placed by the kings alone. Still the fact was not changed into a matter of right, and continued to pass for an abuse. The kings themselves admit this on many occasions. The church, by degrees, regained the election; but she also gave way in her turn; she granted that after the election the confirmation of the king was necessary. The bishop, who formerly took possession of his see, from the time that he was consecrated by the archbishop, now ascended not his throne until after obtaining the sanction of royalty. Such is not only the fact, but the religious and civil law.

"Let no person be permitted," orders the council of Orleans in 549, "to acquire a see by means of money; but with the consent of the king, let him who shall have been elected by the clergy and the people, be consecrated bishop by the archbishop and his suffragans."

"Upon the death of a bishop," says Clotaire II., in 615, "he who is to be ordained in his place by the archbishop and his suffragans, shall be elected by the clergy and the people and ordained by the order of the prince."

The contest between election and royal nomination was often reproduced; but in every case the necessity of confirmation was acknowledged.

2nd. As under the Roman empire, councils could not be convoked but with the consent of the prince, and he threatened the bishops when they attempted to evade it. "We have learnt from public report," wrote king Sigbert to Didier, bishop of Cahors, in the seventh century, "that you have been convoked by . . . the bishop of Vulfoleud, to hold a council in our kingdom, the 1st of September . . . with the others . . . bishops of your province . . . Although we desire to maintain the observance of the canons and ecclesiastical rules, as they were preserved by our ancestors, still, *because we have not been made acquainted with the convocation of this assembly, we have agreed, with our great men, not to suffer this council to be held without our knowledge in our states;* and that no bishops of our kingdom shall assemble at the approaching calends of September. In future, if we have timely intimation of the object of a council, whether it meets in order to regulate the discipline of the church, or for the good of the state, or for other affairs, we shall not refuse our consent to its meeting; provided, however, that information is first given us of it. The reason we write you this letter is, to forbid your attending this assembly." The monuments, the very acts of thirteen councils assembled in the sixth and seventh centuries, formally express that they were convoked by the order, and held with the consent of the king.[1] I do not doubt, however, but in this, the fact was very often contrary to the acknowledged right, and that a number of councils,

[1] These are:

1.	The council of	Orleans,	in	511.
2.	— „	Orleans,	in	533.
3.	— „	Clermont,	in	535.
4.	— „	Orleans,	in	549.
5.	— „	Paris,	in	556.
6.	— „	Tours,	in	567.
7.	— „	Lyons,	in	575.
8.	— „	Châlons,	in	579.
9.	— „	Mâcon,	in	581.
10.	— „	Valencia,	in	584.
11.	— „	Verdun,		——.
12.	— „	Paris,	in	615.
13.	— „	Châlons,	in	650.

especially the mere provincial councils, met and regulated their affairs without any authorization.

3rd. Some writers[1] have thought that the independence of the church also suffered from an institution which was more developed among the Franks than elsewhere; I mean the chapel of the king, and the priest who had the direction of it, under the name of *Archicapellanus, Abbas regii oratorii Apocrisiarius.* At first charged only with the exercise of worship in the interior of the palace, this superior of the chapel assumed gradually more importance, and became, to speak in the language so little applicable of our own times, a kind of minister of ecclesiastical affairs for the whole kingdom: it is supposed these were managed almost entirely by his intermediation, and that by his means royalty exercised a great influence over them. It may be that this influence was real at certain times, under such or such a king, under Charlemagne, for example; but I very much doubt that in general, and of itself, the institution was efficacious; it would serve rather the power of the church over the king, than that of the king in the church.

4th. There was something more real in the restrictions to which, at this epoch, the ecclesiastical privileges were subjected. They were numerous and important. For example, it was forbidden any bishop to ordain a free man as priest without the consent of the king.[2] Priests were exempt from military service; the king did not choose that free men should relieve themselves at will by means of this title. The church, therefore, at this epoch was peopled with slaves; it was especially among her own slaves, among the serfs and labourers of her domains, that she recruited herself; and this circumstance, perhaps, is one of those which have not least contributed to the efforts of the church for ameliorating the condition of the serfs. Many priests were taken from among them; and, independently of religious motives, they knew the miseries of their situation, they bore some sympathy for those who were plunged in it. In criminal matters, the priests in the west had not obtained the privilege which Heraclius had granted to those in the east; they were tried by the ordinary lay

[1] Among others, M. Planck, in his *History of the Constitution of the Christian Church* (in German), a work of rare science and impartiality. See vol. ii. 147.

[2] Council of Orleans, in 511, can. 6.

judges. In civil matters the clergy judged itself, but only in cases where the cause interested simply priests; if the difference was between a priest and a layman, the layman was not bound to appear before the bishop; on the contrary, he had the priest before his judges. With regard to public charges, there were certain churches whose domains were exempt, and the number of these daily increased; but the immunity was by no means general. Upon the whole, immediately after the invasion, in its principal relations with the temporal power, the clergy of Frankish Gaul seemed less independent, and invested with less privileges, than it was in Roman Gaul.

But means were not wanting both to regain in time advantages, and to assure herself of large compensations. By not in any way interfering in dogmatical points, that is, in the intellectual government of the church, the barbaric kings left to her the most fertile source of power. She knew how to draw largely upon it. In the east, the laity took part in theology and in the influence which it conferred. In the west, the clergy alone addressed itself to minds, and alone was master of them. It alone spoke to the people, and alone rallied them around certain ideas which became laws. It was by this means especially that it re-acquired power, and repaired the losses to which the invasion had subjected it. Towards the end of the epoch upon which we are occupied, this had already become visible. The church evidently recovered from the shocks which had been given her by the disorder of the times and the brutal avidity of the barbarians. She made her right of asylum acknowledged and consecrated. She acquired a kind of right of superintendence and revision over the lay judges of an inferior order. The consequences of her jurisdiction over all sins were developed. By wills and marriages, she penetrated more and more into the civil order. Ecclesiastical judges were associated with lay judges every time a priest was concerned in the suit. Lastly, the presence of the bishops, whether with the king, in the assembly of great men, or in the hierarchy of proprietors, assured them a powerful participation in the political order; and if the sovereign power meddled in church affairs, the church, in her turn, extended her action and power more and more into the affairs of the world.

This is the dominant character of this epoch, as regards the reciprocal situation of the civil and religious society. The temporal and spiritual powers approached, penetrated, and encroached more and more upon each other. Before the invasion, when the Empire was still erect, although the two societies were already strongly entwined with one another, still there was a profound distinction. The independence of the church was sufficiently complete in what directly concerned her; and in temporal matters, although she had much influence, she had hardly any direct action except upon the municipal system, and in the midst of cities. For the general government of the state, the emperor had his machinery all prepared, his councils, magistrates, and armies; in a word, the political order was complete and regular, apart from the religious society and its government. After the invasion, amidst the dissolution of the political order, and the universal trouble, the limits of the two governments vanished; they lived from day to day without principles,without settled conditions; they encountered everywhere, clashing, confounded, disputing the means of action, struggling together in darkness and by chance. Of this irregular co-existence of temporal and spiritual power, this fantastical entanglement of their attributes, these reciprocal usurpations, this uncertainty as to their limits, all this chaos of church and state, which has played so great a part in our history, which has brought forth so many events and theories, it is to the epoch which now occupies us that the origin must be assigned; that only is its most striking feature.

In our next lecture we shall occupy ourselves with the internal organization of the church, and the changes which happened in it during the same period.

THIRTEENTH LECTURE.

Of the internal organization and state of the Gallo-Frankish church, from the sixth to the eighth century—Characteristic facts of the Gaulish church at the fifth century—What became of them after the invasion—The exclusive domination of the clergy in the religious society continues—Facts which modify it: 1. Separation of ordination and tenure; priests not ecclesiastics—2. Patronage by laymen of the churches which they founded—3. Oratories, or particular chapels—4. Advocates of the churches—Picture of the general organization of the church—Parishes and their priests—Archpriests and archdeacons—Bishops—Archbishops—Attempts to establish the patriarchates in the west—Fall of the archbishops—Preponderance and despotism of the episcopacy—Struggle of the priests and parishes against the bishops—The bishops triumphant—Despotism corrupts them—Decline of the secular clergy—Necessity for a reformation.

We have seen what were the relations between the church and the state, and their principal modifications, in Frankish Gaul, from the sixth to the eighth century. We shall now examine the peculiar and internal organization of the church at the same epoch; it is curious and full of vicissitudes.

It will be recollected that a religious society may be constituted according to two principal systems. In one, the faithful, the laymen, as well as the priests, take part in the government; the religious society is not under the exclusive empire of the ecclesiastical society. In the other system, power belongs to the clergy alone; laymen are strangers to it; it is the ecclesiastical society which governs the religious society.

This fundamental distinction once established, we have seen that in each of these two great systems, totally various modes of organization might be developed: where religious society governed itself, for example, it might be—1st, that the local associations were united in one general church, under the direction of one or more assemblies, where the ecclesiastics and the laity were together; 2ndly, that there should be no general and sole church, that each particular congregation, each local church should govern itself; 3rdly, that there should be no clergy, properly so called, no men invested with permanent spiritual power; that the laity should fulfil the religious functions. These three modes of organization have been realized by the presbyterians, the independents, and the quakers.

If the clergy alone dominates, if the religious society is under subjection to the ecclesiastical society, this latter may be monarchically, aristocratically, or democratically constituted and governed, by the papal power, the episcopacy, or by assemblies of priests, equal among themselves. The example of these various constitutions is likewise met with in history.

In fact, in the Gaulish church of the fifth century, two of these principles had already prevailed: 1st, the separation of the religious society and the ecclesiastical society, of the clergy and the people, was consummated; the clergy alone governed the church—a domination, however, palliated by some remains of the intervention of the faithful in the election of bishops. 2ndly, in the bosom of the clergy, the aristocratical system prevailed; episcopacy alone dominated; a domination which was likewise palliated, on one hand by the intervention of the simple priests in the election of bishops, on the other by the influence of councils, a source of liberty in the church, although none but bishops sat in them.

Such were the dominant facts, the characteristic features of the Gaulish church at the time of the invasion: what did they become after the invasion: did they remain or disappear? to what modifications were they subjected from the sixth to the eighth century? These are the questions which must occupy us at present.

I. And, first, there cannot be a doubt but that the separation of the clergy and the people, the exclusive domination of the ecclesiastics over the laity, was kept up. Immediately after the invasion, it appeared to waver for a moment; in the common peril, the clergy and the people were brought together. This fact is nowhere positively written and visible; but it is seen by glimpses, it is everywhere felt: in going over the documents of this epoch, one is struck with I know not what new intimacy between the priests and the faithful; these latter lived in the churches, so to speak: on numberless occasions, the bishop met them, spoke with them, consulted them: the solemnity of the times, the community of sentiments and destinies, obliged the government to establish itself in the midst of the population; it sustained the power which protected it: in sustaining it, it took part therein.

This effect was of short duration. You will recollect the principal cause to which I have attributed the exclusive domination of the clergy over the people. It appeared to me especially to result from the inferiority of the people, an inferiority of intellect, of energy, of influence. After the invasion, this fact did not alter, it was rather aggravated. The miseries of the time made the Gaulish-Roman population fall still lower. The priests, on their side, when once the conquerors were converted, no longer felt the same want of close union with the conquered; the people, therefore, lost the momentary importance which it seemed to have acquired. The barbarians inherited none of it, they were in no way capable of associating with the government of the church; they had not the least wish so to do; and kings were soon the only laymen who took part in it.

Many facts, however, combated this isolation of the ecclesiastical society in the religious society, and gave influence to the laity in default of power.

1st. The first, which, in my opinion, has been too little marked, and which has had enduring and important consequences, was the separation of ordination and tonsure. Down to the sixth century, the tonsure took place at the time of entering into orders; it was regarded as the sign of ordination, *signum ordinis.* Dating from the sixth century, we find the tonsure conferred without any admission into orders; instead of being *signum ordinis*, it was called *signum destinationis ad ordinem.* The principle of the church had hitherto been, *tonsura ipsa est ordo*, "tonsure is the order itself," She maintained this principle, with this explanation:

Tonsure is the order itself, but in the largest sense of the term, and as a preparation to the divine service. In a word, everything attests that, from that time, tonsure and ordination were distinct; and that many men were tonsured without entering into orders, became clerks without becoming ecclesiastics.[1]

They wished to participate in the immunities of the church; she received them into her ranks in the same way as she opened her temples to the proscribed; she thereby gained an extension of her credit and her forces. But the religious society gained thereby, in its turn, a means of action upon the ecclesiastical society; those who were merely tonsured did not share completely either the interests or the *esprit-de-corps*, or the life of the clergy, properly so called; they preserved, to a certain degree, the habits and feelings of the lay population, and introduced them into the church. More numerous than they are generally supposed, this class of men has played a considerable part in the history of the middle ages. Bound to the church without belonging to her, enjoying her privileges without falling under the yoke of her interests and manners, protected and not enslaved, it was in its breast that that spirit of liberty was developed which we shall see burst forth towards the end of the eleventh century, and of which Abailard was then the most illustrious interpreter. From the eighth century, it mitigated that separation of the clergy and the people which was the dominant characteristic of the epoch, and prevented it from bearing all its fruit.

2ndly. A second fact concurred to the same result. From the time that Christianity became powerful, it was, as you know, a frequent custom to found and to endow churches. The founder enjoyed, in the church which owed its origin to him, certain privileges which, at first, were purely honorary; they inscribed his name in the interior of the church, they prayed for him, they even granted him some influence over the choice of the priests charged with the divine offices. It

[1] M. Plank even says that they often gave the tonsure to children; and he refers to the 6th canon of the 10th council of Toledo, held in 656, which forbids its being conferred before the age of ten. But there is some confusion in this: this canon only concerns children brought up in monasteries, and whom the tonsure devoted to a religious life. This fact has no analogy with that which occupies us, and to the support of which M. Plank invokes it.—Hist. de la Constit. de l'Egliso Chrětienne, ii. p. 13, not. 8. Labbé, Conc., t. vi. col. 463.

happened that bishops wished to found churches beyond their diocese, whether in their native town, in the midst of some domain, or from some other motive. Their right to choose the priest called to perform the duties was unhesitatingly recognised; many councils occupied themselves in regulating the exercise of this right, and the relations of the bishop who founded the church with the bishop in the diocese where the foundation was situated.

"If a bishop," says the council of Orange, "wishes to build a church in the territory of a city, whether for the interest of his domains, for the benefit of the Church, or for any other reason, after having obtained permission for this, which cannot be denied him without crime, let him not meddle with its consecration, which is absolutely reserved to the bishop of the see where the new church is situated. But this grace shall be granted to the bishop who founded it, that the bishop of the place shall ordain whatever priests the founder may desire to see in his foundation; or, if they be already ordained, the said bishop of the place shall accept them.[1]

This ecclesiastical patronage soon led to a lay patronage of the same nature. Foundations by the laity became more and more frequent. Their conditions and forms were very various. Sometimes the founder reserved a portion of the revenues with which he endowed his church; he sometimes even went so far as to stipulate that he should enter into a participation of the offerings which the church should acquire in addition; so that men founded and endowed churches out of speculation, to run the chance of their fortune, and to associate themselves in their future prosperity. The councils took measures against this abuse, but they recognised and consecrated the right of the founders, whether laymen or ecclesiastics, to influence the choice of the official priests.

"Moved by a pious compassion," say the bishops of Spain, met in council at Toledo, "we have decided that as long as the founders of churches shall live they shall be permitted to have the care of them, and they must especially make it their

[1] Council of Orange, in 441, c. 20.

business to present, for the ordination of bishops, worthy priests for these churches; if they do not propose such, then those whom the bishop of the place shall judge pleasing to God shall be consecrated to his worship, and, with the consent of the founders, shall officiate in their church. If, in contempt of the founders, the bishop performs an ordination, it shall be null, and he shall be constrained, to his shame, to ordain for the place suitable persons chosen by the founders."[1]

By this means, therefore, the laity exercised a certain influence in the church, and took some part in her government.

3rdly. At the same time, and in proportion as the social state became a little fixed, the custom was introduced among the great proprietors in the country, and even in the towns, of instituting at home, in the interior of their house, an oratory, a chapel, and of having a priest to officiate in it. These chaplains soon became the object of lively solicitude on the part of the bishops. They were placed under the dependence of their lay patron far more than under that of the neighbouring bishops; they were likely to participate in the feelings of the house where they lived, and separate more or less from the church. This was, besides, a means for the powerful laity to procure the assistance of religion, and of fulfilling its duties without depending wholly on the bishop of the diocese. We accordingly find the councils of this epoch carefully watching this non-embodied clergy, disseminated in the lay society, and of which they seemed to fear sometimes the serviture, sometimes the independence.

"If any one," orders the council of Agde, "wishes to have an oratory on his own ground, besides the parish church, we allow that in ordinary festivals he shall there cause mass to be said for the accommodation of his own people; but Easter, Christmas, Epiphany, Ascension, Pentecost, the birth of St. John the Baptist, and all the other days which should be held as great festivals, must only be celebrated in certain churches. The priests who, without the order or

[1] Ninth council of Toledo, held in 655, c. 2. I shall often cite the Spanish councils, because they have committed to writing more explicitly and more clearly facts which took place also in Gaul.

permission of the bishop, shall, on the above enumerated festivals, say or hear mass in oratories, shall be excluded from the communion."[1]

"If rectories," says the council of Orleans, "are established in the houses of powerful men, and the priests who officiate there, warned by the archdeacon of the city, neglect, in favour of the power of the master of the house, that which, according to the degree of their order, is their duty in the house of the Lord, let them be corrected according to ecclesiastical discipline. And if by the agents of the lords, or by the lords themselves, the said priests are opposed in the performance of any ecclesiastical duty, let the authors of such iniquity be removed from the holy ceremonies until, being amended, they shall re-enter into the peace of the church."[2]

"Many of our brothers and bishops," says likewise the council of Châlons, "have complained to the holy convocation, upon the subject of the oratories, long since constructed in the country houses of the great men of the state. Those to whom these houses belong, dispute with the bishops property which has been given to these oratories, and do not allow that even the priests who officiate in them are under the jurisdiction of the archdeacon; it is important that this should be reformed: accordingly, let the property of the oratories, and the priests who officiate in them, be under the power of the bishop, in order that he may acquit himself of what is due to these oratories and to the divine service; and if any one oppose himself thereto, let him be excommunicated, according to the tenour of the ancient canons."[3]

It was not without reason that the bishops, having an eye to their power, looked upon this domestic clergy with so much mistrust: an example of it is met with in modern times, which shows us its effects. In England, under the reign of Charles I., before the breaking out of the revolution, during the struggle between the English church and the puritan party, the bishops drove from their cures all the ecclesiastics suspected of puritan opinions. What was the consequence?—the gentry, the great proprietors, who shared these opinions, took into their houses, under the name of chaplains, the expelled

[1] Council of Agde, in 506, c. 21. [2] Council of Orleans, in 541, c. 26.
[3] Council of Châlons, in 650, c. 14.

ministers. A large portion of the clergy who were suspected by the bishops, accordingly, placed themselves under the patronage of the lay society, and there exercised an influence formidable to the official clergy. In vain the English church pursued her adversaries, even into the interior of families; when tyranny is forced to penetrate so deep, it soon becomes enervated, or hastens towards its ruin: the inferior nobility, the high bourgeoisie of England, defended their chaplains with the most persevering energy; they concealed them, they changed them from house to house; they eluded or they braved the episcopal anathemas. The bishops might manœuvre, oppress; they were no longer the only, the necessary clergy; the population harboured in its breast a clergy foreign to the legal church, and more and more at enmity with it. From the sixth to the eighth century, the danger was not the same; the bishops had to fear neither schism nor insurrection. Still the institution of the chaplains had an analogous effect: it tended to form an inferior clergy, less closely united to the body of the church, nearer to the laity, more disposed to share their manners, in fine, to make common cause with the age and the people. Accordingly, they did not cease attentively to overlook and curb the chaplains. They, however, by no means destroyed them; they dared not attempt it: the development of the feudal system even gave to this institution a fixity which at first was wanting to it: and this was also one of the ways by which the laity regained that influence in the government of the religious society, which its legal and internal constitution refused to it.

4thly. The bishops themselves were constrained to open another way to it. The administration of the temporal affairs and property of the church, was often a source of embarrassment and danger to them; they had not only differences to decide, and suits to maintain, but, in the fearful disorder of the time, the property of the church was exposed to continual devastations, engaged and compromised in numerous quarrels, in private wars; and when it was necessary to make a defence, when the church, in behalf of her domains or her rights, had some robbery to repel, some legal proof, perhaps even, in some cases, a judicial combat to maintain, pious menaces, exhortations, excommunications even did not always suffice; she wanted temporal and worldly arms.

In order to procure them, she had recourse to an expedient. For some time past certain churches, especially in Africa, had been in the habit of selecting defenders who, under the name of *causidici, tutores, vice-domini,* were charged with the duty of appearing for them before justice, and of protecting them *adversus potentias divitum.* An analogous necessity, and one far more pressing, led the churches of Frankish-Gaul to seek among their neighbouring laity a patron who, under the name of *advocatus*, took their cause in hand and became their man, not only in judicial disputes, where they had need of him, but against any robberies which might threaten them. From the sixth to the eighth century, the *advocates* of the church did not yet appear with the development nor under the forms which they received at a later period, in the feudal system; we do not as yet distinguish the *advocati sagati,* or armed, from the *advocati togati,* charged merely with civil affairs. But the institution was not the less real and efficacious; we find numerous churches choosing *advocates;* they were careful to take powerful and brave men; kings sometimes gave them to churches who as yet had no *advocates,* and the laity were thus called in to participate in the temporal administration of the church, and to exercise an important influence over her affairs.

It was generally by granting them certain privileges, especially in giving them the usufruct of some domain, that the churches thus solicited the support, and paid the services of some powerful neighbour.

We may already see, if I may so express myself, four doors opened to religious society to enter the ecclesiastical society, and there exercise some power; the separation of ordination and tonsure, that is to say, the introduction into the church of many clerks who were not ecclesiastics; the rights attached to the foundation and to the patronage of churches; the institution of private oratories; and lastly, the intervention of advocates in the administration of the temporal interests of the church; such were the principal causes which, at the epoch which occupies us, combated the exclusive domination of ecclesiastical society over religious society, and weakened or retarded its effects. I might point out many others which I omit, because they were less general and less evident. *A priori,* such a fact was easy to presume: this separation of the governing and the governed could not be so absolute as the official institutions of the church at this epoch would lead us to suppose. If it had been so, if the body of the faithful had been strangers to the body of priests to such a degree, and deprived of all influence over its government, the government, in its turn, would have soon found itself a stranger to its people, and deprived of all power. It must not be supposed that servitude is complete wherever the forms or even the principles of tyranny are found. Providence does not permit evil to be developed in all the rigour of its consequences; and human nature, often so weak, so easily vanquished by whomsoever wishes to oppress it, has yet infinite ability and a wonderful power for escaping from the yoke which it seems to accept. There can be no doubt but that, from the sixth to the eighth century, the religious society bore that of the ecclesiastical society, and that the separation of the clergy and the people, already a source of much evil, one day was to cost both of them dearly; but it was much less complete than it appeared; it only took place with a crowd of restrictions and modifications which alone rendered it possible, and alone can explain them.

II. Let us now enter into the bosom of ecclesiastical society itself, and let us see what became of its internal organization from the fifth to the eighth century, especially of that preponderance of the episcopacy which in the fifth century was its dominant characteristic.

The organization of the clergy at this epoch was complete, and almost the same, at least in its essential forms, as it has remained up to modern times. I can therefore place it before you in its *ensemble;* you will so better follow the variations.

The clergy comprehended two orders, the minor orders and the major orders. The first were four in number: the acolytes, the porters, the exorcists, and the readers. They called major orders, the under-deacons, the deacons, and the priests. The inequality was great; the four minor orders were preserved scarcely more than in name, and out of respect for ancient traditions; although they were reckoned as clergy, they did not, truly speaking, form a part of it; they had not imposed upon them, they were not even recommended to celibacy; they were looked upon rather as servants than as members of the clergy. When, therefore, the clergy and the ecclesiastical government of this epoch is spoken of, it is only the major orders that are meant.

Even in the major orders the influence of the first two named, the under-deacons and deacons, was weak; the deacons were occupied rather in administering the property of the church, and the distribution of her alms than in religious government properly so called. It is to the order of priests, truly speaking, that this government was confined; neither the minor orders, nor the two others of the major orders, really participated in it.

The body of priests were subject, in the first six centuries, to numerous and important vicissitudes. The bishop, in my opinion, ought to be considered as its primitive and fundamental element; not that the same functions, the same rights, have always been indicated by this word; the episcopacy of the second century greatly differed from that of the fourth; it is no less the starting point of ecclesiastical organization. The bishop was, originally, the inspector, the chief of the religious congregation of each town. The Christian church took birth in towns; the bishops were its first magistrates.

When Christianity spread into the rural districts, the municipal bishop no longer sufficed. Then appeared the chorepiscopi, or rural bishops, moving, ambulatory bishops, *episcopi vagi*, considered, sometimes as the delegates, sometimes as the equals, the rivals even of the metropolitan bishops, and whom the latter attempted at first to subject to their power, and afterwards to abolish.

They succeeded therein: the rural districts once Christian, the chorepiscopi in their turn no longer sufficed: something more fixed, more regular, was necessary; something less contested by the most influential magistrates of the church, that is to say, the metropolitan bishops. Then parishes were formed; each Christian agglomeration at all considerable became a parish, and had a priest for its religious head, naturally subordinate to the bishop of the neighbouring town, from whom he received and held all his powers; for it seems that originally parish priests acted absolutely only as representatives, as delegates of the bishops, and not in virtue of their own right.

The union of all the agglomerated parishes around a town, in a circumscription for a long time vague and variable, formed the diocese.

After a certain time, and in order to bring more regularity and completeness into the relations of the diocesan clergy, they formed a small association of many parishes under the name of the *rural chapter*, and at the head of the rural chapter was placed an archpriest. At a later period many rural chapters were united in a new circumscription under the name of *district*, which was directed by an archdeacon. This last institution had scarcely arisen at the epoch of which we treat: it is true that long before we find archdeacons in the dioceses; but there was but one, and he did not preside over a territorial circumscription; established in an episcopal town, in the same town with the bishop, he took his place, sometimes in the exercise of his jurisdiction, sometimes in the visitation of the diocese. It was only at the end of the seventh, or, at least, at the commencement of the eighth century, that we see many archdeacons in the same diocese, residing at a distance from the bishop, and each placed at the head of a district. We still encounter at this epoch, in Frankish Gaul, some chorepiscopi; but the name and charge were not long in disappearing.

The diocesan organization was then complete and definitive. The bishop, as you see, had been its source, as he remained its centre. He was much changed himself, but it was around him, and under his influence, that almost all other changes were brought about.

All the dioceses in the civil province formed the ecclesiastical province, under the direction of the metropolitan or archbishop. The quality of the archbishop was but the expression of this fact. The civil metropolis was generally more wealthy, more populous than the other towns of the province; its bishop had more influence; people met around him on all important occasions; his residence became the chief place of the provincial council; he convoked it, and was the president of it; he was moreover charged with the confirmation and consecration of the newly elected bishops of the province; with receiving accusations brought against bishops, and the appeals from their decisions, and with carrying them, after having made a first examination, to the provincial council, which alone had the right of judging them. The archbishops unceasingly attempted to usurp this right, and make a personal power of it. They often succeeded;

but, in truth, as to all important circumstances, it was to the provincial council that it appertained; the archbishops were only charged with superintending the execution of it.

In some states finally, especially in the east, the organization of the church extended beyond the archbishops. As they had constituted parishes into the diocese, and the dioceses into the province, they undertook to constitute provinces into national churches, under the direction of a patriarch. The undertaking succeeded in Syria, in Palestine, in Egypt, in the Eastern Empire; there was a patriarch at Antioch, at Jerusalem, at Constantinople; he was, with regard to archbishops, what archbishops were to bishops; and the ecclesiastical organization corresponded in all degrees of the hierarchy with the political organization.

The same attempt took place in the west, not only on the part of the bishops of Rome, who laboured at an early period to become the patriarchs of the whole west, but independently of their pretensions, and even against them. There are scarcely any of the states formed after the invasion, which did not attempt, from the sixth to the eighth century, to become a national church, and to have a patriarch. In Spain, the archbishop of Toledo; in England, the archbishop of Canterbury; in Frankish Gaul, the archbishop of Arles, of Vienne, of Lyons, of Bourges, bore the title of primate or patriarch of Gaul, of Great Britain, of Spain, and attempted to exercise all its rights. But the attempt everywhere failed: the western states had scarcely taken rise; their limits, their government, their very existence were incessantly in question. Gaul, particularly, was divided between many nations, and, in the heart of each nation, between the sons of the kings; the bishops of a kingdom were unwilling to acknowledge the authority of a foreign primate; the civil government was equally opposed to it. Besides, the bishop of Rome, already in possession of great influence, even where his official supremacy was not acknowleged, warmly contested the establishment of the patriarchs; in Gaul, the principle upon which he acted was constantly to transfer the primacy from one metropolitan to another, so as to prevent its remaining too long attached to one particular see; at one time he favoured the pretensions to the primacy of the metropolitan of Vienne, then those of the bishop of

Arles; at another time those of the bishop of Lyons; and then again those of the bishop of Sens; so as, by this constant fluctuation and uncertainty in the religious and civil order, to prevent the institution from attaining force or fixity.

The same causes which operated against this particular institution, extended their influence beyond it; in the same way that they had prevented the system of the patriarchate from taking root, they weakened and finally broke down the archiepiscopal system. From the sixth to the eighth century, the metropolitan bishops fell from time to time lower and lower; so that, at the accession of the Carlovingians, they could hardly be said to exist at all. The circumstance alone of the parcelling out of Gaul into different states, was calculated to be of fatal consequence to them. The circumscription of the religious society no longer agreed with that of the civil society. Within the province of the archbishop of Lyons, for instance, there were bishops subject to the kingdom of the Visigoths, and to the kingdom of the Franks, and who, on all occasions, eagerly availed themselves of this pretext for evading their spiritual superior's authority, quite certain of being supported by the temporal sovereign. Moreover, as you have seen, the preponderance of the metropolitans was based upon that of the town in which they respectively resided, and upon its former quality as a metropolis. Now, in the general disorder occasioned by the invasion, considerable changes took place in the relative importance of towns; rich, important cities, metropoles, truly so called, became poor and depopulated. Others, on whom fortune smiled more favourably, acquired a wealth and population previously unknown to them. With the disappearance from a city of its importance, disappeared the cause which had rendered its bishop a metropolitan, and the word metropolitan became, by degrees, a falsehood, a circumstance highly dangerous to the power which it outwardly expressed. Besides, it was in the very nature of the institution to be assailed at once, on the one hand, by the bishops, who were not desirous of having a spiritual superior; on the other, by the bishop of Rome, who naturally wished to have no rivals; the result was what might have been expected. The bishops preferred, as their general metropolitan, the bishop of Rome, who lived at a distance, and took care to conciliate them, not having them as yet within his power, adopted the course of supporting the bishop of Rome against their more immediate metropolitans. Thus attacked on both sides, the metropolitans daily declined in influence and power; the bishops ceased to pay any attention to their mandates, or even to their exhortations; the body of the church to have recourse in any way to their intervention; and when, in 744, Pepin-le-Bref consulted pope Zachary on the best means of restoring order to the confused and agitated church, one of his first questions was, what course he should adopt for procuring respect for the metropolitans at the hands of the bishops and parochial priests.

In point of fact, the whole government of the church, at this period, was in the hands of the bishops and of the priests: they were the only members of it who were at all active and powerful. What were their mutual relations? how was power divided between them?

The general manifest fact was, the exclusive domination and, we may say, despotism, of the bishops. Let us seek closely for the causes of this: it is the best means of properly understanding the situation of the church.

1. And first, the fall of the metropolitans left the bishops without superiors, or very nearly so. With the head of the ecclesiastical province declined the provincial synod, which it was his privilege to assemble and preside over. These synods, heretofore the unquestionable superiors of the bishops, to which appeals were carried from the decisions of the bishops, and which took cognizance of all the causes which the bishops could not of themselves decide, became rare and inactive. In the course of the sixth century, there were held in Gaul fifty-four councils of every description; in the seventh century, only twenty; in the first half of the eighth century, only seven, and five of these were held in Belgium, or on the banks of the Rhine.[1]

[1] *Table of the Gaulish Councils of the Sixth Century.*

Date.	*Place.*	*Present.*
506	Agde................	25 bishops, 8 priests, 2 deacons, representing their bishops.
507	Toulouse	
511	Orleans	32 bishops.
515	St. Maurice	4 bishops, 8 counts.

Table of the Gaulish Councils of the sixth century—continued.

Date.	Place.	Present.
516	Lyons	
517	Place uncertain	16 bishops.
517	Epaonense	25 bishops.
517	Lyons	11 bishops.
524	Arles	14 bishops, 4 priests.
527	Carpentras	19 bishops.
529	Orange..............	14 bishops, 8 *viri illustres*
529	Valencia.	
529	Vaison	11 or 12 bishops.
530	Angers	5 bishops.
533	Orleans	26 bishops, 5 priests.
535	Clermont	15 bishops.
538	Orleans..............	19 bishops, 7 priests.
540	Orleans.	
541	Orleans..............	38 bishops, 11 priests, 1 abbot.
545	Arles.	
549	Orleans..............	5 bishops, 21 priests, archdeacons, or abbots.
549	Arles	10 bishops.
550	Toul.	
550	Metz.	
554	Arles................	11 bishops, 8 priests, deacons, or archdeacons.
555	Place uncertain in Brittany.	
555	Paris	27 bishops.
557	Paris................	16 bishops.
563	Saintes.	
567	Lyons	8 bishops, 5 priests, 1 deacon.
567	Tours	7 bishops.
573	Paris	32 bishops, 1 priest
575	Lyons	
577	Paris.	
578	Auxerre	The bishop of Auxerre, 7 abbots, 34 priests, 3 deacons, all of the diocese of Auxerre
579	Châlons.	
579	Saintes.	
580	Braines.	
581	Lyons.	
581	Màcon	21 bishops.
583	Lyons	8 bishops, 12 delegates of bishops.
584	Valencia.	
585	Màcon	43 bishops, 15 delegates, 16 bishops without sees
587	Andelot.	
588	Clermont.	
588	Place uncertain.	
589	Sourcy near Soissons.	
589	Châlons.	

Table of the Gaulish Councils of the sixth century—continued.

Date.	*Place.*	*Present.*
589	Narbonne............	7 bishops.
590	Upon the confines of Auvergne, of Rouergue, and of Givaudan.	
590	Poictiers.	6 bishops.
590	Metz.	
591	Nanterre.	
594	Châlons.	

Table of the Councils of Gaul in the Seventh Century.

Date.	*Place*	*Present.*
603	Châlons.	
615	Paris.	
shortly afterwards	Place uncertain.	
625	Rheims............	41 bishops.
627	Màcon.	
628	Clichy	Bishops and high laymen.
633	Clichy	15 bishops, Dagobert, great men.
638	Paris	9 bishops, Dagobert, great men.
648	Bourges.	
650 or 645	Orleans.	
650	Châlons	38 bishops, 5 abbots, 1 archdeacon.
658	Nantes.	
664	Paris..............	25 bishops.
669	Clichy	Bishops and great men.
670	Sens..............	30 bishops.
670	Autun.	
679	Place uncertain.	
684 or 685	In the palace of the king.	
688	Ibid.	
692 or 682	Rouen	16 bishops, 4 abbots, 1 legate, 3 archdeacons, many priests and deacons.

Table of the Councils of Gaul in the first half of the Eighth Century.

Date.	*Place.*	*Present.*
719	Maestricht.	
742	In Germany.	
743	Septines.	
744	Soissons	23 bishops, many priests and high laymen.
745	In Germany.	
748	Ibid.	
752	Vermeric.	

Thus gradually freed from individual superiors, and from assemblies of their equals, the bishops found themselves in an almost entirely independent position. There was a change, too, in the system of episcopal elections. You have seen that the election by the clergy and the people, although still legal and of frequent occurrence at the epoch which occupies us, was still far more uncertain and far less real. A foreign force, royalty, constantly interfered therein, in order to bring trouble and impotence into it: kings unceasingly directly nominated bishops, despite the continual protestations of the church, and, in all cases, the elected required their confirmation. The ties which united the bishops to their priests became accordingly very much weakened; it was almost solely by election that the clergy influenced the episcopacy, and this influence, if it was not destroyed, was at least enervated and disputed.

2ndly. There resulted from this another circumstance which still more separated the bishops from their priests: when the clergy elected them, it took them from its own bosom; it selected men already known and accredited in the diocese. When, on the contrary, a crowd of bishops received their title from kings, the greater part arrived strangers, unknown, alike without credit and without affection among the clergy whom they had to govern. Taken even in the diocese, they were there often destitute of consideration; intriguers who had succeeded, by disgraceful means, or even by money, in obtaining the royal preference. Thus were still farther broken the ties which united the bishops to the clergy; thus the episcopal power, which no longer possessed any superior power, was alike released from the influence of its people; as the clergy was separated from the lay population, so was the episcopacy separated from the clergy.

3rdly. This is not all: the clergy itself declined; not only did it lose its power, but its position, and, so to speak, its quality was diminished. You have seen that, at this epoch, a great number of slaves entered into the church, and by what causes. The bishops soon perceived that a clergy thus formed was without principle, without power, far more easy to govern and to conquer, if it attempt to resist. In many dioceses they took care to recruit it from the same source, to aid themselves the natural course of things; this origin of a crowd of priests long contributed to the sovereignty of the episcopacy.

4thly. Here we have a fourth cause, even more powerful and extensive. The bishops were the sole administrators of the property of the church. This property was of two kinds: on one side, foundation property, every day more considerable, for it was under this form that the greater part of donations to churches were made; on the other, the offerings of the faithful in the churches themselves. I shall say a word, in passing, of a third kind of ecclesiastical revenue, which at a later period played an important part, but which, at the seventh century, was not yet well established; I mean the tithe. From the earliest ages, the clergy made continual efforts to bring back or to generalise this Hebrew institution; it preached it, it praised it; it recalled the Jewish traditions and manners. Two Gaulish councils of the sixth century, that of Tours, in 567, and that of Mâcon, in 585, made it the subject of formal provisions. But they felt, by their very tone, that these dispositions were rather exhortations than laws: "We urgently caution you," writes the council of Tours to the faithful, "that, following the examples of Abraham, you do not fail to offer to God the tenth of all your property, to the end that you may preserve the rest;"[1] and these exhortations were but of little effect.

It was at a later period, and only under the Carlovingians, that, with the aid of the civil power, the clergy attained its end, and rendered the tithe general and regular. At the epoch of which we treat, the foundation property and the offerings were her only revenues. Now it must not be supposed, that these revenues belonged to a particular church or parish, where the source of them lay: the produce of all the adjacent domains, of all offerings received in the diocese, formed a mass of which the bishop alone had the disposition:

"Let the domains, estates, vineyards, slaves, the peculium, ... which are given to parishes," says the council of Orleans, "remain in the power of the bishop."[2] Charged with the cost of dispensing worship and the maintenance of the priests, in the whole diocese, it was the bishop who determined the part allotted to each parish. Certain rules, it

[1] Labbe, vol. v. col. 868. [2] Council of Orleans, in 611, c. 14, 15.

is true, were soon established with regard to this matte.. three parts were usually made of the revenues of a parish; one third was appropriated to the priests who performed its duties; another to the expense of worship, and a third returned to the bishop. But in spite of this legal injunction, often repeated by the canons, the centralization of the ecclesiastical revenues continued; the general administration belonged to the bishop, and it was easy to foresee the extension of this means of power.

5th. He disposed of persons almost as of things, and the liberty of the parish priests was scarcely better guaranteed than their revenue. The principle of the servitude of the glebe, if I may so express myself, was introduced into the church; we read in the acts of the councils:

"It is said, in the law concerning the labourers of the field, that each must remain wherever he began to live. The canons likewise order, that the priests who work for the church remain where they commenced."[1]

"Let no bishop raise in degree a strange priest."[2]

"Let no one ordain a priest who does not first promise to remain where he shall be placed."[3]

Never was power over persons more expressly established.

6th. The progress of the political importance of the bishops turned equally to the profit of their religious domination. They entered into the national assemblies; they surrounded and counselled kings. How could the poor priests struggle with any advantage against such superiors? Besides, such was the disorder of the times, and both the difficulty and the necessity of maintaining some general tie, some unity in the administration of the church, that the course of things agreeing with the passions of men, tended to strengthen the central power. The despotism of the episcopal aristocracy prevailed by the same causes which caused that of the feudal aristocracy to prevail; this was, perhaps, at this epoch, the common and dominant want, the only means of maintaining society.

But it redounds to the honour and safety of human nature, that an evil, although inevitable, is never accomplished without resistance, and that liberty, incessantly protesting

[1] Council of Seville, in 619, c. 3. [2] Council of Angers, in 453, c. 9.
[3] Council of Valencia, in 524, c. 6.

and struggling against necessity, prepares the enfranchisement, even at the moment that it submits to the yoke. The bishops strangely abused their immense power: the priests, and the revenues of their diocese were the prey to violences and exactions of all kinds: the acts of the councils, composed of bishops only, are, in this respect, the most unexceptionable testimony.

"We have learned," says the council of Toledo, "that the bishops treat their parishes, not episcopally, but cruelly; and while it has been written 'neither as being lords over God's heritage, but being ensamples to the flock,' they load their dioceses with loss and exactions. It is for this reason that the things which the bishops appropriate to themselves are to be refused them, with the exception of what the ancient institutions grant them; let the priests, whether parochial or diocesan, who shall be tormented by the bishop, carry their complaints to the metropolitan, and let the metropolitan delay not to repress such excesses."[1]

"Those who have already obtained ecclesiastical degrees, that is to say, the priests," says the council of Braga, "must in no way be subject to receive blows, except for grave and deadly faults. It is not suitable that each bishop should, according to his inclination and when it pleases him, strike with blows and cause his honourable ministers to suffer, for fear he lose the respect which is his due from those who are subject to him."[2]

The priests did not lose all respect for the bishops, nor any more did they accept all their tyranny. An important fact, and one too little remarked, is seen here and there during the course of this epoch: this is the contest of the parochial priests against the bishops. Three principal symptoms in the acts of the councils must not be overlooked:

1st. The parochial priests, the inferior clerks, leagued among themselves to resist: they formed *conjuratios* against the bishops similar to those conjuratios, to those fraternities formed at a later period by the burghers against their lords.

"If any priests, as has happened lately in many places, at the instigation of the devil should rebel against authority, unite in a conspiracy, should take a common oath among themselves,

[1] Council of Toledo, in 589, c. 20. [2] Council of Braga, in 675, c. 7.

or unite in a common bond, let such audacity be concealed under no pretext, and, the thing once known, let the bishops, assembled in synod, punish the guilty according to their rank and quality."[1]

"If any priests, for the purposes of revolt, should combine in a common bond, whether verbal, or written, and should cunningly lay snares for their bishop, and, once warned to give up these practices, should refuse to obey, let them be degraded from their rank."[2]

2nd. The priests have constantly recourse against their bishops, to the aid of the laity, probably to that of the lord of the manor, or any other powerful person in the district with whom they are in connexion. We find this injunction repeatedly in the acts of the councils:

"Let not the priests rise up against their bishops by the aid of secular power."[3]

3rd. But while repeating this prohibition, while proscribing the *conjurationes* of the priests, the councils themselves endeavoured to apply some remedy to the evils combined against: complaints were constantly addressed to them from all quarters, to which they felt themselves compelled to pay attention; a few passages from their acts will be more elucidatory on this point than any comments of ours:

"As some complaints have reached us, of certain bishops having taken possession of things given by the faithful for the use of their parishes, so that little or nothing is left to the churches upon which these gifts were really bestowed, it has appeared to us just and reasonable, and we hereby declare that, if the church of the city wherein the bishop resides is so well provided, that, by the grace of Christ, it wants for nothing, all that remains to the parishes should be distributed among the clerks who officiate in them, or employed in repairing their churches. But if the bishop is involved in much expense, without sufficient revenue to meet it, there shall be given to the richer parishes that which is fitting and reasonable, whether for priests, or for the support of the

[1] Council of Orleans, in 538, c. 28.

[2] Councils of Rheims in 625, c. 2; see also the council of Narbonne, in 589, c. 5.

[3] Council of Clermont, in 535, c. 4.

buildings, and let the bishop appropriate the surplus to his own use, in order that he may provide for his expenses."[1]

"If offerings have been made to the basilicas established in cities, of lands, goods, or any other things whatsoever, let them be at the disposition of the bishop, and let him be free to employ what is suitable, whether in the repair of the basilica, or in the support of priests who officiate in it. With regard to parochial property or basilicas established in boroughs, dependent upon cities, let the custom of each place be observed."[2]

"It has been decided that no bishop, in the visitation of his diocese, shall receive from any church anything beyond what is due to him, as a mark of honour to his see; he shall not take the third of all the offerings of the people in the parish churches, but this third shall remain for the lighting and repairs of the churches; and each year the bishop shall have an account of it. For if the bishop take this third, he robs the church of its light and the support of its roof."[3]

"Avarice is the root of all evil, and this guilty thirst seizes even the hearts of the bishops. Many of the faithful, from love for Christ and the martyrs, raise basilicas in the parishes of the bishops, and deposit offerings therein; but the bishops seize upon them and turn them to their own use. Thence it follows that priests are wanting to perform Divine service, because they do not receive their fees. Dilapidated cathedrals are not repaired because sacerdotal avarice has carried off all the funds. The present orders, therefore, that bishops govern their churches without receiving more than is due to them according to the ancient decrees, that is to say, the third of the offerings and of the parochial revenues; if they take more than this, the council will cause it to be returned on the demand of either the founders of the church themselves if they be living, or of their descendants. Nevertheless, the founders of churches are not to suppose that they retain any power whatever over the property with which they have endowed the said churches, seeing that according to the canons, not only the church itself, but the property with which it is endowed, is under the jurisdiction, duly administered, of the bishop."[4]

[1] Council of Carpentras, in 527.
[2] Council of Orleans, in 538, c. 5.
[3] Council of Braga, in 572, c. 2.
[4] Council of Toledo, in 638, c. 33.

"Among the things which it behoves us to regulate by common consent, it is more especially necessary to meet discreetly, the complaints of the parochial priests of the province of Galicia, touching the rapacity of their bishops, which has grown to such a height as to compel the priests to demand public inquiry into them; such inquiry having been made, it has clearly resulted that these bishops overwhelm their parochial churches with their exactions; and that while they themselves wallow in luxury, they have brought many of the churches to the verge of ruin; in order to put a stop to such abuses we order that, according to the regulations of the synod of Braga, each of the bishops of the said province shall receive annually from each of the churches in his diocese the sum of two *solidi*,[1] and no more. And when the bishop visits his diocese, let him be burdensome to no one from the multitude of his attendants, let him have no more than five carriages with him, and let him stay no longer than one day at each church."[2]

The extracts here given are amply sufficient to prove the oppression and the resistance, the evil and the attempt to remedy it;—the resistance was abortive, the remedy ineffectual: episcopal despotism continued to take deeper and wider root. Thus, at the commencement of the eighth century, the church had fallen into a state of disorder almost equal to that prevalent in civil society. Without superiors, without inferiors at all to be dreaded—relieved from the superintendence of the metropolitans and of the councils, rejecting the influence of the priests—a crowd of bishops were seen yielding themselves up to the most scandalous excesses. Masters of the ever increasing wealth of the church, ranking amongst the great landed proprietors, they adopted their interests and their manners; they relinquished their ecclesiastical character and led a wholly secular life; they kept hounds and falcons, they went from place to place surrounded by an armed retinue, they took part in the national warfare; nay more, they undertook, from time to time, expeditions of violence and rapine against their neighbours on their own account. A crisis was inevitable; everything prepared the necessity for reformation, everything proclaimed it, and

[1] About 13s. [2] Council of Toledo, in 646, c. 4.

you will see that in point of fact, shortly after the accession of the Carlovingians, an attempt at reformation was made by the civil power, but the church herself contained the germ of a remedy: side by side with the secular clergy, there had been rising up another order, influenced by other principles, animated with another spirit, and which seemed destined to prevent that dissolution with which the church was menaced; I speak of the monks. Their history from the sixth to th eighth century will be the object of our next lecture.

FOURTEENTH LECTURE.

History of the regular clergy, or the monks, from the sixth to the eighth century—That the monks were at first laymen—Importance of this fact—Origin and progressive development of the monastic life in the east—First rules—Importation of the monks into the west—They are ill received there—Their first progress—Difference between eastern and western monasteries—Opinion of Saint Jerome, as to the errors of the monastic life—General causes of its extension—State of the monks in the west in the fifth century—Their power and their want of coherence—Saint Benedict—His life—He founds the monastery of Monte Cassino—Analysis and estimate of his rule—It diffuses itself throughout the west, and becomes predominant in almost all the monasteries there.

Since we resumed the history of religious society in Frankish Gaul, we have considered: 1, the general dominant fact which characterized the church from the sixth to the eighth century—that is to say, its unity; 2, its relations with the state; 3, its internal organization, the mutual position of the governors and the governed, the constitution of the government—that is to say, of the clergy.

We have seen that, towards the middle of the eighth century, the government of the church, the clergy, had fallen into a state of great disorder and decay. We have recognised a crisis, the necessity for reformation; I mentioned to you that a principle of reform already existed in the bosom of the clergy itself; I named the regular clergy, the monks; it is with their history at the same period that we are now about to occupy ourselves.

The term, regular clergy, is calculated to produce an illusory effect, it gives one the idea that the monks have always been ecclesiastics, have always essentially formed a part of the clergy, and this is, in point of fact, the general notion which has been applied to them indiscriminately, without regard to time, or place, or to the successive modifications of the institution. And not only are monks regarded as ecclesiastics, but they are by many people considered as, so to speak, the most ecclesiastical of all ecclesiastics, as the most completely of all clerical bodies separated from civil society, as the most estranged from its interest and from its manners. This, if I mistake not, is the impression which the mere mention of their name at present, and for a long time past, naturally arouses in the mind; it is an impression full of error: at their origin, and for at least two centuries afterwards, the monks were not ecclesiastics at all; they were mere laymen, united together indeed by a common religious creed, in a common religious sentiment, and with a common religious object, but altogether apart from the ecclesiastical society, from the clergy, especially so called.

And not only was such the nature of the institution at its origin, but this primitive character which is so generally unheeded, has prominently influenced its whole history, and alone enables us to comprehend its vicissitudes. I have already made some remarks upon the establishment of monasteries in the west, more especially in the south of Gaul. I will now, in renewing the subject, trace back the facts to their remotest sources, and follow them more closely in their development.

You are all aware it was in the east that the monks took their rise. The form in which they first appeared, was very different from that which they afterwards assumed, and in which the mind is accustomed to view them. In the earlier years of Christianity, a few men of more excitable imaginations than their fellows, imposed upon themselves all sorts of sacrifices and of extraordinary personal austerities; this, however, was no Christian innovation, for we find it, not only in a general tendency of human nature, but in the religious manners of the entire east, and in several Jewish traditions. The *ascetes* (this was the name first given to these pious enthusiasts; *ασκησις, exercises, ascetic life,*) were the first form of monks. They did not segregate, in the first instance, from civil society; they did not retire into the deserts; they only condemned themselves to fasting, silence, to all sorts of austerities, more especially to celibacy.

Soon afterwards they retired from the world; they went to live far from mankind, absolutely alone, amidst woods and deserts, in the depths of the Thebaïd. The ascetes became hermits, anchorites; this was the second form of the monastic life.

After some time, from causes which have left no traces behind them—yielding, perhaps, to the powerful attraction of some more peculiarly celebrated hermit, of Saint Anthony, for instance, or perhaps simply tired of complete isolation, the anchorites collected together, built their huts side by side, and while continuing to live each in his own abode, performed their religious exercises together, and began to form a regular community. It was at this time, as it would seem, that they first received the name of monks.[1]

By and bye they made a further step; instead of remaining in separate huts, they collected in one edifice, under one roof: the association was more closely knit, the common life more complete. They became *cenobites*;[2] this was the fourth form of the monastic institution, its definitive form, that to which all its subsequent developments were to adapt themselves.

At about this period we see arising, for the conduct of these houses of cenobites, for these monasteries, a certain discipline mutually agreed upon, certain written rules, directing the exercises of these small societies, and laying down the obligations of their members; among these primitive rules of the eastern monks, the most celebrated are those of Saint Anthony, Saint Macharius, Saint Hilarius, and Saint Pacomus; all these rules are brief and general, directed to a few leading circumstances of life, but without any pretension to govern the whole life; they are precepts, in fact, rather than rules, customs, rather than laws. The ascetes, the hermits, and the other different classes of monks, continued to subsist, concurrently with the cenobites, in all the independence of their first condition.

The spectacle of such a life, of so much rigidity and enthusiasm, of sacrifice and of liberty, strongly excited the imagi-

[1] Monachus, μοναχος, from μονος, alone.

[2] Cenobitæ, κοινοβιοι, from κοινος, common, and βιος, life.

nation of the people. The monks were multiplied with a prodigious rapidity, and varied to infinity. As you may suppose, I shall not enter into the detail of all the forms which under this name, were taken by the exaltation of the faithful; I shall only indicate the extreme terms, so to speak, of the career which it ran through, and its two effects, at once the most strange and the most various. While, under the name of *Messalians*, or *οὐχιτα*, numerous bands of fanatics overran Mesopotamia, Armenia, &c., rejecting the legal worship, merely celebrating irregular spontaneous prayer, and abandoning themselves in the towns, upon public places, to all sorts of extravagancies; others, in order to separate themselves more completely from all human intercourse, established themselves, after the example of Saint Simeon of Antioch, on the summit of a column, and under the name of *stylites*, devoted their life to this fantastical isolation; and neither one nor the other were in want of admirers and imitators.[1]

In the last half of the fourth century, the rule of Saint Basil brought some regularity into the new institution. Digested into the form of answers to questions of all kinds,[2] it soon became the general discipline of the monasteries of the west—of all those, at least, which had neither any entirety or fixity. Such could not fail to be the result of the influence of the secular clergy over the monastic life, of which the most illustrious bishops, Saint Athanasius, Saint Basil, Saint Gregory Nazianzen, and numerous others, then declared themselves the patrons. This patronage could not fail to introduce into it more order and system. Still, the monasteries remained purely lay associations—strangers to the clergy, to its functions, to its rights. For the monks, there was no ordination, no ecclesiastical engagements. Their dominant characteristic was always religious exaltation and liberty. They entered into the association, they went out from it, they chose their own abode, their own austerities; enthusiasm took the form and entered the path which pleased it. The monks, in a word, had nothing in common with the priests, except their doctrines and the respect with which they inspired the population.

[1] There were stylites in the east down to the twelfth century.
[2] It contained 203 questions, and as many answers.

Such was the state of the monastic institution in the east at the last half of the fourth century. It was somewhere about this period that it was introduced into the west. Saint Athanasius, driven from his see, retired to Rome;[1] he took there with him some monks, and there celebrated their virtues and glory. His accounts, and the spectacle offered by the first monks, or those who followed their example, were ill received by the western population. Paganism was still very strong in the west, especially in Italy. The superior classes who had abandoned its doctrines wished at least to preserve its manners, and a part of the inferior orders still preserved its prejudices. The monks, at their first appearance, were then an object of contempt and of anger. At the funeral of Blesilla, a young Roman nun, who died, it was said, from excessive fasting, in 384, the people cried: "When will they drive this detestable race of monks from the town? Why do they not stone them? Why don't they throw them into the river?" It is St. Jerome who records these popular ebullitions.[2]

"In the cities of Africa," says Salvienus, "and more especially in Carthage, no sooner did a man in a cloak make his appearance, pale, and with his head shaved, than the miserable infidel populace assailed him with curses and abuse; and if some servant of God, from the monasteries of Egypt, or the holy city of Jerusalem, or the venerable retreat of some hermitage, proceeded to that city to fulfil some pious duty, the people pursued him with odious insults, ridiculing and hissing him.[3]

I have already mentioned Rutilius Numatianus, a Gaulish poet, who resided for a long time at Rome, and has left us a poem, celebrating his return to his native country; in the course of this poem, he says, in reference to the Isle of Gorgona:

"I detest those rocks, scene of the recent shipwreck of one I hold dear: it was there a fellow-townsman of my own descended living into the tomb. He was one of our own nobles, possessor of a splendid fortune, blessed in a happy and dignified marriage; but, impelled by madness, he abandoned

[1] In 341. [2] Letters to Paul, Lett. 22, *al.* 25.

[3] *De Gubernatione Dei.* viii. 4.

God and men, and now, a credulous exile, foolishly takes delight in a foul retreat in this island. Unfortunate man, who seeks celestial food amidst filthy garbage, and, more cruel to himself than are his offended gods, persists in his miserable solitude. This Christian sect, with its delusions, is more fatal than are the poisons of Circe: these only change the body; that perverts the mind."[1]

Rutilius, I admit, was a pagan, but numbers of men in the west were so too, and received the same impressions.

Meantime, the revolution which had filled the east with monks, pursued its course in the west, bringing about gradually the same results. Paganism after awhile disappeared, and the new creed, the new manners, took possession of society at large; and the monastic life, as in the east, had soon the greatest bishops for patrons, the whole population for admirers. St. Ambrose at Milan, St. Martin at Tours, St. Augustin in Africa, celebrated its praises, and themselves founded monasteries. St. Augustin drew up a sort of rule for the nuns of his diocese, and ere long the institution was in full vigour throughout the west.

It assumed there, however, from the outset, as I have already had occasion to observe, a peculiar character. Undoubtedly the original desire was to imitate what had taken place in the east; and minute inquiries were made into the discipline and manners of the eastern monasteries; a description of these, as you are aware, formed the materials of two books, published at Marseilles by Cassienus; and in the establishment of many of the new monasteries, great pains were taken to conform to them. But the genius of the western character differed far too widely from that of the east for the difference not to be stamped upon the respective regulations. The desire for retirement, for contemplation, for a marked rupture with civil society, was the source and fundamental trait of the eastern monks: in the west, on the contrary, and especially in southern Gaul, where, at the commencement of the fifth century, the principal monasteries were founded, it was in order to live in common, with a view to conversation as well as to religious edification, that the first monks met. The monasteries of Lerens, of Saint Victor, and

[1] Itin. i. 517.

many others, were especially great schools of theology, the focuses of intellectual movement. It was by no means with solitude or with mortification, but with discussion and activity, that they there concerned themselves.

And not only was this diversity of situation and turn of mind in the east and west real, but contemporaries themselves observed it, paid attention to it; and in labouring to extend the monastic institution in the west, clear sighted men took care to say that it was not necessary to servilely imitate the east, and to explain the reasons why. In point of fasts and austerities, the rules of the western monasteries were, in general, less rigid. "Much eating," said Sulpicius Severus, "is gormandizing among the Greeks, natural among the Gauls."[1]

"The rigour of winter," says Cassien also, "does not permit us to be contented with light stockings, nor with a coat without sleeves, nor with a mere tunic; and he who shall present himself clothed in a small cloak, or in a thin mantle of goat's hair, will be laughed at instead of edifying."[2]

Another cause no less contributed to give a new direction to the monastic institution in the west. It was only in the first half of the fifth century that it spread and really established itself there. Now, at this epoch, the monasteries of the east had already taken their full development; all the extravagancies of ascetic exaltation had already there given a spectacle to the world. The great bishops of the west, the chiefs of the church and of mind in Europe, whatever their religious ardour, were struck by these excesses of the rising monachism, the acts of folly to which it led, the vices which it often covered. Certainly no native of the west had more religious enthusiasm, a more lively, more oriental imagination, nor a more fiery character, than Saint Jerome. He was, however, by no means blind to the faults and dangers of the monastic life, such as it was offered by the east. I will read some passages in which he expresses his thoughts upon this subject; they are among the number of the most interesting documents of the period, and which give us the best information upon it. "There are monks," says he, "who, from the dampness of the cells, from immoderate fasts, from the weari-

[1] Sulp. Sev. Dial. i. 8. [2] Cassien, *de Instit. cœnob.* l. ii.

ness of solitude, from excess of reading, fall into melancholy, and have more need of the remedies of Hippocrates, than of our advice . . . I have seen persons of both sexes, in whom the understanding has been affected with too much abstinence, especially among those who live in cold and damp cells; they no longer knew what they did, nor how to conduct themselves, nor when they should speak, nor when keep silence."[1]

And elsewhere:—

"I have seen men who, renouncing the age only in habits and name, have changed nothing of their old way of life. Their fortune is rather increased than diminished. They have the same cohorts of slaves, the same pomp of banquets. It is gold that they eat upon miserable dishes of delph or clay; and amid the swarms of their servants, they have themselves called solitaries."[2]

"Avoid also men whom thou shalt see loaded with chains, with the beard of a goat, a black cloak, and feet naked in spite of cold . . . They enter into the houses of the nobles; they deceive poor women loaded with sins; they are always learning and never arrive at the knowledge of truth; they feign sorrow, and, apparently abandoned to long fasts, they make amends at night by secret feasts."[3]

And again:—

"I blush to say it, from the bottom of our cells we condemn the world; while rolling in sackcloth and ashes, we pronounce our sentences upon bishops. What means this pride of a king under the tunic of a penitent? . . . . Pride quickly creeps into solitude: that man has fasted a little; he has seen no one; he already thinks himself a weighty personage; he forgets what he is, whence he came, where he goes; and his heart and language already wander on all sides. Contrary to the will of the apostle, he judges other people's servants; he goes wherever his gluttony leads him; he sleeps as long and as often as he pleases; he respects no one; he does whatever he chooses; he looks down on every one else as inferior

[1] Saint Jerome, lett. 95, (*al.* 4, *ad Rusticum,* 97, (*al.* 8,) *ad Demetriadem.*

[2] Saint Jerome, lett. 95, (*al.* 7,) *ad Rusticum.*

[3] Saint Jerome, lett. 18, (*al.* 22,) *ad Eustochium.*

from himself; he is oftener out in the town than in his cell, and while he affects retiring modesty amongst his brethren, in the public streets he thrusts himself against any passenger."[1]

Thus, the most impassioned, the most enthusiastic of the fathers of the west was not unacquainted either with the insanity, hypocrisy, or the intolerable pride which from that time the monastic life gave birth to; and characterized them with that indignant good sense, that satirical and passionate eloquence which is his characteristic; and he denounced them loudly, for fear of the contagion.

Many of the most illustrious bishops of the west, Saint Augustin among others, had the same foresight, and wrote in the same strain; they also applied themselves to the prevention of the absurd extravaganciesin to which the monks of the east had fallen. But in attending to this, in marking the insanity or hypocrisy of which the monastic life served as the groundwork, they incessantly laboured to propagate it. It was a means for them of drawing away from pagan civil society, always the same in fact, despite its apparent conversion, a portion of the laity. Without entering into the clergy, the monks followed the same path, served the same influence; the patronage of the bishops could not be wanting to them. Had it been wanting to them, their progress probably would not have been diminished. It was not to any ecclesiastical combination, nor even to the movement and the particular direction that Christianity might impress upon men's imaginations, that the monastic life owed its origin. The general state of society at this epoch, was its true source. It was tainted with three vices, idleness, corruption, and unhappiness. Men were unoccupied, perverted, and a prey to all kinds of miseries; this is the reason that we find so many turning monks. A laborious, honest, or happy people, would never have entered into this life. When human nature could not fully and harmoniously display itself, when man could not pursue the true aim of his destiny, it was then that his development became eccentric, and that, rather than accept ruin, he cast himself, at all risks, into the strangest situations.

[1] Saint Jerome, lett. 15, (*al.* 77,) *ad Marcum*; 97 (*al.* 4,) *ad Rusticum*

In order to live and act in a regular and reasonable manner, mankind requires that the facts, in the midst of which it lives and acts, should be, to a certain degree, reasonable, regular; that its faculties should find employment, that its condition should not be too austere, that the spectacle of general corruption and abasement should not rebel against, should not desolate strong souls, in which morality cannot be deadened. The weariness, the disgust at an enervated perversity, and the desire to fly from the public miseries, is what made the monks of the east far more than the particular character of Christianity or an access of religious exaltation. These same circumstances existed in the west; Italian, Gaulish, African society, amidst the fall of the Empire, and the devastations of the barbarians, was as unhappy, as depraved, as idle, as that of Asia Minor or Egypt. The true causes of the continual extension of the monastic life were, therefore, the same in both countries, and must have produced in them the same effects.

Despite the diversities which I have remarked, the similitude was also very great, and the counsels of the most illustrious bishops did not prevent the extravagancies of the monks of the east from finding imitators in the west. Neither hermits, recluses, nor any of the pious follies of the ascetic life were wanting in Gaul. Saint Senoch, a barbarian by birth, retired into the environs of Tours, inclosed himself within four walls, so close together, that he could make no movement with the lower part of his person, and lived many years in this situation, an object of veneration to the surrounding population.

The recluses, Caluppa in Auvergne, Patroclus in the territory of Langres, Hospitius in Provence, were not quite so admirable; still their celebrity was great, as were their austerities.[1] Even the stylites had competitors in the west; and the account which Gregory of Tours has left us concerning them, paints the manners of the times with so much truth and interest, that I must read it to you entire. Gregory gives an account of his own conversation with the monk Wulfilaïch, doubtless a barbarian, as his name indicates, and who was

[1] See Gregory of Tours, vol. i. p. 231, 312, in my *Collection des Mémoires relatifs à l'Histoire de France.*

the first in the west to attempt setting up as a rival for Saint Simeon of Antioch.

"I went into the territory of Treves," says Wulfilaïch to Gregory; "'I there constructed, with my own hands, upon this mountain, the little dwelling which you see. I found there an image of Diana, which the people of the place, still infidels, adored as a divinity. I raised a column upon which I remained with great suffering, and without any kind of shoes or stockings; and when the winter season arrived, I was so affected with the rigours of the frost, that very often the nails have fallen from my feet, and frozen water has hung from my beard in the form of candles; for this country has the reputation of often having very severe winters.' We earnestly asked him to say what was his nourishment and drink, and how he had overthrown the idol of the mountain; he said:—'My food was a little bread and herbs, and a small quantity of water. But a large number of people from the neighbouring villages began to flock towards me; I continually preached to them that Diana did not exist; that the idol and the other objects to which they thought it their duty to address worship, were absolutely nothing. I also repeated to them that those canticles which they usually sang while drinking, and amidst their debaucheries, were unworthy of the Divinity, and that it would be far better if they offered the sacrifices of their praises to the all-powerful God who made heaven and earth; I also often prayed the Lord to deign to overthrow the idol, and draw these people from their errors. The mercy of the Lord worked upon those gross minds, and disposed them, lending an ear to my words, to quit their idols, and follow the Lord. I assembled some of them, in order that I might, with their help, throw down the immense image which I could not destroy by my own strength. I had already broken the other idols, which was more easy. Many assembled around the statue of Diana; they threw cords around it, and began to pull; but all their efforts could not break it. I then went to the cathedral, threw myself upon the ground, and with tears implored the Divine mercy to destroy by the powers of Heaven, what earthly efforts did not suffice to throw down. After my prayer I left the cathedral, and immediately returned to the labourers; I took the cord, and we immediately recommenced pulling. At the first effort the idol fell to the ground; it was afterwards broken, and reduced to powder with iron mallets . . . . . I felt disposed to return to my ordinary way of life; but the bishops, who wished to strengthen me, in order that I might continue more perfectly the work which I had commenced, came to me and said:—'The way that you have chosen is not the right way; you are unworthy, and cannot be compared with Saint Simeon of Antioch, who lived upon his column. Besides, the situation of the place does not permit of a like amount of suffering; descend rather, and live with the brothers that you have assembled.' At these words, that I might not be accused of disobedience towards the bishop, I descended, and I went with them, and also took some repast with them. One day, the bishop having despatched me to some distance from the village sent labourers with hatchets, chisels, and hammers, and threw down the column on which I used to live. When I returned the next day, I found all destroyed; I wept bitterly; but I did not wish to re-establish what was destroyed, for fear of being accused of going against the orders of the bishops; and from that time I have remained here, and contented myself with living with my brothers.' "[1]

All is equally remarkable in this account, both the energetic devotion and the inward enthusiasm of the hermit, and the good sense, perhaps with a touch of jealousy, of the bishops; we meet in it at once the influence of the east, and the peculiar character of the west. And as the bishop of Treves repressed the insanity of the stylites, so Saint Augustin assailed hypocrisy wandering under the monkish cloak.

" The subtle enemy of mankind," says he, " has everywhere dispersed hypocrites under the features of monks; they overrun the provinces, where no one has sent them, wandering in every direction, not establishing themselves, staying nowhere. Some go about selling relics of martyrs; that is to say, if they be relics of martyrs; others show their robes and their phylacteries![2]"

I might cite many other examples in which this two-fold fact, the resemblance and the difference of the east and the west, is likewise marked. Amidst these eccentricities,

[1] Greg. of Tours, vol. i. p. 440—444.
[2] Saint Augustin, *de Opere Monac.* c. 28.

through these alternations of folly and wisdom, the progress of the monastic institution continued; the number of monks went on increasing; they wandered or became fixed, they excited the nation by their preachings, or edified it by the spectacle of their life. From day to day they received greater admiration and respect; the idea became established that this was the perfection of Christian conduct. They were proposed as models for the clergy; already some of them had been ordained, in order to make them priests or even bishops; and yet they were still laity, preserving a great degree of liberty, contracting no kind of religious engagement, always distinct from the clergy, often even purposely separating from it.

"It is the ancient advice of the fathers," says Cassier "advice which endures, that a monk, at any cost, must fly bishops and women; for neither women, nor bishops, allow a monk who has once become familiar with them, to rest in peace in his cell, nor to fix his eyes on pure and celestial doctrine, contemplating holy things."[1]

So much liberty and power, so strong an influence over the people and such an absence of general forms, of regular organization, could not fail to give rise to great disorder. The necessity of putting an end to it, of assembling these missionaries, these solitaries, these recluses, these cenobites, who every day became more numerous, and were neither of the people nor the clergy, under a common government, under one discipline, was strongly felt.

Towards the end of the fifth century, in 480, there was born in Italy, at Nursia, in the duchy of Spoleto, of a wealthy and considerable family, the man destined to resolve this problem, to give to the monks of the west the general rule for which they waited; I speak of Saint Benedict. At the age of twelve years he was sent to Rome to prosecute his studies. This was the time of the fall of the Empire, and the great troubles of Italy; the Heruli and the Ostrogoths disputed for its possession; Theodoric drove out Odoacer; Rome was incessantly taken, re-taken, threatened. In 494, Benedict, scarcely twelve years of age, left it with Cyrilla, his nurse; and a short time afterwards we find him a hermit

[1] Cassien, *de Instit. cœnob.* xi. 17.

in the depths of a cavern, at Subiaco, in the Campagna di Roma.

As to why this child retired there, how he lived, nothing is known; for his legend, our only account, places at every step a moral wonder, or a miracle, properly so called. However this may have been, at the end of a certain period, the life of Benedict, his youth and his austerities, attracted the shepherds of the neighbourhood; he preached to them; and the power of his word and the authority of his example, the always numerous concourse of auditors, soon rendered him celebrated. In 510, the neighbouring monks of Vicovaro wished to have him for their chief; he at first refused, telling the monks that their conduct was disorderly, that they abandoned themselves in their house to all kinds of excesses, that they should undertake reformation and submit themselves to a very severe rule. They persisted, and Benedict became abbot of Vicovaro.

He, in effect, undertook with invincible energy the reformation which he had spoken of; as he had foreseen, the monks were soon tired of a reformer. The struggle between them and him became so violent that they attempted to poison him in the chalice. He perceived it by a miracle, says the legend; quitted the monastery, and retook to his hermit life at Subiaco.

His renown spread far; not only the shepherds, but laymen of every condition, and wandering monks, assembled to live near him. Equitius and Tertullus, noble Romans, sent their sons, Maurus and Placidus to him; Maurus at the age of twelve, Placidus quite an infant. He founded monasteries around his cavern. In 520, it appears that he had founded twelve, each composed of twelve monks, in which he began to try the ideas and institutions by which, in his opinion, the monastic life should be regulated.

But the same spirit of insubordination and jealousy which had driven him from the monastery of Vicovaro was soon manifested in those which he had himself just founded. A monk named Florentius raised up enemies against him, laid snares for him. Benedict was irritated, and a second time renounced the struggle, and, taking some of his disciples, among others, Maurus and Placidus, he retired, in 528, to the frontiers of the Abruzzi and the Terra di lavoro, near Cassino.

He there found what the hermit Wulfilaïch, whose history I have just mentioned, found near Treves, paganism still in existence, and the temple and statue of Apollo standing on Mount Cassino, a hill which overlooks the town. Benedict overthrew the temple and the statue, extirpated paganism, collected numerous disciples, and founded a new monastery.

It was here, where he remained and ruled to the end of his life, that he entirely applied himself to, and published, his Rules of Monastic Life. It soon became, as every one knows, the general, and almost only law of the monks of the west. It was by this rule of Saint Benedict that the western monastical institution was reformed, and received its definitive form. Let us stop here, then, and examine with some care this small code of a society which has played so important a part in the history of Europe.

The author commences by explaining the state of the western monks at this epoch; that is to say, at the beginning of the sixth century:

"It is well known," says he, "that there are four kinds of monks: firstly, the *cenobites*, those who live in a monastery, under a ruler or abbot. The second kind is that of the anchorites, that is to say, hermits; those who, not from the fervour of a novice, but by long proof of the monastic life, have already learned to the great profit of many people, to combat against the devil, and who, well prepared, go out alone from the army of their brothers to engage in a single combat. . . . . . . The third kind of monks is that of the *sarabaïtes*, who, not being tried by any rule, nor by any lessons of experience, as gold is tried in the furnace, and similar rather to the soft nature of lead, by their works keep fealty to the age, and lie to God by their tonsure. We meet these to the number of two, three, or more, without pastor, not caring about the sheep of the Lord, but merely their own particular flock; their law is their desire; what they think or prefer, that they call holy; what does not please them they say is not permitted. The fourth kind is that of the monks who are called *gyrovagi*, who, during their whole life, inhabit various cells for three or four days, in various provinces, always wandering—never settled, obeying the bent of their luxuries and the debaucheries of gormandizing, and in every respect worse than the sarabaïtes. It is much better to hold our peace than to speak of their miserable way of life: passing them in silence, let us, with God's aid, regulate the strong association of the cenobites."

The facts thus established, the rule of Saint Benedict is divided into seventy-three chapters, namely:

Nine chapters concerning the moral and general duties of the brothers.

Thirteen concerning religious duties and offices;

Twenty-nine concerning discipline, faults, penalties, &c.;

Ten concerning the internal government and administration;

Twelve concerning various subjects, as guests, brothers travelling, &c.;

That is,—1. nine chapters on the moral code; 2. thirteen on the religious; 3. twenty-nine of the penal code or discipline; 4. ten of the political code; 5. twelve upon various subjects.

Let us take each of these small codes, and see what principles dominate in them, what was the meaning and compass of the reformation which their author brought about.

1. With regard to the moral and general duties of monks, the points upon which the whole rule of Saint Benedict rests are, self-denial, obedience, and labour. Some of the monks of the west had often endeavoured to introduce labour into their life; but the attempt had never become general, was never followed up. This was the great revolution which Saint Benedict made in the monastic institution; he especially introduced manual and agricultural labour into it. The Benedictine monks were the agriculturists of Europe; they cleared it on a large scale, associating agriculture with preaching. A colony, a swarm of monks, not very numerous at first, transported themselves into uncultivated places, or almost so, often into the midst of a still pagan population, into Germany, for example, or Brittany; and there, at once missionaries and labourers, they accomplished their two-fold task, often attended with as much danger as fatigue. This is how Saint Benedict regulated the employment of the day in his monasteries; you will see that labour there occupied a great place:

"Laziness is the enemy of the soul, and consequently the brothers should, at certain times, occupy themselves in manual labour; at others, in holy reading. We think that this should be thus regulated. From Easter to the month of October, after the first prime, they should work, nearly to the fourth hour, at whatever may be necessary: from the fourth hour, nearly to the sixth, they shall apply themselves to reading. After the sixth hour, on leaving the table, they shall repose quietly in their beds; or if any one wishes to read, let him read, but in such a manner as not to disturb others: and let nones be said at the middle of the eighth hour. Let them work till vespers at whatever there may be to do; and if the poverty of the place, necessity, or the harvest keep them constantly employed, let them not mind that, for they are truly monks if they live by manual labour, as our brothers the apostles did; but let everything be done with moderation, for the sake of the weak.

"From the month of October, until the beginning of Lent, let them be occupied in reading until the second hour; at the second let them sing tierce, and until nones let all work at what is enjoined them; at the first stroke of nones let them quit work and be ready the moment the second stroke shall sound. After repast, let them read or recite the psalms.

"During Lent, let them read from the morning until the third hour, and let them then work as they shall be ordered, until the tenth hour. During Lent, all shall receive books from the library, which they shall read one after another all through. These books shall be given at the commencement of Lent. Especially let one or two ancients be chosen to go through the monastery at the hours when the brothers are occupied in reading, and let them see if they find any negligent brother who abandons himself to repose, or to conversation, who in no way applies himself to reading, who is not only useless to himself, but who distracts the others. If one of the kind is found, let him be reprimanded once or twice; if he do not amend, let him be subjected to the regulated correction, in order to intimidate the others. On Sunday let all be occupied in reading, except those who are selected for various functions. If any one be negligent or lazy, so that he neither wishes nor is able to meditate or read, let some labour be enjoined upon him, so that he may not remain doing nothing. As regards infirm or delicate brothers, let some work or employment be imposed, so that they may neither be lazy nor loaded with the severity of the work. . . . . Their weakness should be taken into consideration by the abbot."[1]

Together with labour, Saint Benedict prescribes passive obedience of the monks to their superiors: a rule less new, and which prevailed also among the monks of the east, but which he laid down in a much more express manner, and more vigorously developing its consequences. It is impossible, in studying the history of European civilization, not to be astonished at the part which is there played by this idea, and not curiously to seek its origin. Of a surety, Europe received it neither from Greece, ancient Rome, the Germans, nor from Christianity, properly so called. It began to appear under the Roman empire, and arose out of the worship of the imperial majesty. But it was in the monastic institution that it was truly aggrandized and developed; it is from thence that it set out to spread itself into modern civilization. That is the fatal present that the monks made to Europe, and which so long altered or enervated its virtues. This principle is incessantly repeated in the rule of Saint Benedict. Many chapters, entitled, *De obedientia, de humilitate*, &c., announce and comment upon it in detail. Here are two which will show to what a point the rigour of application was pressed. Chapter sixty-eight, entitled, *If a brother is ordered to do anything impossible*, is thus expressed:

"If by chance anything difficult or impossible be imposed upon a brother, let him receive with all mildness and obedience the command which is imposed upon him. If he sees that the thing entirely surpasses the extent of his power, let him explain fitly and patiently to his superior the reason of the impossibility, not inflamed with pride, not resisting, not contradicting. If, after his observation, the prior persists in his opinion and his command, let the disciple know that it ought to be so, and, confiding in the aid of God, let him obey."

Chapter sixty-nine is entitled, *That in a monastery no one must defend another*, and goes on to say:—

"It is necessary to be very careful that, upon no pretext, a monk dare in the monastery defend another, or, so to speak, protect him, even when he shall be related by the ties

[1] Reg. S. Bened. c. 48.

of blood; let this in no manner be dared by the monks, because it might lead to grave and scandalous occurrences. If any one transgress in this, let him be severely reprimanded."

Self-denial is the natural consequence of passive obedience. Whoever is bound to obey absolutely, and on every occasion, exists not; all personality is torn from him. The rule of Saint Benedict formally establishes the interdiction of all property as well as all personal will.

"It is especially necessary to extirpate from the monastery, and unto the very root, the vice of any one possessing anything in particular. Let no person dare to give or receive without the order of the abbot, nor have anything of his own peculiar property, not a book, nor tablets, nor a pen, nor anything whatsoever; for it is not permitted them even to have their body and their will under their own power."[1]

Can individuality be more completely abolished?

2. I shall not detain you with the thirteen chapters which regulate worship and the religious offices; they do not give rise to any important observation.

3. Those which treat of discipline and penalties, on the contrary, require our best attention. It is here that perhaps the most considerable of the changes brought about by Saint Benedict into the monastic institution appears, the introduction of solemn and perpetual vows. Hitherto, although the entering into the monastery gave reason to presume the intention of remaining there, although the monk contracted a kind of moral obligation which daily tended to take great fixity, still no vow, no formal engagement, was yet pronounced. It was Saint Benedict who introduced them, and made them the basis of the monastic life, of which the primitive character thus entirely disappeared. This character was exaltation and liberty; perpetual vows, which could not long delay being placed under the care of the public power, substituted a law, an institution.

"Let him who is to be received," says the rule of Saint Benedict, "promise in the oratory, before God and his saints,

[1] Reg. S. Bened. c.33

the perpetuity of his stay, the reformation of his manners and obedience. Let a deed be made of this promise, in the name of the saints whose relics are deposited there, and in presence of the abbot. Let him write this deed with his own hand, or, if he cannot write, let another, at his request, write it for him, and let the novice put a cross to it, and with his own hand deposit the deed upon the altar." [1]

The word *novice* reveals another innovation to us; a noviciate was, in fact, the natural consequence of the perpetuity of vows, and Saint Benedict, who, to an exalted imagination and an ardent character, joined much good sense, and practical sagacity, failed not to prescribe it. Its duration was more than a year. They read by degrees the whole rule to the novice, saying to him: "Here is the law under which you wish to strive; if you can observe it, enter; if you cannot, go freely." Upon the whole, the conditions and forms of trial are evidently conceived in a spirit of sincerity, and with the intention of being well assured that the will of the candidate was real and strong.

4. As regards the political code, the government itself of the monasteries, the rule of Saint Benedict offers a singular mixture of despotism and liberty. Passive obedience, as you have just seen, is its fundamental principle; at the same time the government is elective; the abbot is always chosen by the brothers. When once this choice is made, they lose all liberty, they fall under the absolute domination of their superior, but of the superior whom they have elected, and of no other.

Moreover, in imposing obedience on the monks, the rule orders that the abbot consult them. Chapter III., entitled, *That the advice of the brothers must be taken*, expressly says:

"Whenever anything of importance is to take place in the monastery, let the abbot convoke the whole congregation, and say what the question is, and after having heard the advice of the brothers, he shall think of it apart, and shall do as appears to him most suitable. We say call all the brothers to the council, because God often reveals by the youngest what is most valuable. Let the brothers give

[1] Reg. S. Bened. c. 58.

their advice in all submission, and let them not venture to defend it obstinately; let the affair depend upon the will of the abbot, and let all obey what he thinks beneficial. But as it is suitable that the disciple should obey the master, so it is desirable that the latter should regulate all things with prudence and justice. Let the rule be followed in everything, and let no one dare to break it.

"If trifling things are to be done in the interior of the monastery, let them take the advice of the ancients alone."

Thus in this singular government, election, deliberation, and absolute power were coexistent.

5. The chapters which treat of various subjects have nothing remarkable, except a character of good sense and mildness, which is also seen in many other parts of the rule, and with which it is impossible not to be struck. The moral thought and general discipline of it are severe; but, in the details of life, it is humane and moderate; more humane, more moderate than the Roman law, than the barbaric laws, than the general manners of the times. I do not doubt but that the brothers, confined within a monastery, were governed by an authority, upon the whole more reasonable, and in a manner less severe, than they would have been in civil society.

Saint Benedict was so impressed with the necessity for a mild and moderate rule, that the preface which he has annexed to it finishes with these words:

"We wish thus to institute a school for the service of the Lord, and we hope we have not put into this institution anything harsh or painful; but if, after the council of equity, anything for the correction of vice, or maintenance of charity, is found in it which is rather too harsh, do not, alarmed at that, flee the path of salvation; at its commencement it is always narrow; but by the progress of a regular life, and faith, the heart dilates, and runs with an ineffable sweetness into the way of God's commandments."

It was in 528 that Saint Benedict gave forth his rule: in 543, the time of his death, it had already spread into all parts of Europe. Saint Placidus carried it into Sicily, others into Spain. Saint Maurus, the cherished disciple of Saint Benedict, introduced it into France. At the request of Innocent, bishop of Mans, he set out from Mount Cassino at the end of the year 542, while Saint Benedict still lived. When he arrived at Orleans, in 543, Saint Benedict no longer lived, but the institution did not the less pursue its course. The first monastery founded by Saint Maur was that of Glanfeuil, in Anjou, or Saint Maur-sur-Loire. At the end of the sixth century, the greater part of the French monasteries had adopted the same rule; it had become the general system of the monastic order, so that towards the end of the eighth century, Charlemagne caused it to be asked in the various parts of his empire, if there existed any other kind of monks than those of the order of Saint Benedict?

We have as yet not studied more than half, so to speak, of the revolutions of the monastic institutions at this epoch, its internal revolutions, the changes in the regime and legislation of monasteries, their relations on the one hand with the state, on the other with the clergy, their situation in civil society, and in ecclesiastical society. This will form the subject of our next lecture.

FIFTEENTH LECTURE.

The relations of the monks with the clergy, from the fourth to the eighth century—Their primitive independence—Causes of its decline—1. In proportion as the number and the power of the monks were augmented, the bishops extended their jurisdiction over them — Canons of the councils—2. The monks demand and obtain privileges—3. They aspire to enter into the clergy—Differences and contests among the monks themselves upon this subject—The bishops at first repulse their pretensions—They give way to them—In entering into the clergy the monks lose their independence—Tyranny of the bishops over the monasteries—Resistance of the monks—Charters granted by the bishops to some monasteries—The monks have recourse to the protection of the kings, to that of the popes—Character and limits of the intervention—Similarity between the struggle of the monasteries against the bishops and that of the commons against the feudal lords.

We have studied the internal system of monasteries from the fourth to the eighth century; at present let us occupy ourselves with their external condition in the church in general, with their relations with the clergy.

As people have been deceived as to the internal state and system of monasteries, by forgetting the primitive character of monks, who were at first laymen and not ecclesiastics, so have they been greatly deceived concerning their situation in the church, by forgetting their equally primitive character, which was liberty, independence.

The foundation of a great number of monasteries belonged to an epoch, when the monks were already, and for a long time had been, incorporated with the clergy; many were founded by a patron, lay or ecclesiastical, sometimes a bishop, sometimes a king, or a great nobleman; and we see them, from their very origin, subject to an authority to which they owed their existence.

It is supposed that it had always been thus, that all the monasteries had been the creation of some will foreign and superior to that of the congregation itself, and which, more or less, had retained its influence. This is entirely to overlook the primitive situation of these establishments, and the true mode of their formation.

The first monasteries were not founded by any one,—they founded themselves. They were not, as at a later period, the pious work of some rich and powerful man who was desirous of building an edifice, joining a church to it, endowing it, and calling other men to it, in order that they might there lead a religious life. The monastical associations formed themselves spontaneously, among equals, by the impulsive movement of soul, and without any other aim than that of satisfying it. The monks preceded the monastery, its edifices, its church, its endowment; they united, each of his own will, and on his own account, without depending upon any one beyond, as free as they were disinterested.

In meeting, they naturally found themselves, in all that related to manners, to doctrines, to religious practices, placed under the inspection of the bishops. The secular clergy existed before the monasteries; it was organised; it had rights, a recognised authority; the monks were subject to it, like other Christians. The moral and religious life of the faithful was the object of episcopal inspection and censure; that of the monks was in the same case: the bishop was not invested with any jurisdiction with regard to them, with any particular authority; they were in the general condition of the laity—living, however, in great independence, electing their superiors, administering the property which they possessed in common, without any obligation to any one, without any burden upon any one, governing themselves, in a word, as they chose.

Their independence, and the analogy between their situation and the rest of the laity was such, that they had no particular church, for instance, no church attached to their monastery, no priest who celebrated Divine service for them especially; they went to the church of the neighbouring city or parish, like all the faithful, united to the mass of the population.

This was the primitive state of the monasteries, the starting point of their relations with the clergy. They did not long remain there: many causes soon concurred to change their independence, and unite them more intimately with the ecclesiastical corporation. Let us attempt to recognise them, and to mark the various degrees of their transition.

The number and power of the monks continually increased. When I say power, I speak of their influence, their moral action on the public: for power, properly so called, legal, constituted power, the monks were entirely without; but their influence was daily more visible and more strong. For this reason alone, they attracted a more assiduous and attentive inspection on the part of the bishops. The clergy very quickly understood that it had in them, either formidable rivals, or useful instruments. They applied themselves, therefore, at an early period to confine them, and to make use of them. The ecclesiastical history of the fifth century attests the continual efforts of the bishops to extend and to confirm their jurisdiction over the monks. The general inspection which they had a right to exercise over all the faithful, furnished them with a thousand occasions and means. The very liberty enjoyed by the monks lent them aid, for it gave rise to many disorders; and the episcopal authority was, of all others, most naturally called upon to interfere for their repression. It interposed, therefore, and the acts of the councils of the fifth century abound in canons, whose only object is to confirm and establish the jurisdiction of the bishops over monasteries. The most fundamental is a canon of the œcumenical council held at Chalcedonia in 451, and which enacts:

"Those who have sincerely and really embraced the solitary life shall be suitably honoured; but as some, under the appearance and name of monks, disturb civil and ecclesiastical affairs, overrunning towns, and attempting even to institute monasteries for themselves, it has pleased us to order that no one build or found a monastery without the consent of the bishop.

"Monks, in every city or district, shall be subject to the bishop, remain tranquil, only apply themselves to fastings and prayer, and ' ain in the place where they have renounced the world. Let them not meddle with ecclesiastical and civil affairs, and interfere in nothing out of doors, and not quit their monasteries, unless, for some necessary work, it be so ordered by the bishop of the city."[1]

This text proves that, hitherto, the greater part of the monasteries were freely founded by the monks themselves; but this fact was already considered as an abuse, and the authority of the bishop was formally required. Its necessity, in fact, became a law, and we read in the canons of the council of Agde, held in 506:

"We forbid that new monasteries be founded without the consent of the bishop."[2]

In 511, the council of Orleans orders:

"Let the abbots, according to the humility which is suitable to the religious life, be subject to the power of the bishops; and if they do anything against the rule, let them be reprimanded by the bishops; and being convoked, they shall meet once a year in the place chosen by the bishop."[3]

Here the bishop goes further, he makes himself the ruling minister even in the interior of monasteries; it was not from him that they held it; he was not the monastical legislative power; but he took the right of surveying the execution of the law there.

The same council adds: "Let no monk, abandoning, through ambition or vanity, the congregation of the monastery, dare to construct a separate cell without the permission of the bishop, or the consent of his abbot."[4]

New progress of the episcopal authority: hermits, anchorites, recluses, attracted more admiration and popular favour than the cenobites: the most zealous monks were always disposed to quit the interior of the monasteries in order to give themselves up to these proud austerities. For some time no authority interfered to prevent it, not even that of the abbot; you now see the repressive power sanctioned, not only that of the abbot, but of the bishop; he, too, charged both with keeping the monks within the interior of the house, and with repressing the external effects of exaltation.

[1] Coun. of Chalcedonia, in 451. c. 4. [2] Ib. c. 58.
[3] Ib. c. 19. [4] Coun. of Orleans, c. 22.

In 352, a new council of Orleans decrees :

"Let abbots who slight the orders of the bishops, not be admitted, unless they humbly retract this rebellion."[1]

And a year afterwards:

"Let the monastery and the discipline of monks be under the authority of the bishop of the district in which they are situated.

"Let it not be permitted to abbots to go far from their monastery without the permission of the bishop. If they do so, let them be regularly corrected by their bishop, according to the ancient canons.

"Let the bishops take under their care, nunneries established in their city; and let them not allow any abbess to do aught against the rule of her monastery."[2]

When all these rules were proclaimed, although they did not contain anything very precise, although, as you see, the jurisdiction of the bishops was not exactly determined, still it was established; it interfered in the principal points of the existence of the monks, in the foundation of monasteries, in the observation of their discipline, in the duties of the abbots; and, recognised in principle, although often repulsed in fact, it strengthened itself by exercise.

The monks themselves concurred to its progression. When they had acquired more importance, they claimed a separate existence. They complained of being assimilated with the simple laity, and confounded with the mass of the faithful; they desired to be established as a distinct corporation, a positive institution. Independence and influence were not sufficient for them—privilege was necessary. Now, from whom could they obtain it, except from the clergy? The authority of the bishops could alone constitute them separate from the religious society in general, and privilege them in its bosom. They demanded these privileges, and obtained them, but by paying for them. There was one, for instance, very simple, that of not going to the church of the parish, of constructing one in the interior of the monastery, and there celebrating divine service. They granted it to them without difficulty; but it was necessary that priests should do duty

[1] Coun. of Orleans, c. 22. [2] Coun. of Orleans, in 554, c. 1, 2, 3. 5.

in these churches; now the monks were not priests, and had not the right of doing duty. They gave them priests, and the external clergy from that time had a place in the interior of monasteries; men were there sent from it as delegates, inspectors. By this fact alone, the independence of the monks already endured a serious blow: they saw, and attempted to remedy, the evil; they demanded that instead of priests sent from without, the bishop should ordain some monks priests. The clergy consented to it, and under the name of *hieromonachi*, the monasteries had priests chosen from out of their own body. They were rather less strangers than those who came from without, but still they belonged to the secular clergy, took its spirit, associated themselves with its interests, separated themselves more or less from their brothers; and by this simple distinction, established between the simple monks and the priests, between those who were present at the service, and those who performed it, the monastic institution already lost part of its independence and of its homogeneity.

The loss was so real that more than one superior of a monastery, more than one abbot perceived it, and attempted to repair it, at least to limit it. The rules of many monastic orders speak of priests established in the monastery with distrust, and apply themselves sometimes to restrain their number, sometimes the influence of them.

Saint Benedict in his formally inserted two chapters on this subject:

"If an abbot," says he, "wishes to have a priest or a deacon ordained for him, let him select from among his people one who is worthy to perform the sacerdotal functions. But let him who is ordained guard against all pride, and let him not contend against anything which shall be enjoined him by the abbot; let him know that he is even more subject to the regular discipline than any other; that the priesthood is not a reason for him to forget obedience and rule; but let him more and more advance in God, and always keep to the functions by which he entered into the monastery, except the duties of the altar, when even, by choice of the congregation, and the will of the abbot, he shall be, by reason of the merits of his life, raised to a more elevated rank. Let him know that he must observe the rule established by the deans and priors; that if he dare to act otherwise, he shall not be judged as a priest, but as a rebel. And if, after having been frequently warned, he does not correct himself, let the bishop himself be called as witness. If he do not amend, and his faults be glaring, let him be driven from the monastery, in case he will not still submit, nor obey the rule."[1]

"If any one of the order of priests ask to be received into the monastery, let it not be immediately consented to; if he persist in his request, let him know that he shall submit to the whole discipline and rule, and that nothing shall be abated him."[2]

This rather jealous fear, this vigilance to repress the arrogance of priests, to subject them to the life of monks, was also manifested elsewhere, and by other symptoms; they only the better prove the progress of the external clergy in the interior of monasteries, and the danger in which it placed their ancient independence.

It had to submit to an entirely different check. Not content with being separated from the lay society, and being raised above it by their privileges, the monks conceived the ambition of entering fully into the ecclesiastical society, of participating in the privileges and power of the clergy. This ambition was shown in the monastical institution at a very early period. It was not approved of by all. The exalted and austere monks, those whose imagination was strongly filled with the holiness of the monastic life, and aspired to all its glories, were averse to receiving the sacred orders. Some regarded the clerical as a worldly life, which deterred them from the contemplation of divine things; the others thought themselves unworthy of the priesthood, and did not find themselves in a sufficiently perfect state to celebrate divine service. Hence arose some singular incidents in the relations between the monks and the clergy. In the fourth century, while Saint Epiphanus was bishop in the island of Cyprus, there was a monk in the island named Paulinianus, celebrated for his virtues, and in great reputation for sanctity. They frequently proposed making him a priest; he always declined, saying that he was not worthy

[1] Reg. S. Bened. c. 62. [2] Ib. c. 60.

of it; but Saint Epiphanus positively insisted upon consecrating him. He proceeded in the following manner: it is himself who gives the account:

"While they celebrated mass in the church of a village near our monastery, without his being aware of it, or in the least expecting it, we had him seized by a number of deacons, and had his mouth held, for fear that, wishing to escape, he should adjure us in the name of Christ. We at first ordained him deacon, and summoned him, by the fear he had for God, to fulfil the office. He strongly resisted, maintaining that he was unworthy. It was almost necessary to force him, for we had great difficulty in persuading him by testimonies of the Writings, and in citing the commands of God. And when he had performed the duties of deacon in the holy sacrifice, we again had his mouth held, with great difficulty; we ordained him priest, and, for the same reasons which we had already impressed upon him, we decided him to take a place among the priests."[1]

They rarely came to such violent extremities; but I might cite many other examples of monks who were sincerely repugnant to becoming priests, and obstinately refused.

Such, however, was far from being their general character. The greater part were very anxious to enter into orders, for the clergy was the superior body: to be received into its bosom was to be raised. "If the desire to become a priest excite you," says Saint Jerome to a monk, "learn, that you may be able to teach; pretend not to be a soldier without having been a militiaman, and a master before having been a disciple."[2] In fact, the desire to become priests so keenly excited the monks, that Cassienus ranks it among the temptations with which the demon pursued them, and especially among those which he attributes to the demon of vain glory.

"Sometimes," says he, "the demon of vain glory inspires a monk with a desire for the degrees of the clergy, the priesthood, or the deaconship. According to him, if he be invested with it, despite himself, he will fill the duties with so much rigour, that he might offer examples of holiness even to other priests, and might gain many people over to the

[1] Saint Epiphanus, lett. to John, bishop of Jerusalem, vol. ii. p. 312.

[2] Saint Jerome, lett. 4, *ad Rusticum*.

church, not only by his admirable way of living, but by his doctrine and discourses."[1] And he relates the following anecdote upon this subject—a singular proof, truly, of the passion with which certain monks aspired to become priests, and of the empire which this desire possessed over their imagination:

"I remember," says he, "that during my stay in the solitude of Scythia, an old man told me, that going one day to the cell of a certain brother, to visit him, as he approached the door, he heard him within pronouncing certain words; he stopped a little, wishing to know what he read of the Scripture, or else what he repeated from memory, according to usage. And as this pious spy curiously listened, with his ear at the door, he perceived that the spirit of vain glory tempted the brother, for he spoke as if he addressed a sermon to the people in the church. The old man still stopped, and he heard that the brother, after having finished his sermon, changed his office, and did the duties of deacon at the mass of the catechumens. He at last knocked at the door, and the brother came to meet him with his accustomed veneration, and introduced him into his cell. Then, rather troubled in his conscience at the thoughts which had occupied him, he asked him how long he had been there, fearing, without doubt, that he had insulted him by keeping him waiting at the door; and the old man answered, smiling: 'I arrived just as you celebrated the mass of the catechumens.'"

Of a surety men preoccupied to such a degree by such a desire, would unhesitatingly have sacrificed their independence to it. Let us see how they attained their end, and what result this success had for them.

The clergy at first looked upon the ambition of the monks with a good deal of jealousy and distrust. At the fourth century, some bishops, more vigorous and discerning than others, or with some particular end in view, received them favourably. Saint Athanasius, for example, bishop of Alexandria, engaged in his great contest against the Arians, visited the monasteries of Egypt, loaded the monks with distinction, and selected many to ordain as priests, and even to make bishops of. The monks were orthodox, eager, popular.

[1] Cassienus, *de Cœnob. inst.* xi. 14. [2] Ibid. 15.

Athanasius saw that in them he should have powerful and devoted allies. His example was followed by some bishops in the west, especially by Saint Ambrose at Milan, and by Eusebius, bishop of Verceil. But the episcopacy in general behaved differently; it continued to treat the pretensions of the monks coldly, scornfully, and to combat them underhand. Proofs of it are in writing down to the seventh century. At the end of the fourth, for example, the bishop of Rome, Saint Siricius (384—398), allowed holy orders to be conferred upon them, but with many stipulations, lest too large a number of monks should penetrate into the clergy. In the middle of the following century, Saint Leo (440—460) engaged Maximus, patriarch of Antioch, not too easily to allow permission to preach to the monks of his diocese, even to the most holy, because their preaching might have serious consequences for the influence of the clergy. At the end of the sixth century, Saint Gregory the Great recommended the bishops to ordain monks as parish priests but rarely, and to employ them with reserve. Upon the whole, amidst even the favours which it exhibits towards them, the episcopacy always shows itself jealous of the monks, and inclined to separate them from the clergy.

But the progress of their popularity surmounted this secret resistance. It was soon acknowledged that theirs, of all lives, was the Christian life; that it surpassed in merit that of the external clergy, who could not do better than imitate them, and that a priest, or even a bishop, in becoming a monk, advanced in the paths of holiness and salvation. The councils themselves, composed of bishops, proclaimed these maxims:

"If priests," says a council of Toledo, "desiring to follow a better life, wish to embrace the rule of the monks, let the bishop give them free access into the monasteries, and in no way obstruct the design of those who wish to give themselves up to contemplation."[1]

When they were generally recognised, there was no longer any means of resisting the invasion of the monks, nor of parsimoniously granting them the priesthood and episcopacy. At the commencement of the seventh century, Boni-

[1] Coun. of Toledo, in 633, c. 60.

face IV. proclaims that they are *plus quam idonei*, more than fitted for all the functions of the clergy; and gradually events and minds progressed in this direction; the monks found themselves incorporated in the clergy; and while preserving a distinct existence, associated on every occasion with its privileges and power. It is impossible to determine exactly the date of this admission; it was progressive, and for a long time incomplete; even in the eighth century, the monks were at times still called laymen, and considered as such. Still it may be said that, about the end of the sixth and at the beginning of the seventh century, the revolution for which they had laboured from the end of the fourth century was consummated. Let us see what were the results of it, as regards their external condition, what was the condition of the monks in the clergy, when they decidedly formed a part of it.

It is evident that they must have lost there a great deal of independence, and that the authority of the bishops over monasteries was necessarily extended and confirmed. You know what the power of the episcopacy was over parish priests from the seventh to the eighth century. The fortune of monks was no better. Those little associations which we have just seen so independent, over which the bishops had scarcely a moral jurisdiction, which they laboured with so much care to draw beneath their empire, see how they were treated at the seventh century. I shall leave the councils to speak for themselves:

"It has been given out at the present council that monks, by order of the bishops, are subject to servile labours, and that, against the canonical orders, the rights of monasteries are usurped with an illegitimate audacity; so that a monastery becomes almost a domain, and that illustrious part of the body of Christ is almost reduced to ignominy and servitude. We therefore warn the chiefs of the churches that they no longer commit anything of the kind; and that the bishops do nothing in monasteries except what the canons direct them, that is, exhort the monks to a holy life, appoint the abbots and other officers, and reform such things as shall be against rule."[1]

[1] Coun. of Toledo, in 633, c. 51.

"As regards presents that are made to a monastery, let not the bishops touch them."[1]

"A most deplorable thing there is, which we are forced to extirpate by a severe censure. We have learnt that certain bishops unjustly establish as prelates in certain monasteries some of their relations or favourites, and procure them iniquitous advantages, to the end that they may receive, through them, both what is in fact regularly due to the bishop of the diocese, and all that the violence of the exactor whom they have sent can seize from the monasteries."[2]

I might greatly multiply these quotations: all would equally attest that, at this epoch, the monasteries were subjected to an odious tyranny on the part of the bishops.

They, however, had means of resistance, and they made use of them. In order to explain the nature of these means satisfactorily, allow me to leave the monks for a moment, and call your attention to an analogous fact, and one much better known.

Every one is aware that, from the eighth to the tenth century, the cities, large or small, which still existed in Gaul, were induced to enter into the feudal society, to assume the characteristics of the new system, to take a place in its hierarchy, to contract its obligations in order to possess its rights, to live under the patronage of a lord. This patronage was harsh, oppressive, and the cities impatiently supported its weight. At a very early period, when they first engaged in feudalism, they attempted to shake it off, to regain some independence. What were their means? In the boroughs there was the wreck of the ancient municipal system: in their miserable condition, they still selected some obscure magistrates: some property remained to them; they administered this property themselves: in a word, they preserved, in some respects, an existence distinct from that which they had assumed in entering the feudal society, an existence which was connected with institutions, with principles, and with a social state, all of them entirely different. These remains of their ancient existence, these wrecks of the municipal system, became the fulcrum by the aid of which the boroughs struggled against the feudal master

[1] Coun. of Lerida, in 524, c. 3. [2] Coun of Toledo, in 655, c. 3.

who had invaded them, and progressively regained some degree of liberty

An analogous fact was brought about in the history of monasteries, and of their relations with the clergy. You have just seen the monks entering into the ecclesiastical society, and falling under the authority of the bishops, as the commons entered at a later period into the feudal society, and fell under the authority of the lords. But the monks also retained some of their primitive existence, of their original independence; for example, they had had domains given them: these domains were not confounded with those of the bishop in whose diocese the monastery was situated; they were not lost in the mass of church property of which the bishop had the sole administration; they remained the distinct and personal property of each establishment. The monks accordingly continued to exercise some of their rights; the election of their abbot and other monastic affairs, the interior administration of the monastery, &c. In the same way, therefore, as the boroughs retained some wreck of the municipal system, and of their property, and made use of them in order to struggle against feudal tyranny, so did the monks preserve some remnants of their internal constitution and of their property, and made use of them in struggling against episcopal tyranny. So that the boroughs followed the route and in the steps of the monasteries; not that they imitated them, but because the same situation led to the same results.

Let us follow in its vicissitudes the resistance of the monks against the bishops; we shall see this analogy developed more and more.

The contest was at first limited to complaints, to protestations, carried either before the bishop himself, or before the councils. Sometimes the councils received them, and issued canons to put a stop to the evil: I have just read to you texts which prove it. But a written remedy is of little efficacy. The monks felt the necessity of recurring to some other means. They openly resisted their bishop; they refused to obey his injunctions, to receive him in the monastery; more than once they repulsed his envoys by force of arms. Still their resistance weighed heavily upon them; the bishop excommunicated them, interdicted their priests: the struggle was grievous for all. They treated. The monks promised to resume order, to make presents to the bishop, to cede to him some part of the domain, if he was willing to promise to respect the monastery thenceforward, not to pillage their property, to leave them in peaceful enjoyment of their rights. The bishop consented, and gave a charter to the monastery. They are regular charters, these immunities, these privileges conferred upon monasteries by their bishop, the use of which became so frequent that we find an official compilation of them in the *Formula* of Marculf. I will read it: you will be struck with the character of these acts:

"To the holy lord and brother in Christ, the abbot of —— or to the whole congregation of —— monastery, built at —— by ——, in honour of Saint ——, bishop, ——. The love which we bear you has impelled us, by Divine inspiration, to regulate for your repose things which assure us eternal recompence, and, without turning us from the right road, or overstepping any limit, to establish rules which may obtain by the aid of the Lord an eternal duration, for we do not insure the least recompence from God in applying ourselves to what must come to pass in future times, without giving succour to the poor in the present time. . . . We think it our duty to insert in this sheet what you and your successors should do with the assistance of the Holy Spirit, or rather that to which the bishop of the holy church himself is bound; namely, that those of your congregation who are to exercise the holy services in your monastery, when they shall be presented by the abbot and all the congregation, receive from us or our successors the sacred orders, without making any gift for this honour; that the said bishop, out of respect for the place, and without receiving any recompence, consecrate the altar of the monastery, and grant, if it be demanded of him, the holy oil each year; and when, by Divine will, one abbot shall pass from the monastery to God, let the bishop of the place, without expecting recompence, elevate to the rank of abbot, the monk most remarkable for the merits of his life, whom he shall find selected by the brethren. And let them take nothing which has been offered by God-fearing men to the abbey. And unless requested by the congregation or the abbot, to go there for the sake of prayer, let none of us enter into the interior of a monastery, nor overstep its enclosure. And if, after having been begged so to do by the monks, the bishop come for the purposes of prayer, or to be useful to them in anything, after the celebration of the holy mysteries, and after having received simple and brief thanks, let him set about regaining his dwelling without being required so to do by any one, so that the monks who are accounted solitaries may, with the help of God, pass the time in perfect tranquillity, and that, living under a holy rule, and imitating the holy fathers, they may the more perfectly implore God for the good of the church, and the salvation of the country. And if any monks of this order conduct themselves with indifference, and not as they should, if it is necessary let them be corrected according to rule by their abbot; if not, the bishop of the town must restrain them, in order that the canonical authority be deprived of nothing which tends to the repose of the servants of the faith. If any of our successors, (which God forbid,) full of perfidy, and impelled by cupidity, desire, in a spirit of audacity, to violate the things herein contained, overwhelmed by the blow of divine vengeance, let him be anathematized and excluded from the communion of the brotherhood for three years, and let this privilege be not the less eternally immovable for his conduct. In order that this constitution may remain always in vigour, we and our brothers, the lords bishops, have confirmed it with our signatures.

"Done, this —— day of ——the year of our Lord ——."[1]

When we come to the history of the commons, you will see that many of the charters which they wrested from their lords, seem to have been framed upon this model.

It happened to the monasteries as it was afterwards to happen to the commons: their privileges were constantly violated or altogether abolished. They were obliged to have recourse to a higher guarantee, and they invoked that of the king: a natural pretext presented itself; the kings themselves founded monasteries, and in founding them took some precautions for shielding them from the tyranny of the bishops; they retained them under their especial protection, and prohibited any usurpation of the property or rights of the monks on the part of the bishops. Thus originated the intervention of royalty between the monasteries and the clergy. By and bye, monasteries

[1] Marculf, b. i. f. 1

which had not been founded by kings had recourse to their protection, and attained it for money or some other consideration. The kings in no way interfered with the jurisdiction of the bishops, they disputed none of their religious rights; the protection accorded by them had exclusive reference to monastic property; as this protection was more or less efficacious, the bishops used every effort to elude it; they refused to recognise the letters of protection and immunity granted by the king; sometimes they falsified them by the assistance of some treacherous brother, or even wholly abstracted them from the archives of the monastery. After a while, in order more fully to possess themselves of the constantly augmenting wealth of these establishments, they thought of another plan: they procured their own nomination as abbots of the more valuable monasteries: an opening to this encroachment presented itself; many monks had become bishops, and for the most part, bishops of the diocese in which their own monastery was situated; in this monastery they had taken care to keep up friends, partizans; and the post of abbot becoming vacant, frequently found no difficulty in securing it for themselves. Thus, at once bishops and abbots, they gave themselves up without restraint to the most monstrous abuses. The monasteries in every direction were sorely oppressed, were recklessly despoiled by their heads; the monks looked around for a new protector, they addressed themselves to the pope. The papal power had been long strengthening and extending itself, and it eagerly availed itself of every opportunity of still further extending itself; it interposed as royalty had interposed, keeping, at all events for a long time, within the same limits, making no attempt to narrow the spiritual jurisdiction of the bishops, and abridging them of no spiritual right; applying itself only to repress their aggressions upon property and persons, and to maintain inviolate the established monastic rules. The privileges granted by the popes to certain monasteries of Frankish-Gaul previously to the commencement of the eighth century kept strictly within these limits, in no case removing them from the episcopal to the papal jurisdiction. The monastery of Fulda presents us with the first instance of such a transfer, and this took place by the consent of the bishop of the diocese, Saint Boniface, who himself placed the monastery under the direct authority of the holy see. This is the first instance of such a proceeding that we meet with; neither popes nor kings had ever before interfered, except for the purpose of keeping the bishops within the just limits of their authority.

Such were the changes through which, in the interval I have described, the monastic associations passed, in their relations with the clergy. Their original condition was that of independence; this independence was lessened the moment that they obtained from the clergy some of the privileges which they had solicited from that body. The privileges so obtained, only served to augment their ambition: they became bent upon entering the ecclesiastical corporation: they did enter it, after a while, and found themselves thenceforward subject, like the priests, to the ill-defined, the unlimited authority of the bishops. The bishops abused their authority, the monasteries resisted, and in virtue of what still remained to them of their original independence, procured guarantees, charters. The charters being slighted, the monks had recourse to the civil authority, to royalty, and royalty confirmed the charters, and took the monks under its protection. This protection proving inadequate, the monks next addressed themselves to the pope, who interposed by another title, but without any more decisive success. It is in this struggle of royal and papal protection against episcopal tyranny, that we leave the monasteries in the middle of the eighth century. Under the Carlovingian race, they had to experience still more terrible shocks, assaults which it required their utmost efforts to overcome. We will speak of these at the proper time; at present, the analogy between the history of the monasteries and that of the commons, which manifested itself two centuries later, is the fact which most peculiarly calls for an observation.

We have now completed the history of social civilization, from the sixth to the middle of the eighth century. We have gone through the revolutions of civil and of religious society,—viewed each of them in their various elements. We have still to study the history, during the same period, of purely intellectual and moral civilization; of the ideas which then occupied men's minds, the works which these ideas gave birth to—in a word, the philosophical and literary history of France at this epoch. We will enter upon this study in our next lecture.

SIXTEENTH LECTURE.

From the sixth to the eighth century all profane literature disappeared; sacred literature alone remained—This is evident in the schools and writings of this epoch—1. Of the schools in Gaul from the sixth to the eighth century—Cathedral schools—Rural schools—Monastic schools—What they taught there—2. Of the writings of the day—General character of literature—It ceased to be speculative, and to seek more especially science and intellectual enjoyments; it became practical; knowledge, eloquence, writings, were made means of action—Influence of this characteristic upon the idea formed of the intellectual state at this epoch—It produced scarcely any works, it has no literature properly so called; still minds were active—Its literature consists in sermons and legends—Bishops and missionaries—1st, Of Saint Cesaire, bishop of Arles—Of his sermons—2nd, Of Saint Columban, missionary, and abbot of Luxeuil—Character of sacred eloquence at this epoch.

In studying the state of Gaul at the fourth and fifth centuries,[1] we found two literatures, the one sacred, the other profane. The distinction was marked in persons and in things; the laity and the ecclesiastics studied, meditated, wrote; and they studied, they wrote, they meditated, upon lay subjects, and upon religious subjects. Sacred literature dominated more and more, but it was not alone, profane literature still existed.

From the fourth to the eighth century, there is no longer any profane literature; sacred literature stands alone; priests only study or write; and they only study, they only write, save some rare exceptions, upon religious subjects. The general character of the epoch is the concentration of intellectual development in the religious sphere. The fact is

[1] Lecture 4th, vol. i. p. 346—389.

H 2

evident, whether we regard the state of the schools which still existed, or the works which have come down to us.

The fourth and fifth centuries, you will remember, were in no want of civil schools, of civil professors, instituted by the temporal power, and teaching the profane sciences. All those great schools of Gaul, the organization and names of which I have mentioned to you, were of this description. I have even pointed out to you, that as yet there were no ecclesiastical schools, and that religious doctrines, which daily became more powerful over minds, were not regularly taught, had no legal and official organ. Towards the end of the sixth century, everything is changed: there are no longer civil schools; ecclesiastical schools alone subsist. Those great municipal schools of Trèves, of Poictiers, of Vienne, of Bordeaux, &c., have disappeared; in their place have arisen schools called cathedral or episcopal schools, because each episcopal see had its own. The cathedral school was not always alone; we find in certain dioceses other schools, of an uncertain nature and origin, wrecks, perhaps, of some ancient civil school, which, in becoming metamorphosed, had perpetuated itself. In the diocese of Reims, for example, there existed the school of Mouzon, some distance from the chief place of the diocese, and in high credit, although Reims had a cathedral school. The clergy began also, about the same epoch, to create other schools in the country, also ecclesiastical, destined to form young readers who should one day become priests. In 529, the council of Vaison strongly recommended the propagation of country schools; they were, indeed, multiplied very irregularly, numerous in some dioceses, scarcely any in others. Finally, there were schools in the great monasteries: the intellectual exercises were of two kinds; some of the most distinguished monks gave direct instruction to the members of the congregation, and to the young people who were being brought up at the monastery; it was, moreover, the custom, in a large number of monasteries, that after the lectures at which the monks were bound to attend, they should have conferences among themselves upon whatever had been made the subject of the lecture; and these conferences became a powerful means of intellectual development and instruction.

The most flourishing of the episcopal schools from the sixth to the middle of the eighth century were those of:

1. *Poictiers.* There were many schools in the monasteries of the diocese, at Poictiers itself, at Ligugé, at Ansion, &c.
2. *Paris.*
3. *Le Mans.*
4. *Bourges.*
5. *Clermont.* There was another school in the town where they taught the Theodosian code; a remarkable circumstance, which I do not find elsewhere.
6. *Vienne.*
7. *Châlons-sur-Saone.*
8. *Arles.*
9. *Gap.*

The most flourishing of the monastic schools of the same epoch were those of:

1. *Luxeuil*, in Franche-Comté.
2. *Fontenelle*, or Saint *Vandrille*, in Normandy; in which were about 300 students.
3. *Sithiu*, in Normandy.
4. *Saint Médard*, at Soissons.
5. *Lerens.*

It were easy to extend this list; but the prosperity of monastic schools was subject to great vicissitudes; they flourished under a distinguished abbot, and declined under his successor.

Even in nunneries, study was not neglected; that which Saint Cesaire founded at Arles contained, at the commencement of the sixth century, two hundred nuns, for the most part occupied in copying books, sometimes religious books, sometimes, probably, even the works of the ancients.

The metamorphosis of civil schools into ecclesiastical schools was complete. Let us see what was taught in them. We shall often find in them the names of sciences formerly professed in the civil schools, rhetoric, logic, grammar, geometry, astrology, &c.; but these were evidently no longer taught except in their relations to theology. This is the foundation of the instruction: all was turned into commentary of the Scriptures, historical, philosophical, allegorical, moral, commentary. They desired only to form priests; all studies, whatsoever their nature, were directed towards this result.

Sometimes they went even further: they rejected the profane sciences themselves, whatever might be the use made of them. At the end of the sixth century, Saint Dizier, bishop of Vienne, taught grammar in his cathedral school. Saint Gregory the Great sharply blamed him for it. "It is not fit," he writes to him, "that a mouth sacred to the praises of God, should be opened for those of Jupiter." I do not know exactly what the praises of God or of Jupiter had to do with grammar; but what is evident, is the crying down of the profane studies, although cultivated by the priests.

The same fact is visible, and far more plainly, in the written literature. No more philosophical meditations, no more learned jurisprudence, no more literary criticism; save some chronicles, some occasional poems, of which I shall speak at a later period, we have nothing belonging to this time except religious works. Intellectual activity appears only under this form, displays itself only in this direction.

A still more important revolution, and less perceived, is manifested: not only did literature become entirely religious, but, religious, it ceased to be literary; there was no longer any literature, properly so called. In the finest times of Greece and Rome, and in Gaul, up to the fall of the Roman empire, people studied, they wrote, for the mere pleasure of studying, of knowing, in order to procure for themselves and for others intellectual enjoyment. The influence of letters over society, over real life, was only indirect; it was not the immediate end of the writers; in a word, science and literature were essentially disinterested, devoted to the research for the true and the beautiful, satisfied with finding them, with enjoying them, and pretending to nothing more.

At the epoch which now occupies us it was otherwise; people no longer studied in order to know; they no longer wrote for the sake of writing. Writings and studies took a practical character and aim. Whoever abandoned himself hereto, aspired to immediate action upon men, to regulate their actions, to govern their life, to convert those who did not believe, to reform those who believed and did not practice. Science and eloquence were means of action, of government. There is no longer a disinterested literature, no longer any true literature. The purely speculative character of philosophy, of poetry, of letters, of the arts, has vanished; it is no longer the beautiful that men seek; when they meet with it, it no longer serves merely for enjoyment; positive application, influence over men, authority is now the end, the triumph of all works of mind, of all intellectual development.

It is from not having taken proper heed to this characteristic of the epoch upon which we are occupied, that, in my opinion, a false idea has been formed of it. We find there scarcely any works, no literature, properly so called, no disinterested intellectual activity distinct from positive life. It has been thence concluded, and you have surely heard it said, you may everywhere read, that this was a time of apathy and moral sterility, a time abandoned to the disorderly struggle of material forces, in which intellect was without development and without power.

It was not so. Doubtless nothing remains belonging to this age, either of philosophy, poetry, or literature, properly speaking; but it does not follow that there was no intellectual activity. It was in an eminent degree otherwise; only it was not produced under the same forms as at other epochs; it did not lead to the same results. It was an activity entirely of application, of circumstance, which did not address itself to the future, which had no design to bequeath literary monuments to it, calculated to charm or to instruct; the present, its wants, its destinies, contemporaneous interests and life, that was the circle to which it confined itself, wherein the literature of this epoch spent itself. It produced few books, and yet it was fertile and powerful over minds.

One is therefore highly astonished when, after having heard it said, and having oneself thought that this time was sterile and without intellectual activity, we find in it, upon looking nearer, a world, as it were, of writings, not very considerable, it is true, and often little remarkable, but which, from their number and the ardour which reigns in them, attest a rare movement of mind and fertility. They are sermons, instructions, exhortations, homilies, and conferences upon religious matters. Never has any political revolution, never has the liberty of the press, produced more pamphlets. Three-fourths, nay, perhaps ninety-nine in a hundred, of these little works have been lost: destined to act at the very moment, almost all improvised, rarely collected by their authors or by others, they have not come down to us; and yet an immense number remains to us; they form a true and rich literature.

The sermons, homilies, instructions, &c., of this epoch, may be ranged under four classes. The one class consists of explanations, of commentaries upon the Scriptures. A passionate interest was attached to these monuments of the common faith; men saw everywhere among them purposes, allusions, lessons, examples; they sought in them hidden meanings, moral meanings, will or allegory. The most elevated, the most subtle mind incessantly found there something to exercise itself upon; and the people received with avidity these applications of books, which had all their respect, the actual interests of their conduct and life.

The sermons of the second class relate to the primitive history of Christianity, to the festivals and solemnities which celebrate its great events, such as the birth of Jesus Christ, his passion, his resurrection, &c.

The third class comprehend sermons for the festivals of the saints and martyrs; a kind of religious panegyrics, sometimes purely historical, sometimes turned into moral exhortations.

Finally, the fourth class is that of the sermons destined to apply religious doctrines to the practice of life; that is to say, sermons upon religious morality.

I have no intention to detain you long upon this literature. To really understand it, to estimate the degree of development taken by the human mind, and to appreciate the influence which it has exercised over mankind, a lengthened study is necessary, often tedious, although full of results. The number of these compositions passes all conception: of Saint Augustin alone there remain three hundred and ninety-four sermons; and he preached many others, of which we only have fragments, and again many others which are entirely lost. I shall confine myself to the selecting two of the men who may be considered as the most faithful representatives of this epoch, and to the placing before you some fragments of their eloquence.

There were two classes of preachers—the bishops and the missionaries. The bishops in their cathedral town, where they almost constantly resided, preached several times a week, some even every day. The missionaries, who were chiefly monks, perambulating the country, preaching both in churches and in public places, in the midst of the assembled people.

The most illustrious of the bishops of the epoch which occupies us was Saint Cesaire, bishop of Arles; the most illustrious of the missionaries was Saint Colomban, abbot of Luxeuil. I will endeavour to give you an idea of their life and preaching.

Saint Cesaire was born at the end of the 5th century, in 470, at Châlons-sur-Saône, of a considerable family, and already celebrated for its piety. In his infancy his tendencies, both intellectual and religious, attracted the attention of the bishop of Châlons, Saint Silvestre, who tonsured him in 488, and devoted him to an ecclesiastical life. He made his first appearance in the abbey of Lerens, where he passed many years, abandoning himself to great austerities, and often charged with preaching and teaching in the interior of the monastery. His health suffered from it; the abbot of Lerens sent him to Arles to get re-established, and in 501, amid the unanimous acclamations of the people, he became bishop of that place.

He occupied the see of Arles for forty-one years, from 501 to 542, during the whole of which period he was one of the most illustrious and influential of the bishops of southern Gaul. He presided at, and directed the principal councils of this epoch, the councils of Agde in 506, of Arles in 524, of Carpentras in 527, of Orange in 529, all the councils in which the great questions concerning the doctrine and discipline of the time were treated of, among others, that of semi-Pelagianism. It appears even that his activity was no stranger to politics. He was twice exiled from his diocese; in 505, by Alaric, king of the Visigoths, and in 513, by Theodoric, king of the Ostrogoths, because, they said, he wished to abandon Provence, and especially the city of Arles, to the king of the Burgundians, under whose empire he was born. Whether the accusation was or was not well founded, Saint Cesaire was quickly restored to his diocese, which passionately recalled him.

His preaching there was powerful, and one of the principal sources of his celebrity. About a hundred and thirty of his sermons have reached us, a number far inferior to that which he preached. They may be distributed into the four classes which I have just pointed out, and by a circumstance which reflects honour on Saint Cesaire, the sermons on doctrine or religious morality are more numerous than mystical allegories, or panegyrics of the saints. It is from among the former that I shall take some passages calculated to make you acquainted with this kind of literature and eloquence.[1]

In a sermon, entitled *Advice to the faithful that they read the divine writings*, Saint Cesaire urges them not to devote themselves exclusively to their temporal affairs, to watch their souls, to be occupied solicitously with them.

"The care of our soul, my dear brothers," says he, "strongly resembles the cultivation of the earth: as in the earth, we pluck up some things in order to sow others which shall be good, so should it be for our soul; what is evil should be rooted up, what is good should be planted; let pride be plucked away, and humility take its place; let avarice be rejected, and mercy cultivated.... No one can plant good things in his ground, until he has cleared it of evil things; accordingly thou canst not plant the holy germs of virtue in thy soul, unless thou first pluck out the thorns and thistles of vice. Tell me, I pray thee, thou who saidst even now that thou couldst not accomplish the commandments of God because thou canst not read, tell me, who has taught thee to dress thy vine, at what time to plant a new one? who has taught it thee? Hast thou read it, or hast thou heard speak of it, or hast thou asked it of able cultivators? Since thou art so occupied with thy vine, why art thou not so with thy soul? Give heed, my brother, I pray you, there are two kinds of fields, one of God, the other of man; the domain of God is thy soul; is it, then, just to cultivate thy domain, and to neglect that of God? When thou seest the earth in a good state, thou rejoicest; wherefore, then, dost thou not weep at seeing thy soul lie fallow? We have but few days to live in this world upon the fruits of our earth; let us turn, therefore, our greatest attention towards our souls. . . . let us labour with all our power, with the aid of God, to the end that when he shall come to his field, which is our soul, he may find it cultivated, arranged

[1] The greater part of the sermons of Saint Cesaire were inserted in the appendix to the sermons of Saint Augustin, at the end of vol. v. of his works, fol. 1683.

in good order; let him find crops, not thorns, wine, not vinegar, and more wheat than tares."[1]

Comparisons borrowed from common life, familiar antitheses, singularly strike the imagination of the people; and Saint Cesaire makes great use of them. He recommends the faithful to conduct themselves properly at church, to avoid all distraction, to pray with attention:

"Although in many respects, my dear brothers," says he, "we have often to rejoice at your progress in the way of salvation, still there are some things of which we must caution you, and I pray you to receive our observations willingly, according to your custom. I rejoice, and I return thanks to God, for that I see you flock faithfully to the church to hear the divine lectures; but if you wish to complete your success and our joy, come here earlier: you see tailors, goldsmiths, blacksmiths, rise early in order to provide for the wants of the body; and we, we cannot go before day to church to solicit pardon for our sins.... Come then, at an early hour, I pray you, and once arrived, try, with the aid of God, to prevent any foreign thought from gliding amidst our prayers, for fear of our having one thing upon our lips, and another in our hearts, and that while our language is addressed to God, our minds go astray upon all sorts of subjects.... If thou wished to urge any affair important to thyself with some powerful man, and suddenly turning thyself from him, and interrupting the conversation, thou wert to occupy thyself with all sorts of trifles, what an insult wouldst thou not be guilty of towards him? what would his anger not be towards thee? If then, when we are occupied with a man, we employ all our care not to think of anything else for fear of offending him, ought we not to be ashamed, when we are occupied with God in prayer, when we have to defend ourselves to his Holy Majesty for miserable sins, should we not be ashamed to allow our mind to wander here and there, and to turn from his divine countenance? Every man, my brothers, takes for his God that which absorbs his thought at the moment of prayer, and seems to adore it as his Lord.... This one, while praying, thinks of the public place, it is the public place that he adores; another has before his eyes the house which he

[1] *S. Aug. Op.* vol. v. col. 509, 510.

is constructing or repairing; he adores what he has before his eyes; another thinks of his vine, another of his garden.... What will it be if the thought which occupies be an ill thought, an illegitimate thought? if, in the midst of our prayers, we allow our mind to run upon cupidity, rage, hate, luxury, adultery?... I implore you, therefore, my cherished brothers, if you wish entirely to avoid these distractions of the soul, let us endeavour, with the aid of God, not to yield to them."[1]

Even in treating of the most elevated subjects, in addressing the gravest counsel to his people, the tone of St. Cesaire's preaching is always simple, practical. foreign to all literary pretension, only destined to act upon the soul of his auditors. He wishes to excite in them that ardour for good works, that active zeal, which incessantly pursues good.

" Many people, my dear brothers," says he, " think that it is sufficient for eternal life, if they have done no evil; if, perchance, any one has deceived himself by this false tranquillity, let him know, positively, that it is not sufficient for a Christian merely to have avoided evil, if he has not accomplished, as far as in him lies, things which are good; for He who said: *Depart from evil,*—also said to us . *Do good.*

" He who thinks that it is sufficient not to have done evil, although he has done no good, let him tell me if he would desire from his servant what he does to his Lord. Is there any one who would wish that his servant should do neither good nor evil? We all require that our servants should not only not do the evil which we interdict them, but that they should acquit themselves of the labours that we impose upon them. Thy servant would be more seriously guilty if he should rob thee of thy cattle, but he would not be exempt from fault if he neglected to guard it. It is not just that we should be towards God as we would not wish our servants to be towards us. . . .

" Those who think that it is sufficient that they do no evil are accustomed to say: ' May it please God that I should merit being found, at the hour of death, the same as when I left the sacrament of baptism.' Doubtless, it is good for

[1] *S. Aug. Op.* vol. v. col. 471—473.

each to be found free from faults at the day of judgment, but it is a grave one not to have progressed in good. To him alone who left the world as soon as he received baptism. may it suffice to be the same as when leaving baptism; he had not time to exercise good works; but he who has had time to live, and is arrived at the age to do good, it will not suffice him to be exempt from faults, if he wishes also to be exempt from good works. I wish that he who desires to be found the same at death as he was when he received the sacrament of baptism would tell me, if, when he plants a new vine, he wishes that at the end of ten years it should be the same as the day when he planted it. If he grafts an olive plant, would it suit him that it should be the same after many years as on the day when he grafted it? If a son be born to him, let him consider whether he would wish, that after five years he should be of the same age and the same size as at the day of his birth. Since, then, there is no one to whom this would be agreeable for the things which belong to him, in the same way that he would be sorrowful if his vine, his olive plant, or his son, should make no progress, so let him sorrow if he find that he himself has made no progress from the moment he was born in Christ."[1]

And elsewhere, in a sermon upon charity:—

"It is not without reason, you must suppose, that I so often discourse with you upon truth and perfect charity. I do it because I know no remedy so wholesome, or so efficacious for the wounds of sin. Let us add that, however powerful may be this remedy, there is no one who may not procure it, with the aid of God. For other good works omitted, one may find some excuse; there is none for omitting the duty of charity. One may say to me, 'I cannot fast;' 'I cannot love?' They may say, 'From the weakness of my body, I cannot abstain from meat and wine;' but who can say to me, 'I cannot love my enemies, nor pardon those who have offended me?' Let no one deceive himself, for no one can deceive God. . . . There are many things which we cannot draw from our granary or our cellar, but it would be disgraceful to say that there is something which we cannot draw from the treasure of our heart;

[1] *S. Aug. Op.* vol. v. col. 431, 432.

for here our feet have not to run, our eyes to look, our ears to listen, nor our hands to work. We can allege no fatigue as an excuse; men do not say to us: 'Go to the east to seek charity; sail to the east, and thence bring back affection.' It is into ourselves and into our hearts that they order us to enter; it is there that we shall find everything. . .

"But, says some one, I cannot, in any way, love my enemies. God tells thee in the Scriptures that thou canst; and thou answerest that thou canst not. Now, look; should we believe God or thee? . . . How then? So many men, so many women, so many children, so many delicate young girls have supported with a firm heart, for the love of Christ, the flames, the sword, wild beasts; and we cannot support the insults of some foolish persons! and for some petty ills which the wickedness of men has done us, we pursue against them to their death the vengeance of our injuries. Truly, I know not with what face and with what conscience we dare ask to share eternal beatitude with the saints, we who cannot follow their example even in the slightest things."[1]

This is not devoid of energy; the feeling of it is lively, the turns picturesque; it almost amounts to eloquence.

Here is a passage which is even more touching. It is doubtful whether the sermon from which I borrow it is by Saint Cesaire. It contains some almost verbal imitations from the eastern fathers, especially Eusebius and Saint Gregory: but this matters little; it is certainly by some preacher of the time, and characterizes it as well as that which I have just cited. It was preached on Easter-day; it celebrates Christ's descent into hell, and his resurrection:

"Behold," says the preacher, "you have heard what was done of his own free-will by our Saviour, the Lord of Vengeance. When, like a conqueror, burning and terrible, he reached the countries of the kingdom of darkness, at the sight of him the impious legions of hell, affrighted and trembling, began to ask each other, saying:—'What is this terrible figure resplendent with the whiteness of snow? Never has our Tartarus received his like; never has the world cast into our caverns any one resembling him; this is an invader, not a debtor; he exacts, he

[1] *S. Aug. Op.* vol. v. col. 451, 452.

does not ask; we see a judge, not a suppliant; he comes to command, not to succumb; to take away, not to remain. Did our porters sleep when this triumpher attacked our gates? If he was a sinner, he would not be so powerful; if any fault sullied him, he would not illuminate our Tartarus with such brilliancy. If he is God, wherefore has he come? if he is man, how has he dared? If he is God, what does he in the sepulchre? if he is man, why does he deliver sinners? whence comes he, so dazzling, so powerful, so radiant, so terrible? . . . Who is he, that with so much intrepidity he oversteps our frontiers, and that not only he does not bear our punishments, but that he delivers others from our chains? Should not this be he by whose death our prince lately said we should gain the empire over the whole universe? But if this be he, the hope of our prince has deceived him; where he thought to conquer, he has been conquered and thrown down. O, our prince, what hast thou done, what hast thou wished to do? Behold him who, by his splendour, has dissipated thy darkness; he has overthrown thy dungeons, broken thy chains, delivered thy captives, and changed their sorrow into joy. Behold those who were accustomed to groan under our torments insult us because of the salvation which they have received; and not only do they not fear us, but they even menace us. Have any seen hitherto the dead become proud, the captives rejoice? Why hast thou desired to lead hither him whose coming has called back joy to those who late were in despair? We no longer hear their accustomed cries, none of their groans resound!' "[1]

Surely, even were you to find such a passage in *Paradise Lost*, you would not be astonished, for this discourse is not unworthy of the hell of Milton.

It is not, however (and this is a good reason for not attributing it to him), in the general tone of the preaching of Saint Cesaire. This is in general more simple, less ardent; it addresses itself to the common incidents of life, to the natural feelings of the soul. There reigns in it a mild kindness towards a genuine intimacy with the population to whom the preacher addresses himself; he not only speaks a language suited to his auditors, the language which he believes best

[1] *S. Aug. Op.* vol. v. col. 283, 284.

calculated to act upon them; but he pays attention to the effect of his words; he wishes to take from them anything which they may possess likely to wound,—all bitterness; he in a manner claims indulgence for his severity.

"When I make these reflections, I fear that some will rather be irritated against us than against themselves: our discourse is offered to your charity as a mirror; and as a matron, when she regards herself in her mirror, corrects what she sees defective in her person, and does not break the mirror; so, when any one shall recognise his deformity in a discourse, it is just that he should rather correct himself than be irritated against the preacher as against a mirror. Those who receive a wound are more disposed to nurse it than to irritate themselves against the remedies; let no persons irritate themselves against spiritual remedies; let each receive, not only patiently, but with a good heart, what is said to him with a good heart. It is well known that he who receives in a good spirit a salutary correction, already avoids evil; he who is displeased with his faults, begins to have an inclination for what is good, and in proportion as he departs from vice, he approaches virtue."[1]

He pushes his solicitude so far as to desire that his auditors should interrogate him, and enter into conversation with him.

"It was a cause of great joy to him," say his biographers, "when men induced him to explain any obscure point; and he himself frequently excited us to it, by saying to us—'I know that you do not understand all that we say; why do you not interrogate us, to the end that you may be able to comprehend? The cows do not always run to the calves—often, even the calves run to the cows, that they may appease their hunger at the dugs of their mother. You should act in precisely the same manner, so that by interrogating us, you may seek the means of extracting the spiritual honey for yourselves.'"[2]

One can scarcely suppose but that such language would exercise great influence over the mass of the people; that of

[1] *S. Aug. Op.* vol. v. col. 480.

[2] *Vita S. Cæsarii*, c. 30; *dans les Acta sanct. ord. S. Bened.* vol. i. p. 667.

Saint Cesaire was great indeed, and everything attests that few bishops possessed the soul of their auditors as he did.

I pass to a preaching of another kind, less regular, less wise, but not less powerful—to that of the missionaries. I have named Saint Colomban as the type of this class of men. He was born in 540, not in Gaul, but in Ireland, in the province of Leinster; he prosecuted his ecclesiastical studies, and became a monk in the monastery of Benchor, situated in the North of Ireland, in Ulster. What he had to do as a common monk, and in Ireland, did not satisfy his activity; and in 585, already forty-five years of age, he passed into France with twelve monks of his monastery, with the sole aim of visiting it and preaching there. He preached, indeed, while travelling from west to east, with enormous success, attracting everywhere the concourse of the people, and the attention of the great. A short time after his arrival in Burgundy, the king, Gontran, implored him to remain there. He established himself amidst the mountains of Vosges, and there founded a monastery. At the end of a very short period, in 590, the increasing number of his disciples, and the affluence of people, obliged him to seek a more extensive and more accessible place; he descended to the foot of the mountains, and there founded the monastery of Luxeuil, which soon became very considerable. The successes of Saint Colomban were less peaceable than that of Saint Cesaire—they were accompanied by resistance and trouble; he preached the reformation of manners, the zeal of faith, without caring for any consideration or circumstance, falling out with princes, with bishops, casting the Divine fire on all sides, without troubling himself about the conflagration. Accordingly, his influence, which he exercised with a good intention, was uncertain, unequal, and incessantly disturbed. In 602, he got into a quarrel with the neighbouring bishops, about the day of the celebration of Easter, and not choosing to yield anything to the local customs, he made enemies of them. About 609, a violent storm was raised against him at the court of the king of Burgundy, Theodoric II., and, with his accustomed energy, he preferred to abandon his monastery rather than yield for an instant. Fredégaire has accurately preserved the account of this contest; I will read it entire·

the character and the situation of the missionary are strongly shown in it :—

"The fourth year of the reign of Theodoric, the reputation of Saint Colomban increased in the cities and in all the provinces of Gaul and Germany. He was so much celebrated and venerated by all, that king Theodoric often visited him at Luxeuil, to ask with humility the favour of his prayers. As he went there very often, the man of God began to rebuke him, asking him why he gave himself up to adultery with concubines, rather than enjoying the sweetness of a legitimate marriage, so that the royal race might proceed from an honourable queen, and not from an evil place. As already the king obeyed the word of the man of God, and promised to abstain from all illicit things, the old serpent glided into the soul of his grandmother Brunehault, who was a second Jezebel, and excited her against the saint of God with the sting of pride. Seeing Théodoric obey the man of God, she feared that if her son, slighting the concubines, put a queen at the head of the court, she would see herself, by this event, retrenched of a part of her dignity and honours. It happened one day that Colomban visited the court of Brunehault, which was then in the domain of Bourcheresse.[1] The queen having seen him enter the court, led to him the sons that Theodoric had had by his adulteries. Having looked at them, the saint asked what they wanted with him. Brunehault said to him—'These are the sons of the king—give them the favour of thy benediction.' Colomban said to her—'Know that they will never bear the royal sceptre, for they have come from an ill place.' She, in a fury, ordered the children to retire. The man of God having left the court of the queen, at the moment that he passed the threshold a terrible noise from above was heard, but did not repress the fury of this miserable woman, who prepared to set snares for him. . . . . Colomban, seeing the royal anger raised against him, promptly repaired to the court, to repress by his admonitions this unworthy rancour. The king was then at Epoisse, his country house. Colomban arrived as the sun went down; they announced to the king that the man of God was there, and that he was not willing to enter into the house of the king. Then Theodoric said,

[1] Between Châlons and Autun.

that he had rather properly honour the man of God than provoke the anger of the Lord by offending one of his servants; he therefore ordered his people to prepare everything with royal pomp, and to go to the servant of God. They ran therefore, and, according to the order of the king, offered their presents. Colomban, seeing that they presented him dishes and cups with royal splendour, asked what they wanted. They said to him—'This is what the king sends thee.' But, driving them back with malediction, he answered —'It is written, the Most High rejecteth the gifts of the wicked; it is not fit that the lips of the servants of God should be soiled with his meat—of his who interdicts their entry, not only into his dwelling, but that of others.' At these words, the vases fell to pieces, the wine and the beer ran over the ground, and everything was scattered about. Some servants, terrified, went to tell the king what had happened. He, seized with fright, repaired, at break of day, with his grandmother, to the man of God; they implored him to pardon them for what they had done, and promised to correct themselves in future. Colomban was appeased, and returned to the monastery. But they did not long observe their promises; their miserable sins recommenced, and the king gave himself up to his usual adulteries. At the news of this, Colomban sent him a letter full of reproaches, menacing him with excommunication if he would not correct himself. Brunehault, again enraged, excited the mind of the king against Colomban, and strove to deprive him of all his power; she prayed all the lords and great men of the court to animate the king against the man of God; she also dared to solicit the bishops, in order that they might raise suspicions concerning his religion, and blame the rule which he imposed upon his monks. The courtiers, obeying the discourse of this miserable queen, excited the mind of the king against the saint of God, and persuaded him to cause him to come and prove his religion. The king hurried away, sought the man of God at Luxeuil, and asked him why he deviated from the customs of other bishops, and also why the interior of the monastery was not open to all Christians. Colomban, with a haughty soul and full of courage, answered the king that it was not customary to open the entrance of the dwelling-place of the servants of

God to secular men and strangers to religion, but that he had places prepared and destined to receive all guests. The king said to him—'If thou desire to acquire the gifts of our bounty and the help of our protection, thou must allow every one to enter into all parts of thy monastery.' The man of God answered—'If thou wouldst violate what has hitherto been subject to the rigour of our rules, and if thou art come here to destroy the retreats of the servants of God, and overthrow the rules of discipline, know that thy empire shall crumble to the ground, and that thou shalt perish with all thy royal race;' which the event afterwards confirmed. Already, with a rash step, the king had penetrated into the refectory; terrified at these words, he quickly returned. He was then assailed with the warm reproaches of the man of God, to whom Theodoric said: 'Thou hopest I shall give thee the crown of a martyr; know that I am not sufficiently foolish to commit so great a crime. Return to a view of things which will be far more profitable for thee, and let him who has renounced the manners of secular men resume the path he has quitted.' The courtiers all cried, with one voice, that they could not tolerate in that place a man who would not associate with all. But Colomban said that he would not go beyond the boundary of the monastery, unless taken away by force. The king then departed, leaving a certain lord named Bandulf, who immediately drove the saint of God from the monastery, and conducted him in exile to the town of Besançon, until the king should decide upon the sentence which it might please him to pass."

The struggle was prolonged for some time; the missionary was finally obliged to quit Burgundy. Theodoric had him conducted to Nantes, where he attempted to embark in order to return to Ireland; an unknown circumstance, of which his biographers have made a miracle, prevented him crossing the sea; he resumed the route of the countries of the east, and established himself in the states of Teodebert, brother of Theodoric, in Switzerland. on the borders of the lake of Zurich; then on the lake of Constance, and finally on the lake of Geneva. New troubles drove him from this abode; he passed into Italy, and there founded, in 612, the monastery of Bobbio, where he died on the 21st of November, 615, an object of veneration to all the people among whom he had brought his tempestuous activity.

It is shown in his eloquence: few monuments of it remain to us; such preaching was far more improvised, far more fugitive, than that of a bishop. Belonging to Saint Colomban we have only the rule which he instituted for his monastery, some letters, some poetical fragments, and sixteen *Directions*, which are really sermons, preached either during some mission, or in the interior of his monastery. The character of them is entirely different from that of the sermons of Saint Cesaire; there is much less mind and reason in them; a less fine and varied knowledge of human nature and the different situations of life, less care taken to model the religious instruction upon the wants and capacities of the auditors. But on the other hand, the flights of imagination, the pious transports, the rigorous application of principles, the warfare declared against all vain or hypocritical compromise, give to the words of the orator that passionate authority which does not always and surely reform the soul of his auditors, but which dominates over them, and, for some time at least, sovereignly disposes of their conduct and their life. I shall cite but one passage from them, so much the more remarkable, as being what one would least expect to find there. It was the age when fasts, mortifications, austerities of all kinds were multiplied in the interior of monasteries, and Saint Colomban recommends them, like others; but, in the sincerity of his enthusiasm, he soon perceived that neither sanctity nor faith existed therein, and he attacked the errors of the monastical rigours, in the same way that he had attacked the baseness of worldly effeminacy:

"Do not suppose," says he, "that it suffices for us to fatigue the dust of our body with fasts and vigils, if we do not also reform our manners. . . . To mortify the flesh, if the soul fructifies not, is to labour incessantly at the earth without making it produce any harvest; it is to construct a statue of gold outside, and of mud within. To what purpose were it to go far abroad to make war, if the interior be left a prey to ruin? What would be said of the man who should dig all round his vineyard and leave it inside full of brambles and bushes?. . . . A religion consisting merely of gestures and movements of the body is vain; the suffering of the body alone is vain; the care which a man takes of his exterior is vain, if he does not also watch and take care of his soul. True piety resides in the humility, not of the body, but of the heart. To what purpose are those combats, which are fought with the passions by the servant when these live in peace with the master? . . . . It does not suffice any more to hear speak of the virtues, or to read of them. . . . Is it by words alone that a man cleanses his house of filth? Is it without labour and without sweat that a daily work can be accomplished? . . . . Therefore strengthen yourself, and cease not to combat; no one obtains the crown, unless he has courageously fought."[1]

We do not find many passages in the Instructions of Saint Colomban, so simple as this. The transports of imagination are there always mixed with subtlety of mind; still the foundation is often energetic and original.

Compare this sacred eloquence of the sixth century with the eloquence of the modern pulpit, even in its finest period; at the seventeenth century, for example. I said but now that, from the sixth to the eighth century, the characteristic of literature was that of ceasing to be literature, that it had become an action, a power; that in writing, in speaking, men only concerned themselves with positive and immediate results ; that they sought neither science nor intellectual pleasures, and that, for this reason, the epoch produced scarcely anything but sermons, or works analogous to them. This fact, which is shown in the general literature, is imprinted on the sermons themselves. Open those of modern times, they have evidently a character more literary than practical; the orator aspires far more to beauty of language, to the intellectual satisfaction of his auditors, than to influence them to the bottom of their souls, to produce real effects, true reformation, efficacious conversion. There is nothing of this kind, nothing literary, in the sermons which I have just spoken of; no anxiety about speaking well, about artistically combining images, ideas; the orator goes to the facts; he desires to act: he turns and returns in the same circle; he fears not repetitions, familiarity, or even vulgarity; he speaks briefly, but he begins again each morning. It is not sacred eloquence, it is religious power.

There was at this epoch a literature which has not been

[1] *S. Colomban. Inst.* 2. *Bibl. patr.* vol. xii. p. 10.

remarked, a veritable literature, essentially disinterested, which had scarcely any other end in view but that of procuring intellectual, moral pleasure to the public; I mean the lives of the saints, the legends. They have not been introduced into the literary history of this epoch: they are, however, its true, its only literature, for they are the only works which had the pleasures of the imagination for their object. After the battle of Troy, almost every town in Greece had poets who collected the traditions and adventures of the heroes, and made a diversion of them for the public, a national diversion. At the epoch which occupies us, the lives of the saints played the same part for the Christians. There were men who occupied themselves in collecting them, writing them, and recounting them for the edification, no doubt, but more especially for the intellectual pleasure of the Christians. That is the literature of the time, properly so called. In our next lecture, I shall lay some of those before you, as well as some monuments of profane literature, which we likewise meet there.

SEVENTEENTH LECTURE.

Preface of the *Old Mortality* of Walter Scott—Robert Patterson—Preface of the *Vie de Saint Marcellin*, bishop of Embrun, written at the commencement of the sixth century—Saint Ceran, bishop of Paris—Eagerness of the Christians of these times to collect the traditions and monuments of the life of the saints and martyrs—Statistics of this branch of sacred literature—Collection of the Bollandists—Cause of the number and popularity of legends—They almost alone satisfy at this epoch—1. The wants of the moral nature of man—Examples · Life of Saint Bavon, of Saint Wandregisilus, of Saint Valery—2. The wants of physical nature—Examples: Life of St. Germain of Paris, of Saint Wandregisilus, of Saint Rusticulus, of Saint Sulpicius of Bourges—3. The wants of the imagination—Examples: Life of Saint Seine, of Saint Austregesilus—Literary defects and merits of legends.

HEADING the *Puritans* of Walter Scott is a preface which the French translators have omitted, I know not why, and from which I take the following details:

"The tombs of the puritan martyrs, scattered in large numbers, especially in some counties of Scotland, are still objects for the respect and devotion of their partisans. It is sixty years ago that a man living in the county of Dumfries, named Robert Patterson, a descendant, it was supposed, of one of the victims of the persecution, quitted his house and small inheritance, in order to devote himself to the task of keeping these modest tombs in repair. . . He contrived to discover them in the most secret places, in the mountains and rocks where the insurgent puritans had taken refuge, and where, often surprised by troops, they perished sword in hand, or were shot after the combat. He freed the funeral stone from the moss which covered it, he renewed the half effaced inscription where the pious friends of the dead had expressed, in scriptural style, both the celestial joys which awaited him, and the malediction which should for ever pursue his murderers. Every year he visited all the tombs: no season stopped him; he begged not, nor had he any need so to do; hospitality was always assured him in the families of the martyrs or zealots of the sect. For nearly thirty years he continued this painful pilgrimage; and it is scarcely more than twenty-five years since he was found exhausted with fatigue, and breathing his last sigh upon the high road, near Lockerby; by his side was his old white horse, the companion of his labours. In many parts of Scotland, Robert Patterson is still remembered, and the people, ignorant of his real name, designated him, from the employment to which he devoted his life, by that of *Old Mortality*, (man of the dead of olden times.)"

I go back from the eighteenth to the sixth century, and I read at the head of the *Life of Saint Marcellin*, bishop of Embrun, this little prologue:

"By the bounty of Christ, the combats of the illustrious martyrs, and the praises of the blessed confessors, have filled the world to such a degree, that almost every town may boast of having as patrons martyrs born within its bosom. Hence it happens, that the more they write and propagate the inestimable recompence which they received for their virtues, the more will the gratitude of the faithful increase. Accordingly, I find my pleasure in seeking everywhere the palms of these glorious champions; and while travelling with this view, I arrived at the city of Embrun. There I found that a man, long since sleeping with the Lord, still performs signal miracles. . . . . . I asked, curiously, what had been the kind of life of this holy man from his infancy, what was his country, by what proofs and by what marvels of virtue he had been raised to the sublime charge of pontiff; and all declared with one voice what I have here committed to writing. Men even whose age has been prolonged to a very late period, and some of whom have attained ninety, and even a hundred years, have given me unanimous answers concerning the holy pontiff. . . . I wish, therefore, to transmit his memory to future ages, although I feel my weakness succumb under such a burden."[1]

[1] *Vie de Saint Marcellin*, in the *Acta Sanctorum* of the Bollandists, 20th April, vol. ii. p. 751.

Behold the Robert Patterson of the sixth century: this unknown man performed the same travels, and fulfilled almost the same office for the Christian heroes of this epoch, as *Old Mortality* did for the martyrs of Scotch puritanism. It was a taste, a general need of the age, that of seeking all the traditions, all the monuments of the martyrs and saints, and transmitting them to posterity. Saint Ceraune, or Ceran, bishop of Paris at the beginning of the seventh century, likewise devoted his life to this task. He wrote to all the priests whom he thought learned in the pious traditions of their country, praying them to collect such for him: we know, among others, that he addressed himself to a priest of the diocese of Langres, called Warnacher, and that this latter sent him the acts of three sainted brothers of one birth, Speusippius, Eleusippius, and Meleusippus, martyrised in that diocese shortly after the middle of the second century; and of Saint Didier, bishop of Langres, who underwent the same fate about one hundred years later. It would be easy to find many analogous facts in the history of Christianity, from the fourth to the tenth century.

Thus were amassed the materials of the collection commenced in 1643 by Bolland, a Jesuit of Belgium, since continued by many other scholars, and known under the name of *Recueil des Bollandistes.* All monuments relative to the life of the saints are there collected and classed by month and day. The enterprise was interrupted in 1794 by the Belgian revolution; so the work is finished only for the first nine months of the year, and the first fourteen days of the month of October. The end of October, and the months of November and December are wanting; but the materials for them were prepared: they have been found, and it is said that no time will be lost in publishing them.

In its actual state, this collection contains 53 volumes folio, of which the following is the distribution:—

January . . .	2	volumes	July . . .	7	volumes
February . .	3	„	August . .	6	„
March . . .	3	„	September .	8	„
April . . .	3	„	October (up to the fourteenth day) . . .	6	„
May	8	„			
June	7	„			

Would you have an idea of the number of lives of the saints, long or succinct, contemporaneous or not, which fill these 53 volumes? Here is the list, day by day, of those of the month of April:—

April 1. . . .	40 Saints		April 17. . . .	42 Saints
2. . . .	41		18. . . .	46
3. . . .	26		19. . . .	38
4. . . .	26		20. . . .	57
5. . . .	20		21. . . .	24
6. . . .	55		22. . . .	62
7. . . .	35		23. . . .	42
8. . . .	25		24. . . .	74
9. . . .	39		25. . . .	30
10. . . .	30		26. . . .	48
11. . . .	39		27. . . .	56
12. . . .	141		28. . . .	45
13. . . .	39		29. . . .	58
14. . . .	46		30. . . .	126
15. . . .	41			
16. . . .	81			1472

I have not made the calculation for the fifty-three volumes; but according to this amount of one month, and judging by approximation, they contain more than 25,000 lives of saints. I must add that many, doubtless, have been lost, and that many others still remain unpublished in the libraries. This simple statistic shows you the extent of this literature, and what prodigious activity of mind it presupposes in the sphere of which it is the object.

Such an activity, such a fertility, surely did not proceed from the mere fancy of the authors; there were general and powerful causes for it. It is customary to see them only in the religious doctrines of this epoch, in the zeal which they inspired: assuredly, they conspired thereto; and nothing of the kind was done without their influence; still they did not do all. In other times, also, these doctrines were diffused, were energetic without producing the same result. It was not merely to faith and to religious exaltation; it was also, and perhaps more especially, to the moral state of society and of man, from the fifth to the tenth century, that the literature of legends owes its richness and popularity.

You know the character of the epoch which we have just studied: it was a time of misery and extreme disorder, one of those times which weigh, in some measure, in all directions upon mankind, checking and destroying it. But however bad the times may be, whatever may be the external circumstances which oppress human nature, there is an energy, an elasticity in it, which resists their empire; it has faculties, wants which make their way through all obstacles; a thousand causes may curb them, turn them from their natural direction, suspend or divert their development for a greater or less length of time; nothing can abolish them, reduce them to a state of complete impotence: they seek and always find some issue, some satisfaction.

It was the merit of the pious legends to give to some of those powerful instincts, those invincible wants of the human soul, that issue, that satisfaction, which all elsewhere refused them.

And first you know to what a deplorable state Frankish-Gaul had arrived, what depravation or what brutality reigned there. The view of the daily recurring events revolted or suppressed all the moral instincts of man; everything was abandoned to chance or to force; we scarcely meet, in the interior world, with that empire of idea of duty, that respect for right, which is the foundation of the security of life and the repose of the soul. They were found in the legends. Whoever will cast a glance, on the one hand, upon the chronicles of civil society, on the other, upon the lives of the saints,—whoever, in the History of Gregory of Tours alone, will compare the civil traditions and the religious traditions, will be struck with their difference; in the one, morality only appears, so to speak, in spite of mankind and without their knowledge; interests and passions alone reign: people are plunged into their chaos and darkness; in the others, amidst a deluge of absurd fables, morality bursts forth with an immense influence; it is seen, it is felt; this sun of intellect shines upon the world in the bosom of which it lives. I might refer you almost indifferently to all the legends; you would everywhere meet with the fact I point out. Two or three examples will make it fully evident.

Saint Bavon, or Bav, hermit and patron of the town of Ghent, who died in the middle of the seventh century, had at first led a worldly life; I read in his history, written by a cotemporary.

"One day he saw a man come to him, whom formerly, and while he still led a worldly life, he had himself sold. At this sight, he fell into a violent fit of despair for having committed so great a crime towards this man; and, turning towards him, he fell upon his knees, saying, 'It is I by whom thou wast sold, tied with thongs; remember not, I implore thee, the evil that I have done to thee, and grant me one prayer. Strike my body with rods, shave my head as thou wouldst that of a robber, and cast me in prison as I deserve, with my feet and hands tied; may be, if thou dost this, the Divine mercy will grant me his pardon.' The man .... says that he dare not do such a thing to his master; but the holy man, who spoke eloquently, strove to induce him to do what he asked. Finally, constrained, and despite himself, the other, overcome by his prayers, did as he required him; he tied the hands of the godly man, shaved his head, tied his feet to a stick, and conducted him to the public prison; and the holy man remained there many days, deploring day and night those acts of a worldly life, which he had always before his mind's eye, as a heavy burden."[1]

The exaggeration of these details is of little importance; even the material truth of the history is of little importance: it was written at the beginning of the seventh century, to those men of the seventh century who incessantly had under their observation servitude, the sale of slaves, and all the iniquities, all the sufferings, which ensued from their condition. You can understand what a charm this simple recital possessed for them. It was a real moral relief, a protest against odious and powerful facts, a weak but precious echo of the rights of liberty.

Here is a fact of another nature: I take it from the *Life of Saint Wandregisilus, Abbot of Fontenelle*, who died in 667, and who, before embracing the monastic life, had been count of the palace of king Dagobert:—

"While he still led a lay life, as he was travelling one day accompanied by his people, he arrived at a certain place on

[1] In 653 or 657. Life of Saint Bavon, § 10, *Acta Sanct. Ord. S. Ben.*, vol. ii. p. 400.

his road; the people in insurrection abandoned themselves to all the transports of fury against the holy man: impelled by a barbarous and insensate rage, and fallen into the condition of beasts, a crowd of people rushed towards him, and much blood would have been shed, if his intervention and the power of Christ had not provided a remedy. He implored the succour of Him to whom it is said: 'Thou art my refuge against tribulations;' and trusting to words instead of his sword, he placed himself under the shield of Divine mercy. Divine help did not fail him, when human help was wanting; this crowd of madmen stood immoveable. The discourse of the holy man then dispersed and saved them at the same time; they came in fury, and they retired in quiet."[1]

Would you suppose that at this epoch it would have occurred to any barbarian, to any man a stranger to religious ideas, thus to manage the multitude, to employ only persuasion and words, in order to appease a disturbance. It is very probable that he would have had immediate recourse to force. The rash employment of force was repugnant to a pious man, preoccupied with the idea that he had to do with souls; instead of physical force, he invoked moral force; before massacre, he tried a sermon.

I now take an example in which the relations of men shall be nothing, in which no attempt shall be made to substitute moral for physical force, nor to protest against social iniquity; in which there is no question concerning anything but individual, private sentiments, of the internal life of man. I read in the life of Saint Valery, who died in 622, abbot of Saint Valery, in Picardy:

"As this godly man returned on foot from a certain place," says Cayeux, "to his monastery, in the winter season, it happened, by reason of the excessive rigour of the cold, that he stopped to warm himself in the dwelling of a certain priest. This latter and his companions, who should have treated such a guest with great respect, began, on the contrary, boldly to hold unsuitable and ill discourse with the judge of the place. Faithful to his custom always to put the salutary remedy of the Divine word upon corrupted and

[1] Life of Saint Wandregisilus, § 4, in the *Acta Sanct. Ord. S. Ben.*, vol. ii. p. 535.

frightful wounds, he attempted to check them, saying: 'My sons, have you not seen in the Evangelist that at the day of judgment you will have to account for every idle word?' But they, scorning his admonition, abandoned themselves more and more to gross and obscene discourse, for the mouth speaks from the overflowing of the heart. As for him, he said: 'I desired, by reason of the cold, to warm my fatigued body a little at your fire; but your guilty discourse forces me to depart, all frozen as I am.' And he left the house."[1]

Of a surety the manners and language of the men of this age were very coarse, disorderly, impure; still, doubtless, respect, a taste even for gravity, for purity, both in thought and word, was not abolished; and when they found an occasion, many among them certainly took pleasure in satisfying that taste. The legends alone furnished them with the means. There was presented the image of a moral state, highly superior, in every respect, to that of the external society, of common life; the human mind might there repose, relieved from the view of crimes and vices which assailed it on all sides. Perhaps it scarcely itself sought this relief; I doubt if it ever made account of it; but, when it came upon it, it eagerly enjoyed it; and this, no doubt, was the first and most powerful cause of the popularity of this literature.

This was not all: it also answered to other wants of our nature, to those wants of affection, of sympathy, which proceed, if not from morality, properly so called, at least from moral sensibility, and which exercise so much influence over the soul. The sensible faculties had much to suffer at the epoch which occupies us; men were hard, and were treated harshly; the most natural sentiments, kindness, pity, friendship, both of family and of choice, took but a weak or painful development. And yet they were not dead in the heart of man: they often sought to display themselves; and the sight of their presence, of their power, charmed a population condemned to so little enjoyment of them in real life. The legends gave them this spectacle; although by a very false idea, in my opinion, and one which has produced deplorable extravagances, the religion of the time often commanded the sacrifice, even the contempt of the most legitimate feelings, still

[1] Life of Saint Valery, § 25, in the *Acta Sanct. Ord. S. Ben.*, vol. ii. p. 86.

it did not stifle, it did not interdict the development of human sensibility; while very often ill directing its application, it favoured rather than suppressed its exercise. We find, in the lives of the saints, more benevolence, more tenderness of heart, a larger part given to the affections, than in any other monument of this epoch. I will place before you some instances; I am convinced you will be struck with the development of our sensible nature, which breaks forth amidst the theory of sacrifice and self-denial.

The ardent zeal of Saint Germain, bishop of Paris in the last half of the sixth century,[1] for the redemption of slaves, is known by every one; many pictures have perpetuated it, but the touching details of it must be read in his life:

"Were even the voices of all united in one, you could not say how prodigal were his alms; often contenting himself with a tunic, he covered some poor naked object with the rest of his clothes, so that while the beggar was warm, the benefactor was cold. It is impossible to enumerate in how many places, or in what number, he redeemed captives. The neighbouring nations, the Spaniards, the Scotch, the Britons, the Gascons, the Saxons, the Burgundians, may attest in what way recourse was had, on all sides, to the name of the Saint, in order to be delivered from the yoke of slavery. When he had nothing more left, he remained seated, sorrowful and restless, with a more grave visage, and a more solemn conversation. If by chance any one then invited him to a repast, he excited the guests, or his own servants, to concert the manner of delivering a captive, and the soul of the bishop escaped a little from its despondency. If the Lord, in any way, sent means to the saint, immediately, seeking in his mind, he was accustomed to say: 'Let us return thanks to the Divine clemency, for the means of effecting redemption has arrived,' and at once, without hesitation, the effect followed the words. When, therefore, he had thus received anything, the wrinkles on his forehead disappeared, his countenance was more serene, he walked with a lighter step, his discourse was more copious and lively; so much so that one would have thought that, in redeeming others, this man delivered himself from the yoke of slavery."[2]

[1] Died in 576.

[2] Life of Saint Germain, bishop of Paris, § 74, in the *Acta Sanct. Ord. S. Ben.*, vol. i. p. 244.

Never has the passion of goodness been painted with a more simple and a truer energy.

In the life of Saint Wandregisilus, abbot of Fontenelle, of whom I have just spoken, I find this anecdote:

"As he repaired one day to king Dagobert, just as he approached the palace, there was a poor man whose cart had been overthrown before the very gate of the king: many people passed in and out, and not only they did not lend him any aid, but many passed over him, and trod him under foot. The man of God, when he arrived, saw the impiety which these children of insolence committed, and, immediately descending from his horse, he held his hand out to the poor man, and, both together, they raised the cart. Many of those present, seeing him all soiled with mud, mocked and insulted him; but he cared not, following with humility the humble example of his Master; for the Lord himself has said in the Gospel: 'If they have called the master of the house Beelzebub, how much more shall they call them of his household?'"[1]

Here is another taken from the Life of Saint Sulpicius the Pious, bishop of Bourges, in which breathes, amidst the most puerile credulity, a benevolence and a mildness certainly very foreign to the general manners of the epoch.

"One night, a ruffian, doubtless poor, introduced himself violently into the pantry of the holy man: he soon seized upon what, in his criminal heart, he proposed stealing, and hastens to get out; but he finds no opening, he is imprisoned within the surrounding walls, and confined on all sides. The night slipt away fruitlessly to this man who had entered so easily, and who could not see the slightest outlet. However, the light of day began to light the world; the man of God called one of his guards, ordered him to take a comrade, and to bring to him the man they should find in the office, plunged in crime, and as if bound.

"The servant went without delay to seek a companion, and repaired to the office: there they found the guilty man, and seized him to carry him off; the knave escaped from their hands; and seeing himself loaded with crimes, surrounded with people, preferring a speedy death to the punishment of

[1] Life of Saint Wandregisilus, § 7, in the *Acta Sanct. Ord. S. Ben*, vol. ii. p. 528.

his long transgressions, he rushed into a well nearly eighty cubits deep, which he saw near him; but at the moment when he fell into the abyss, he implored the prayers of the blessed bishop. The man of God ran quickly, and ordered one of his servants to descend into the well by means of a cord, enjoining him expressly immediately to draw up the criminal who had thrown himself in. All exclaimed that any one whom such an abyss had swallowed could not live, and that surely he was dead already; but the holy man ordered his servant to obey him without delay. The latter waited no longer, and, strengthened with the benediction of the saint, he found him whom they believed dead sound and safe. Having surrounded him with cords, he drew him captive on to his native soil. The walls could not contain the crowd; almost the whole town had hastened to such a spectacle, and all made a great noise with their cries and plaudits. The criminal, as if shaking off a profound stupor, threw himself at the feet of the saint, and implored his pardon. The latter, full of charity, immediately granted it to him, and even gave him what he had need of, recommending him to ask, for the future, instead of taking, and saying that he would rather make him presents than be robbed by him. Who can express the perfect humility of this man, the prompt mercy, the holy simplicity, patience, and forbearance."[1]

If we desire examples of the development of sensibility alone, without any precise application, without any beneficial or direct result, the life of Saint Rusticula, abbess of the monastery that Saint Cesaire had founded at Arles, will furnish us with two which seem to me to have a lively interest. Saint Rusticula was born in Provence, in the territory of Vaison: her parents had already one son.

"One night, when her mother Clemence was asleep, she saw herself, in a dream, nursing, with great affection, two small doves, one as white as snow, the other of a mixed colour. As she occupied herself about them with much pleasure and tenderness, she thought that her servants came to tell her that Saint Cesaire, bishop of Arles, was at her gate. Hearing this, and delighted at the arrival of the

[1] Life of Saint Sulpicius. § 28 and 29, in the *Acta Sanct. Ord. S. Ben.*, vol. ii. p. 175.

saint, she ran joyfully to him, and eagerly saluting him, humbly prayed him to grant to her house the blessing of his presence. He entered, and blessed her. After having done him the due honours, she prayed him to take some nourishment, but he answered—'My daughter, I only desire thee to give me this dove, which I have seen thee rearing so carefully.' Hesitating within herself, she thought whence he could know that she had this dove; and she denied that she possessed anything of the kind. He then answered—'Before God, I tell thee I will not leave this place till thou grant me my request.' She could no longer excuse herself; she showed her doves, and offered them to the holy man. He joyfully took that which was of a brilliant white, and, congratulating himself, put it into his bosom; and after taking leave of her, he departed. When she awoke, she reflected upon what all this signified, and she sought in her soul why he who was no more had appeared to her. She knew not that Christ had chosen her daughter in marriage, he who has said, 'A city that is set on an hill cannot be hid. Neither do men light a candle, and put it under a bushel, but on a candlestick, and it giveth light unto all that are in the house.'"[1]

There is certainly nothing remarkable in the incidents of this account; the foundation is little conformable to natural sentiments, since it is concerning a daughter being taken from her mother; and yet there reigns in it a general tinge of sensibility, of sweet and lively tenderness, which penetrates even into the allegory by which this sacrifice is asked of the mother, and sheds much charm and grace over it.

Saint Rusticula governed her abbey with great success, and especially inspired a deep affection in her nuns: in 632, she was ill, and near to death:

"It happened one Friday, that after having, according to her custom, sung the vespers with her daughters, and feeling fatigued, she went beyond her powers in giving her accustomed reading: she knew that she only went quicker to the Lord. The Saturday morning she was rather cold, and had lost all strength in her limbs. Then laying down in her little bed, she was seized with a severe fever: she, how-

[1] Life of Saint Rusticula, § 3, in the *Acta Sanct. Ord. S. Ben.*, vol. ii p. 140.

ever, did not cease to praise God, and, fixing her eyes on heaven, she recommended to his care her daughters, whom she left orphans, and, with a firm voice consoled those who wept around her. On the Sunday she found herself worse; and as it was customary to make her bed only once a year, the servants of God asked her to allow herself a rather softer couch, in order to spare her body so rough a fatigue; but she would not consent thereto. On Monday, the day of Saint Lawrence the martyr, she still lost strength, and her chest made a great noise. To this sight the sorrowful virgins of Christ answered with tears and sighs. As it was the third hour of the day, and as, in its affliction, the nuns read the psalms in silence, the holy mother asked why she did not hear the psalms: the nuns answered they could not sing by reason of their sorrow: 'Sing still louder,' said she, 'that I may receive the help of it, for it is very sweet to me.' The following day, when her body was almost without motion, her eyes, which preserved their vigour, still shone like stars, and looking on all sides, and being unable to speak, she imposed silence with her hand, on those who wept, and gave them consolation. When one of the sisters touched her feet to see if they were warm or cold, she said: 'It is not yet the hour.' But shortly after, at the sixth hour of the day, with a serene countenance, with eyes shining, and as if she smiled, this glorious, blest soul, passed to heaven, and associated with the innumerable choirs of saints."[1]

I know not if any of you have ever opened a collection, entitled *Mémoires pour servir a l'Histoire de Port Royal*,[2] which contains the account of the life and death of the principal nuns of that celebrated abbey; among others, of the two Angelique Arnaulds, who successively governed it. Port-Royal, the branch for women as well as that for men, was, as you know, the asylum for the most ardent, the most independent souls, as well as for the most elevated minds, that honoured the age of Louis XIV. Perhaps human sensibility is nowhere displayed with more richness and energy than in the moral history of these pious women, of whom many shared at once the intellectual development of Nicolle and

[1] Life of Saint Rusticula, § 31, p. 146.
[2] Three vols. 12mo. Utrecht, 1742.

of Pascal. Well; the recital of their last moments a good deal resembles what I have just read: we find there the same emotions of piety and friendship, almost the same language; and the sensible nature of mankind appears to us, in the seventh century, almost as lively, and as developed, as that of the seventeenth, amidst the most passionate characters of the age.

I might greatly multiply these examples; but we must proceed. I have some to present to you of another kind.

Independently of the satisfaction which they gave to morality and human sensibility, the condition of which in the external world was so bad, the legends also corresponded to other faculties, to other wants. Much is at present said concerning the interest, the movement which, in the course of what is vaguely called the middle ages, animated the life of nations. It seems that great adventures, spectacles and recitals incessantly excited the imagination; that society was a thousand times more varied and amusing than it is among us. It may have been so for some men placed in the superior ranks, or thrown into peculiar situations; but for the mass of the population, life was, on the contrary, prodigiously monotonous, insipid, wearisome; its destiny went on in the same place, the same scenes were produced before the eyes; there was scarcely any external movement, still less movement of mind; its pleasures were as few as its blessings, and the condition of its intellect was not more agreeable than its physical existence. It nowhere so much as in the lives of the saints, found nourishment for this activity of imagination, this inclination for novelty, for adventures, which exercises so much influence over men. The legends were to the Christians of this age, (let me be allowed this purely literary comparison,) what those long accounts, those brilliant and varied histories, of which the *Thousand and One Nights* gives us a specimen, were to the Orientals. It was there that the popular imagination wandered freely in an unknown, marvellous world, full of movement and poetry. It is difficult for us, in the present day, to share the pleasure which was taken in them twelve centuries since; the habits of mind have changed; distractions beset us: but we may at least understand that there was therein a source of powerful interest for this literature. In the immense number of adventures and scenes with which it charmed the Christian people, I have selected two which will perhaps give you some idea of the kind of attraction which they had for it. The first is taken from the life of Saint Seine, (Saint Sequanus,) the founder, in the sixth century, of the abbey in Burgundy, which took his name, and it describes the incident which induced him to select its site:

"When Seine found himself—thanks to his laudable zeal —well instructed in the dogmas of the divine scriptures, and learned in monastical rules, he sought a place suited for building a monastery; as he went over all the neighbouring places, and communicated his project to all his friends, one of his relations, Thiolaif, said to him: 'Since thou interrogatest me, I will point out a certain place where thou mayest establish thyself, if what thou desirest to do is inspired by the love of God. There is an estate which, if I do not deceive myself, belongs to me by hereditary right; but the people around feed themselves, like ferocious beasts, with human blood and flesh; this renders it difficult to go among them, unless one pays a troop of armed men.' The blessed Seine answered him: 'Show me the place, to the end that if my desires have been conceived by a divine instinct, all the ferocity of these men may be changed into the mildness of the dove.' Having, therefore, taken his companions, he arrived at the place of which they had spoken. It was a forest, the trees of which almost touched the clouds, and whose solitude had not for a long time been interrupted: they asked themselves how they could penetrate into it, when they saw a winding foot-path, so narrow, and full of briars, that they could scarcely place their feet upon the same line, and from the thickness of the branches, it was with difficulty that one foot followed the other. However, with much labour, and having their clothes torn, they got into the depths of this rough forest; then, bending towards the ground, they began to watch the profound darkness with an attentive eye.

"Having for some time looked with attention, they perceived very narrow openings to a cavern, obstructed by stones and plants; besides which, the interlaced branches of the trees rendered the cavern so dark, that wild beasts themselves would have hesitated to enter it. This was the cavern of the robbers, and the resort of unclean spirits. When they approached it, Seine, agreeable to God, bent his knees at the entry, and extending his body over the bushes, addressed a prayer to God, mixed with tears, saying—'Lord, who hast made Heaven and earth, which thou givest to the wishes of him who implores thee, and who originatest all good, and without whom all the weak efforts of humanity are useless, if thou orderest me to live in this solitude, make the same known unto me, and lead to good the beginnings which thou hast granted to my devotion.' When he had finished his prayer, he arose, and raised his hands towards heaven, and his eyes, which were moist with tears. Knowing then that it was under the conduct of the Saviour that he had repaired into this dark forest, after having blessed the place, he immediately set about placing the foundations of a cell where he had kneeled to pray. The report of his arrival came to the ears of the neighbouring inhabitants, who, each exhorting the other, and impelled by a Divine movement, repaired near him. When they had seen him, from wolves they became lambs, so that those who were formerly a source of terror were henceforth ministers of help; and, from that time, this place, which was the resort for divers cruel demons and robbers, became the abode of innocents."[1]

Should we not suppose that we were reading the account of the establishment of some colonists in the heart of the most distant forests of America, or of some pious missionaries amidst the most savage hordes?

Here is an account of a different character, but which is no less full of movement and interest.

Still young, and before entering into the ecclesiastical order, Saint Austregesilus, bishop of Bourges, at the commencement of the seventh century, manifested a lively desire to forsake the world, and not to marry.

" Hearing him speak thus, his parents began to press him earnestly to obey them in this respect. He, in order that he might not see them discontented, whom he desired to see satisfied, promised to do as they asked him, if such was the will of God.

[1] Life of Saint Seine, § 7 and 8. *Acta Sanct. Ord. S. Ben.*, vol. i. p. 264.

"When, therefore, he was occupied in the king's service, he began to return to this business, and to seek what would best befit him to do. He recollected three men of the same nation, and of equal fortune. He wrote their names upon three tablets, and put them under the cover of the altar in the cathedral of Saint John, near the town of Châlons, and made a vow to pass three nights in prayer without sleeping. After the three nights, he was to put his hands upon the altar, taking the tablet which the Lord should deign to make him find first, and demand in marriage the daughter of the man whose name should be upon the tablet. After having passed one night without sleep, the next night he found himself overcome by it, and towards the middle of the night, unable to resist any longer, his limbs gave way, and he fell asleep upon a seat. Two old men presented themselves to his view. One said to the other: 'Whose daughter is Austregesilus to marry?' The other answered: 'Art thou ignorant that he is already married?' 'To whom?' 'To the daughter of judge Just.' Austregesilus then awoke, and applied himself to finding out who this Just was, of what place he was judge, and if he had a virgin daughter. As he could not find him, he repaired, according to custom, to the king's palace. He arrived in a village where there was an inn. Some travellers were assembled there, among others, a poor veteran with his wife. When this woman saw Austregesilus, she said to him:

"'Stranger, stop an instant, and I will tell thee what I have lately seen concerning thee in a dream; it appeared as if I heard a great noise, like that of the singing of psalms, and I said to my host: 'Man, what is this that I hear? what festival is now being celebrated by the priests, that they make this procession?' He answered: 'Our guest Austregesilus is being married.' Full of joy, I was eager to see the young bride, and to view her face and form. When the priests, clothed in white, carrying crosses, and singing psalms in the usual manner, were passed, thou camest out, and all the people followed behind; for me, I looked with curiosity, and I saw no woman, not even the girl whom thou wert to marry; I said to thy host: 'Where is the virgin whom Austregesilus is to marry?' he answered: 'Do you not see her in his hands?' I looked, and I only saw in thy hands the book of the gospel.' Then the saint understood by his vision and the dream of this woman, that the voice of God called him to the priesthood."[1]

There is here no miracle, properly so called; all is confined to dreams; but you see what movement of imagination is connected with all the sentiment, with all the incidents of a religious life, and with what eagerness the people received them.

These are the true sources of this literature; it gave to the moral, physical, and poetical nature of man, a nourishment, a satisfaction which it found nowhere else; it elevated and agitated his soul; it animated his life. Hence its fertility and its credit.

If it were our purpose to consider it under a purely literary point of view, we should find its merits neither very brilliant nor very varied. Truth of sentiment and *naiveté* of tone are not wanting to it; it is devoid of affectation and pedantry. The narrative is not only interesting, but it is often conceived under a rather dramatic form. In the eastern countries, where the charm of narration is great, the dramatic form is rare; we there meet with few conversations, few dialogues, with little getting up, properly speaking. There is much more of this in the legends; dialogue is there habitual, and often progresses with nature and vivacity. But we should in vain seek a little order in them, any art of composition; even for the least exacting minds, the confusion is extreme, the monotony great; credulity continually descends to the ridiculous, and the language has arrived at a degree of imperfection, of corruption, of coarseness, which in the present day pains and wearies the reader.

I wish to say a few words also on a portion (very inconsiderable, it is true, but which, however, I ought not to omit) of the literature of this period, that is, its profane literature. I have observed that, dating from the 6th century, sacred literature was alone, that all profane literature had disappeared; there were, however, some remains of it; certain chronicles, certain occasional poems which belonged not to religious society, and which merit a moment's attention. In our next lecture, I shall present to you, on some of those monuments so little known in the present day, developments which appear to me not uninteresting.

[1] Life of Saint Austregesilus, § 2, in the *Acta Sanct Ord. S. Ben.*, vol. ii. p. 95.

EIGHTEENTH LECTURE.

Some wrecks of profane literature from the sixth to the eighth century—Of their true character—1st, Prose writers—Gregory of Tours—His life—His *Ecclesiastical History of the Franks*—The influence of the ancient Latin literature unites with that of the Christian doctrines—Mixture of civil and religious history—Frédégaire—His *Chronicle*—2ndly, Poets—Saint Avitus, bishop of Vienne—His life—His poems on the Creation—Original sin—The condemnation of man—The Deluge—The passage of the Red Sea—The praise of virginity—Comparison of the three first with the *Paradise Lost* of Milton—Fortunatus, bishop of Poictiers—His life—His relations with Saint Radegonde—His poems—Their character—First origin of French literature.

I MENTIONED in our last lecture that we should now occupy ourselves with the wrecks of profane literature, scattered here and there, from the sixth to the eighth century, amidst sermons, legends, theological dissertations, and escaping from the universal triumph of sacred literature. I shall, perhaps, be a little embarrassed with my promise, and with this word *profane*, which I have applied to the works of which I mean to speak. It seems to say, in fact, that their authors or their subjects are of a lay character, that they belong not to the religious sphere. Yet, see the names of the writings, and of the authors. There are two prose writers, and two poets· the prose writers are Gregory of Tours, and Frédégaire; the poets—Saint Avitus, and Fortunatus. Of these four men, three were bishops: Gregory at Tours, Saint Avitus at Vienne, and Fortunatus at Poictiers; all three were canonized; the fourth, Frédégaire, was probably a monk. With regard to the persons, there can scarcely be anything less profane; assuredly they belong to sacred literature. As regards the works themselves, that of Gregory of Tours bears the title of *Ecclesiastical History of the Franks*; that of Frédégaire is a simple chronicle; the poems of Saint Avitus turn upon the Creation, Original Sin, the Expulsion from Paradise, the Deluge, the Passage of the Red Sea, the Praise of Virginity; and although in those of Fortunatus many treat of the incidents of a worldly life, as the marriage of Sigebert and Brunehault, the departure of queen Galsuinthe, &c., still the greater part relate to religious events or interests, as the dedications of cathedrals, the praise of saints or bishops, the feasts of the church, &c., so that, to judge by appearances, the subjects as well as the authors enter into sacred literature, and it seems that there is nothing to which the name of profane can be suitable.

I might easily allege that some of these writers were not always ecclesiastics; that Fortunatus, for example, for a long time lived a layman; that many of his poems date from this period of his life. It is not certain that Frédégaire was a monk. Gregory of Tours formally expressed his intention of mixing the sacred and the profane in his history. But these would be poor reasons. I had far rather admit that, in some respects, the works I intend to speak of at present belong to sacred literature; and still I maintain what I have said; they belong to profane literature; they bore its character in more than one respect, and they should bear its name. And here is the reason:

I have just passed before you the two principal kinds of the sacred literature of this epoch, on one hand sermons, on the other, legends. Nothing of this kind had existed in antiquity; neither the Greek nor Latin literature furnished a model of similar compositions. They took their rise from Christianity—from the religious doctrines of the age; they were original; they constituted a new and truly religious literature, for it had no impress of ancient literature, of the profane world, neither in form nor groundwork.

The works of which I am about to speak are of another nature: the authors and the subjects are religious, but the character of the compositions, the manner in which they are conceived and executed, belong not to the new religious literature; the influence of pagan antiquity is clearly shown in them; we incessantly find there the imitation of the Greek or Latin writers; it is visible in the turn of the imagination;

in the forms of the language; it is sometimes direct and avowed. This is nothing like that truly new Christian mind, foreign, even hostile, to all ancient recollections, which is visible in the sermons and legends: here, on the contrary, and even in the most religious subjects, one feels the traditions, the intellectual customs of the pagan world, a certain desire to be connected with profane literature, to preserve and reproduce its merits. It is hence that the name is applied correctly to the works of which I speak, and that they form in the literature from the sixth to the eighth century a separate class, which in a measure unites the two epochs, the two societies, and claims especial inquiry.

Let us pass in review the four writers I have just named: we shall recognise this characteristic in their writings.

I begin by the prose writers, and by Gregory of Tours, incontestably the most celebrated.

You will recollect whether historical compositions had fallen in the Roman empire: high history, the poetical, political, philosophical history, that of Livy, that of Polybius, and that of Tacitus, had equally vanished; they could only keep a register, more or less exact, more or less complete, of events and men, without retracing their concatenation or moral character, without uniting them to the life of the state, without seeking therein the emotions of the drama, or of the true epopee. History, in a word, was no more than a chronicle. The last Latin historians, Lampridius, Vopiscus, Eutropius, Ammianus Marcellinus himself, all are mere chroniclers. The chronicle is the last form under which history presents itself in the profane literature of antiquity.

It is likewise under this form that it re-appears in the rising Christian literature: the first Christian chroniclers, Gregory of Tours among others, did nothing but imitate and perpetuate their pagan predecessors.

George Florentius, who took the name of Gregory from his great grandfather, bishop of Langres, was born on the 3rd of November, 539, in Auvergne, in the bosom of one of those families which called themselves senatorial, and which formed the decaying aristocracy of the country. The one to which he belonged was noble in the civil and the religious order: he had many illustrious bishops for ancestors and relations, and he was descended from a senator of Bourges, Vettius

Epagatus, one of the first and most glorious martyrs of Christianity in Gaul. It appears (and this fact is so commonly met with in the history of celebrated men, that it becomes matter of suspicion), it appears that from his infancy, by his intellectual and pious tendencies, he attracted the attention of all around him, and that he was brought up with particular care as the hope of his family and of the church, among others by his uncle, Saint Nizier, bishop of Lyons, Saint Gal, bishop of Clermont, and Saint Avitus, his successor. He had very ill health, and, already ordained deacon, he made a journey to Tours, in the hope of being cured at the tomb of Saint Martin. He was actually cured, and he returned to his country. We find him, in 573, at the court of Sigebert I., king of Austrasia, to whom Auvergne belonged. He received news that the clergy and people of Tours, doubtless struck with his merits during the sojourn which he had made among them, had just elected him bishop. After some hesitation, he consented, was consecrated the 22nd of August by the bishop of Reims, and immediately repaired to Tours, where he passed the rest of his life.

He, however, often left it; and even on affairs foreign to those of the church. Gontran, king of Burgundy, and Childebert II. king of Austrasia, employed him as a negotiator in their long quarrels; we find him in 585 and in 588, travelling from one court to another to reconcile the two kings. He appeared likewise at the council of Paris, held in 577, to judge Pretextat. archbishop of Rouen, whom Chilperic and Frédégonde wished to expel, and whom in fact they did expel from his diocese.

In his various missions, and especially at the council of Paris, Gregory of Tours conducted himself with more independence, good sense, and equity, than was evinced by many other bishops. Doubtless, he was credulous, superstitious, devoted to the interests of the clergy: still few ecclesiastics of his time had a devotion, I will not say as enlightened, but less blind, and kept to so reasonable a line of conduct in what concerned the church.

In 592, according to his biographer, Odo of Cluny, who wrote his life in the tenth century, he made a journey to Rome to see pope Gregory the Great. The fact is doubtful, and of little interest: still the account of Odo of Cluny contains a rather piquant anecdote, and one which proves what a high estimation Gregory and his contemporary were held in at the tenth century. He was, as I have said, remarkably weak and puny.

"Arrived in the presence of the pontiff," says his biographers, "he kneeled and prayed. The pontiff, who was of a wise and deep mind, admired within himself the secret dispensations of God, who had placed so many divine graces in so small and puny a body. The bishop, internally advised, by the will on high, of the thought of the pontiff, arose, and regarding him with a tranquil air, said to him: 'It is the Lord who makes us, and not ourselves; it is the same with the great and with the small.' The holy pope, seeing that he thus answered to his thought, conceived a great veneration for him, and took so much to heart the dignifying of the see of Tours, that he presented a chair of gold to it, which is still preserved in that church."[1]

Close upon his return from his journey to Rome, if it is true that he made one, Gregory died at Tours, the 17th of November, 593, very much regretted in his diocese, and celebrated throughout western Christendom, where his works were already spread. That which interests us most in the present day was certainly not at that time the most ardently sought for. He composed, 1st, a treatise of the *Glory of the Martyrs*, a collection of legends, in one hundred and seven chapters, devoted to the recital of the miracles of martyrs; 2. A treatise on the *Glory of the Confessors*, in one hundred and twelve chapters; 3. A collection entitled *Lives of the Fathers*, in twenty chapters, and which contains the history of twenty-two saints, of both sexes, of the Gaulish church; 4. A treatise on the *Miracles of Saint Julianus*, bishop of Brioude, in fifty chapters; 5. A treatise on the *Miracles of Saint Martin of Tours*, in four books; 6. A treatise on the *Miracles of Saint Andrew*. These were the writings which rendered his name so popular. They have no distinguishing merit amid the crowd of legends, and nothing which requires us to stop at them.

The great work of the bishop of Tours, that which has brought his name down to us, is his *Ecclesiastical History of*

[1] *Vita S. Gregorii*, &c., by Odo, abbot of Cluny, § 24.

the Franks. The mere title of the book is remarkable, for it points out its character to be at once civil and religious; the author did not wish to write a history of the church merely, nor of the Franks alone; he thought that the destinies of the laity and those of the clergy should not be separated.

He says, "I shall indiscriminately combine, and without any other order than that of time, the virtues of the saints and the disasters of the people. I am not of opinion that it should be regarded as unreasonable to mix the felicities of the blessed with the calamities of the miserable in the account, not for the convenience of the writer, but in order to conform with the progress of events . . . . Eusebius, Severus, Jerome, and Orosius have mixed up in like manner in their chronicles, the wars of kings and the virtues of martyrs."[1]

I shall have recourse to no other testimony than that of Gregory of Tours himself, for distinguishing in his work that influence of ancient literature, that mixture of profane and sacred letters, which I pointed out at the beginning. He protests his contempt for all pagan traditions; he eagerly repudiates all heritage of the world in which they reigned.

"I do not occupy myself," he says, "with the flight of Saturn, nor the rage of Juno, nor the adulteries of Jupiter; I despise all such things which go to ruin, and apply myself far rather to Divine things, to the miracles of the gospel."[2]

And elsewhere, in the *Preface* of his history, we read:

"The cultivation of letters and the liberal sciences were declining, were perishing in the cities of Gaul, amidst the good and evil actions which were then committed; while the barbarians abandoned themselves to their ferocity, and the kings to their fury, while the churches were alternately enriched by pious men, and robbed by the infidels, we find no grammarian able in the art of logic, who undertook to describe these things either in prose or verse. Many men accordingly groan, saying: 'Unhappy are we! the study of letters perishes among us, and we find no person who can describe in his writings present facts.' Seeing this, I have thought it advisable to preserve, although in an uncultivated

[1] Gregory of Tours, vol. i. p. 39, in my *Collection des Mémoires sur l'Histoire de France.*

[2] *Article upon Greg. of Tours*, vol. i. p. 22, in my *Collection.*

language, the memory of past things, in order that future men may know them."[1]

What does the writer lament? the fall of the liberal studies, of the liberal sciences, of grammar, of logic. There is nothing Christian there; the Christians never thought of them. On the contrary, when the mere Christian spirit dominated, men scorned what Gregory calls the liberal studies; they called them profane studies.

It is the ancient literature which the bishop regrets, and which he wishes to imitate as far as his weak talent will allow him; it is that which he admires, and which he flatters himself with the hope of continuing

You see here the profane character breaks through. Nothing is wanting to this work to place it in sacred literature: it bears the name of *Ecclesiastical History*, it is full of the religious doctrines, traditions, the affairs of the church. And still civil affairs likewise find a place in it, and it is a chronicle very like the last of the pagan chronicles; and respect and regret for pagan literature, as formally expressed in it, with the design of imitating it.

Independently of the narrative, the book is very curious from the double character which unites it to the two societies, and marks the transition from one to the other. As to the rest, there is no art of composition, no order; even the chronological order, which Gregory promises to follow, is incessantly forgotten and interrupted. It is merely the work of a man who has collected all he has heard said, all that passed in his time, traditions and events of every kind, and has inserted them, good and bad, in a single narration. The same enterprise was executed, and in the same spirit, at the end of the eleventh century, by a Norman monk, Orderic Vital. Like Gregory of Tours, Orderic collected all the recollections, all facts, both lay and religious, which came within his knowledge, and inserted them promiscuously, connected by a small thread, and, to complete the resemblance, he also gave his work the title of *Ecclesiastical History of Normandy*. I shall speak minutely of it when we arrive at the civilization of the eleventh century; I merely wished here to point out the analogy. The work of the bishop of

[1] *Art. on Greg. of Tours*, vol. i. p. 23, in my *Collection*.

Tours, precisely by reason of this shadow of ancient literature, which we may catch a glimpse of in the distance, is superior to that of the Norman monk. Although the Latin is very corrupt, the composition very defective, and the style undignified, it has still some merit in the narration, some movement, some truth of imagination, and a rather acute knowledge of men. It is, upon the whole, the most instructive and amusing chronicle of the three centuries. It begins at the year 377, at the death of Saint Martin, and stops in 591.

Frédégaire continued it. He was a Burgundian, probably a monk, and lived in the middle of the eighth century. This is all that is known of him, and even his name is doubtful. His work is very inferior to that of Gregory of Tours; it is a general chronicle, divided into five books, and commences at the creation of the world. The fifth book only is curious; it is there that the narration of Gregory of Tours is taken up, and continued up to 641. This continuation is of no value except for the information which it contains, and because it is almost the only work there is upon the same epoch. For the rest, it has no literary merit, and, except two passages, contains no picture the least detailed, nor does it cast any light upon society and manners. Frédégaire himself was struck, I will not say with the mediocrity of his work, but with the intellectual decay of his time.

"We can only draw with trouble," says he, "from a source which does not still run. Now the world ages, and the force of mind deadens in us: no man in the present age is equal to the orators of past times, and no one dare even pretend to emulate them."[1]

The distance between Gregory of Tours and Frédégaire, is, in fact, great. In the one, we still feel the influence, and, as it were, the breath of Latin literature; we recognise some traces, some tinges of a taste for science and elegance in mind and manners. In Frédégaire all recollection of the Roman world has vanished; he is a barbarous, ignorant, and coarse monk, whose thought, like his life, is inclosed within the walls of his monastery.

[1] *Preface* to Frédégaire, vol. ii. p. 164, of my *Collection*.

From the prose writers let us pass to the poets; they are worthy of our attention.

I just now called to your recollection what had been the last state, the last form of history, in Latin literature, from the third to the fifth century. Without falling quite so low, the decay of poetry was profound. All great poetry had disappeared, that is, all epic, dramatic, or lyrical poetry; the epopee, the drama, and the ode, those glories of Greece and Rome, were not even aimed at. The only kinds still slightly cultivated, were: 1, didactic poetry, sometimes taking that philosophic tone, of which Lucretius gave the model, and more frequently directed towards some material object, the chase, fishing, &c.; 2, descriptive poetry, the school of which Ausonius is the master, and in which are found numerous narrow but elegant minds; 3, lastly, occasional poetry, epigrams, epitaphs, madrigals, epithalamiums, inscriptions, all that kind of versification, sometimes in mockery, sometimes in praise, whose only object is to draw some momentary amusement from passing events. This was all that remained of the poetry of antiquity.

The same kinds, the same characteristics, appear in the semi-profane, and the semi-Christian poetry of this epoch. In my opinion, the most distinguished of all the Christian poets from the sixth to the eighth century, although he may not be the most talked of, is Saint Avitus, bishop of Vienne. He was born about the middle of the fifth century, like Gregory of Tours, of a senatorial family in Auvergne. Episcopacy was there a kind of inheritance, for he was the fourth generation of bishops; his father Isique preceded him in the see of Vienne. Alcimus Ecdicius Avitus mounted it in 490, and occupied it until the 5th of February, 525, the time of his death. During all that period, he played an important part in the Gaulish church, intervened in events of some importance, presided at many councils, among others, at that of Epaone in 517, and especially took a very active part in the struggle between the Arians and the orthodox. He was the chief of the orthodox bishops of the east and south of Gaul. As Vienne belonged to the Burgundian Arians, Saint Avitus had often to struggle in favour of orthodoxy, not only against his theological adversaries, but also against the civil power; he got out of it happily and wisely, respecting and managing the masters of the country without ever abandoning his opinion. The conference which he had at Lyons, in 499, with some Arian bishops in presence of king Gondebald, proved his firmness and his prudence. It is to him that the return of king Sigismond to the bosom of orthodoxy is attributed. However this may be, it is as a writer, and not as a bishop, that we have to consider him at present.

Although much of what he wrote is lost, a large number of his works remains; a hundred letters on the events of his times, some homilies, some fragments of theological treatises, and lastly, his poems. Of these there are six, all in hexameter verses. 1. Upon the Creation, in 325 verses; 2. Upon Original Sin, in 423 verses; 3. On the Judgment of God and the Expulsion from Paradise, 435 verses; 4. Upon the Deluge, 658 verses; 5. On the Passage of the Red Sea, 719 verses; 6. In praise of Virginity, 666 verses. The first three, The Creation, Original Sin, and The Judgment of God, together form a triad, and may be considered as three parts of one poem, that one might—indeed, that one ought to call, to speak correctly, Paradise Lost. It is not by the subject alone that this work recals to mind that of Milton; the resemblances in some parts of the general conception, and in some of the more important details, is striking. It does not follow that Milton was acquainted with the poems of Saint Avitus; doubtless, nothing proves the contrary; they were published at the beginning of the sixteenth century, and the classical and theological learning of Milton was very great, but it is of little importance to his glory whether or not he was acquainted with them. He was one of those who imitate when they please, for they invent when they choose, and they invent even while imitating. However it may be, the analogy of the two poems is a rather curious literary fact, and that of Saint Avitus deserves the honour of being closely compared with that of Milton.

The first part, entitled, *Of the Creation*, is essentially descriptive; the descriptive poetry of the sixth century appears there in all its development. It singularly resembles the descriptive poetry of our time, the school, of which the abbé Delille is the chief, that we have seen so flourishing, and which at present scarcely counts a few languishing inheritors. The essential characteristic of this kind is to excel in con quering difficulties which are not worth being conquered, to describe what has no need of being described, and thus to arrive at a rather rare literary merit, without it resulting in any truly poetical effect. There are some objects which it is sufficient to name, occasions in which it is sufficient to name the objects, in order that poetry may take rise, and the imagination be struck; a word, a comparison, an epithet, place them vividly before one's eyes. Descriptive poetry, such as we know it, is not content with this result: it is scientific more than picturesque; it troubles itself less with making objects seen, than with making them known; it minutely observes, and surveys them as a designer, as an anatomist, is intent upon enumerating them, upon displaying every part of them; and this being the fact, that which, simply named or designated by a single stroke, by a general image, would be real and visible to the imagination, appears only decomposed, cut up, dissected, destroyed. This is the radical vice of modern descriptive poetry, and the trace of it is imprinted in its happiest works. It is found in that of the sixth century; the greater part of the descriptions of Saint Avitus have the same fault, the same character.

God works at the creation of man: "He places the head on the most elevated place, and adapts the countenance, pierced with seven outlets, to the wants of the intellect. From thence are exercised the senses of smell, hearing, sight, and taste: that of touch is the only sense which feels and judges by the whole body, and whose energy is spread through all its members. The flexible tongue is attached to the roof of the mouth, so that the voice, driven into this cavity as if struck by a bow, resounds with various modulations through the moved air. From the humid chest, placed before the body, extends the robust arms with the ramifications of the hands. After the stomach comes the belly, which upon each side surrounds the vital organs with a soft envelopment. Below, the body is divided into two thighs, in order to walk more easily by an alternate movement. Behind, and below the occiput, descends the nape of the neck, which everywhere distributes its innumerable nerves. Lower and on the inside are placed the lungs, which must be separated by a light air, and which, by a strong breath, alternately receives and returns it."[1]

[1] Poems of Avitus, l. i. *De Init ie Mundi*. v. 82—107.

Are we not in the workshop of a mechanic? are we not present at that slow and successive labour which announces science and excludes life? In this description, there is great accuracy of facts, the structure of the human body, and the agency of the various organs are very faithfully explained, everything is there, except man and the creation.

It would be easy to find, in modern descriptive poetry, perfectly analogous passages.

Do not suppose, however, that there is nothing but things of this kind, and that, even in this description of poetry, Saint Avitus has always executed as badly as this. This book contains many of the most happy descriptions, many most poetical, those especially which trace the general beauties of nature, a subject far more within the reach of descriptive poetry, much better adapted to its means. I will quote, for an example, the description of Paradise, of the garden of Eden, and I will at the same time place before you that of Milton, universally celebrated.

"Beyond India, where the world commences, where it is said that the confines of heaven and earth meet, is an elevated retreat, inaccessible to mortals, and closed with eternal barriers, ever since the author of the first crime was driven out after his fall, and the guilty saw themselves justly expelled their happy dwelling. . . . No changes of season there bring back frost; there the summer sun is not succeeded by the ice of winter; while elsewhere the circle of the year brings us stifling heat, or fields whitened by frost, the kindness of Heaven there maintains an eternal spring; the tumultuous South wind penetrates not there; the clouds forsake an air always pure, and a heaven always serene. The soil has no need of rains to refresh it, and the plants prosper by virtue of their own dew. The earth is always verdant, and its surface, animated by a sweet warmth, resplendent with beauty. Herbs never abandon the hills, the trees never lose their leaves; and although constantly covered with flowers, they quickly repair their strength by means of their own sap. Fruits, which we have but once in the year, there ripen every month; there the sun does not wither the splendour of the lily; no touch stains the violet; the rose always preserves its colour and graceful form. . . . Odoriferous balm continually runs from fertile branches. If, by chance, a slight wind arises, the beautiful forest, skimmed by its breath, with a sweet murmur agitates its leaves and flowers, from which escape and spread afar the sweetest perfumes. A clear fountain runs from a source of which the eye with care penetrates to the bottom; the most polished gold has no such splendour; a crystal of frozen water attracts not so much light. Emeralds glitter on its shores; every precious stone which the vain world extols, are there scattered like pebbles, adorn the fields with the most varied colours, and deck them as with a natural diadem."[1]

Now see that of Milton; it is cut into numerous shreds, and scattered throughout the fourth book of his poem; but I choose the passage which best corresponds to that which I have just quoted from the bishop of Vienne:

"Thus was this place
A happy rural seat of various view;
Groves whose rich trees wept odorous gums and balm;
Others whose fruit, burnished with golden rind,
Hung amiable, Hesperian fables true,
If true, here only, and of delicious taste:
Betwixt them lawns, or level downs, and flocks
Grazing the tender herb, were interpos'd,
Or palmy hillock; or the flowery lap
Of some irriguous valley, 'spread her store,
Flowers of all hue, and without thorn the rose;
Another side, umbrageous grots and caves
Of cool recess, o'er which the mantling vine
Lays forth her purple grape, and gently creeps
Luxuriant; meanwhile, murmuring waters fall
Down the slope hills, dispers'd, or in a lake,
That to the fringed bank with myrtle crown'd,
Her crystal mirror holds, unite their streams.
The birds their quire apply; airs, vernal airs,
Breathing the smell of field and grove, attune
The trembling leaves, while universal Pan,
Knit with the graces and the hours in dance,
Led on the eternal spring."[2]

The description of Saint Avitus is certainly rather superior

[1] L. i. *De Initio Mundi*, v. 211—257.
[2] Milton, Paradise Lost, iv. 246—68.

than inferior to that of Milton; although the first is much nearer to paganism, he mixes far fewer mythological recollections in his pictures: the imitation of antiquity is perhaps less visible, and the description of the beauties of nature appears to me at once more varied and more simple.

In the same book I find a description of the overflowing of the Nile, which also deserves quotation. You know that, in all religious traditions, the Nile is one of the four rivers of Paradise; it is for this reason that the poet names it, and describes its annual inundations.

"Whenever the river, by swelling, extends over its banks and covers the plains with its black slime, its waters become fertile, heaven is calm, and a terrestrial rain spreads on all sides. Then Memphis is surrounded with water, is seen in the midst of a large gulph, and the navigator is seen upon his fields, which are no longer visible. There is no longer any limit; boundaries disappear by the decree of the river, which equalises all and suspends the labours of the year; the shepherd joyfully sees the fields which he frequents swallowed up; and the fish, swimming in foreign seas, frequent the places where the herds fed upon the verdant grass. At last, when the water has espoused the altered earth and has impregnated all its germs, the Nile recedes, and re-collects its scattered waters: the lake disappears; it becomes a river, returns to its bed, and incloses its floods in the ancient dyke of its banks."[1]

Many features of this description are marked with faults of style; we find many of those laboured comparisons, those artificial antitheses, which he takes for poetry: "*the terrestrial rain*," for example, "*the water espouses the sea*," &c.; still the picture is not devoid of truth and effect. In his poem upon *the Deluge*, Saint Avitus has described an analogous phenomenon, but far more vast and terrible, the fall of the waters of Heaven, and the simultaneous overflow of all the waters of the earth, with much vigour and effect; but the length of the passage forbids my quoting it to you.

In the second book, entitled, *Of the Original Sin*, the poet follows, step by step, the sacred traditions; but they do not subdue his imagination, and he sometimes even elevates himself to poetical ideas, in which he quits them without positively

[1] Avitus, l. i. v. 266—281.

contradicting them. Every one knows the character with which Milton has invested Satan, and the originality of that conception which has preserved in the demon the grandeur of the angel, carrying down to the pit of evil the glorious traces of goodness, and thus shedding, over the enemy of God and man, an interest, which, however, has nothing illegitimate or perverse. Something of this idea, or rather of this intention, is found in the poem of Saint Avitus: his Satan is by no means the demon of mere religious traditions, odious, hideous, wicked, a stranger to all elevated or affectionate feeling. He has preserved in him some traits of his first state, a certain moral grandeur; the instinct of the poet has overcome the doctrine of the bishop; and although his conception of the character of Satan is far inferior to that of Milton, although he could not bring forth in it those combats of the soul, those fierce contrasts which render the work of the English poet so admirable, still his is not devoid of originality and energy. Like Milton, he has painted Satan at the time when he enters Paradise and perceives Adam and Eve for the first time

"When he saw," says he, "the new creatures in a peaceful dwelling, leading a happy and cloudless life, under the law which they had received from the Lord, with the empire of the universe, and enjoying, amidst delicious tranquillity, all which was subjected to them, the flash of jealousy raised a sudden vapour in his soul, and his burning rage soon became a terrible fire. It was then not long since he had fallen from Heaven, and had hurried away with him, into the low pit, the troop attached to his fate. At this thought, and reviewing his recent disgrace in his heart, it seemed that he had lost more, since he saw another possessed of such happiness; and shame mixing itself with envy, he poured out his angry regrets in these words:

"'O sorrow! this work of earth is suddenly raised before us, and our ruin has given birth to this odious race! I, Virtue! I possessed heaven, and I am now expelled it, and dust has succeeded to the honour of angels! A little clay, arranged under a pitiful form, will here reign, and the power torn from us is transferred to him! But we have not entirely lost it; the greatest portion thereof remains; we can and we know to injure. Let us not delay then; this combat pleases me; I will engage them at their first appearance, while their simplicity, which has as yet experienced no deceit, is ignorant of everything, and offers itself to every blow. It will be easier to mislead them while they are alone, before they have thrown a fruitful posterity into the eternity of ages. Let us not allow anything immortal to come out of the earth; let us destroy the race at its commencement: O that the defeat of its chief may become the seed of death; that the principle of life may give rise to the pangs of death; that all may be struck in one; the root cut, the tree will never raise itself. These are the consolations which remain to me in my fall. If I cannot again mount to the heavens, they will at least be closed for these creatures: it seems to me less harsh to be fallen, if the new creatures are lost by a similar fall; if, the accomplices of my ruin, they become companions of my punishment, and share with us the fire which I now catch a glimpse of. But, in order to attract them without difficulty, it is needful that I myself, who have fallen so low, should show them the route which I myself travelled over; that the same pride which drove me from the celestial kingdom, may chase men from the boundaries of Paradise.' He thus spoke, and, heaving a sigh, became silent."[1]

Now for the Satan of Milton, at the same time, and in the same situation:

"O hell, what do mine eyes with grief behold!
Into our room of bliss, thus high advanc'd,
Creatures of other mouldy earth, born, perhaps,
Not spirits, yet to heavenly spirits bright
Little inferior; whom my thoughts pursue
With wonder, and could love, so lively shines
In them Divine resemblance, and such grace
The hand that form'd them on their shape hath pour'd.
Ah, gentle pair, ye little think how nigh
Your change approaches, when all these delights
Will vanish, and deliver ye to woe;
More woe, the more your taste is now of joy;
Happy, but for so happy, ill secur'd
Long to continue, and this high seat your Heav'n,
Ill fenc'd for Heaven to keep out such a foe
As now is enter'd; yet no purpos'd foe

[1] Avitus, l. ii. v. 60—117.

To you, whom I could pity thus forlorn,
Though I unpitied: league with you I seek,
And mutual amity so strait, so close,
That I with you must dwell, or you with me
Henceforth; my dwelling haply may not please,
Like this fair Paradise, your sense; yet such
Accept your Maker's work; he gave it me,
Which I as freely give: Hell shall unfold,
To entertain you two, her widest gates,
And send forth all her kings; there will be room,
Not like these narrow limits, to receive
Your numerous offspring; if no better place,
Thank him who puts me loath to this revenge
On you, who wrong me not, for him who wrong'd.
And should I at your harmless innocence
Melt as I do, yet public reason just,
Honour and empire with revenge enlarg'd
By conquering this new world, compels me now
To do what else, though damn'd, I should abhor."

Here the superiority of Milton is great. He gives to Satan far more elevated, more impassioned, more complex feelings —perhaps even too complex—and his words are far more eloquent. Still there is a remarkable analogy between the two passages; and the simple energy, the menacing unity of the Satan of Saint Avitus, seem to me to be very effective.

The third book describes the despair of Adam and Eve after their fall, the coming of God, his judgment, and their expulsion from Paradise. You will surely remember that famous passage of Milton, after the judgment of God, when Adam sees everything overthrown around him, and expects to be driven out of Paradise; he abandons himself to the harshest rage against the woman:

"Whom thus afflicted when sad Eve beheld,
Desolate where she sat, approaching nigh,
Soft words to his fierce passion she assay'd:
But her with stern regard he thus repell'd:
'Out of my sight, thou serpent! that name best
Befits thee with him leagu'd, thyself as false
And hateful; nothing wants, but that thy shape,

[1] Milton, Paradise Lost, iv. 358—392.

Like his, and colour serpentine, may show
Thy inward fraud, to warn all creatures from thee
Henceforth; least that too heavenly form pretended
To hellish falsehood, snare them. But for thee
I had persisted happy; had not thy pride
And wandering vanity, when least was safe,
Rejected my forewarning, and disdained,
Not to be trusted; longing to be seen,
Though by the devil himself; him overweening
To overreach; but with the serpent meeting,
Fool'd and beguil'd; by him, thou, I by thee,
To trust thee from my side, imagin'd wise,
Constant, mature, proof against all assaults;
And understood not all was but a show,
Rather than solid virtue; all but a rib
Crooked by nature, bent, as now appears,
More to the part sinister, from me drawn;
Will if thrown out as supernumerary,
To my just number found. O! why did God,
Creator wise, that peopled highest Heaven
With spirits masculine, create at last
This novelty on earth, this fair defect
Of nature, and not fill the world at once
With men and angels, without feminine;
Or find some other way to generate
Mankind? This mischief had not then befall'n,
And more that shall befall; innumerable
Disturbances on earth through female snares,
And strait conjunction with this sex."[1]

The same idea occurred to Saint Avitus; only that it is to God himself, not to Eve, that Adam addresses the explosion of his rage:

"When thus he saw himself condemned, and that the most just inquiry had made evident all his fault, he did not humbly ask his pardon and pray; he answered not with shrieks and tears; he sought not to deter, with suppliant confession, the deserved punishment; already miserable, he invoked no pity. He erected himself, he irritated himself, and his pride broke out into insensate clamours: 'It was then to bring my ruin that this woman was united to my fate? That which, by thy

[1] Milton, Paradise Lost, x. 863—897.

first law, thou hast given for a dwelling: it is she who, overcome herself, has conquered me with her sinister councils; it is she who has persuaded me to take that fruit which she herself already knew. She is the source of evil; from her came crime. I was credulous; but thou, Lord, taught me to believe her by giving her to me in marriage, in joining me to her by sweet knots. Happy if my life, at first solitary, had always so run on, if I had never known the ties of such an union, and the yoke of this fatal companion!'

"At this outburst of irritated Adam, the Creator addressed these severe words to desolate Eve: 'Why, in falling, hast drawn down thy unhappy spouse? Deceitful woman, why, instead of remaining alone in thy fall, hast thou dethroned the superior reason of the man?' She, full of shame, her cheeks covered with a sorrowful blush, said that the serpent had persuaded her to touch the forbidden fruit."[1]

Does not this passage appear at least equal to that of Milton? It is even free from the subtle details which disfigure the latter, and diminish the progress of the sentiment.

The book terminates with the prediction of the advent of Christ, who shall triumph over Satan. But with this conclusion the poet describes the very leaving of Paradise, and these last verses are, perhaps, the most beautiful in the poem:

"At these words, the Lord clothes them both with the skins of beasts, and drives them from the happy retreat of Paradise. They fall together to the earth; they enter upon the desert world, and wander about with rapid steps. The world is covered with trees and turf; it has green meadows, and fountains and rivers; and yet its face appears hideous to them after thine, O Paradise! and they are horror-struck with it; and, according to the nature of men, they love better what they have lost. The earth is narrow to them; they do not see its limits, and yet they feel confined, and they groan. Even the day is dark to their eyes, and under the clear sun, they complain that the light has disappeared."[2]

The three other poems of Saint Avitus, *the Deluge*, *the Passage of the Red Sea*, and *the Praise of Virginity*, are very inferior to what I have just quoted; still some remarkable fragments may be found in them, and certainly we have

[1] Avitus, l. iii. v. 96—112. [2] Ibid. v. 195—207.

reason to be astonished that a work which contains such beauties should remain so obscure. But the age of Saint Avitus is all obscure, and he has fallen under the general decay in the midst of which he lived.

I named a second poet, Fortunatus, bishop of Poictiers. He was not of Gaulish origin; he was born in 530, beyond the Alps, near Ceneda, in the Trevisan; and about 565, a little before the great invasion of the Lombards, and the desolation of the north of Italy, he passed into Gaul, and stopped in Austrasia at the time of the marriage of Sigebert and Brunehault, daughter of Athanagilde, king of Spain. It appears that he remained there one or two years, making epithalaniums, laments, a court poet there, devoted to the celebration of its adventures and pleasures. We then find him at Tours, paying his devotions to Saint Martin; he was then a layman. Saint Radegonde, wife of Clotaire I., had just retired, and founded a monastery of nuns. Fortunatus connected himself with her in close friendship, entered into orders, and soon became her chaplain, and almoner of the monastery. From this period, no remarkable incident of his life is known. Seven or eight years after the death of Saint Radegonde, he was made bishop of Poictiers, and there died at the beginning of the seventh century, after having long celebrated with his verses all the great men of his age, and having been in assiduous correspondence with all the great bishops.

Independently of seven lives of saints, of some letters or theological treatises in prose, of four books of hexameters on the life of Saint Martin of Tours, which are merely a poetical version of the life of the same saint by Sulpicius Severus, and some trifling works which are lost, there remain of him two hundred and forty-nine pieces of verse in all kinds of metres, of which two hundred and forty-six were collected by himself in eleven books, and three are separate. Of these two hundred and forty-nine pieces, there are fifteen in honour of certain churches, cathedrals, oratories, &c., composed at the time of their construction or dedication; thirty epitaphs; twenty-nine pieces to Gregory of Tours, or concerning him; twenty-seven to Saint Radegonde, or to sister Agnes, abbess of the monastery of Poictiers, and one hundred and forty-eight other pieces to all sorts of persons, and upon all sorts of subjects.

The pieces addressed to Saint Radegonde, or to the abbess Agnes, are incontestably those which best make known and characterise the turn of mind, and the kind of poetry, of Fortunatus. On these only I shall dwell.

One is naturally led to attach to the relations of such persons the most serious ideas, and it is, in fact, under a grave aspect that they have been described: It has been mistakenly; do not suppose that I have here to relate some strange anecdote, or that this history is subject to the embarrassment of some scandal. There is nothing scandalous, nothing equivocal, nothing which lends the slightest malignant conjecture, to be met with in the relations between the bishop and the nuns of Poictiers; but they are of a futility, of a puerility which it is impossible to overlook, for even the poems of Fortunatus are a monument of them.

These are the titles of sixteen of the twenty-seven pieces addressed to Saint Radegonde, or to Saint Agnes:

Book VIII., piece 8, to Saint Radegonde upon violets.
„ 9, upon flowers put on the altar.
„ 10, upon flowers which he sent her.
Book XI., piece 4, to Saint Radegonde for her to drink wine.
11, to the abbess upon flowers.
13, upon chesnuts.
14, upon milk.
15, *idem.*
16, upon a repast.
18, upon sloes.
19, upon milk and other dainties.
20, upon eggs and plums.
22, upon a repast.
23, *idem.*
24, *idem.*
„ 25, *idem.*

Now see some samples of the pieces themselves; they prove that the titles do not deceive us.

"In the midst of my fasting," writes he to Saint Radegonde, "thou sendest me various meats, and at the sight of them thou painest my mind. My eyes contemplate what the doctor forbids me to use, and his hand interdicts what my mouth desires. Still when thy goodness gratifies us with this milk, thy gifts surpass those of kings. Rejoice, therefore, I pray thee, like a good sister with our pious mother, for at this moment I have the sweet pleasure of being at table."[1]

And elsewhere, after having a repast: "Surrounded by various delicacies, and all kinds of ragouts, sometimes I sleep, sometimes I eat; I open my mouth, then I close my eyes, and I again eat of everything; my mind was confused, believe it, most dear ones, and I could not easily either speak with liberty, or write verses. A drunken man has an uncertain hand; wine produced the same effect upon me as upon other drinkers; methinks I see the table swimming in pure wine. However, as well as I am able, I have traced in soft language this little song for my mother and my sister, and although sleep sharply presses me, the affection which I bear for them has inspired what the hand is scarcely in a state to write."[2]

It is not by way of amusement that I insert these singular quotations, which it would be easy for me to multiply; I desire, on the one hand, to place before your eyes a view of the manners of this epoch, which are but little known; and on the other, to enable you to see, and, so to speak, to touch with your finger, the origin of a kind of poetry which has held rather an important place in our literature, of that light and mocking poetry which, beginning with our old fabliaux, down to *Ver-vert*, has been pitilessly exercised upon the weakness and ridiculous points of the interior of monasteries. Fortunatus, to be sure, did not mean to jest; actor and poet at the same time, he spoke and wrote very seriously to Saint Radegonde and the abbess Agnes; but the very manners which this kind of poetry took for a text, and which so long provoked French fancy, that puerility, that laziness, that gluttony, associated with the gravest relations,—you see them begin here with the sixth century, and under exactly the same traits with those which Marot or Gresset lent to them ten or twelve centuries later.

However, the poems of Fortunatus have not all of

[1] *Tertun Carm.*, l. xi. No. 19; Bib. Pat., vol. v. p. 596.
[2] Ibid. No. 24; ibid.

them this character. Independently of some beautiful sacred hymns, one of which, the *Vexilla Regis*, was officially adopted by the church, there is in many of these small lay and religious poems a good deal of imagination, of intellect, and animation. I shall only quote a passage from an elegiac poem of three hundred and seventy-one verses, about the departure of Galsuinthe, sister of Brunehault, from Spain, her arrival in France, her marriage with Chilperic, and her deplorable end; I select the lamentations of Galsuinthe, her mother, wife of Athanagilde; she sees her daughter about to quit her, embraces her, looks at her, embraces her again, and cries:

"Spain, so full of inhabitants, and too confined for a mother, land of the sun, become a prison to me, although thou extendest from the country of Zephyr to that of the burning Eous, from Tyrhenia to the ocean—although thou sufficest for numerous nations, since my daughter is not longer here, thou art too narrow for me. Without thee, my daughter, I shall be here as a foreigner and wanderer, and, in my native country, at once a citizen and an exile. I ask, what shall these eyes look at which everywhere seek my daughter? . . . Whatever infant plays with me will be a punishment; thou wilt weigh upon my heart in the embraces of another: let another run, step, seat herself, weep, enter, go out, thy dear image will always be before my eyes. When thou shalt have quitted me, I shall hasten to strange caresses, and, groaning, I shall press another face to my withered breast; I shall dry with my kisses the tears of another child; I shall drink of them; and may it please God that I may thus find some refreshment for my devouring thirst! Whatever I do, I shall be tormented, no remedy can console me; I perish, O Galsuinthe, by the wound which comes to me from thee! I ask what dear hand will dress, will ornament thy hair? Who, when I shall not be there, will cover thy soft cheeks with kisses? Who will warm thee in her bosom, who carry thee on her knees, surround thee with her arms? Alas! when thou shalt be without me, thou wilt have no mother. For the rest, my sad heart charges thee at the time of thy departure: be happy, I implore thee; but leave me: go: farewell: send through the air some consolation to thy impatient mother; and, if the wind bears me any news, let it be favourable."[1]

[1] *Fortun. Carm.*, l. vi. No. 7; Bib. Pat., vol. x. p. 562

The subtlety and affectation of bad rhetoric are to be found in this passage; but its emotion is sincere, and the expression ingenious and vivid. Many pieces of Fortunatus have the same merits.

I shall prosecute this inquiry no further; I think I have fully justified what I said in commencing: sacred literature is not there; the habits, and even the metrical forms of the dying pagan literature, are clearly stamped upon them. Ausonius is more elegant, more correct, more licentious than Fortunatus; but, speaking literally, the bishop is a continuation of the consul; Latin tradition was not dead; it had passed into the Christian society; and here commences that imitation which, amid the universal overthrow, unites the modern to the ancient world, and, at a later period, will play so considerable a part in all literature.

We must pause: we have just studied the intellectual state of Frankish Gaul from the sixth to the eighth century. This study completes for us that of the development of our civilization during the same period, that is, under the empire of the Merovingian kings. Another epoch, stamped with the same character, began with the revolution which raised the family of the Pepins to the throne of the Franks. In our next lecture I shall attempt to describe the revolution itself; and we shall then enter into the new paths which it forced France to take.

NINETEENTH LECTURE.

The causes and the character of the revolution which substituted the Carlovingians for the Merovingians—Recapitulation of the history of civilization in France under the Merovingian kings—The Frankish state in its relations with the neighbouring nations—The Frankish state in its internal organization—The aristocratical element prevailed in it, but without entirety or regularity—The state of the Frankish church—Episcopacy prevails in it, but is itself thrown into decay—Two new powers arise—1st. The Austrasian Franks—Mayors of the palace—The family of the Pepins—2. Papacy—Circumstances favourable to its progress—Causes which drew and united the Austrasian Franks to the popes—The conversion of the Germans beyond the Rhine—Relations of the Anglo-Saxon missionaries, on the one hand with the popes, on the other, with the mayors of the palace of Austrasia—Saint Boniface—The popes have need of the Austrasian Franks against the Lombards—Pepin-le-Bref has need of the pope to make himself king—Their alliance and the new direction which it impressed upon civilization — Conclusion of the first part of the course.

We have arrived at the eve of a great event, of the revolution which threw the last of the Merovingians into a cloister, and carried the Carlovingians to the throne of the Franks. It was consummated in the month of March 752, in the semi-lay and semi-ecclesiastical assembly held at Soissons, where Pepin was proclaimed king, and consecrated by Boniface, archbishop of Mayence. Never was a revolution brought about with less effort and noise; Pepin possessed the power: the fact was converted into right; no resistance was offered him; no protest of sufficient importance to leave a trace in history. Everything seemed to remain the same; a title, merely, was changed. Yet there can be no doubt but that a great event was thus accomplished; there can be no doubt but that this change was the indication of the end of a particular social state, of the commencement of a new state, a crisis, a veritable epoch in the history of French civilization.

It is this crisis that I wish to bring before you at present. I wish to recapitulate the history of civilization under the Merovingians, to indicate how it came to end in such a result, and to represent the new character, the new direction which it was obliged to take under the Carlovingians, by plainly setting forth the transition and its causes.

Civil society and religious society are evidently the two-fold subject of this recapitulation. We have studied them separately, and in their relations; we shall so study them in the period upon which we are about to enter. It is necessary that we should know exactly at what point they had each arrived at the crisis which now occupies us, and what was their reciprocal situation.

I commence with civil society. From the opening of this course, we have been speaking of the foundation of modern states, and in particular of the Frank state. We marked its origin at the reign of Clovis; it is even by concession that we are permitted not to go farther back, not to go to Pharamond. Let it be understood, however, that even in the epoch at which we have arrived, at the end of the Merovingian race, there was nothing established which the Franko-Gaulish society had, nothing invested with a somewhat stable and general form, that no principle prevailed in it so completely as to regulate it; that neither within nor without did the Frankish state exist; that in Gaul there was no state at all.

What do we mean by a State? a certain extent of territory having a determinate centre, fixed limits, inhabited by men who have a common name, and live involved, in certain respects, in the same destiny. Nothing like this existed in the middle of the eighth century, in what we now call France.

You know how many kingdoms had there alternately appeared and disappeared. The kingdoms of Metz, Soissons, Orleans, Paris, had given place to the kingdoms of Neustria, Austrasia, Burgundy, Aquitaine, incessantly changing masters, frontiers, extent, and importance; reduced at length to two, the kingdoms of Austrasia and Neustria, even these two had nothing stable or regular, their chiefs and their limits continually varied; the kings and the provinces continually passed from one to the other; so that even in the interior of the territory occupied by the Frankish population, no political association had any consistency or firmness.

The external frontiers were still more uncertain. On the east and north the movement of the invasion of the German nations continued. The Thuringians, the Bavarians, the Allemandi, the Frisons, the Saxons, incessantly made efforts to pass the Rhine, and take their share of the territory which the Franks occupied. In order to resist them, the Franks crossed the Rhine; they ravaged, at several times, the countries of the Thuringians, the Allemandi, and the Bavarians, and reduced these nations to a subordinate condition, doubtless very precarious, and incapable of exact definition. But the Frisons and Saxons escaped this semi-defeat, and the Austrasian Franks were forced to maintain an incessant warfare against them, which prevented their frontiers from gaining the least regularity on this side.

On the west, the Britons and all the tribes established in the peninsula known under the name of Armorica, kept the frontiers of the Neustrian Franks in the same state of uncertainty.

In the south, in Provence, Narbonnese, and Aquitaine, it was no longer from the movement of the barbarous and half wandering colonies that the fluctuation proceeded; but there was fluctuation. The ancient Roman population incessantly laboured to regain its independence. The Franks had conquered, but did not fully possess these countries. When their great incursions ceased, the towns and country districts rebelled, and confederated in order to shake off the yoke. A new cause of agitation and instability was joined to their efforts. Mohammedanism dates its rise from the 16th of July, 622; and at the end of the same century, or at least at the commencement of the eighth, it inundated the south of Italy, nearly the whole of Spain, the south of Gaul, and made on this side a still more impetuous effort than that of the German nations on the borders of the Rhine. Thus, on all points, on the north, the east, the west, and the south, the Frankish territory was incessantly invaded, its frontiers changed at the mercy of incessantly repeated incursions. Upon the whole, there can be no doubt but that, in this vast extent of country, the Frankish population dominated; it was the strongest, the most numerous, the most established; but still it was without territorial consistency, without political unity; as distinct frontier nations, and under the point of view of the law of nations, the state, properly so called, did not exist.

Let us enter into the interior of the Gaulo-Frankish society; we shall not find it any more advanced; it will offer us no greater degree of entirety or fixedness.

You will recollect that, in examining the institutions of the German nations before the invasion, I showed that they could not be transplanted into the Gaulish territory, and that the free institutions, in particular the government of public affairs by assemblies of free men, become inapplicable to the new situation of the conquerors, had almost entirely perished. Even the class of free men, that condition of which individual independence and equality were the essential characteristics, continually diminished in number and importance; it was evidently not this class, nor the system of institutions and influences analogous to its nature, that was to prevail in the Gaulo-Frankish society, and govern it. Liberty was then a cause of disorder, not a principle of organization.

In the first periods following the invasion, royalty, as you have seen, made some progress; it collected some wreck of the inheritance of the empire; religious ideas gave it some power: but this progress soon stopped; the time of the centralization of power was still far distant; all means of gaining obedience were wanting; obstacles arose on all sides. The speedy and irremediable humiliation of the Merovingian royalty proves how little capable the monarchical principle was of possessing and regulating the Gaulo-Frankish society. It was nearly as impotent as the principle of free institutions.

The aristocratical principle prevailed: it was to the great proprietors, each on his domain, to the companions of the king, the antrustions, leudes, *fideles*, that the power actually belonged. But the aristocratical principle itself was incapable of giving any stable or general organization to society; it prevailed in it, but with as much disorder as would have flowed from any other system, without conferring any more simple or regular form. Consult all modern historians who have attempted to describe and explain this epoch.

Some have sought its key in the struggle of the free men against the leudes, that is, the conquering nation against that which was to become the nobility of the court; others adhere to the diversity of races, and will speak of the struggle of the Germans against the Gauls; others, again, attach great importance to the struggle of the clergy against the laity, the bishops against the great barbarian proprietors, and there see the secret of most of the events. Others, again, especially insist upon the struggle of the kings themselves against their companions, their leudes, who aspired to the rendering themselves independent, and annulling and invading the royal power. All, in some measure, have a different word for the enigma which the social state of this epoch presents: a great reason for presuming that no word can explain it. All these struggles in fact existed; all these forces contested without any of them gaining enough of the ascendancy to dominate with any regularity. The aristocratic tendency, which must have arisen later than the feudal system, was certainly dominant; but no institution, no permanent organization, could yet arise from it.

Thus, within and without, whether we consider the social order or the political order, everything was restless, incessantly brought into question; nothing appeared destined to a long or powerful development.

From civil society let us pass to religious society; the recapitulation, if I mistake not, will show it to be in the same state.

The idea of the unity of the church was general and dominant in minds; but in facts it was far from having the same extension, the same power. No general principle, no government, properly so called, reigned in the Gaulo-Frankish church; it was, like civil society, an entire chaos.

And first, the remains of the free institutions which had presided at the first development of Christianity, had almost entirely disappeared. You have seen them gradually reduced to the participation of the clergy in the election of bishops, to the influence of councils in the general administration of the church. You have seen the election of bishops, and the influence of councils decline, and almost vanish in their turn. At the commencement of the eighth century, a mere vain shadow remained of them; the bishops, for the most part, owed their elevation to the orders of kings, of or the mayors of the palace, or to some such form of violence. Councils scarcely ever met. No legal, constituted liberty preserved any real power in the religious society.

We have seen the dawn of universal monarchy; we have seen papacy take a marked ascendancy in the west. Do not suppose, however, that at the epoch which occupies us, and in Gaul especially, this ascendancy resembled a real authority, a form of government. Nay, at the end of the seventh century it was in a rapid decay. When the Franks were established in Gaul, the popes tried to preserve with these new masters the credit which they had enjoyed under the Roman empire. At the fifth century the bishop of Rome possessed considerable domains in southern Gaul, especially in the diocese of Arles, a powerful means of relation and influence with those countries. They remained to him under the Visigoth, Burgundian, or Frank kings, and the bishop of Arles continued to be habitually his vicar, as much for his personal interests, as for the general affairs of the church. Thus the relations of the popes with the Frank kings were frequent in the sixth and at the beginning of the seventh century; numerous monuments of them have come down to us; among others, a letter from Gregory the Great to Brunehault: and upon some occasions, the Franks themselves had recourse to the intervention of papacy. But in the course of the seventh century, by a multitude of rather complex causes, this intervention almost entirely ceased. We find from Gregory the Great to Gregory II. (from the year 604 to the year 715) scarcely a single letter, a single document, which proves any correspondence between the masters of Frankish Gaul and the papacy.

The prodigious disorder which then reigned in Gaul, the instability of all kingdoms, and of all kings, doubtless contributed to it: no one had any time to think of contracting or keeping up relations so distant; everything was decided at once upon the spot, and on direct and immediate motives. Beyond the Alps almost equal disorder reigned; the Lombards invaded Italy, and menaced Rome; a personal and pressing danger retained the attention of the papacy within the circle of its own peculiar interests. Besides, the composition of the episcopacy of the Gauls was no longer the same; many barbarians had entered into it, strangers to all the recollections, all the customs which had so long united the Gaulish bishops to the bishop of Rome. All circumstances concurred to make null the religious relations between Rome and Gaul; so that at the end of the seventh century, the Gaulo-Frankish church was no more governed by the principle of universal monarchy, than by that of common deliberation; papacy was scarcely more powerful than liberty.

There, as elsewhere, in religious society as in civil society, the aristocratical principle had prevailed. It was to episcopacy that the government of the Gaulo-Frankish church belonged. It was administered during the fifth and sixth century, with a good deal of regularity and continuity; but in the course of the seventh, from the causes which I have already spoken of, the episcopal aristocracy fell into the same corruption, the same anarchy which seized upon the civil aristocracy; the metropolitans lost all authority; mere priests lost all influence; many bishops reckoned more on their influence as proprietors, than on their mission as chiefs of the church. Many of the laity received or usurped the bishoprics as private domains. Each occupied himself with his temporal or diocesan interests; all unity vanished in the government of the secular clergy. The monastic order presented a similar aspect; the rule of Saint Benedict was commonly adopted in it, but no general administration connected the various establishments among themselves; each monastery ruled and governed itself apart; so that, at the end of the seventh century, the aristocratical system, which dominated alike in church and state, was here almost as disordered, almost as incapable of giving rise to any approach to a general and regular government.

Nothing, therefore, was established at this epoch, in either one or other of the two societies from which modern society has arisen. The absence of rule and public authority was, perhaps, more complete than immediately after the fall of the empire; then, at all events, the wrecks of Roman and German institutions still subsisted, and maintained some kind of social order amidst the most agitated events. When the fall of the Merovingian race approached, even these wrecks had fallen into ruin, and no new edifice had as yet arisen; there was scarcely a trace of the imperial administration, or of the *mals* or assemblies of the free men of Germany, and the feudal organization was not seen. Perhaps at no epoch has the chaos been so great, or the State had so little existence.

Still, under this general dissolution, two new forces, two principles of organization and government, were being prepared in civil and religious society, destined to approach each other and to unite, in order, at last, to make an attempt to put an end to the chaos, and to give to church and state the entirety and fixity which they wanted.

Whoever will observe, attentively, the distribution of the Franks over the Gaulish territory, from the sixth to the eighth century, will be struck with a considerable difference between the Franks of Austrasia, situated on the borders of the Rhine, the Moselle, and the Meuse, and that of the Franks of Neustria, transplanted into the centre, the west and the south of Gaul. The first were probably more numerous, and certainly less dispersed. They still kept to that soil whence the Germans drew their power and fertility, so to speak, as Antæus did from the earth. The Rhine alone separated them from ancient Germany; they lived in continual relation, hostile or pacific, with the German and partly Frankish colonies who inhabited the right bank. Still they were well established in their new country, and wished firmly to guard it. They were also less separated from the manners of the ancient German society than were the Neustrian Franks, and, at the same time, having become proprietors, they daily more and more contracted the wants and habits of their new situation, and of the social organization which might be adapted to it. Two facts, apparently contradictory, bring out into bold relief this particular characteristic of the Austrasian Franks. It was more especially from Austrasia that those bands of warriors set out whom we see, in the course of the sixth and seventh centuries, still spreading over Italy and the south of Gaul, and there abandoning themselves to a life of incursion and pillage; and yet it is in Austrasia that the most remarkable monuments of the passage of the

Franks into the condition of proprietors are seen; upon the borders of the Rhine, the Moselle, and the Meuse, are the strongest of those habitations of theirs which became castles, so that Austrasian society is the most complete and faithful image of the ancient manners and the new situation of the Franks; it is there that one least meets with Roman or heterogeneous elements; it is there that the spirit of conquest and the territorial spirit, the instincts of the proprietor and those of the warrior are allied, and display themselves with the greatest energy.

A fact so important could not fail to become evident, and to exercise a great influence over the course of events; the Austrasian society could not but give rise to some institution, some power, which expressed and developed its character. This was the part taken of its mayors of the palace, and in particular by the family of the Pepins.

The mayor of the palace is met with in all the Frankish kingdoms. I shall not enter here into a long history of the institution, I shall confine myself to remarking its character and general vicissitudes. The mayors were at first merely the first superintendents, the first administrators of the interior of the palace of the king; the chiefs whom he put at the head of his companions, of his leudes, still united around him. It was their duty to maintain order among the king's men, to administer justice, to look to all the affairs, to all the wants, of that great domestic society. They were the men of the king with the leudes; this was their first character, their first state.

Now for the second. After having exercised the power of the king over his leudes, his mayors of the palace usurped it to their own profit. The leudes, by grants of public charges and fiefs, were not long before they became great proprietors. This new situation was superior to that of companions of the king; they detached themselves from him, and united in order to defend their common interests. According as their fortune dictated, the mayors of the palace sometimes resisted them, more often united with them, and, at first servants of the king, they at last became the chiefs of an aristocracy, against whom royalty could do nothing.

These are the two principal phases of this institution: it gained more extension and fixedness in Austrasia, in the family of the Pepins, who possessed it almost a century and a half, than anywhere else. At once great proprietors, usufructuaries of the royal power, and warlike chiefs, Pepin-le-Vieux, Pepin l'Heristal, Charles Martel, and Pepin-le-Bref, by turns defended these various interests, appropriated their power to themselves, and thus found themselves the representatives of the aristocracy, of royalty, and of that mind, at once territorial and conquering, which animated the Franks of Austrasia, and secured to them the preponderance. There resided the principle of life and organization which was to take hold of civil society, and draw it, at least for some time, from the state of anarchy and impotence into which it was plunged. The Pepins were the depositories of its power, the instrument of its action.

In the religious society, but out of the Frank territory, a power was also developed capable of introducing, or at least of attempting to introduce, order and reformation into it: this was papacy.

I shall not repeat here what I have already said of the first origin of papacy, and of the religious causes to which it owed the progressive extension of its power. Independently of these causes, and in a purely temporal point of view, the bishop of Rome found himself placed in the most favourable situation. Three circumstances, you will recollect, especially contributed to establish the power of the bishops in general: 1st, their vast domains, which caused them to take a place in that hierarchy of great proprietors to which European society had belonged for so long a period; 2nd, their intervention in the municipal system, and the preponderance which they exercised in cities, by being directly or indirectly receiving the inheritance of the ancient magistracies; 3rd, their quality as councillors of the temporal power; they surrounded the new kings, and directed them in their attempts at government. Upon this triple base the episcopal power raised itself in the rising states. The bishop of Rome was, more than any other, prepared to profit by it. Like others, he was a great proprietor. At a very early period he possessed considerable domains in the Campagna di Roma, in the south of Italy, and upon the borders of the Adriatic sea. Considered as a councillor of the temporal power, no one had so good a chance: instead, like the Frank, Spanish, Anglo-Saxon, bishops, of being the servant of a king present, he was the representative, the vicar of a king absent; he depended on the emperor of the east, a sovereign who rarely cramped his administration, and never eclipsed it. The Empire, it is true, had other representatives than the pope in Italy; the exarch of Ravenna, and a duke who resided at Rome, were the real delegates with regard to the civil administration; but, in the interior of Rome, the attributes of the bishop in civil matters, and in default of attributes, his influence in other respects, conferred almost all the power upon him. The emperors neglected nothing to retain him in their dependence; they carefully preserved the right of confirming his election; he paid them certain tributes, and constantly maintained at Constantinople, under the name of Apocrisiary, an agent charged to manage all his affairs there, and to answer for his fidelity. But if these precautions retarded the complete and external emancipation of the popes, it did not prevent their independence being great, nor, under the title of delegates of the emperor, their daily approaching nearer to becoming its successors.

As municipal magistrates, as chiefs of the people within the walls of Rome, their situation was not less advantageous. You have seen that in the remainder of the west, particularly in Gaul, and as the inevitable effect of the disasters of the invasion, the municipal system was declining; there certainly remained its wrecks, and the bishop almost alone disposed of them; but they were only wrecks; the importance of the municipal magistrates was daily lowered under the violent blows of counts, or other barbarous chiefs. It was far from being thus in Rome: there the municipal system, instead of being weakened was fortified. Rome in no way remained in the possession of the barbarians; they only pillaged it in passing; the imperial power was too distant to be real; the municipal system soon became the only government; the influence of the Roman people in its affairs was much more active, much more efficacious, at the sixth and seventh centuries, that it had been in preceding ages. The municipal magistrates became political magistrates; and the bishop who, under forms more or less fixed, by means more or less direct, was in some measure their chief, took the first lead in this general and unperceived elevation towards a kind of sovereignty, while elsewhere the episcopal power arose not beyond the limits of a narrow and doubtful administration.

Thus, as proprietors, councillors of sovereign, and as popular magistrates, the bishops of Rome had the best chances; and while religious circumstances tended to increase their power, political circumstances had the same result, and impelled them in the same paths. Thus, in the course of the sixth and seventh centuries, papacy gained a degree of importance in Italy, which it had formerly been very far from possessing; and although at the end of this epoch it was a stranger to Frankish Gaul, although its relations both with the kings and with the Frank clergy had become rare, yet, such was its general progress, that in setting foot again in the monarchy of the Frankish church, it did not fail to appear there with a force and credit superior to all rivalry.

Here, then, we see two new powers which were formed and confirmed amidst the general dissolution; in the Frank state, the mayors of the palace of Austrasia; in the Christian church, the popes; here are two active, energetic principles, which seem disposed to take possession, the one of civil society, the other of religious society, and capable of attempting some work of organization, of establishing some government therein.

It was, in fact, by the influence of these two principles, and of their alliance, that, in the middle of the eighth century, the great crisis of which we seek the character shone forth.

After the fifth century, papacy took the lead in the conversion of the pagans; the clergy of the various states of the west, occupied both in its religious local duties, and in its temporal duties, had almost abandoned this great enterprise: the monks alone, more interested and less indolent, continued to occupy themselves arduously in it. The bishop of Rome undertook to direct them, and they in general accepted him for a chief. At the end of the sixth century, Gregory the Great accomplished the most important of these conversions, that of the Anglo-Saxons established in Britain. By his orders, Roman monks set out to undertake it. They began with the county of Kent, and Augustin, one among them, was the first archbishop of Canterbury. The Anglo-Saxon church was thus, at the seventh century, the only one in the west which owed its origin to the Romish church. Italy, Spain, and Gaul, had become Christians without the help of papacy; their churches were not bound to that of Rome by a filial power; they were her sisters, not her daughters. Britain, on the contrary, received her faith and her first preachers from Rome. She was, therefore, at this epoch, far more than any other church in the west, in habitual correspondence with the popes, devoted to their interests, docile to their authority. By a natural consequence, and also by reason of the similitude of idioms, it was more especially with the Anglo-Saxon monks that the popes undertook the conversion of the other pagan nations of Europe, among others, of Germany. One need only glance over the lives of the saints of the seventh and eighth centuries to be convinced that the greater part of the missionaries sent to the Bavarians, the Frisons, the Saxons, Willibrod, Rupert Willibald, Winfried, came from Britain. They could not labour at this work without entering into frequent relations with the Austrasian Franks, and their chiefs. The Austrasians on all sides bordered the nations beyond the Rhine, and were incessantly struggling to prevent them from again inundating the west. The missionaries were obliged to traverse their territory, and to obtain their support, in order to penetrate into the barbarous countries. They therefore failed not to claim that support. Gregory the Great even ordered the monks whom he sent into Britain to pass through Austrasia, and recommended them to the two kings, Theodoric and Theodebert, who then reigned at Châlons and at Metz. The recommendation was far more necessary and pressing when the matter in hand was to convert the German colonies. The Austrasian chiefs on their side, Arnoul, Pepin l'Herital, and Charles Martel, were not long in foreseeing what advantages such labours might have for them. In becoming Christians, these troublesome colonies were obliged to become fixed, to submit to some regular influence, at least to enter into the path of civilization. Besides, the missionaries were excellent explorers of those countries with which communication was so difficult of accomplishment; by their mediation could be procured information and advice. Where could be found such skilful agents, such useful allies? Accordingly, the alliance was soon concluded. It was in Austrasia that the missionaries who were spread over Germany found their principal fulcrum; it was from thence that they set, to it that they returned; it was to the kingdom of Austrasia that they annexed their spiritual conquests; it was with the masters of Austrasia on the one hand, and with the popes on the other, that they were in intimate and constant correspondence. Glance at the life, follow the works of the most illustrious and most powerful among them, namely, Saint Boniface, and you will recognise all the facts of which I have just spoken.

Saint Boniface was an Anglo-Saxon, born about 680, at Crediton, in the county of Devon, and called Winfried. A monk in the monastery of Exeter at a very early period, and later, in that of Nutsell, it is not known whence came his design of devoting himself to the conversion of the German nations; perhaps he merely followed the example of many of his compatriots. However this may be, from the year 715, we find him preaching amidst the Frisons; incessantly renewed warfare between them and the Austrasian Franks drove him from their country; he returned to his own, and re-entered the monastery of Nutsell. In 718, we encounter him at Rome, receiving from pope Gregory II. a formal mission, and instructions for the conversion of the Germans. He goes from Rome into Austrasia, corresponds with Charles Martel, passes the Rhine, and pursues his enormous enterprise with indefatigable perseverance among the Frisons, the Thuringians, the Bavarians, the Catti, and the Saxons. His entire life was devoted to it, and it was always with Rome that were connected his works. In 723, Gregory II. nominated him bishop; in 732, Gregory III. conferred upon him the titles of archbishop and apostolic vicar; in 738, Winfried, who no longer bore the name of Boniface, made a new journey to Rome, in order to regulate definitively the relations of the Christian church which he had just founded, with Christianity in general; and for him Rome is the centre, the pope is the chief of Christianity. It was to the profit of papacy that he sent in all directions the missionaries placed under his orders, erected bishoprics, conquered nations. Here is the oath which he took when the pope nominated him archbishop of Mayence, and metropolitan of the bishoprics which he should found in Germany.

"I, Boniface, bishop by the grace of God, I promise to thee, blessed Peter, prince of the apostles, and to thy vicar, the holy Gregory, and to his successors, by the Father, the Son, and the Holy Ghost, the holy and indivisible Trinity, and by thy sacred body, here present, always to keep a perfect fidelity to the holy catholic faith; to remain, with the aid of God, in the unity of that faith, upon which, without doubt, depends the whole salvation of Christians; not to lend myself, upon the instigation of any one, to anything which can be against the universal church, and to prove, in all things, my fidelity, the pureness of my faith, and my entire devotion to thee, to the interests of thy church, who hast received from God the power to tie and to untie, to thy said vicar, and to his successors: and if I learn that the bishops are against the ancient rule of the holy fathers, I promise to have no alliance nor communion with them, any more than to repress them if I am able; if not, I will at once inform my apostolic lord. And if (which God forbid!) I ever, whether by will or occasion, do anything against these my promises, let me be found guilty at the eternal judgment—let me incur the chastisement of Ananias and of Sapphira, who dared to lie unto you, and despoil you of part of their property. I, Boniface, a humble bishop, have with my own hand written this attestation of oath, and depositing it on the most sacred body of the sacred Peter, I have, as it is prescribed, taking God to judge and witness, made the oath, which I promise to keep."[1]

To this oath I add the statement which Boniface himself has transmitted to us of the decrees of the first German council held under his presidence in 742:

"In our synodal meeting, we have declared and decreed that to the end of our life we desire to hold the catholic faith and unity, and submission to the Roman church, Saint Peter, and his vicar; that we will every year assemble the synod; that the metropolitans shall demand the *pallium* from the see of Rome, and that we will canonically follow all the precepts of Peter, to the end that we may be reckoned among the number of his sheep, and we have consented and subscribed to this profession. I have sent it to the body of Saint Peter, prince of the apostles, and the clergy and the pontiff have joyfully received it.

"If any bishop can correct or reform anything in his diocese, let him propose the reformation in the synod before the archbishops and all there present, even as we ourselves

[1] *S. Bonif. Epist.*, ep. 118; *Bib. Pat.*, vol. xiii., p. 119; ed. of Lyons.

have promised with oath to the Roman church. Should we see the priests and people breaking the law of God, and we are unable to correct them, we will faithfully inform the apostolic see, and the vicar of Saint Peter, in order to accomplish the said reform. It is thus, if I do not deceive myself, that all bishops should render an account to the metropolitan, and he to the pontiff of Rome, of that which they do not succeed in reforming among the people, and thus they will not have the blood of lost souls upon their heads."[1]

Of a surety, it is impossible more formally to submit the new church, the new Christian nations to the papal power.

A scruple, which I must express, impedes my progress: I fear that you are tempted to see more especially in this conduct of Saint Boniface the influence of temporal motives, of ambitious and interested combinations: it is a good deal the disposition of our time; and we are even a little inclined to boast of it, as a proof of our liberty of mind and our good sense. Most certainly let us judge all things in full liberty of mind; let the severest good sense preside at our judgments; but let us feel that, wherever we meet with great things and great men, there are other motives than ambitious combinations and personal interests. Let it be known that the thought of man can be elevated, that its horizon can be extended only when he becomes detached from the world and from himself; and that, if egoism plays a great part in history, that of disinterested and moral activity is, in the eyes of the most rigorous critic, infinitely superior to it. Boniface proves it, as well as others. All devoted as he was to the court of Rome, he could, when need was, speak truth to it, reproach it with its evil, and urge it to take heed to itself. He learned that it granted certain indulgences, that it permitted certain licences which scandalised severe consciences. He wrote to the pope Zachary:

"These carnal men, these simple Germans, or Bavarians, or Franks, if they see things done at Rome which we forbid, suppose that it has been permitted and authorised by the priests, and turn it against us in derision, and take advantage of it for the scandal of their life. Thus, they say that every

[1] Labbé, *Counc.*, vol. xi., col. 1544-45.

year, in the calends of January, they have seen, at Rome, both day and night, near the church, dancers overrunning the public places, according to the custom of the pagans, and raising clamours, after their fashion, and singing sacrilegious songs; and this day, they say, and till night-time, the tables are loaded with meats, and no one will lend to his neighbour either fire or iron, or anything in his house. They say also, that they have seen women carry phylacteries, and fillets attached to their legs and arms, and offer all sorts of things for sale to the passers by; and all these things, seen by carnal men, and those but little instructed, are subjects of derision, and an obstacle to our preaching, and to the faith. . . . If your paternity interdict these pagan customs in Rome, it will acquire a great reputation, and will assure us a great progress in the doctrine of the church."[1]

I might cite many other letters, written with as much freedom, and which prove the same sincerity. But a fact speaks louder than all the letters in the world. After having founded new bishoprics and many monasteries, at the highest point of his success and glory, in 753, that is, at seventy-three years of age, the Saxon missionary demanded and obtained authority to quit his bishopric of Mayence, and to place therein his favourite disciple Lullus, and to again prosecute the works of his youth among the still pagan Frisons. He in fact went amid woods, morasses, and barbarians, and was massacred in 755, with many of his companions.

At his death, the bringing over of Germany to Christianity was accomplished, and accomplished to the profit of papacy. But it was also to the profit of the Franks of Austrasia, to the good of their safety and their power. It follows that it was for them as much as for Rome, that Boniface had laboured; it was upon the soil of Germany, in the enterprise of converting its tribes by Saxon missionaries, that the two new powers, which were to prevail, the one in the civil society, the other in the religious society, encountered each other, the mayors of the palace of Austrasia, and the popes. In order to consummate their alliance, and to make it bear all its

[1] *S. Bonif. Ep. ad Zacharium*, ep. 132; *Bib. Pat.*, vol. xiii., p. 125, ed. of Lyons.

fruits, an occasion was only wanting on either side; it was not long in presenting itself.

I have already spoken of the situation of the bishop of Rome with regard to the Lombards, and of their incessant efforts to invade a territory which daily became more positively his domain. Another real, although less pressing danger, also approached him. As the Franks of Austrasia, with the Pepins at their head, had on the north to combat the Frisons and the Saxons, and on the south the Saracens, so the popes were pressed by the Saracens and the Lombards. Their situation was analogous; but the Franks achieved victory under Charles Martel; the papacy, not in a condition to defend herself, everywhere sought soldiers. She tried to obtain them from the emperor of the east: he had none to send her. In 739, Gregory III. had recourse to Charles Martel. Boniface took charge of the negotiation; it was without result: Charles Martel had too much to do on his own account; he cared not to involve himself in a new war; but the idea was established at Rome that the Franks alone could defend the church against the Lombards, and that sooner or later they would cross the Alps for her good.

Some years after, the chief of Austrasia, Pepin, son of Charles Martel, in his turn, had need of the pope. He wished to get himself declared king of the Franks, and, however well his power might be established, he wanted a sanction to it. I have many times remarked, and am not tired of repeating it, that power does not suffice to itself; it wants something more than success, it wants to be converted into right; it demands that characteristic, sometimes of the free assent of men, sometimes of religious consecration. Pepin invoked both. More than one ecclesiastic, perhaps Boniface, suggested to him the idea of getting his new title of king of the Franks sanctioned by the papacy. I shall not enter into the details of the negotiation undertaken upon this subject; it offers some rather embarrassing questions and chronological difficulties: it is not the less certain that it took place, and that Boniface conducted it, as his letters to the pope often show; we see him, among others, charge his disciple Lullus to inform the pope of certain important affairs which he would rather not commit to writing. Lastly, in 751,

"Burchard, bishop of Wurtzburg, and Fulrad, a chaplain

priest, were sent to Rome to pope Zachary, in order to consult the pontiff touching the kings who were then in France, and who had merely the name without any power. The pope answered by a messenger, that he thought that he who already possessed the power of the king, was the king; and giving his full assent, he enjoined that Pepin should be made king. . . Pepin was then proclaimed king of the Franks, and anointed for this high dignity with the sacred unction by the holy hand of Boniface, archbishop and martyr of happy memory, and raised upon the throne, according to custom of the Franks, in the town of Soissons. With regard to Childeric, who invested himself with the false name of king, Pepin had him shaved and put in a monastery."[1]

Such was the progressive march of the revolution; such were the indirect and true causes of it. It has been represented in later times[2] (and I myself have contributed to propagate this idea[3]) as a new German invasion, as a recent conquest of Gaul by the Franks of Austrasia, more barbarians, more Germans, than Franks of Neustria, who had gradually amalgamated with the Romans. Such was in fact the result, and, so to speak, the external character of the event; but its character does not suffice to explain it; it had far more distant and more profound causes than the continuation or renewal of the great German invasion. I have just placed them before you. The civil Gallo-Frankish society was in a complete dissolution; no system, no power had come to establish itself in it, and to found it in ruling it. The religious society had fallen almost into the same state. Two principles of regeneration were gradually developed; the mayor of the palace among the Franks of Austrasia; and the papacy at Rome. These new powers were naturally drawn together by the mediation of the conversion of the German tribes, in which they had a common interest. The missionaries, and especially the Anglo-Saxon missionaries, were the agents of this junction. Two particular circumstances, the perils in which the Lombards involved the papacy, and the need which Pepin had of the pope in order to get his title of king sanc-

[1] Annales d'Eginhard, vol. iii., p. 4, in my *Collection des Memoires relatifs a l'Histoire de France.*

[2] *Histoire des Français*, by M. de Sismondi, vol. ii., p. 168—171.

[3] See my *Essais sur l'Histoire de France*, third *Essai*, p. 67—85.

tioned, made it a close alliance. It raised up a new race of sovereigns in Gaul, destroyed the kingdom of the Lombards in Italy, and impelled civil and religious Gallo-Frankish society into a route which tended to make royalty prevail in the civil order, and papacy in the religious order. Such will appear to you the character of the attempts at civilization made in France by the Carlovingians, that is to say, by Charlemagne, the true representative of that new direction, although it failed in its designs, and did nothing but throw, as it were, a bridge between barbarism and feudalism. This second epoch, the history of civilization in France under the Carlovingians, in its various phases, will be the subject of the following lectures.

TWENTIETH LECTURE.

Reign of Charlemagne—Greatness of his name—Is it true that he settled nothing? that all that he did has perished with him?—Of the action of great men—They play a double part—That which they do, in virtue of the first, is durable; that which they attempt, under the second, passes away with them—Example of Napoleon—Necessity of being thoroughly acquainted with the history of events under Charlemagne, in order to understand that of civilization—How the events may be recapitulated in tables—1. Charlemagne as a warrior and conqueror: Table of his principal expeditions—Their meaning and results—2. Charlemagne as an administrator and legislator—Of the government of the provinces—Of the central government—Table of national assemblies under his reign—Table of his capitularies—Table of the acts and documents which remain of this epoch—3. Charlemagne as a protector of intellectual development: Table of the celebrated cotemporaneous men—Estimation of the general results, and of the character of his reign.

We enter into a second great epoch of the history of French civilization, and as we enter, at the first step, we encounter a great man. Charlemagne was neither the first of his race, nor the author of its elevation. He received an already established power from his father Pepin. I have attempted to make you understand the causes of this revolution and its true character. When Charlemagne became king of the Franks, it was accomplished; he had no need even to defend it. He, however, has given his name to the second dynasty; and the instant one speaks of it, the instant one thinks of it, it is Charlemagne who presents himself before the mind as its founder and chief. Glorious privilege of a great man! No one disputes that Charlemagne had a right to give name to his race and age. The homage paid to him is often blind and undistinguishing; his genius and glory are extolled without discrimination or measure; yet, at the same time, persons repeat, one after another, that he founded nothing, accomplished nothing; that his empire, his laws, all his works, perished with him. And this historical common-place introduces a crowd of moral common-places on the ineffectualness and uselessness of great men, the vanity of their projects, the little trace which they leave in the world, after having troubled it in all directions.

Is this true? Is it the destiny of great men to be merely a burden and a useless wonder to mankind? Their activity so strong, so brilliant, can it have no lasting result? It costs very dear to be present at the spectacle; the curtain fallen, will nothing of it remain? Should we regard these powerful and glorious chiefs of a century and a people, merely as a sterile scourge, or at very best, as a burdensome luxury? Charlemagne, in particular, should he be nothing more?

At the first glance, the common-place might be supposed to be a truth. The victories, conquests, institutions, reforms, projects, all the greatness and glory of Charlemagne, vanished with him; he seemed a meteor suddenly emerging from the darkness of barbarism, to be as suddenly lost and extinguished in that of feudality. There are other such examples in history. The world has more than once seen, we ourselves have seen an empire like it, one which took pleasure in being compared to that of Charlemagne, and had a right so to be compared; we have likewise seen it fall away with a man.

But we must beware of trusting these appearances. To understand the meaning of great events, and measure the agency and influence of great men, we need to look far deeper into the matter.

The activity of a great man is of two kinds; he performs two parts; two epochs may generally be distinguished in his career. First, he understands better than other people the wants of his time; its real, present exigences; what, in the age he lives in, society needs, to enable it to subsist and attain its natural development. He understands these wants better than any other person of his time, and knows better than any other how to wield the powers of society, and direct them skilfully towards the realization of this end. Hence proceed his power and glory; it is in virtue of this, that as soon as he appears; he is understood, accepted, followed; that all give their willing aid to the work which he is performing for the benefit of all.

But he does not stop here. When the real wants of his time are in some degree satisfied, the ideas and the will of the great man proceed further. He quits the region of present facts and exigencies; he gives himself up to views in some measure personal to himself; he indulges in combinations more or less vast and specious, but which are not, like his previous labours, founded on the actual state, the common instincts, the determined wishes of society, but are remote and arbitrary. He aspires to extend his activity and influence indefinitely, and to possess the future as he has possessed the present. Here egoism and illusion commence. For some time, on the faith of what he has already done, the great man is followed in his new career; he is believed in and obeyed; men lend themselves to his fancies; his flatterers and his dupes even admire and vaunt them as his sublimest conceptions. The public, however, in whom a mere delusion is never of any long continuance, soon discovers that it is impelled in a direction in which it has no desire to move. At first the great man had enlisted his high intelligence and powerful will in the service of the general feeling and wish; he now seeks to employ the public force in the service of his individual ideas and desires; he is attempting things which he alone wishes or understands. Hence disquietude first, and then uneasiness; for a time he is still followed, but sluggishly and reluctantly; next he is censured and complained of; finally, he is abandoned and falls; and all which he alone had planned and desired, all the merely personal and arbitrary part of his work, perishes with him.

I shall avoid no opportunity of borrowing from our age the torch which it offers, in this instance, in order to enlighten a time so distant and obscure. The fate and name of Napoleon at present belong to history. I shall not feel the least embarrassed in speaking of it, and speaking of it freely.

Every one knows that at the time when he seized the power in France, the dominant, imperious want of our country was security—without, national independence; inwardly, civil life. In the revolutionary troubles, the external and internal destiny, the state and society, were equally compromised. To replace the new France in the European confederation, to make her avowed and accepted by the other states, and to constitute her within in a peaceable and regular manner,—to put her, in a word, into the possession of independence and order, the only pledges of a long future, this was the desire, the general thought of the country. Napoleon understood and accomplished it.

This finished, or nearly so, Napoleon proposed to himself a thousand others: potent in combinations, and of an ardent imagination, egoistical and thoughtful, machinator and poet, he, as it were, poured out his activity in arbitrary and gigantic projects, children of his own,—solitary, foreign to the real wants of our time, and of our France. She followed him for some time, and at great cost, in this path which she had not selected; a day came when she would follow no further, and the emperor found himself alone, and the empire vanished, and all things returned to their proper condition, to their natural tendency.

It is an analogous fact which the reign of Charlemagne offers us at the ninth century. Despite the immense difference of time, situation, form, even groundwork, the general phenomenon is similar: these two parts of a great man, these two epochs of his career, are found in Charlemagne as in Napoleon. Let us endeavour to state them.

Here I encounter a difficulty which has long pre-occupied me, and which I do not hope to have completely surmounted. At the commencement of the course, I engaged to read you a general history of France. I have not recounted events to you; I have sought only general results, the concatenation of causes and effects, the progress of civilization, concealed under the external scenes of history; as regards the scenes themselves, I had taken it for granted that you know them. Hitherto I have cared little to know if you had taken this precaution; under the Merovingian race, events, properly so called, are of rare occurrence—so monotonous, that it is less necessary to regard them nearly: general facts only are important, and they may, up to a certain point, be brought to light and understood without an exact knowledge of the details. Under the reign of Charlemagne, it is entirely different: wars, political vicissitudes of all kinds, are numerous and brilliant; they occupy an important place, and general facts are concealed far behind the special facts which occupy the front of the scene. History, properly so called, envelops and covers the history of civilization. The latter will not be clear to you unless the former is presented to you; I cannot give you an account of events, and yet you require to know them.

I have attempted to sum them up in tables, to present under that form the special facts of this epoch; those, at least, which approach nearly to general facts, and immediately concern the history of civilization. Statistical tables are looked upon in the present day, and with good reason, as one of the best means of studying the state of a society, under certain relations; why should not the same method be applied to the past? it does not produce them with vividness and animation, like recital; but it raises their frame-work, so to speak, and prevents general ideas from floating in vagueness and at chance. In proportion as we advance in the course of civilization, we shall often be obliged to employ it.

Three essential characteristics appear in Charlemagne: he may be considered under three principal points of view: 1st, as a warrior and a conqueror; 2nd, as an administrator and legislator; 3rd, as a protector of sciences, letters, arts, of intellectual development in general. He exercised a great power, outwardly by force, inwardly by government and laws; he desired to act, and in fact did act, upon mankind itself, upon the human mind as upon society. I shall endeavour to make you understand him in these three respects, by presenting to you, in tables, the facts which relate to him, and from which the history of civilization may be deduced.

I commence with the wars of Charlemagne, of which the following are the most essential facts:

Table of the principal Expeditions of Charlemagne.

	Date.	*Enemies.*	*Observations.*
1	769	Against the Aquitani.	He goes to the Dordogne.
2	772	,, the Saxons.	He goes beyond the Weser.
3	773	,, the Lombards.	He goes to Pavia and Verona.
4	774	Idem.	He takes Pavia, and goes to Rome.
5	774	,, the Saxons.	
6	775	Idem.	
7	776	,, the Lombards.	He goes to Treviso.
8	776	,, the Saxons.	He goes to the sources of the Lippe.

	Date.	*Enemies.*	*Observations.*
9	778	Against the Arabs of Spain.	He goes to Saragossa.
10	778	„ the Saxons.	
11	779	Idem.	He goes into the country of Osnabruck.
12	780	Idem.	He goes to the Elbe.
13	782	Idem.	He goes to the conflux of the Weser and the Aller.
14	783	Idem.	He goes to the Elbe.
15	784	Idem.	He goes to the Sale and the Elbe.
16	785	Idem.	He goes to the Elbe.
17	785	„ the Thuringians.	He does not go in person.
18	786	„ the Bretons.	Idem.
19	787	„ the Lombards of Benevento.	He goes to Capua.
20	787	„ the Bavarians.	He goes to Augsburg.
21	788	„ the Huns, or Avares.	He goes to Ratisbon.
22	789	„ the Slavonian Wiltzes.	He goes between the Lower Elbe and the Oder.
23	791	„ the Huns or Avares.	He goes to the conflux of the Danube and the Raab.
24	794	„ the Saxons.	
25	795	Idem.	
26	796	Idem.	
27	796	„ the Huns or Avares.	Under the orders of his son Louis, king of Italy.
28	796	„ the Arabs.	Under the orders of his son Pepin, king of Aquitaine.
29	797	„ the Saxons.	He goes to the Lower Weser and the Lower Elbe.
30	797	„ the Arabs.	By his son Louis.
31	798	„ the Saxons.	He goes beyond the Elbe.
32	801	„ the Lombards of Benevento.	By his son Pepin to Chieti.
33	801	„ the Arabs of Spain.	By his son Louis to Barcelona.
34	802	„ the Saxons.	By his sons beyond the Elbe.
35	804	Idem.	He goes between the Elbe and the Oder. He transplants tribes of Saxons into Gaul and Italy.
36	805	„ the Slavonians of Bohemia.	By his eldest son, Charles.
37	806	Idem.	By his son Charles.
38	806	„ the Saracens of Corsica.	By his son Pepin.
39	806	„ the Arabs of Spain.	By his son Louis.
40	807	„ the Saracens of Corsica.	By Generals.
41	807	„ the Arabs of Spain.	Idem.

	Date.	Enemies.	Observations.
42	808	Against the Danes and Normans.	
43	809	„ the Greeks.	In Dalmatia, by his son Pepin.
44	809	„ the Arabs of Spain.	
45	810	„ the Greeks.	Idem.
46	810	„ the Saracens in Corsica and Sardinia.	
47	810	„ the Danes.	He goes in person to the conflux of the Weser and the Aller.
48	811	Idem.	
49	811	„ the Avares.	
50	811	„ the Bretons.	
51	812	„ the Slavonian Wiltzes.	He goes between the Elbe and the Oder
52	812	„ the Saracens in Corsica.	
53	813	Idem.	

That is, in all, fifty-three expeditions, namely:

1 against the Aquitani.
18 — Saxons.
5 — Lombards.
7 — Arabs of Spain.
1 — Thuringians.
4 — Avares.
2 — Bretons.
1 — Bavarians.
4 — Slavonians beyond the Elbe.
5 — Saracens in Italy.
3 — Danes.
2 — Greeks.

Without counting numerous other small expeditions, of which no distinct and positive monuments are left.

From this table alone it is clearly seen that these wars did not the least resemble those of the first race; they are not the dissensions of tribe against tribe, of chief against chief; expeditions undertaken with a view of establishment or pillage; they are systematic and political wars, inspired by an intention of government, commanded by a certain necessity.

What is this system? What is the meaning of these expeditions?

You have seen various German nations—Goths, Burgundians, Franks, Lombards, &c.—established upon the Roman territory. Of all these tribes or confederations, the Franks were the strongest, and occupied the central position in the new establishment. They were not united among themselves by any political tie; they incessantly make war. Still, in some respects, and whether they knew it or not, their situation was similar, and their interests common.

You have seen that, from the beginning of the eighth century, these new masters of western Europe, the Roman-Germans, were pressed on the north-east, along the Rhine and the Danube, by new German, Slavonian, and other tribes proceeding to the same territory; on the south by the Arabs spread on all the coasts of the Mediterranean; and that thus a two-fold movement of invasion menaced with an approaching fall the states but just rising out of the ruins of the Roman empire.

Now let us see what was the work of Charlemagne in this situation: he rallied against this two-fold invasion, against the new assailants who crowded upon the various frontiers of the empire, all the recently-established inhabitants of his territory, ancient or modern, Romans or Germans. Follow the course of his wars. He begins by definitively subduing, on one side, the Roman population, who still attempted to free themselves from the barbarian yoke, as the Aquitani in the south of Gaul; on the other, the later-arrived German population, the establishment of whom was not consummated, as the Lombards in Italy, &c. He snatched them from the various impulsions which animated them, united them all under the domination of the Franks, and turned them against the two-fold invasion, which, on the north-east and south, menaced all alike. Seek a dominant fact which shall be common to all the wars of Charlemagne; reduce them all to their simple expression: you will see that their true meaning is, that they are the struggle of the inhabitants of the ancient empire, conquering or conquered, Romans or Germans, against the new invaders.

They are therefore essentially defensive wars, brought about by a triple interest of territory, race, and religion. It was the interest of territory which especially broke out against the nations of the right bank of the Rhine, for the Saxons and Danes were Germans, like the Franks and the Lombards:

there were Frankish tribes among them, and some learned men think that many pretended Saxons may have been only Franks, established in Germany. There was, therefore, no diversity of race; it was merely in defence of the territory that war took place. The interest of territory and the interest of race were united against the wandering nations beyond the Elbe, or on the banks of the Danube, against the Slavonians and the Avares. Against the Arabs who inundated the south of Gaul, there was interest of territory, of race, and of religion, all together. Thus did the various causes of war variously combine; but, whatever might be the combinations, it was always the German Christians and Romans, who defended their nationality, their territory, and their religion against nations of another origin or creed, who sought a soil to conquer. All their wars have this character—all are derived from this triple necessity.

Charlemagne had in no way reduced this necessity into a general idea or theory; but he understood and faced it: great men rarely do otherwise. He faced it by conquest; defensive war took the offensive form; he carried the struggle into the territory of nations who wished to invade his own; he laboured to reduce the foreign races, to extirpate the hostile creeds. Hence arose his mode of government, and the foundation of his empire: offensive war and conquest required this vast and formidable unity.

At the death of Charlemagne, the conquests cease, the unity disappears, the empire is dismembered and falls to pieces; but is it true that nothing remained, that the warlike exploits of Charlemagne were absolutely sterile, that he achieved nothing, founded nothing? There is but one way to resolve this question; it is, to ask ourselves if, after Charlemagne, the countries which he had governed found themselves in the same situation as before; if the two-fold invasions which, on the north and on the south, menaced their territory, their religion, and their race, recommenced after being thus suspended; if the Saxons, Slavonians, Avares, Arabs, still kept the possessors of the Roman soil in perpetual disturbance and anxiety. Evidently it was not so; true, the empire of Charlemagne was broken up, but into separate states, which arose as so many barriers at all points where there was still danger. Up to the time of Charlemagne, the frontiers of Germany, Spain, and

Italy were in continual fluctuation; no constituted public force had attained a permanent shape; he was compelled to be constantly transporting himself from one end to the other of his dominions, in order to oppose to the invaders the moveable and temporary force of his armies. After him, the scene is changed; real political barriers, states more or less organized, but real and durable, arose; the kingdoms of Lorraine, of Germany, Italy, the two Burgundies, Navarre, date from that time; and in spite of the vicissitudes of their destiny, they subsist, and suffice to oppose effectual resistance to the invading movement. Accordingly, that movement ceases, or continues only in the form of maritime expeditions, most desolating at the points which they reach, but which cannot be made with great masses of men, nor produce great results.

Although, therefore, the vast domination of Charlemagne disappeared with him, it is not true that he founded nothing; he founded all the states which sprung from the dismemberment of his empire. His conquests entered into new combinations, but his wars attained their end: the foundation of the work subsisted, although its form was changed. It is thus that the action of great men is in general exercised. Charlemagne, as an administrator and legislator, appears to us under the same aspect.

His government is more difficult to sum up than his wars. Much has been said of the order which he introduced into his states, of the great system of administration which he attempted to found. I indeed believe he attempted it, but he was very far from succeeding in his attempt: despite the unity, despite the activity of his thought and of his power, the disorder around him was immense and invincible; he repressed it for a moment on one point, but the evil reigned wherever his terrible will did not come; and when it had passed, recommenced the moment it was at a distance. We must not allow ourselves to be deceived by words. Open, in the present day, the *Almanac Royal;* you may read the system of the administration of France: all the powers, all the functionaries, from the last step to the most elevated, are there indicated and classed according to their relations. And there is no illusion — the things pass, in fact, as they are written; the book is a faithful image of the reality. It would be easy to construct a similar administrative chart for the empire of Charlemagne, to place in it dukes, counts, vicars, centeniers, sheriffs (*scabini*), and to distribute them, hierarchically organized, over the territory. But this would only be a vast fiction: more frequently, in most places, these magistrates were powerless, or themselves disorderly. The effort of Charlemagne to institute them and to make them act was continual, but as incessantly failed. Now that you are warned, and on your guard against the systematic appearances of this government, I may sketch the features—you will not conclude too much from them.

The local government must be distinguished from the central government.

In the provinces, the power of the emperor was exercised by two classes of agents—one local and permanent, the other sent to a distance, and transitory.

In the first class were included—first, dukes, counts, vicars of courts, centeniers, *scabini*, all resident magistrates nominated by the emperor himself or by his delegates, and charged in his name to raise forces, to render justice, to maintain order, to receive tribute; second, beneficiaries, or vassals of the king, who held from him, sometimes hereditarily, more frequently for life, still more frequently without any stipulation or rule, estates or domains, throughout the extent of which they exercised, mostly in their own name, partly in that of the emperor, a certain jurisdiction, and almost all the rights of sovereignty. Nothing was well determined or very clear with regard to the situation of beneficiaries, and the nature of their power: they were at once delegates and independent, proprietors and usufructuaries; and one or other of these characters prevailed in them alternately. But however that may be, they were, without doubt, in habitual relation with Charlemagne, who made use of them everywhere in order to convey and execute his will.

Above the local and resident agents, magistrates, or beneficiaries, were the *missi dominici*, temporary ambassadors, charged, in the name of the emperor, to inspect the provinces, authorized to penetrate into conceded domains, as well as into free lands, invested with the right of reforming certain abuses, and called upon to render an account of everything to their master. The *missi dominici* were for

Charlemagne, at least in the provinces, the principal medium of order and administration.

With regard to the central government, putting aside for a moment the action of Charlemagne himself, and of his personal counsellors, that is to say, with regard to the true government, the national assemblies, to judge from appearances, and if we may believe almost all modern historians, occupied an important place. They were, indeed, frequent and active under his reign. The following is a table of those which are expressly mentioned by the chroniclers of the time:

	Date.	Place.
1	770	Worms.
2	771	Valenciennes.
3	772	Worms.
4	773	Geneva.
5	775	Duren.
6	776	Worms.
7	777	Paderborn
8	779	Duren.
9	780	Ehresburg.
10	781	Worms.
11	782	At the source of the Lippe.
12	785	Paderborn.
13	786	Worms.
14	787	Ibid.
15	788	Ingelheim.
16	789	Aix-la-Chapelle.
17	790	Worms.
18	792	Ratisbon.
19	793	Ibid.
20	794	Frankfort.
21	795	Kuffenstein.
22	797	Aix-la-Chapelle.
23	799	Lippenheim.
24	800	Mayence.
25	803	Ibid.
26	804	At the source of the Lippe
27	805	Thionville.
28	806	Nimeguen.
29	807	Coblentz.
30	809	Aix-la-Chapelle.
31	810	Verden.
32	811	Ibid.
33	812	Boulogne.
34	812	Aix-la-Chapelle.
35	813	Ibid.

To know the number and periodical regularity of these great meetings, doubtless, is something; but what passed within their breast, and what was the character of their political intervention? this is an important point.

A very curious monument remains upon this subject; one of the cotemporaries and counsellors of Charlemagne, his cousin-german, Adalhard, abbot of Corbie, wrote a treatise entitled *De Ordine Palatii*, destined to make known the internal government of Charlemagne, and more especially the general assemblies. This treatise is lost; but, towards the end of the ninth[1] century, Hincmar, archbishop of Reims, reproduced it almost complete in a letter of instruction written at the request of some great men of the kingdom, who had had recourse to his counsel for the government of Carloman, one of the sons of Louis-le-Begue. Certainly, no document merits more confidence. Here we read—

"It was the custom of the time to hold two councils every year . . . . in both of them, and in order that they might not appear convoked without motive,[2] they submitted to the examination and deliberation of the nobles . . . . and, in virtue of the orders of the king, the articles of the law named *capitula*, which the king himself had drawn up by the inspiration of God, or the necessity of which had been made manifest to him in the interval between the meetings."

The proposition of the capitularies, or, to speak in modern phraseology, the initiative, therefore, emanated from the emperor. It must have been so: the initiative is naturally exercised by him who wishes to regulate, to reform, and it was Charlemagne who had conceived this design. Still I do not doubt any the more that the members of assembly might have made any propositions which appeared desirable to them; the constitutional mistrusts and artifices of our times were, certainly, unknown to Charlemagne, too sure of his power to fear the liberty of deliberations, and who saw in

[1] In 882.

[2] *Ne quasi sine causa convocari viderentur.* This phrase indicates that most of the members of those assemblies looked upon the obligation of repairing thither as a burden; that they had but little desire to share in the legislative power, and that Charlemagne wished to legitimate their convocation by giving them something to do, far rather than that he subjected himself to the necessity of obtaining their adhesion

these assemblies a means of government far more than a barrier to his authority. I resume the text of Hincmar:

"After having received these communications, they deliberated upon them one, two, three, or even a greater number of days, according to the importance of the matter. Messengers from the palace, going and coming, received their questions and reported the answers; and no stranger approached the place of their meeting, until the result of their deliberations had been put before the eyes of the great prince, who then, with the wisdom which he received from God, adopted a resolution to which all obeyed."

The definitive resolution always depended therefore on Charlemagne alone; the assembly only gave him information and counsel. Hincmar continues:

"The things, accordingly, went on thus for one, two, or more capitularies, until, with the aid of God, all the necessities of the times were provided for.

"While his affairs were treated of in this manner out of the presence of the king, the prince himself, amidst the multitude which generally came to the general councils, was occupied in receiving presents, saluting the most considerable men, discoursing with those whom he rarely saw, testifying an affectionate interest in the more aged, making merry with the younger; and doing these and similar things alike for ecclesiastics as for seculars. Still, if those who deliberated upon matters submitted to their examination manifested a desire therefor, the king repaired to them, remained with them as long as they wished; and they reported to him with complete familiarity what they thought of everything, and what were the friendly discussions which had been raised among them. I must not forget to mention that, if the weather was fine, all this passed in the open air; if not, in distinct buildings, where those who had to deliberate upon the propositions of the king were separated from the multitude of persons who came to the assembly, and then the less considerable men could not enter. The places destined for the meeting of the lords were divided into two parts, so that the bishops, abbots, and priests, high in dignity, could be united without any mixture of the laity. In the same way the counts and other principal men of the state were separated, in the morning, from the rest of the multitude, until, the king present or absent, they were all met together; and the abovementioned lords, the priests on their side, and the laity on theirs, repaired to the hall assigned to them, and where they had honourably prepared their seats. When the lay and ecclesiastical lords were thus separated from the multitude, it remained in their option to sit together, or separately, according to the affairs of which they had to treat—ecclesiastical, secular, or both. So if they wished any one to come, whether to demand nourishment, or to ask a question, and again to dismiss him, after having received what they wanted, they could do so. Thus passed the examination of the affairs which the king proposed to their deliberations.

"The second occupation of the king was to demand of every one what he had to report to him, or to teach him concerning the part of the kingdom whence he came. Not only was this permitted to every one, but they were strictly recommended to inquire, in the intervals of the assemblies, what passed within or without the kingdom; and that they should seek to know this from foreigners as well as countrymen, enemies as well as friends, sometimes by employing envoys, and without taking much care as to how the intelligence was acquired. The king wished to know whether, in any part, any corner of the kingdom, the people murmured and were agitated, and what was the cause of its agitation, and whether it had come to a disturbance upon which it was necessary that a general council should be employed, and other similar details. He also wished to know if any of the subdued nations thought of revolting; if any of those who had revolted seemed disposed to submit; if those who were still independent menaced the kingdom with any attack, &c. Upon all these matters, wherever a disturbance or a danger became manifest, he principally asked what were its motives or occasion." [1]

I shall have no need of long reflections in order to make you recognise the true character of these assemblies; it is clearly shown in the picture which has been traced by Hincmar. Charlemagne alone fills it; he is the centre and soul of all things; it is he who says that the assemblies shall meet, that they shall deliberate; it is he who occupies himself about the state of the country, who proposes and sanctions laws; in him reside the will and impulsion; it is from him that all emanated, in order to return to him. There was

[1] Hincm. *App. de Ordine Palatii*, vol. ii. p. 201—215.

there no great national liberty, no true public activity; but there was a vast means of government.[1]

This means was by no means sterile. Independently of the force which Charlemagne drew from it for current affairs, you have seen that it was there that the *capitularies* were generally drawn up and decreed. In our next lecture I shall occupy you more especially with this celebrated legislation. I desire at present merely to give you an idea of it.

While waiting for more details, here is a table of the capitularies of Charlemagne, with their number, their extent, and their object:

Table of the Capitularies of Charlemagne.

	Date.	Place.	Articles.	Civil Legislation.	Religious Legislation.
1	769	. . . .	18	1	17
2	779	Duren	23	15	8
3	788	Ratisbon.	8	7	1
4	789	Aix-la-Chapelle . .	80	19	61
5	Id.	. . . .	16	...	16
6	Id.	. . . .	23	14	9
7	Id.	. . . .	34	20	14
8	793	. . . .	17	15	2
9	794	Frankfort	54	18	36
10	797	Aix-la-Chapelle . .	11	11	
11	799	. . . .	5	...	5
12	Before 800	. . . .	70		
13	800	. . . .	5	5	
14	801	. . . .	8	8	
15	Id.	. . . .	1	...	1
16	Id.	. . . .	22	...	22
17	802	. . . .	41	27	14
18	Id.	. . . .	23	18	5
19	803	Aix-la-Chapelle . .	7	...	7
20	Id.	Idem.	1[2]	...	1
21	Id.	Idem.	1	...	1
22	Id.	. . . .	11	11	
23	Id.	. . . .	29	27	2
24	Id.	. . . .	12	12	

[1] See my *Essais sur l'Histoire de France*, p. 315—344.

[2] Domestic and Rural Legislation. This is the capitulary *De Villis.*

Table of the Capitularies of Charlemagne—continued.

	Date.	Place.	Articles.	Civil Legislation.	Religious Legislation.
25	803	. . . .	22	20	2
26	Id	. . . .	8	8	
27	Id.	. . . .	13	11	2
28	Id.	Worms	3	...	3
29	804	Seltz	8	...	8
	Id.	Idem	12	...	12
30	805	Thionville	16	...	16
31	Id.	Idem	25	23	2
32	Id.	Idem	16	14	2
33	Id.	Idem	1	...	1
34	806	. . . .	20[1]		
35	Id.	. . . .	8	7	1
36	Id.	. . . .	6	6	
37	Id.	. . . .	8	7	1
38	Id.	Nimeguen	19	18	1
39	Id.	. . . .	23	...	23
40	807	. . . .	7	7	
41	808	. . . .	30	28	2
42	809	Aix-la-Chapelle . .	37	36	1
43	Id.	Idem	16	15	1
44	810	Idem	18	14	4
45	Id.	. . . .	16	13	3
46	Id.	. . . .	5	5	
47	811	. . . .	12	7	5
48	Id.	. . . .	13	...	13
49	Id.	. . . .	9	9	
50	812	. . . .	9	9	
51	Id.	Boulogne	11	11	
52	Id.	. . . .	13	13	
53	813	. . . .	28	9	19
54	Id.	Aix-la-Chapelle . .	20	19	1
55	Id.	Idem	46	46	
56	Date uncertain.	. . . .	59	26	33
57	Id.	. . . .	14	...	14
58	Id.	. . . .	13	...	13
59	Id.	. . . .	13	12	1
60	Id.	. . . .	9	...	9
		Total . .	1126	621	415

[1] Political Legislation. Division of States.

Surely such a table gives evidence of great legislative activity; and yet it says nothing of the revision which Charlemagne caused to be made of the ancient barbarous laws, especially the Salic and Lombard laws. In fact, activity, an universal, indefatigable activity, the desire to think of everything, of introducing everywhere at once animation and rule, is the true, the great characteristic of the government of Charlemagne—the character which he himself, and he alone, impressed on his times. I am about to place before you a new proof of this. This was not a time (allow me the expression) for much writing and scribbling; of a surety, the multitude of official acts drawn up under a reign would not prove any great things in favour of the genius of a monarch in the present day. It was different with those of Charlemagne. There can be no doubt but that the large number of public acts of all kinds which have come down to us from it, is an incontestable testimony of the immense and contagious activity, which was, perhaps, his greatest superiority and his surest power. The following is a table and classification of those acts—of those, at least, which have been printed in learned collections. Many others are doubtless lost; others, perhaps, remain in manuscript, and unknown.

Table of the Principal Diplomas, Documents, Letters, and various Acts emanated from Charlemagne or other great men, Lay or Ecclesiastical, under his Reign.

Date.	Number.	Of Charlemagne.	Of Others.	Acts of Civil Government.	Acts of Religious Government.	Donations and Concessions to Churches.	Donations and Concessions to Monasteries.	Letters.	Various Acts.
769	23	6	17	...	3	4	14	2	
770	16	3	13	...	...	5	8	3	
771	9	1	8	...	2	...	7		
772	33	7	26	1	2	12	16	1	1
773	18	2	16	...	2	9	6	...	1
774	21	7	14	2	1	3	7	6	2
775	19	8	11	...	2	6	7	4	
776	20	4	16	...	1	3	10	4	2
777	18	4	14	1	...	5	11	1	
778	16	5	11	...	...	6	8	2	

Table of the Principal Diplomas, &c.—continued.

Date.	Number.	Of Charlemagne.	Of others.	Acts of Civil Government.	Acts of Religious Government.	Donations and Concessions to Churches.	Donations and Concessions to Monasteries.	Letters.	Various Acts.
779	19	6	13	1	2	8	8		
780	10	3	7	2	...	2	5	1	
781	12	6	6	2	2	1	5	...	2
782	21	6	15	...	...	6	4	9	2
783	11	1	10	...	...	...	4	5	2
784	6	1	5	...	...	2	2	...	2
785	15	...	15	...	1	...	7	6	1
786	15	4	11	2	4	...	6	2	1
787	26	10	16	2	6	3	5	9	1
788	27	3	24	3	2	2	12	7	1
789	16	7	9	3	2	1	6	1	3
790	22	11	11	2	3	2	14	1	
791	20	1	19	...	1	4	12	2	1
792	7	1	6	...	1	1	5		
793	28	3	25	4	1	1	7	12	3
794	20	8	12	...	7	4	4	3	2
795	14	3	11	...	1	3	5	3	2
796	32	4	28	...	2	3	15	11	1
797	15	8	7	4	1	3	5	2	
798	21	2	19	1	2	2	10	5	1
799	27	3	24	1	4	4	6	6	6
800	23	6	17	3	...	3	12	1	4
801	23	5	18	1	3	4	13	2	
802	30	13	17	4	8	3	9	5	1
803	26	15	11	7	3	7	7	...	2
804	38	5	33	2	2	9	24	...	1
805	15	6	9	2	2	4	7		
806	25	8	17	5	2	3	13	1	1
807	33	3	30	1	1	11	10	2	8
808	29	3	26	1	..	17	7	3	1
809	15	5	10	3	2	5	1	4	
810	19	6	13	3	...	1	6	8	1
811	27	5	22	4	1	7	14	...	1
812	19	7	12	5	...	1	10	...	3
813	42	13	29	4	6	6	26		
814	10	...	...	...	...	7	1	...	2
Year uncertain.	194	19	175	4	2	129	27	21	11
	745	257	878	80	87	322	428	155	73

NOTE—The elements of this table are taken from the "History of the Germanic Empire" of Count Bünau, vol. ii. p. 872—930; Leipzick, 1732.

Such are the facts—at least, such are the frames in which they are placed. Now, I here reproduce the question which I raised just now concerning the wars of Charlemagne. Is it true, is it possible, that of this government, so active and vigorous, nothing remained—that all disappeared with Charlemagne—that he founded nothing for the internal consolidation of society?

What fell with Charlemagne, what rested upon him alone, and could not survive him, was the central government. After continuing some time under Louis le Debonnaire and Charles le Chauve, but with less and less energy and influence, the general assemblies, the *missi dominici*, the whole machinery of the central and sovereign administration, disappeared. Not so the local government, the dukes, counts, vicaires, centeniers, beneficiaries, vassals, who held authority in their several neighbourhoods under the rule of Charlemagne. Before his time, the disorder had been as great in each locality as in the commonwealth generally; landed properties, magistracies were incessantly changing hands; no local positions or influences possessed any steadiness or permanence. During the forty-six years of his government, these influences had time to become rooted in the same soil, in the same families; they had acquired stability, the first condition of the progress which was destined to render them independent and hereditary, and make them the elements of the feudal regime. Nothing, certainly, less resembles feudalism than the sovereign unity which Charlemagne aspired to establish; yet he is the true founder of feudal society! it was he who, by arresting the external invasions, and repressing, to a certain extent, the intestine disorders, gave to local situations, fortunes, influences, sufficient time to take real possession of the country. After him, his general government perished like his conquests; his unity of authority like his extended empire; but as the empire was broken into separate states, which acquired a vigorous and durable life, so the central sovereignty of Charlemagne resolved itself into a multitude of local sovereignties, to which a portion of the strength of his government had been imparted, and which had acquired under its shelter the conditions requisite for reality and durability; so that in this second point of view, in his civil as well as military capacity, if we look beyond first appearances, he accomplished and founded much.

I might show him to you accomplishing and leaving analogous results in the church; there also he arrested dissolution, until his time always increasing: there also he gave society time to rest, to acquire some consistency and to enter upon new paths. But time presses: I have yet at present to speak of the influence of Charlemagne in the intellectual order, and of the place occupied by his reign in the history of the human mind; scarcely shall I be able to point out the principal features.

It is more difficult here than anywhere else to sum up facts and present them in a table. The acts of Charlemagne in favour of moral civilization form no entirety, manifest no systematic form; they are isolated, scattered acts; at times the foundation of certain schools, at times measures taken for the improvement of ecclesiastical offices, and the progress of the knowledge which depends on them; also general recommendations for the instruction of priests and laymen; but most frequently an eager protection of distinguished men, and a particular care to surround himself with them. There is nothing systematic, nothing that can be estimated by the mere juxtaposition of figures and words. I wish, however, with a touch, and without entering into details, to place before you some facts which may give you an idea of that kind of action of Charlemagne, of which more is said than is known. It appears to me that a table of the celebrated men who were born and died under his reign—that is, of the celebrated men whom he employed, and those whom he made—would tend efficiently towards this end; this body of names and of works may be taken as a decided proof, and even as a correct estimate of the influence of Charlemagne over minds

Table of the celebrated men born or who died under the reign of Charlemagne.

Names.	Country.	Birth.	Death.	Condition.	Works.
1. Alcuin (he took the name of [illegible], and the surname of Flac[illegible])	England (co. York.)	About 735	804	Chief of the school of the palace of Charlemagne, abbot of Saint Martin of Tours.	More than 30 works—viz., 1. [illegible] on the Scriptures; 2. Polemical, [illegible], and literary writings; 3. [illegible] writings, letters, and [illegible].
2. Angilbert, (surnamed Homer.)	.. ..	.. ..	814	[illegible] minister of Pepin, king of Italy, duke of maritime France, from the Scheldt to the Seine, secretary of Charlemagne, abbot of Saint Riquieri.	1. [illegible]; 2. An account of what he had done for his monastery while abbot.
3. Leidrade.	Norica.	.. ..	About 816	Archbishop of Lyons, one of the principal *[illegible] dominici* of [illegible].	1. Letters; 2. Theological writings.
4. Smaragde.	.. ...	.. ..	About 820	Abbot of Saint [illegible], employed by Charlemagne in many negotiations.	1. [illegible] of morality; 2. [illegible] on the New Testament; 3. A large [illegible].
5. Saint Benedict d'Aniane.	Septimanie.	751	821	Abbot of Aniane and of Inde; reformer of monasteries.	1. Code of [illegible] rules; 2. [illegible] of [illegible]; 3. Theological writings
6. Theodulph.	Italy (Goth.)	.. ..	821	Bishop of Orleans; *missus* of Charlemagne.	1. [illegible] concerning schools; 2. Theological writings; 3. Poems.

Table of the celebrated men born, or who died under the reign of Charlemagne—continued.

Names.	Country.	Birth.	Death.	Condition.	Works.
7. Adalhard.	Austrasia.	753	826	Counsellor of Pepin, king of Italy, and of Charlemagne; abbot of Corbie.	1. Statutes for the abbey of Corbie: 2. Letters; 3. A treatise *De Ordine Palatii*, reproduced by Hincmar.
8. Ansegise.	Burgundy.	. .	833	Overseer of the buildings of Charlemagne, employed in various missions; abbot of Fontenelle.	The first collection of the capitularies of Charlemagne, and of Louis le Debonnaire, in four books.
9. Wala (surnamed Arséne and Jérémiah.)	Austrasia.	. .	836	Counsellor of Louis le Debonnaire, and abbot of Corbie.	He tok a great part in the revolutions of the reign of Louis le Debonnaire.
10. Amalaire, surnamed Symphosius.	Austrasia.	. .	837	Chief of the school of the palace, and priest at Metz.	1. The rule of the canons; 2. A large treatise of ecclesiastical offices; 3. Letters.
11. Eginhard.	Austrasia.	. .	839	Secretary of Charlemagne, and abbot of Seliegenstadt.	1. The Life of Charlemagne; 2. Annals; 3. Letters.
12. Agobard.	Spain.	779	840	Archbishop of Lyons.	1. Theological writings, stamped with a reforming spirit; 2. Letters; 3. Some Poems

13 Thegan.	Austrasia.	... ...	About 846	Chorepiscopus of Tréves.	The Life of Louis le Debonnaire.
14. Raban Maur.	Austrasia.	776	856	Abbot of Fulda, archbishop of Mayence.	Fifty-one theological, moral, philosophical, philological, chronological works, letters, &c.
15. Walfrid (Strabo.)	Germany.	807	849	Abbot of Reichenau, near Constance.	1. A Commentary on the whole Bible; 2. A Life of Saint Gall; 3. Many [illegible]ther theological [illegible]ks; 4. Poems; among others a descriptive poem, *Hortulus*.
16. Nithard.	Austrasia.	Before 790	About 859	Duke of Maritime France, monk at Saint Riquieri.	History of the dissensions of the sons of Louis le Debonnaire.
17. Florus.	Burgundy.	. .	About 860	Deacon and priest at Lyons.	Many [illegible]ological writings, having for the most part a [illegible] c[illegible]er. The principal is a refutation of John Erigena. Poems; among others a L[illegible]t on the dismem[illegible]nt of the empire, after [illegible]is le Debonnaire.
18. Saint Prudentius, (family name, Galindo.)	Spain.	. .	861	Bishop of Troyes.	Theological writings; among others, up[illegible] p[illegible]i[illegible]on, and against John Erigena.

Table of the celebrated men born, or who died under the reign of Charlemagne—continued.

Names.	Country.	Birth.	Death.	Condition.	Works.
19. Servat-Loup.	Diocese of Sens.	... ...	862	Abbot of Ferrieres, in Gatinois.	1. Theological writings; among others, upon predestination: 2. Letters; 3. A history of the emperors, (lost.)
20. Radbirt (Paschase.)	Diocese of Soissons.	.. .	865	Abbot of Corbie.	o [illegible]al writings; among [illegible]s, his [illegible]k on the sacrament of the [illegible]r, or the body and blood of Jesus Christ.
21. Ratramne.	... ...	... ...	868	Monk at Corbie.	T [illegible]gical writings; [illegible] [illegible]g [illegible]rs on transubstantiation and predestination.
22. Gottschalk.	Saxony.	... ...	869	Monk at Obais.	His writings in support of predestination
23. John, called Scot, or Erigena.	Ireland.	... ...	Between 872 and 879	... .	[illegible]y philosophical works; among others, 1. Of Divine Predestin[illegible]; 2. Of the division of nature.

Surely such a table is sufficient to prove that at this epoch, and under the star of Charlemagne, intellectual activity was great. Recal to your minds the times from whence we set out; call to mind that from the sixth to the eighth century, we had great difficulty in finding any names, any works; that sermons and legends were almost the only monuments which we encountered. Here, on the contrary, you see reappear, and that almost at once, philosophical, historical, philological, and critical writings; you find yourself in the presence of study and science—that is to say, of pure and disinterested intellectual activity, of the real movement of mind. I shall soon discuss with you, in a more detailed manner, the men and the works I have just named, and you will see that they truly commence a new epoch, and merit the most serious attention.

Now, I ask, have we a right to say that Charlemagne has founded nothing, that nothing remains of his works? I have merely given you a glimpse, as in a transient panorama, of their principal results; and yet their permanence is thus shown therein as clearly as their grandeur. It is evident that, by his wars, by his government, and by his action upon minds, Charlemagne has left the most profound traces; that if many of the things he did perished with him, many others have survived him; that western Europe, in a word, left his hands entirely different from what it was when he received it.

What is the general, dominant character of this change, of the crisis over which Charlemagne presided?

Take in at one view, that history of the civilization in France under the Merovingian kings which we have just studied; it is the history of a constant, universal decline. In individual man as in society, in the religious society as in civil society, everywhere we have seen anarchy and weakness extending itself more and more; we have seen everything become enervated and dissolved, both institutions and ideas, what remained of the Roman world and what the Germans had introduced. Up to the eighth century, nothing of what had formerly been could continue to exist; nothing which seemed to dawn could succeed in fixing itself.

Dating from Charlemagne, the face of things changes; decay is arrested, progress recommences. Yet for a long period the disorder will be enormous, the progress partial, but little visible, or often suspended. This matters not: we shall no more encounter those long ages of disorganization, of always increasing intellectual sterility: through a thousand sufferings, a thousand interruptions, we shall see power and life revive in man and in society. Charlemagne marks the limit at which the dissolution of the ancient Roman and barbarian world is consummated, and where really begins the formation of modern Europe, of the new world. It was under his reign, and as it were under his hand, that the shock took place by which European society, turning right round, left the paths of destruction to enter those of creation.

If you would know truly what perished with him, and what, independently of the changes of form and appearance, is the portion of his works which did not survive him, if I mistake not, it is this:

In opening this course, the first fact which presented itself to your eyes, the first spectacle at which we were present, was that of the old Roman empire struggling with the barbarians. The latter triumphed; they destroyed the Empire. In combating it, they respected it; no sooner had they destroyed it, than they aspired to reproduce it. All the great barbaric chiefs, Ataulphe, Theodoric, Euric, Clovis, showed themselves full of the desire of succeeding to the Roman emperors, of adapting their tribes to the frame of that society which they had conquered. None of them succeeded therein; none of them contrived to resuscitate the name and forms of the empire, even for a moment; they were overcome by that torrent of invasion, by that general course of dissolution which carried all things before it; barbarism, incessantly extended and renewed itself, but the Roman empire was still present to all imaginations; it was between barbarism and Roman civilization that, in all minds of any compass at all, the question lay.

It was still in this position when Charlemagne appeared; he also, he especially nursed the hope of resolving it, as all the great barbarians who went before him had wished to resolve it, —that is to say, by reconstituting the empire. What Diocletian, Constantine, Julian, had attempted to maintain with the old wrecks of the Roman legions, that is, the struggle against the invasion, Charlemagne undertook to do with Franks, Goths, and Lombards: he occupied the same territory;

he proposed to himself the same design. Without, and almost always on the same frontiers, he maintained the same struggle; within, he restored its name to the empire, he attempted to bring back the unity of its administration; he placed the imperial crown upon his head. Strange contrast! He dwelt in Germany; in war, in national assemblies, in the interior of his family, he acted as a German; his personal nature, his language, his manners, his external form, his way of living, were German; and not only were they German, but he did not desire to change them. "He always wore," says Eginhard, "the habit of his fathers, the habit of the Franks. . . . Foreign costumes, however rich, he scorned, and suffered no one to be clothed with them. Twice only during the stay which he made at Rome, first at the request of pope Adrian, and then at the solicitation of Leo, the successor of that pontiff, he consented to wear the long tunic, the chlamys, and the Roman sandal." He was, in fact, completely German, with the exception of the ambition of his thought; it was towards the Roman empire, towards Roman civilization that it tended; that was what he desired to establish, with barbarians as his instruments.

This was, in him, the portion of egoism and illusion; and in this it was that he failed. The Roman empire, and its unity, were invincibly repugnant to the new distribution of the population, the new relations. the new moral condition of mankind; Roman civilization could only enter as a transformed element into the new world which was preparing. This idea, this aspiration of Charlemagne, was not a public idea, nor a public want; all that he did for its accomplishment perished with him. Yet even of this vain endeavour something remained. The name of the western empire, revived by him, and the rights which were thought to be attached to the title of emperor, resumed their place among the elements of history, and were for several centuries longer an object of ambition, an influencing principle of events. Even, therefore, in the purely egoistical and ephemeral portion of his operations, it cannot be said that the ideas of Charlemagne were absolutely sterile, nor totally devoid of duration.

Here we must stop; the way is long, and I have proceeded so quickly that I have hardly had time to describe the principal events of the journey. It is difficult, it is fatiguing to have to compress within a few pages what filled the life of a great man. I have as yet only been able to give you a general idea of the reign of Charlemagne, and of his placc in the history of our civilization. I shall probably employ many of the following lectures in making you acquainted with him under certain special relations; though I shall be very far from doing justice to the subject.

TWENTY-FIRST LECTURE.

Object of the lecture—Of capitularies in general—Review of the capitularies of the Carlovingian Frank kings—Of the two forms under which the capitularies have descended to us—Scattered capitularies—Collection of Angesise and of the deacon Benedict—Of the edition of the capitularies by Baluze—Erroneous idea generally entertained as to capitularies—They are not invariably laws—Great variety in these acts—Attempt at classification—Table of contents of the capitularies of Charlemagne: 1. Moral legislation—2. Political legislation—3. Penal legislation—4. Civil legislation—5. Religious legislation—6. Canonical legislation—7. Domestic legislation—8. Incidental legislation—True character of the capitularies.

I ANNOUNCED to you my intention of laying before you a summary of the reign of Charlemagne, and its results, reviewing his government and his influence upon intellectual development. In the first of these respects, the picture I have placed before you appears to me sufficiently complete; it presents, I think, a clear and precise idea of the part filled by the wars of Charlemagne in the history of civilization in the west; and, moreover, I could not enter more fully into the subject, without going through an absolute and continuous narration of events. As to the government of Charlemagne and its action upon mind, what I have said in the last lecture is altogether incomplete, and I may, without losing myself in details, enter more closely into this part of the subject. I will proceed to do so. The legislation of Charlemagne will now occupy our attention: that which he did in protecting intellectual development, with an account of the distinguished men who lived and laboured under his influence, will be the subject of the following lectures.

It is commonly supposed that the term *capitularies* applies only to the laws of Charlemagne; this is a mistake. The word *capitula*, "little chapters," equally applies to all the laws of the Frank kings. I have no remark to make at present respecting the capitularies, in themselves of very slight importance,[1] of the first race; of those of the second race, there have come down to us 152—namely,

5 capitularies of Pepin le Bref, commencing with the year 752, the period of his elevation to the title of king of the Franks.

65 of Charlemagne.
20 of Louis le Debonnaire.
52 of Charles le Chauve,
3 of Louis le Begue.
3 of Carloman.
1 of Eudes.
3 of Charles le Simple.

I reckon here only the acts of such Carlovingians as reigned in France; several descendants of Charlemagne, established in Germany and Italy, also left capitularies, but with these we have nothing to do.

The capitularies enumerated have come down to us in two different forms. We have them, first, in the shape of as many separate acts, scattered through various manuscripts, sometimes with, sometimes without date; and there exists, secondly, a collection of them made in the course of the ninth century, and divided into seven books. The four first of these were compiled by Angesise, abbot of Fontenelle, one of the councillors of Charlemagne, who died in 833. He collected and classified the *capitula* of that prince, and a portion of those of Louis le Debonnaire. The first book contains 162 *capitula* of Charlemagne, relative to ecclesiastical affairs.

The second, forty-eight *capitula* of Louis le Debonnaire, in the same class of subjects.

The third, ninety-one *capitula* of Charlemagne on temporal affairs.

The fourth, seventy-seven *capitula* of Louis le Debonnaire on temporal affairs.

[1] The table in the twentieth lecture mentions only sixty; but there were besides five private acts, which, upon reflection, I think ought to be inserted among the capitularies.

To these four books, which, immediately upon their publication, acquired such credit that Charles le Chauve, in his own capitularies, cites them as an official code, a deacon of Mayence, named Benedict, at the request of his archbishop, Otger, added, about the year 842, three new books, constituting the fifth, sixth, and seventh books of the collection, and which contain:

The fifth, 405 *capitula;* the sixth, 436 *capitula;* the seventh, 478 *capitula.* In all, 1697.

But, besides the capitularies which Angesise had omitted, and those which had been declared since the compilation of his collection, the three books of the deacon Benedict contain a number of acts with which the Carlovingian kings had nothing to do; for instance, fragments of the Roman law, extracted from the Theodosian code, from *Breviarium* of the Visigoths, from Justinian, Julian, &c. We even find there considerable fragments of the famous collection known by the name of *The false Decretals,* pretended canons, and other acts of the first popes—a collection at this time scarcely known, and which Benedict himself was one of the first to bring into vogue; so that many learned persons have assigned their fabrication to him.

Four supplements, added by anonymous compilers at later periods to the seven books already mentioned, extend the number of articles in this collection to 2100.

The capitularies have been published several times under both these forms. The best edition is unquestionably that of Baluze, in two vols. folio, Paris, 1677. It is not only the best as a matter of comparison, but it is excellent in itself. "Of all the sources of the law of the middle ages," says Savigny,[1] "I have found none more fully presented to us than the capitularies in Baluze's excellent edition." And, in fact, it is far more complete, and better edited, than those of Lindenbrog, Pithou, Herold, Du Tillet, &c. Baluze had collected a great number of manuscripts, and he published fragments and whole capitularies previously inedited. His work may fairly be described as a vast and good collection of texts; but there, in truth, its merit ends. The texts themselves have been subjected to no examination, to no critical

[1] ii. 91.

revision. Baluze has given them to us exactly as he found them, without troubling himself to inquire whether or no the copyists had confused them, or filled them with blunders. It would doubtless have been an entire misconception to have sought to introduce into the capitularies an order foreign to the ideas of the primitive legislator, to have classified them systematically, to have curtailed repetitions emanating from the legislator himself, and which are characteristic of his work. But there are, in the various manuscripts, a confusion and a want of accuracy which are manifestly attributable to the copyists alone; a multitude of words are changed, a multitude of articles wrongly placed; various readings of the same manuscript are set down as different *capitula.* I do not by any means propose to go through a list of the blunders of this description, or to discuss the question of their rectification. All I desire to point out to you is the general fact that they exist in abundance, and that Baluze's work, consequently, valuable in many respects, is still only to be regarded as the materials for a really correct and satisfactory edition of the capitularies—an edition, however, which it would require long and arduous and scientific labour to produce.

Let us first consider the capitularies themselves.

At the first glance, it is impossible not to be struck with the confusion which pervades this word: it is indiscriminately applied to all the acts inserted in Baluze's collection; and yet, in point of fact, the greater portion of those acts differ essentially from capitularies, properly so called. What would be the effect, if, some centuries hence, a compiler were to take all the acts of a government of our times, of the French administration for instance, in the last reign, and, throwing them promiscuously together in one heap, under one undistinguishing title, were to give the collection forth as the legislation, the code of the period? The result would manifestly be an utterly absurd and fallacious chaos; laws, ordinances, decrees, briefs of the crown, personal judgments, departmental circulars, would be mixed up together, haphazard, in utter confusion. This has been exactly the case with the capitularies. I will proceed to analyse the collection of Baluze, classifying according to their nature and objects the acts of all kinds which we meet with there. You will at once see how great is their diversity.

We find there under the general title of capitularies:

1. Ancient national laws revised; the Salic law, for example.[1]

2. Extracts from the ancient laws, Salic, Lombard, Bavarian, &c.; extracts evidently made for a particular purpose, a particular place, a particular moment of time, for a special necessity, the nature of which there is no longer anything to indicate to us.[2]

3. Additions to the ancient laws, to the Salic law, for instance,[3] to the law of the Lombards,[4] to that of the Bavarians,[5] &c. These additions seem to have been made in a peculiar form, and with peculiar solemnities; that to the Salic law is preceded, in an ancient manuscript, by these words:

"These are articles which the lord Charles the Great, emperor, caused to be written in his councils, and ordered to be inserted among the other laws."

The legislature, indeed, appears to have required the adhesion of the people to these additions more expressly than to the other parts of the law; thus, in 803, the year in which the additions to the Salic law were made, we find Charlemagne issuing the following direction to his *missi:*

"Let the people be interrogated touching the articles which have recently been added to the law; and after they have all consented to them, let them affix to the said articles their signature in confirmation."[6]

4. Extracts from the acts of the councils, and from the entire body of canonical legislation; the great capitulary enacted at Aix-la-Chapelle, in 789,[7] and a host of articles in the other capitularies are nothing more than such extracts.

5. New laws, of which some were passed by the general assemblies of the people, with the concurrence of the great laymen and great ecclesiastics together, or of the ecclesiastics alone, or of the laymen alone; while the rest appear to

[1] See Baluze, i. col. 281, *sub anno* 798.

[2] Extract from the law of the Lombards, cap. a. 801; Baluze, i. col. 349; from the law of the Ripuarians, cap. a. 803: *id.* col. 395.

[3] Cap. a. 803. *id.* i. 387. [4] Cap. a. 801; *id.* i. 345.

[5] Cap. l. 788; *id.* i. 207.

[6] Cap. a. 803, § 19. i. 394. [7] *Id.* i. 209.

have been the work of the emperor himself, to have been what we now call ordinances. The distinctions between these two classes of laws are not, on a close examination, very precisely marked, but they are perceptible.

6. Instructions given by Charlemagne to his *missi*, on their departure for the provinces, and designed sometimes to regulate the personal conduct of the *missi*, sometimes to guide them in their inquiries, very often as simple communications to the people in particular districts, which the *missi* were to convey. Acts of this description, very foreign, in part, at all events, to our notions of legislation, are of frequent occurrence in the capitularies;[1] articles of a totally different nature are sometimes mixed up with them.

7. Answers given by Charlemagne to questions addressed to him by the counts or bishops, or *missi dominici*, on the occasion of difficulties occurring to them in the course of their administration,[2] and wherein he solves these difficulties, which have reference sometimes to matters which we should call legislative, sometimes to points in executive administration, sometimes to private interests.

8. Questions which Charlemagne proposed to put to the bishops or counts at the next general assembly, and which he had noted down on paper that they might not, meantime, pass out of his recollection. These questions, which are among the most curious documents in the whole collection, bear in general a character of censure and reprimand of those to whom they are to be addressed. I will read a few of them to give you a practical idea of the liberality and good sense which characterized the mind of Charlemagne. My translation is literal:

"How does it happen that, both on the frontiers and with the army, wherever there is any great measure to be taken for the defence of the country, one man will not give aid to another?"[3]

"What is the meaning of these continual suits by which every one appears seeking to wrest from his neighbour that which he possesses?"[4]

[1] Cap. a. 789; Baluze, i. 243; a. 802, i. 351; a. 802, i. 375; a. 803, i. 391; a. 806, i. 449.

[2] 6° Cap. a. 803: *id.* i. 401.

[3] 1 Cap. a. 811, § 1. Baluze, i. 477. [4] *Ib.* § 2.

"To ascertain on what occasions and in what places the ecclesiastics and the laity seek, in the manner stated, to impede each other in the exercise of their respective functions. To inquire and discuss up to what point a bishop or an abbot is justified in interfering in secular affairs, and a count or other layman with ecclesiastical affairs. To interrogate them closely on the meaning of those words of the Apostle: 'No man that warreth for the law, entangleth himself with the affairs of this life.' Inquire to whom these words apply."[1]

"Desire the bishops and abbots to tell us truly what is the meaning of the phrase always in their mouths: 'Renounce the world;' and by what signs we may distinguish those who have renounced the world, from those who still adhere to the world: is it merely that the former do not bear arms, or marry publicly?[2]

"To ask them further, whether he is to be considered as having renounced the world, whom we see labouring, day by day, by all sorts of means, to augment his possessions; now making use, for this purpose, of menaces of eternal flames, now of promises of eternal beatitude; in the name of God or of some saint despoiling simple-minded men of their property, to the infinite prejudice of the lawful heirs, who are, in very many cases, from the misery in which they are thus involved, driven by their necessities to robbing and to all sorts of disorders and crimes?"[3]

Clearly such questions as these do not at all resemble articles of law.

9. Some of the *capitula* are not even questions, but mere notes, memoranda of particular things which Charlemagne from time to time conceived the idea of doing, and which he had put down on paper, lest he should forget them. We read, for instance, at the end of the *capitula*, or instructions to the *missi dominici*, in 803, these two articles:

"Recollect to order that they who send us horses as presents, inscribe their names on each horse. And so with dresses that may be sent us from abbeys.

"Recollect to order that whenever vicarious persons are found doing evil, or suffering it to be done, they be expelled

[1] Cap. II. a. 811, § 4. [2] *Ib.* [3] *Ib.* § 5.

from their post, and replaced by others of a better character."[1]

I could cite many *capitula* of this description.

10. Other articles contain judgments and briefs of the crown and the courts, collected evidently for the purpose of jurisprudence; thus we read in a capitulary of the year 803:

"A man had suborned a slave, induced him to kill his two young masters, the one aged nine, the other eleven; and then killed the slave himself, and threw him into a ditch. Adjudged, that the said man pay a *wehrgeld* for the boy of nine years old, a double *wehrgeld* for the boy of eleven, and a treble *wehrgeld* for the slave; and undergo, moreover, our ban."[2]

This is obviously a judicial decree in a particular case, inserted among the capitularies as a precedent in future cases of a similar description.

11. We meet in like manner with acts of pure domestic financial administration, relative to the management of Charlemagne's own domains, and which enter into the most minute details on this subject. The famous capitulary *De Villis* is an example of this, and there are several other articles of the same character scattered through the collection.[3]

12. Besides the so various acts I have enumerated, the capitularies contain purely political acts, occasional documents, nominations, recommendations, decisions upon personal and passing differences. I look for instance at the capitulary rendered in 794 by the assembly of Frankfort,[4] and among the 54 articles of which it is composed, I find:

(Art. 1.) Letters of pardon granted to Tassilon, duke of the Bavarians, who had revolted against Charlemagne.

(Art. 6.) Arrangements for the settlement of a dispute between the bishop of Vienne, and the archbishop of Arles and others, respecting the limits of the sees of the Tarentaise, Embrun, and Aix. It sets forth that letters from the pope on these matters were read, and that it was determined to consult anew with his holiness.

(Art. 7). As to the justification offered, and the pardon received, by bishop Pierre.

[1] Baluze, i. 395.

[2] Cap. a. 803, § 12; Baluze, i. 398.

[3] Baluze, i. 331.

[4] *Id.*, *ib* 26

(Art. 8). As to the deposition of the pretended bishop Gerbod.

(Art. 53). Charlemagne procures the assent of the assembly of bishops to the pope's licence, authorizing him to retain about his person bishop Hildebold as his minister of ecclesiastical affairs.

(Art. 54). He recommends Alcuin to the good wishes and prayers of the assembly.

There is obviously nothing legislative here.

Thus, at first glance, on the most simple examination of the nature of these various acts, and without entering into any close inspection of their contents, you see how wholly erroneous is the general, the common idea entertained of these capitularies: they constitute anything but a code; they comprise anything but laws. Let us now take a closer view; let us penetrate into the interior of the collection, and examine the articles of which each capitulary is composed; we shall here find the same diversity, the same confusion; we shall here in like manner find how inadequate has been the attention hitherto paid to this study, and how fallacious are most of the results which have been deduced from it.

I have analyzed the sixty-five capitularies of Charlemagne, classifying under eight heads, according to the nature of the provisions, the articles which they comprise. These eight heads are:

1. Moral legislation.
2. Political legislation.
3. Penal legislation.
4. Civil legislation.
5. Religious legislation.
6. Canonical legislation.
7. Domestic legislation.
3. Occasional legislation.

I will first lay this classification before you, and then make some observations upon each head.

Analytical Table of the Capitularies of Charlemagne.

Date.	Articles.	Moral Legislation.	Political Legislation.	Penal Legislation.	Civil Legislation.	Religious Legislation.	Canonical Legislation.	Domestic Legislation.	Occasional Legislation.
769	18	1	3	...	...	3	11		
779	23	...	9	5	2	2	5		
788	1	1							
Id.	1	1							
Id.	8	...	...	4	3	...	1		
789	80	16	5		3	11	45		
Id.	16	...	...	...	...	2	14		
Id.	23	6	9	...	2	1	5		
Id.	34	3	5	18	3	3	5		
793	17	1	6	...	7	...	4		
794	54	...	6	...	4	6	27	...	8
797	10	...	5	5					
799	5	...	...	...	...	...	5		
800	1	..	1						
Id.	70	...	...	...	...	...	...	70	
Id.	5	...	5						
801	8	...	...	5	3				
Id.	1	...	1						
Id.	22	...	2	...	...	...	20		
802	41	9	10	5	...	1	16		
Id.	23	2	13	3	...	...	5		
803	7	...	...	...	...	...	7		
Id.	1	...	...	...	...	...	1		
Id.	1	...	...	...	...	...	1		
Id.	11	...	2	4	5				
Id.	34	...	20	2	8	...	2	...	2
Id.	12	...	3	3	6				
Id.	14	1	6	2	3	1	1		
Id.	8	...	4	...	4				
Id.	13	1	5	1	3	1	2		
Id.	3	...	...	...	...	1	2		
804	20	2	3	...	...	...	15		
Id.	1	1							
805	16	4	...	...	...	...	12		
Id.	25	4	13	3	4	...	1		
Id.	24								
Id.	16								
Id.	1								
806	20	1							
Id.	8	...	...	4	3	...	1		
Id.	6	...	3	1	2				
Id.	8	...	4	1	2				
Id.	19	1	10	...	...	...	2		

Analytical Table of the Capitularies of Charlemagne—continued.

Date.	Articles.	Moral Legislation.	Political Legislation.	Penal Legislation.	Civil Legislation.	Religious Legislation.	Canonical Legislation.	Domestic Legislation.	Occasional Legislation.
806	23	...	...	...	...	7	16		
807	7	...	7	...	...	...	...	...	2
808	30	...	11	10	6	...	1		
809	37	3	15	6	12	...	1		
Id.	16								
810	18	6	8	4					
Id.	16	57	4	3	2	2			
Id.	5	...	5						
811	12	...	4	...	...	...	8		
Id.	13	...	...	...	...	9	4		
Id.	9	...	9						
812	9	...	9						
Id.	11	1	9	...	1				
Id.	13		10	...	3				
813	28	3	2	...	...	...	20		
Id.	20	...	6	2	7	3	2	3	
Id.	46	...	...	39	7				
year uncer-tain.	59	5	13	...	3	9	29		
Id.	14	...	...	...	...	14			
Id.	13	...	...	...	...	9	4		
Id.	13	2	8	...	2	...	1		
Id.	9	...	...	...	...	9	9		
	1150	80	273	130	110	85	309	73	12

Let us now examine a little more closely the contents of this table; the examination will be a very rapid one, but sufficient, I hope, to give you an idea of the true character of the government of Charlemagne, and of the monuments which exist of it in this collection.

I. *Moral Legislation.* — I have classed under this title those articles which are neither commanding nor prohibitory; which, in truth, are not laws at all, but mere advice, suggestions, or moral precepts. For instance:

" Avarice consists in desiring the possessions of others, and in not giving to others a share of that which we ourselves possess: according to the apostle, it is the root of all evil, and it should, therefore, be carefully avoided.[1]

"Those who apply themselves to amass property by all sorts of ways make dishonourable gains.[2]

"All men should practise hospitality.[3]

"Keep clear of theft, of unlawful marriages, of bearing false witness, as we have often exhorted you, and as is exhorted by the Word of God."[4]

The legislator goes even further than this; he seems to thinks himself responsible for the conduct of each individual, and apologises for not being able to fulfil this responsibility to the extent he desires:

"It is necessary," he says, "that every man should seek, to the best of his strength and ability, to serve God and walk in the way of his precepts; for the lord emperor cannot watch over each person individually, with the necessary care, or keep each man in proper discipline."[5]

Is not this pure morality? Such provisions are foreign to the laws of rising societies and to those of perfected societies: open the Salic law and our codes, you will find nothing of the kind there; they in no way address themselves to human liberty in order to give it counsel; they contain merely formally prohibitive or imperative texts. But in the passage from primitive barbarism to civilization, legislation takes another character; morality is introduced into it, and becomes, for a certain period, matter of law. Skilful legislators, founders or reformers of societies, comprehend the empire which the idea of duty exercises over men; the instinct of genius warns them, that without its support, without the free concurrence of the human will, society can neither be maintained nor developed in peace; and they apply themselves to introduce this idea into the souls of men in every kind of way, and they make legislation a kind of preaching, a medium of instruction. Consult the history of every nation, the Hebrews, the Greeks, &c., you will everywhere recognise this fact; you will everywhere find, between the epoch of the primitive laws—which are purely penal, pro-

[1] Cap. a. 806, § 15; Baluze, i. 454. [2] *Ib.* § 16.
[3] Cap. a. 794, § 33; *ib.* 268. [4] *Ib.* 789, § 56; *ib.* 236.
[5] Cap. a. 802 § 3; *ib.* 364.

hibitive, destined to repress the abuses of force—and the epoch of scientific laws, which have confidence in morality, in the reason of individuals, and leave all which is purely moral in the domain of liberty,—between these two epochs, I say, you will always find one in which morality is the object of legislation, in which legislation formally writes and teaches it. Gaulo-Frankish society was at this point when Charlemagne governed it; and this was one of the causes of his close alliance with the church, the only power then capable of teaching and preaching morality.

I accordingly comprehend, under the name of *moral legislation*, all relating to the intellectual development of men; for example, all the provisions of Charlemagne concerning schools, what books to distribute, the reformation of ecclesiastical offices, &c.

II. *Political Legislation.*—This is one of the most considerable portions of the capitularies; it comprehends two hundred and ninety-three articles. Under this head I place—

1. The laws and measures of Charlemagne of all kinds, to ensure the execution of his orders throughout the extent of his states; for example, all provisions relative to the nomination or conduct of his various agents, counts, dukes, vicars, centeniers, &c.; they are numerous, and are constantly repeated.

2. The articles whose object is the administration of justice, the sitting of local courts, the forms to be followed there, the military service, &c.

3. The police legislations, which are very various, and sometimes go into the most minute details; the provinces, the army, the church, merchants, beggars, public places, the interior of the imperial palace, alternately form the object of them. We there meet, for example, with an attempt to fix the price of goods, a veritable attempt at a *maximum* price.

"The most pious lord our king has decreed, with the consent of the holy synod, that no man, ecclesiastic or layman, shall, whether in times of plenty or in times of scarcity, sell provisions dearer than at the price recently fixed by the bushel, namely: a bushel of oats, one denier; of barley, two deniers; of rye, three deniers; of wheat, four deniers. If he desires to sell it in loaves, he shall give twelve loaves of wheat, each of two pounds, for one denier, fifteen loaves of rye, twenty of barley, or twenty-five of oats, of the same weight, also for one denier, &c." [1]

The suppression of mendicity and a poor rate, likewise appear there.

"With regard to vagrant mendicants, we order, that each of our subjects support his own poor, whether on his fees or within his house, and not allow them to go elsewhere to beg. If such beggars are found, and they do no work with their hands, let no one think of giving them anything." [2]

The provisions relative to the internal regulation of the palace give a singular idea of the disorders and violences which were committed there:

"We will and order that none of those who serve in our palace, take upon himself to receive any man who seeks a refuge there, and comes there to conceal himself, on account of robbery, homicide, adultery, or any other crime; that if any free man violate our prohibition, and conceal a malefactor in our palace, he shall be forced to carry him on his shoulders to the public place, and there he shall be attached to the same post as the malefactor. . . . Whoever shall find men fighting in our palace, and cannot or will not put an end to the conflict, he shall pay a share of the damage which they have caused, &c." [3]

The capitularies contain numberless analogous provisions; internal police was evidently of great importance in the government of Charlemagne.

4. I class, also, under the head of political legislation all which concerns the distinction between the lay and the ecclesiastical powers and their relations. Charlemagne made great use of the ecclesiastics—they were, in truth, his principal means of government; but he wished to make use of them, and not for them to make use of him: the capitularies attest his vigilance in governing the clergy himself, and keeping it under his power. You have seen, by some of the questions which he proposed addressing to the bishops in the general assemblies, to what a degree he was impressed with this idea.

[1] Cap. a. 794, § 2, vol. i. col. 263

[2] Cap. a. 806, § 10; vol. i. col. 454.

[3] Cap. a. 800, § 3 and 4; vol. i. col. 343.

5. It seems to me necessary, lastly, to refer to political legislation, the provisions relative to the administration of the sees conceded by Charlemagne, and his relations with the beneficiaries. This was certainly one of the leading features of his government, and one of those to which he most assiduously called the attention of the *missi.*

I need not point out to you that the general character of all this political legislation, in its various parts, is a continual, indefatigable effort towards order and unity.

III. *Penal legislation.* This in general is scarcely more than the renewal, to a certain extent, of the ancient Salic, Ripuarian, Lombard, barbarian, &c. laws. Punishment, repression of crimes, of abuse of force, is, as you have seen, almost the only object, the essential character of those laws. There was, therefore, less to do in this respect than in any other. The new provisions which Charlemagne here and there added, were in general for the object of mitigating the ancient legislation, especially the rigour of the punishments inflicted upon slaves. In some cases, however, he aggravated the punishment, instead of mitigating it—when, for example, punishments were a political instrument in his hands. Thus the punishment of death, so rare in the barbaric laws, recurs in almost every article of a capitulary of the year 789, intended to restrain and convert the Saxons; almost every violation of order, every relapse into idolatrous practices, is punished with death.[1] With these exceptions, the penal legislation of Charlemagne has but little originality or interest.

VI. *The civil legislation* offers but little more. Here, also, the ancient laws, the ancient customs, remained in vigour; Charlemagne had very little to alter in them. He, however, carefully occupied himself, doubtless at the instigation of the ecclesiastics, with the condition of persons, especially with the relations between men and women. It is evident that at this epoch these relations were prodigiously irregular—that a man took and quitted a woman without scruple, and almost without formality. The result was a great disorder in individual morality, and in the state of families. The civil law was thence strongly interested in the reformation of manners, and Charlemagne understood

[1] Bal., vol. i. col. 251.

this. Hence the great number of provisions inserted in his capitularies concerning the conditions of marriages, the degrees of parentage, the duties of husbands towards wives, the duties of widows, &c. The greater portion of these provisions are borrowed from canonical legislation; but it must not be supposed that their motive and origin was purely religious—the interest of civil life, the necessity of fixing and of regulating the family, had evidently a large share therein.

V. *Religious legislation.* By religious legislation, I mean provisions relative, not to the clergy, to ecclesiastics alone, but to the faithful, to the Christian people, and to its relations with the priests. It is thus distinguished from canonical legislation, which concerns only the ecclesiastical society, the relations of the clergy among themselves. The following are some provisions of religious legislation:

"Let care be taken not to venerate the names of false martyrs, or the memory of doubtful saints."[1]

"Let no one suppose that God is only to be prayed to in three languages,[2] for God is adored in all languages, and man is heard if he ask just things."[3]

"Let preaching always be performed in such a manner that the common people may be able to understand it thoroughly."[4]

These provisions have generally a character of good sense, even of liberty of mind, which one would scarcely expect to find in them.

VI. *The canonical legislation* is that which occupies the greatest place in the capitularies, and naturally so; the bishops (as I have already observed) were the principal counsellors of Charlemagne; they sat in the greatest numbers in the general assemblies; their affairs were always attended to first. Accordingly, these assemblies were generally looked upon as councils, and their laws were transmitted to the collection of canons. They are almost all drawn up in the interest of the power of the bishops. You will remember that at the accession of the Carlovingian race, the episcopal aristocracy, strong as it had been, was in complete dissolution.

[1] Cap. a. 789, § 41; a. 794, § 40; vol. i. col. 228, 269.
[2] Probably in Latin, Greek, and the German language.
[3] Cap. a. 794, § 50: vol. i. col. 270.
[4] Cap. a. 813, § 14; vol. i. col. 505.

Charlemagne reconstituted it; under his hand, it regained the regularity, the entirety it had lost, and became, for many centuries, the dominant ruler of the church. At a later period, I shall speak of this more minutely.

VII. The *domestic legislation* contains only what relates to the administration of the private property, the farms of Charlemagne; an entire capitulary, entitled *de Villis*, is a collection of various instructions, addressed at different periods of his reign to the persons employed on his domains, and which have been erroneously assembled under the form of a single capitulary. M. Anton has given, in his *History of German Agriculture in the Middle Ages*,[1] a very curious commentary upon this capitulary, and upon all the domestic details which we find there.

VIII. The *occasional legislation* is inconsiderable in amount; only twelve articles belong to this head, and I have just cited some of them.

Here closes my examination, far too brief in itself, doubtless, but still more detailed, more definite, I think, than any previously made, of the legislation of Charlemagne and its object. I say *legislation*, because I wish to avail myself of words in common use; otherwise, it is quite clear that in all we have gone through there is nothing of what we understand by a code, and that Charlemagne, in his capitularies, did anything but legislate. Capitularies are, properly speaking, the whole acts of his government, public acts of all kinds by which he manifested his authority. It is evident that the collection which has come down to us is far from containing all those acts, and that a large number of them are wanting. There are whole years for which we have no capitularies; in those which we do possess we find provisions which relate to acts which are missing. The collection of Baluze is a mere collection of fragments; they are mutilated wrecks, not of the legislation only, but of the whole government of Charlemagne. This is the point of view under which any one wishing to make an accurate study of the capitularies should view them in order to comprehend and explain them.

In our next lecture, we shall begin to occupy ourselves with the state of mind at the same epoch, and with the influence of Charlemagne over intellectual development.

[1] In German, vol. i. p. 177—243.

TWENTY-SECOND LECTURE.

Of intellectual decay in Frankish Gaul, from the fifth to the eighth century —Of its causes—It ceases under the reign of Charlemagne—Difficulty of describing the state of the human mind at this epoch—Alcuin is its most complete and faithful representative—Life of Alcuin—His labours for the restoration of manuscripts—For the restoration of schools—His teaching in the school of the palace—His relations with Charlemagne—His conduct as abbot of Saint Martin of Tours—His works; 1. Theological; 2. Philosophical and literary; 3. Historical; 4. Poetical—His general character.

I HAVE said, and I consider it established, that, from the fifth to the eighth century, decay in Frankish Gaul was constant and general; that it was the essential character of the time, and only stopped under the reign of Charlemagne.

If this character was anywhere more visible, more signal than elsewhere, it was in the intellectual order, in the history of the human mind at this epoch. Recal to mind through what vicissitudes we have seen it pass. At the end of the fourth century, two literatures, two philosophies, marched, as it were, side by side, profane literature and sacred literature, pagan philosophy and Christian theology. It is true, profane literature and pagan philosophy were dying; but they still breathed. We saw them soon disappear; sacred literature and Christian theology alone remained. We have continued on our way; Christian theology and sacred literature themselves have disappeared; we no longer meet with anything but sermons, legends, monuments of an entirely practical activity, devoted to the wants of actual life, foreign to the research and contemplation of the true and beautiful. This is the state into which the human mind had fallen in the seventh and during the first half of the eighth century.

This decay has been generally attributed to the tyranny of the church, to the triumph of the principle of authority and faith over the principle of liberty and reason. Quite modern writers, men of impartiality and learning—Tennemann, for example, in his *History of Philosophy*[1] — have adopted this explanation. The absolute authority of the church, and the doctrine of pure and simple faith, opposed to that of rational inquiry, have, doubtless, powerfully contributed to weaken the human mind; but it was at a later period that their influence was exercised. At the epoch which occupies us, this cause, I think, had as yet acted but feebly. Recal to mind the picture I placed before you of the state of the Christian church at the fifth century;[2] liberty then was great. Now, from the fifth to the eighth century, the church was not constituted with sufficient regularity or strength to exercise tyranny; none of the means of government by which, at a later period, she dominated over mind were then within her hands; the rising papacy as yet possessed only a power of influence and counsel; episcopacy, although it was the dominant system of the ecclesiastical society, was weak and disordered; councils became rare; no authority was firm and general; if there had been any true energy of mind, doubtless it would easily have forced itself into light. At a later period, from the 11th to the 14th century, the church was strong; her power was regularly organized; the principle of implicit submission to her decision reigned in the minds of men; and yet intellectual activity was far greater. There was then a real danger in struggling against the church, and yet men struggled: they resisted her pretensions, they even assailed her title. The seventh century made no attempt at attack or resistance; the ecclesiastical power and freedom of thought had not even occasion to commence a struggle.

It is not, then, to this cause that the intellectual apathy and sterility of this epoch are to be attributed. The fall of the empire, its disorders and miseries, the dissolution of social relations and ties, the occupations and sufferings of personal interests, the impossibility of permanent labour, of

[1] In German, vol. viii. p. 1—8.
[2] See vol. i., the third and fourth lectures.

tranquil leisure, such were the true causes of the moral, as well as of the political decay, and of the darkness which enveloped the human mind.

Whatever may be the cause of it, the fact is undeniable. If we considered in its entirety the history of the human mind in modern Europe, from the fifth century up to our own days, we should find, I think, that the seventh century is the lowest point to which it has descended, the nadir of its course, so to speak. With the end of the eighth century began its movement of progress.

It is rather difficult to characterize this movement with exactness, and to sum up in a few characteristic words the intellectual state of Frankish-Gaul under Charlemagne. No one simple idea dominates in it. The works which then occupied mind formed no whole, attached themselves to no principle. They are partial, isolated works; the activity is sufficiently great, but manifests itself by no great results; all attempt to systematise this time under a moral point of view—to reduce it to any general and striking fact, would infallibly misrepresent it.

Another method appears to me more suited to make it known and understood. We find in this period a man with a mind doubtless more active and extensive than any around him, except that of Charlemagne; superior in instruction and intellectual activity to any of his contemporaries, without elevating himself much above them by the originality of his knowledge of ideas; in a word, a faithful representative of the intellectual progress of his epoch, which he outstripped in all things, but without ever separating himself from it. This man is Alcuin. It is necessary, as a general rule, to give way only with extreme reserve to the temptation to take a particular man as the image, the representative of an epoch. Such comparisons are more ingenious than solid. On the one hand, a society, however declining and sterile it may be, is almost always, intellectually speaking, greater and richer than an individual. It comprehends a body of ideas, of knowledge of facts, and of moral wants, which are not reproduced within the narrow space of an individual existence. On the other hand, a distinguished man, even when originality is not his pre-eminent characteristic, always differs greatly from the mass of his contemporaries: he is himself, and not a nation; so that, under a twofold relation, the representation is incorrect, and the image fallacious. Care should be taken, in this particular case which occupies us, not to depend too much upon it, though it is, perhaps, here more faithful than in any other instance. Alcuin is, perhaps, one of the men who best represent their epoch; still we must make many reservations. And, at the same time that I place him before you as the expression of the state of the human mind at the end of the eighth century, I should wish to be sure that you will reduce this comparison to its true value.

Alcuin was not a Frenchman. It will be sufficient to cast a glance at the last table in the previous lecture, to see that Charlemagne took great care to attract distinguished foreigners into his states, and that among those who helped to second intellectual development in Frankish Gaul, many came from abroad. Charlemagne even did more. We see, at the seventeenth century, that Louis XIV., not content with protecting letters in his kingdom, extended his encouragement and favour to them throughout Europe. Colbert wrote to learned Germans, Dutch, Alsatians, to announce to them, on the part of the king, presents and pensions, which went sometimes as high as three thousand livres. Analogous facts are met with under Charlemagne; he not only strove to attract distinguished men into his states, but he protected and encouraged them wherever he discovered them. More than one Anglo-Saxon abbey shared his liberality; and learned men who, after following him into Gaul, wished to return to their country, in no way became strangers to him. Peter of Pisa and Paul Warnefried, who remained but a short time in Gaul, experienced this. Alcuin fixed himself there permanently. He was born in England, at York, about 735. The intellectual state of Ireland and England was then superior to that of the continent; letters and schools prospered there more than anywhere else. It is rather difficult to assign any precise causes for this fact; the principal of them, I think, is the following:—Christianity was carried into Ireland by Greek missionaries, and into England by Latin missionaries. In Ireland, during the first ages which followed its introduction, no invasion of barbarians came to stop its progress, to disperse the monasteries and schools, to stifle the intellectual movement which it had set on foot. In England, when the missionaries of Gregory the Great arrived, the barbaric invasion was consummated, the Saxons well established; there also, therefore, Christianity had not to undergo, at least not at this epoch, or until the great incursion of the Danes, any social disorder; its studies and its various works were not violently interrupted. I placed before you, in the beginning of this course,[1] the view of the intellectual state of Gaul in the fourth, and at the commencement of the fifth century; neither schools nor literary men were wanting to it; and if the Visigoths, the Burgundians, the Franks, had not brought chaos and ruin into it, the human mind, although weakened, had not fallen into the state in which we find it at the seventh century. This is the advantage which England possessed at that epoch; society here had not been ravaged or broken up by recent, continual invasions. The establishments for study and science which Christianity had formed there, were still erect, and quietly pursued their labours.

Whether this cause is or is not sufficient to explain it, the fact is incontestable. The schools of England, and particularly that of York, were superior to those of the continent. That of York possessed a rich library, where many of the works of pagan antiquity were found; among others, those of Aristotle, which it is a mistake to say were first introduced to the knowledge of modern Europe by the Arabians, and the Arabians only; for from the fifth to the tenth century, there is no epoch in which we do not find them mentioned in some library, in which they were not known and studied by some men of letters. Alcuin himself informs us of the instruction which they gave in the school of the monastery of York. We read in his poem, entitled, *Pontiffs and Saints of the Church of York*:—

"The learned Ælbert gave drink to thirsty minds at the sources of various studies and sciences. To some he was eager to communicate the art and rules of grammar; for others he made flow the waves of rhetoric. He exercised these in the combats of jurisprudence, and those in the songs of Adonia. Some learned from him to sound the pipes of Castalia, and to strike with a lyric foot the summits of Parnassus

[1] Vol. i., lectures third and fourth.

To others he taught the harmony of heaven, the works of the sun and the moon, the five zones of the pole, the seven wandering stars, the laws of the course of the stars, their appearance and decline, the motions of the sea, the tremblings of the earth, the nature of men, of beasts, and birds, and the inhabitants of woods; he unveiled the various qualities and the combinations of numbers; he taught how to calculate with certainty the solemn return of Easter; and, above all, he explained the mysteries of the holy scriptures."[1]

Reduce this pompous description to simple terms: grammar, rhetoric, jurisprudence, poetry, astronomy, natural history, mathematics, chronology, and the explanation of the holy scriptures, these surely form an extensive course of instruction, more extensive than was found at this epoch in any school in Gaul or Spain. He who taught these, this Ælbert whom Alcuin celebrates, became archbishop of York, and Alcuin succeeded him in his functions.

About this time, before 766, he had already made one, or even two journeys to the continent. The occasion and date of these journeys are very difficult to determine. I will not occupy you with these details of minute and complicated criticism. Some learned men have thought that at that time—at Pavia, perhaps—Alcuin saw Charlemagne. If the fact be true, it is to no purpose, for we know absolutely nothing of their first connexion. But, in 780, on the death of archbishop Ælbert, and the accession of his successor, Eanbald, Alcuin received from him the mission to proceed to Rome for the purpose of obtaining from the pope and bringing to him the *pallium*. In returning from Rome, he came to Parma, where he found Charlemagne. It is not known whether this was the first time of their seeing each other; but, at all events, the emperor at once pressed him to take up his abode in France. After some hesitation, Alcuin accepted the invitation, subject to the permission of his bishop, and of his own sovereign. The permission was obtained, and in 782 we find him established in the court of Charlemagne, who at once gave him three abbeys, those of Ferrieres in Gatinois, of St. Loup at Troyes, and of St. Josse in the county of Ponthieu.

[1] *Pontiffs and Saints of the Church of York*, v. 1431—1447; *Alcuini Opera*, vol. ii. p. 256, ed. Frohben, 1777.

From this time forth, Alcuin was the confidant, the councillor, the intellectual prime minister, so to speak, of Charlemagne. Let us endeavour to form somewhat of a clear and complete idea of his labours.

In doing so, we must observe a distinction between his practical activity and his scientific activity, between the immediate results of his personal influence, and those of his writings.

In the practical point of view, as intellectual prime minister of Charlemagne, Alcuin did, more especially, three things —1. He corrected and restored the manuscripts of ancient literature; 2. He revived public schools and public studies; 3. He himself taught.

1. The historians mention only in passing, and without attaching any importance to it, a fact which really played an important part in the revival of intellectual activity at this period; I mean the revision and correction of ancient manuscripts, both sacred and profane. From the sixth to the eighth century, these had gone through the hands of copyists so ignorant that the texts had become altogether unrecognisable; infinite passages had been mutilated and misplaced; the leaves were in the utmost disorder; all orthographical and grammatical correctness had disappeared; to read and understand the works thus injured, required absolute science, and of science there was less and less every day. To remedy this evil, to restore ancient manuscripts to their proper reading and order, to correct their orthography and their grammar, was one of the first tasks to which Alcuin applied himself; a task which continued to occupy him throughout the remainder of his life, which he constantly recommended to his pupils, and in the fulfilment of which he was supported by Charlemagne's authority. We find among the capitularies an ordinance in these terms:—

"Charles, by the aid of God, king of the Francs and Lombards, and prince of the Romans, to the high ministers of religion throughout our dominions: Having it near at heart that the state of the churches should more and more advance towards perfection, and being desirous of restoring by assiduous care the cultivation of letters, which have almost entirely disappeared from amongst us, in consequence of the neglect and indifference of our ancestors, we would excite by our own example all well-disposed persons to the study of the liberal arts. To this purpose, we have already, by God's constant help, accurately corrected the books of the Old and New Testament, corrupted by the ignorance of the copyists. We could not endure that in the divine services, amidst the sacred lessons, there should occur discordant solecisms, and we therefore conceived the design of reforming these lessons. We entrusted this work to our proved servant, the deacon Paul. We enjoined him diligently to go through the writings of the catholic fathers; to cull amidst those fertile meads the finest and most useful flowers, and to form of these one sweet and beneficial garland. Eager to obey our highness, he reperused the treatises and discoveries of the various catholic fathers, and selecting the best of these, has presented to us, in two volumes, a series of divine readings, freed from inaccuracies, adapted to each sacred day throughout the year. We have examined the texts of these volumes with our sagacity, and having found them worthy of our sanction and authority, we transmit them to you to be read in the churches of Christ under your care."[1]

Whilst he was thus, by the agency of others, collecting and correcting the texts destined for divine services, Alcuin himself laboured at a complete revisal of the sacred writings. He concluded it about the year 801, in the abbey of St. Martin de Tours, and sent it to Charlemagne. "I long meditated," he says, "what present I could offer you, not merely not unworthy of the glory of your imperial power, but which might form some addition to your wealth; for I could not consent that while others were laying at your feet rich gifts of every kind, my humble talents should remain so idle as not to prepare some offering to your beatitude. At length, by an inspiration of the Holy Ghost, I thought of a present at once suitable in me to offer, and calculated to be agreeable to your wisdom. What, indeed, could be more worthy of you than the divine books, which I herewith send to your Most Illustrious Authority, collected into one body, and carefully freed from all errors, to the utmost of my ability and pains. If the devotion of my heart could have devised anything better, I

[1] Constitution of Charlemagne, addressed to the bishops, in 788; Baluze, i. 203.

would have offered it to you with equal zeal for the increase of your glorious fortune."[1]

This present, it would seem, excited the emulation of Charlemagne himself, for we read in Thegau, a contemporary chronicler, that, " in the year which preceded Charlemagne's death, he carefully corrected, by the assistance of certain learned Greeks and Syrians, the four gospels of Jesus Christ."[2]

Such examples, and such orders, could not fail of effect, and the ardour for the reproduction of ancient manuscripts became general; as soon as an exact revision of any work had been completed by Alcuin or one of his disciples, copies of it were transmitted to the principal churches and abbeys, where fresh copies were made for diffusion amongst the lesser churches and abbeys. The art of copying became a source of fortune, of glory even; the monasteries in which the most correct and beautiful copies were executed, attained celebrity on this sole account; and in each monastery, the monks who most excelled in the art were, in like manner, honoured among their brethren. The abbey of Fontenelle, and two of its members, Ovon and Hardouin, were especially renowned in this respect. The fraternities at Reims and at Corbie sought to vie with the famed monks of Fontenelle; instead of the corrupt characters which had been in use for the past two centuries, the small Roman characters were resumed. The monastic libraries soon became very considerable in their extent; a great number of existing manuscripts date from this period; and though its zeal was more peculiarly directed to sacred literature, profane literature was not altogether neglected. Alcuin himself, it is stated, on more than one authority, revised and copied the plays of Terence.

II. At the same time that he was restoring manuscripts, and thus supplying study with sound materials, he laboured with ardour at the re-establishment of schools, which had then fallen everywhere into decay: here again an ordinance by Charlemagne shows us the measures, doubtless suggested by Alcuin himself, which were taken on this subject:

[1] Letters of Alcuin, i. 153, letter 103.

[2] *De la Vie et des Actes de Louis le Debonnaire*, in my *Collection des Memoires relatifs à l'Histoire de France*, III, 281.

"Charles, by the aid of God, &c., to Baugulf, abbot, and his brotherhood, health:

"We beg to inform your Devotion to God that, in concert with our councillors, we have deemed it beneficial that in the bishoprics and monasteries confided by the favour of Christ to our government, care should be taken, not only to live orderly and according to our holy religion, but moreover to instruct in the knowledge of letters, and according to the capacity of individuals, all such as are willing and able to learn, by God's help. For though of the two it is better to be good than to be learned, yet to have knowledge leads to the being good. In the various letters addressed to us from monasteries, announcing that the brethren continued to pray for us in their holy ceremonies, and in their private orisons, we have remarked that for the most part, while the sentiments were excellent, the language in which they were conveyed was generally rude and illiterate; that the fine thoughts and feelings which a pious devotion dictated within, an unskilful and an uneducated tongue mutilated in the delivery. This inspired us with an apprehension that the same want of ability which prevented men from writing properly, must also operate in keeping them from a due understanding of the holy scriptures. It is certain, at all events, that the allegories, emblems, and imagery of the holy writings, will be more readily comprehended in their true spiritual meanings, by those who are versed in general learning. We, therefore, would have you select from among your brethren such as may be deemed best fitted, for first acquiring themselves, and then communicating to others, a knowledge of letters; and let such proceed to their task with the least possible delay. As you value our favour, fail not to communicate copies of this communication to all the suffragan bishops, and all the monasteries around you."[1]

Many contemporary monuments give evidence that this *imperial circular*, as we should now call it, did not remain without effect; that it resulted in the re-establishment of systematic studies in the episcopal cities and in the great monasteries. From this epoch date the majority of the schools, which soon afterwards acquired such celebrity, and from which proceeded

[1] Baluze, 201.

the most distinguished men of the following century; for example, those of Ferrieres in Gatinois, of Fulda in the diocese of Mayence, of Reichenau in that of Constance, of Aniane in Languedoc, of Fontenelle or St. Vandrille, in Normandy; while most of the men who did honour to these establishments at the period in question had been disciples of Alcuin himself, who, amid all his avocations, was a public preacher and a public teacher of great distinction.

III. It was not, however, in a monastery, nor in any public institution, that he taught in the first instance: from 782 to 796, the period of his residence in the court of Charlemagne, Alcuin presided over a private school, called *The School of the Palace*, which accompanied Charlemagne wherever he went, and at which were regularly present all those who were with the emperor. Here, besides many others, Alcuin had for auditors:

1. Charles, son of Charlemagne.
2. Pepin do.
3. Louis do.
4. Adalhard. } Privy councillors of Charlemagne.
5. Angilbert. }
6. Flavius Damætas. }
7. Eginhard. }
8. Riculf, archbishop of Mayence.
9. Rigbod, archbishop of Trèves.
10. Gisla, sister of Charlemagne.
11. Gisla, daughter of Charlemagne.
12. Richtrude, a nun of Chelles.
13. Gundrade, sister of Adalhard; and Charlemagne himself, who took the most lively interest in the lessons given.

It is difficult to say what could have been the course of instruction pursued in this school; I am disposed to believe that to such auditors Alcuin addressed himself generally upon all sorts of topics as they occurred; that in the *Ecole du Palais*, in fact, it was conversation rather than teaching, especially so called, that went on; that movement given to mind, curiosity constantly excited and satisfied, was its chief merit. At such periods, in the days of its new birth, amid the joy of its first progress, the mind is neither regular nor fastidious; it troubles itself very slightly as to the beauty and real utility of its labours; that which it takes most especial delight in is the play of thought; it may be said to disport with itself rather than to study; it is more intent upon its own immediate activity than upon results; so that it is occupied with something which interests it, that is all it asks; let it but discover or produce something new, unexpected, and it is all delight. There has come down to us a singular specimen of the instruction given at this *Ecole du Palais:* it is a conversation entitled *Disputatio*, between Alcuin and Pepin, second son of Charlemagne, at that period a youth of fifteen or sixteen: I will lay before you a literal translation of the greater portion of this; you will judge for yourselves as to its claims to a learned character, and whether it is what we now understand by lessons.

Interlocutors: Pepin, Alcuin.

"Pepin. What is writing?

Alcuin. The keeper of history.

P. What is speaking?

A. The interpreter of the soul.

P. What is it gives birth to speaking?

A. The tongue.

P. What is the tongue?

A. The whip of the air.

P. What is the air?

A. The preserver of life.

P. What is life?

A. Happiness for the happy, misery for the miserable; the expectation of death.

P. What is death?

A. An inevitable event, a doubtful journey, a subject of tears for the living, the confirmation of wills, the robber of men.

P. What is man?

A. The slave of death, a passing traveller, a guest in his own abode.

P. How is man placed?

A. As a traveller exposed to the world.

P. Where is he placed?

A. Between six walls.

P. What are they?

A. That above, that below, that on the right, that on the left, that in front, that behind.

P. What is sleep?

A. The image of death.

P. What is the liberty of man?

A. Innocence.

P. What is the head?

A. The pinnacle of the body.

P. What is the body?

A. The abode of the soul.

(Next follow twenty-six questions relative to the various parts of the human body, which I suppress as wholly destitute of interest. Then Pepin goes on:)

P. What is heaven!

A. A moving sphere, an immense vault.

P. What is light?

A. The torch of all things.

P. What is the day?

A. A call to labour.

P. What is the sun?

A. The splendour of the universe, the beauty of the firmament, the grace of nature, the glory of the day, the distributor of the hours.

(I here again suppress five questions on the stars and elements.)

P. What is the earth?

A. The mother of all that grows, the nurse of all that exists, the granary of life, the gulf which swallows up all things.

P. What is the sea?

A. The highway of the daring, the limits of the earth, the hostelry of rivers, the source of rain.

(Now follow six wholly uninteresting questions as to material objects in nature. Then Pepin goes on:)

P. What is winter?

A. The exile of spring.

P. What is spring?

A. The painter of the earth.

P. What is summer?

A. The power which clothes the earth, and ripens fruits.

P. What is autumn?

A. The granary of the year

P. What is the year?

A. The chariot of the world.

(I here omit five astronomical questions.)

P. Master, I am afraid to go upon the sea

A. What leads you to the sea?

P. Curiosity.

A. If you are afraid, I will accompany you.

P. If I knew what a ship was, I would prepare one, wherein thou mightest accompany me.

A. A ship is a wandering house, an inn ready in all places, a traveller who leaves no trace behind him.

P. What is grass?

A. The robe of the earth.

P. What are vegetables?

A. The friends of the physician, the glory of the cooks.

P. What is it renders bitter things sweet?

A. Hunger.

P. What is that of which men never get weary?

A. Gain.

P. What is the dream of the waking?

A. Hope.

P. What is hope?

A. The refreshment of labour, a doubtful event.

P. What is friendship?

A. The similarity of souls.

P. What is faith?

A. The assurance of unknown and marvellous things.

P. What is marvellous?

A. I saw the other day a man standing, a dead man walking, a man walking who had never breathed.

P. How may that have been? Explain yourself.

A. It was an image reflected in the water.

P. How could I have failed to understand you; I who have so often seen the same thing?

A. As you are a youth of good disposition, and endowed with natural capacity, I will put to you several other unusual questions: endeavour to solve them.

P. I will do my best; if I make mistakes, you must correct them.

A. Doubtless. Some one, who is unknown to me, has conversed with me, having no tongue and no voice; he was not before, he will not be hereafter, and I neither heard nor knew him. What means this?

P. Perhaps you mean a dream, master?

A. Exactly so, my son. Listen, once more: I have seen the dead engender the living, and the dead consumed by the breath of the living.

P. Fire was produced by rubbing together dead branches, and it then consumed the branches.

A. You are quite accurate.

(Then come fourteen more enigmas of the same character, and the conversation terminates as follows):

A. What is that which at one and the same time is and is not?

P. Nothing.

A. How can it be and not be?

P. It exists in name, but not in fact.

A. What is a mute messenger?

P. That which I hold in my hand.

A. What do you hold in your hand?

P. My letter.

A. Read it, my son."[1]

Clearly, as a means of education, these conversations are altogether and strangely puerile: as a symptom and commencement of intellectual movement, they merit all our attention: they evidence that eager curiosity with which mind, in its crude infancy, directs its view upon all things; that so vivid pleasure which it takes in every unexpected combination, in every at all ingenious idea; a tendency which is manifested alike in the life of individuals and in that of nations, and which gives birth to the most fantastic dreams, the vainest subtleties. It was, beyond doubt, dominant in the palace of Charlemagne, and, doubtless, led to the formation of that sort of academy there, whose members all assumed surnames derived from sacred or profane literature—Charlemagne—David, Alcuin—Flaccus, Angilbert—Homer, Friedgies—Nathaniel, Amalaire—Symphosius, Gisla—Lucia, Gundrade,—Eulalia, and so on; and the singular conversation of which I have just laid extracts before you is, in all probability, only a fair specimen of that which habitually took place, and

[1] Alcuini Opera, ii. 352—354.

to their no small delight, among these *beaux-esprits*, half barbarian, half cultivated.

If the influence of Alcuin had been confined within the walls of this academy, it would have effected but little worthy of our notice; but the great business of his life was in connexion with Charlemagne, and the intellectual authority of this extraordinary man was more grave and more productive of results.

To give you an idea of the relations existing between these two men, and of the prodigious movement of mind which Alcuin was entrusted with the direction of, I cannot do better than lay before you the most authentic monument of them which exists—their correspondence. There remain to us, in the whole, two-hundred-and-thirty-two of Alcuin's letters; of these, thirty are addressed to Charlemagne; I will pass these in review before you, sometimes translating passages as I proceed, sometimes merely indicating the nature of their contents.

Review of the Letters of Alcuin to Charlemagne.

No. of the Letter.	Date.	Purport.
14	793	On the Transfiguration of Jesus Christ.
28	796	He congratulates him on his victories over the Huns, (Avares,) and gives him advice as to the manner in which he should proceed for their conversion: 1. By sending among them gentle-mannered missionaries: 2. By not requiring tithe from them: "It is better to lose the tithe than to prejudice the faith; we ourselves, born, bred, and educated in the Catholic religion, scarce consent to surrender a tithe of our goods; how much less readily will such consent be given by the newly-born faith, the doubtful heart and greedy spirit of these tribes?" 3. By observing a certain method of religious instruction: "This method, I think, should be that which the blessed Augustin has laid down in his book *On the Instruction of the Simple-minded.* The pupil should first be taught the general facts of the immortality of the soul, of a future life, and the eternity of our destiny. Then he should be told for what crimes and sins eternal punishment with the devil and his angels will be inflicted on him, and for what

No. of the Letter.	Date.	Purport.
		good actions he will be rewarded, in the presence of Christ, with eternal glory. Finally, he should have carefully inculcated upon him faith in the Holy Trinity, and have explained to him the coming of Jesus Christ into this world, for the salvation of mankind."
32	796	He recommends him to be lenient towards his Hun prisoners, and towards his enemies generally.
38	796	He gives him an account of what he is doing for the prosperity of the school at the Abbey of Tours: "I, your Flaccus, in obedience to your exhortation and wise desire, apply myself in serving out to some of my pupils in this house of Saint Martin, the honey of the holy writings; I essay to intoxicate others with the old wine of antique studies; one class I nourish with the fruits of grammatical science; in the eyes of another, I display the order of the stars. But I am constantly in want of most of those excellent books of scholastic erudition, which I had collected around me in my own country, both by the devoted zeal of my master, and by my own labour. I therefore entreat your majesty to permit me to send some of my people into Britain that they may bring these flowers thence into France .... In the morning of my life I sowed the seeds of learning in Britain; now, in its eventide, though my blood is less warm within me, I do not cease sowing these seeds in France, and I hope that by the grace of God they will prosper in both countries."
61	797	He gives him a detailed explanation of the lunar cycle.
64	798	He recommends several persons to his favour.
65	798	He explains to him the origin of the names of Septuagesima and Sexagesima. (The sixty-sixth letter is a reply from Charlemagne, who puts forward several objections to his views.)
67	798	He recurs to the subject, and defends himself from the imputation of obstinacy. "As to what you say in the conclusion of your letter, in a most friendly spirit, and solely for my good, that, if there be anything to correct in my opinions on the matter, I should correct them promptly and humbly, I would reply that, thanks to God, I have never been obstinately pertinacious in error, nor over confident in my own opinion; I yield without a struggle to superior judgment, attentive to the maxim that it is better to make use of the ears than of the tongue. I entreat your wisdom, then, to believe that I address myself to you, not as to a disciple but as to a judge, and that I offer you my humble ideas, not as to one

No. of the Letter.	Date.	Purport.
		ignorant of the matter, but as to one fully competent to correct the views of others."
68	797	On the course of the sun and the phases of the year; and on the heresy of Felix, bishop of Urgel.
69	798	On astronomy and chronology: he replies to several questions which had been addressed to him by a woman, probably Gisla, Charlemagne's sister.
70	798	On astronomy; he replies to several questions of Charlemagne on the course of the sun, the constellations, &c.
71	798	On the same subject.
80	799	On the state of public affairs; he urges him to be lenient towards the Saxons.
81	799	He excuses himself from accompanying Charlemagne to Rome, on the ground of ill health.
84	800	A complimentary letter, with some astronomical calculations.
85	800	He thanks him for having heard read the pamphlet he (Alcuin) had written against bishop Felix, and sends him some observations on orthography and arithmetic.
90	800	He condoles with him on the death of his wife Liutgarde, and forwards an epitaph.
91	800	On the same subject.
93	800	He congratulates him on his victories; exhorts him to clemency; speaks to him about the health of pope Leo; excuses himself for not having written, and refuses to go to Rome.
102	801	He felicitates himself upon the return of Charlemagne from Italy.
103	801	Forwarding his corrected copy of the holy scriptures.
104	801	He excuses himself from going to court, on the ground of his advanced age.
105	801	He expresses his sorrow for the death of Manfred, solicits materials for the building of a church, and entreats Charlemagne to be careful in avoiding the dangers of the expedition to Benevento: "Though my affection may appear insensate, at least it cannot be charged with want of consistency; and the confidence I have in your proved humility, emboldens me to say to you what I do. Perhaps some one may object: why does he concern himself with that which is not his business? But I humbly interest myself in all that concerns your prosperity, which, I declare to you, is more dear to me than my own life. You are the blessing of the kingdom, the safety of the people, the honour of the church, the protector of all the faithful in Christ; it is under the shadow of your power, the shelter of your

No. of the Letter.	Date.	Purport.
		pious care, that, by Divine grace, we are enabled to pursue a religious life, and to serve God in tranquillity: it is, therefore, just and necessary, that, with an attentive spirit and a devoted heart, we occupy ourselves with your fortune and your health, and pray God to preserve to us in health and prosperity our most excellent and most honour-worthy king David."
106	801	He thanks him for his favours, and entreats him, on account of his infirmities, to allow him to remain at St. Martin's.
115	802 or 803	He excuses himself and the fraternity of St. Martin for having given an asylum to a priest of the church of Orleans, which affair had been the occasion of a great tumult in the church of St. Martin, and of great anger to Charlemagne and Theodulf.
123	Year uncertain.	He replies to questions forwarded by Charlemagne, as to the difference between the terms *eternal* and *sempiternal*, *perpetual* and *immortal*, *age* and *time*.
124	Id.	He replies to questions from Charlemagne, on certain passages of Scripture.
125	Id.	He replies to a question by Charlemagne, why we find in none of the gospels the hymn sung by Jesus Christ after the Last Supper.
126	Id.	He replies to Charlemagne, who has asked him, on the part of a learned Greek, to whom the price of man's redemption was remitted.
127	Id.	He gives advice to Charles on the subjects of capitularies, wills, successions, &c.

It was no easy task for Alcuin to fulfil such varied relations, to satisfy all the intellectual requirements of that indefatigable master, who thought of everything and busied himself with everything—history, morals, theology, astronomy, chronology, grammar—and doubtless regarded it as a matter of course, that in these things, as in all others, his will should in every case, and immediately, be carried into effect.

There is doubtless a powerful charm in the society of a great man; but when the great man is a sovereign, it soon becomes a heavy burden to have to please him at every moment and in everything. No formal text shows it us; but Charlemagne, in his relations with Alcuin, no doubt exhibited that pitiless egoism of a superior and despotic genius, which only considers men, even those whom it best loves, and to whom it attaches the greatest importance, as tools, and progresses towards its end without troubling itself as to how dear it costs those whom it employs in the attainment. A profound weariness seized upon Alcuin—he earnestly solicited permission to retire from the court, and to live in retirement. In 796, he wrote to an archbishop, whose name is unknown:

"Your paternity must know that I your son ardently desire to lay aside the weight of worldly affairs, and to serve God alone. Every man needs with vigilance to prepare to meet God, and how especially so old men, borne down with years and infirmities!" [1]

And to his friend Angilbert:

"On thy departure, I attempted many times to take refuge in the haven of repose; but the King of all things, the Master of souls, has not yet accorded to me what he has so long made me wish." [2]

Charlemagne at length allowed him to depart, and about 796, it seems, he gave him for a retreat the abbey of Saint Martin of Tours, one of the most wealthy in the kingdom.

Alcuin hastened to take possession of it. The retreat was magnificent; there were more than twenty thousand labourers or serfs on the domains of the abbeys which he possessed, and the correspondence which he continued to keep up with Charlemagne animated without burdening his life. He did not remain idle in his new situation; he re-established rule and order in the monastery, enriched the library with manuscripts copied at York by young priests whom he sent for this purpose, and by his own teaching he gave the school a brilliancy which it had never before known. It was at this epoch that many of the most distinguished men of the following century—among others, Raban Maur, who became archbishop of Mayence, and Amalaire, a learned priest of Metz—were formed by his lessons.

Charlemagne attempted several times to recal Alcuin to his side; he wished him, among others, to accompany him to Rome, when he went there, in 800, to assume the empire of the west. "It is a reproach," he writes to him, "to prefer

[1] Lett. of Alcuin, 168th, vol. i. p. 228. [2] Ibid. 21st, vol. i. p. 31.

the smoked roofs of the people of Tours to the gilded palaces of the Romans."[1]

But Alcuin remained firm.

"I do not think," answers he, "that my weak body, broken by daily pains, can support this journey. I should have much desired it, if it were practicable.[2] How can I constrain myself to new combats, and to toil under the weight of arms—I, who am left by my infirmities scarcely in a state to raise them from the earth?[3] . . . I implore you to leave me to finish my career at Saint Martin; all the energy, all the dignity of my body has flown; I admit it; less and less is daily left me, and I shall never again recover it in this world. I had of late desired and hoped once more to see the face of your beatitude, but the deplorable increase of my infirmities has proved to me that I must renounce that hope. I conjure, then, your inexhaustible goodness that the so holy spirit, that the so benevolent will, which are in you, be not irritated against my weakness; grant, with a pious compassion, that a wearied man may repose himself, that he may pray for you in his orisons, and that he may prepare, by confession and tears, to appear before the eternal judge."[4]

Charlemagne, it seems, insisted no longer; and Alcuin, perhaps in order to protect himself from new solicitations, resolved entirely to renounce all activity, even that to which he had given himself up in his retreat. In 801, he resigned his abbeys, and obtained that they should be divided among his principal disciples; and, free from all business, he, till the day of his death, (19th May, 804,) occupied himself only with his health and his salvation.

I have given somewhat of expansion to this account of his relations with Charlemagne, and the various situations of his life; it is there, more especially, that is reflected the image of this time, and that the social movement amidst which he lived is shown. I will now say something to you of his works: a few words and a few extracts will, I hope, suffice to give you at least an idea of them.

They may be divided into four classes: 1, theological

[1] Lett. of Alcuin, 93rd, vol. i. p. 138.
[2] Ibid. 81st letter, p. 120.
[3] Ibid. 104th letter, p. 154.
[4] Ibid. 106th, p. 157.

works; 2, philosophical and literary works; 3, historical works; 4, poetical works.

1. The theological works are of three kinds: 1. Commentaries on various parts of the holy scriptures; commentaries whose especial object is to discover the allegorical meaning, and to determine the moral sense of the sacred writings. 2. Dogmatical treatises, the greater part directed against the heresies of the Adoptians respecting the nature of Jesus Christ; a heresy which played a rather important part at this time, which was condemned by two councils held by the order of Charlemagne, and of which Alcuin was the principal adversary. 3. Liturgical works on the celebration of ecclesiastical offices.

2. The philosophical and literary works are six in number: 1, a kind of treatise of practical morality, entitled *De Virtutibus et Vitüs*, and addressed to count Wido or Guy, in a dedicatory epistle, and a peroration in the following terms:

"I recollect thy request and my promise; thou didst urgently pray me to write thee some exhortations in a concise style, in order that, amidst the occupations given thee by military affairs, thou mightest constantly have before thine eyes a manual of maxims and paternal counsels, where thou mightest examine thyself, and excite thyself to seek eternal beatitude. I very willingly comply with so worthy a request; and be assured that, although these counsels may appear to thee written without eloquence, they are dictated by holy charity. I have divided this discourse into separate chapters, so that my advice may be more easily fixed on the memory of thy piety: for I know thou art much occupied with worldly affairs. Let the holy desire to thy salvation, I beseech thee, make thee often have recourse to this reading, as to a useful refreshment; so that thy soul, fatigued with external cares, may enter into itself, there find enjoyment, and understand properly to what it ought especially to apply itself.

"And do not allow thyself to be deterred by the lay habit which thou wearest, or by the secular life which thou leadest, as though in that habit thou couldst not pass through the gates of celestial life. For as the beatitude of the kingdom of God is preached to all without distinction, so the entry to that kingdom is open equally, with only a distinction as to merits, to each sex, to all ages, to all ranks; there no heed is taken as to whether a man on earth has been layman or priest, rich or poor, young or old, master or slave, but eternal glory crowns each according to his works." [1]

Thirty-five chapters then follow upon the various virtues and vices, wisdom, faith, charity, indulgence, envy, pride, &c. We find nothing here particularly original or profound; but practical utility is aimed at with much good sense, and human nature is sometimes observed and described with a highly intellectual delicacy. The following two chapters prove it.

" *Of Sorrow.*

" There are two kinds of sorrow, the one beneficial, the other pernicious. Sorrow is beneficial when the soul of the sinner is afflicted with his sins, and is so afflicted with them that it aspires to confession and penitence, and desires to be converted to God. Very different is worldly sorrow, which works the death of the soul, become incapable of accomplishing any good; this latter troubles man, and often depresses him to that point that he loses the hope of eternal good. Of this sorrow are born malice, rancour, cowardice, bitterness, and despair, often even disgust at this life. It is conquered by spiritual joy, hope of future blessings, the consolation given by the Scriptures, and by fraternal conversation, animated with spiritual enjoyment." [2]

" *Of Vain glory.*

" That pest, vain glory, is a passion with a thousand forms, which glides on all sides into the heart of the man who is occupied in striving against vices, and even of the man who has conquered them. In the deportment and the beauty of the body, in step, word, action, fasts, prayer, solitude, reading, science, silence, obedience, humility, long-suffering, patience, it seeks a means of overcoming the soldier of Christ; it resembles a dangerous rock concealed under swollen billows, and which prepares a terrible storm for those who sail the most successfully, and when they are all unsuspecting. This man, who does not take pride in fine and splendid clothing, the demon of false glory endeavours to inspire with a pride in the foulness and coarse-

[1] Alcuin Oper. vol. ii. pp. 129, 145.

[2] Chap. 33, vol. ii. p. 153.

ness of common clothing; another has resisted the temptations of ambition, he will be lost by those of humility; a third has not allowed himself to be puffed up by the advantages of science and eloquence, he will be subdued by the gravity of silence. One publicly fasts, and vain glory possesses him; to escape it he fasts in secret; it insinuates its poison into the swelling heart of the internal man; for fear of succumbing he avoids long prayer before his brothers, but what he does in secret does not protect him from the excitements of vanity; it puffs one, because he is very patient in his works and labours; another, because he is very prompt to obey; this man, because he surpasses all others in humility; that, because of his zeal in science; a third, by reason of his application to reading; a fourth, because of the length of his watches. A terrible evil, which strives to sully man, not only in works of the world, but even in his virtues."[1]

There is here a rather skilful observation of human nature, and a tolerable art in expressing the results.

The title of the second work of this class is *De Ratione Animæ* (*of the nature of the soul*), and it is addressed to Gundrade, sister of Adalhard, and surnamed Eulalia, one of the women who were present at the lectures of Alcuin in the school of the palace. It is a more purely philosophical attempt than the preceding, and in which, under all its forms, the idea of the unity of the soul is expressed with subtlety and energy.

"The soul," says he, "bears divers names according to the nature of its operations: inasmuch as it lives and makes live, it is the soul (*anima*); inasmuch as it contemplates, it is the spirit (*spiritus*); inasmuch as it feels, it is sentiment (*sensus*); since it reflects, it is thought (*animus*); as it comprehends, intelligence (*meus*); inasmuch as it discerns, reason (*ratio*); as it consents, will (*voluntas*); as it recollects, memory (*memoria*). But these things are not divided in substance as in name, for all this is the soul, and one soul only."[2]

And elsewhere:

"The soul, in its very nature, has an image, as it were, of the Holy Trinity, for it has intellect, will, and memory. The soul, which is also called the mind, the life, the sub-

[1] Chap. 34, vol. ii. p. 144. [2] Vol. ii. p. 149.

stance which includes these three faculties within itself, is one; these three faculties do not constitute three lives, but one life; not three minds, but one mind; not three substances, but one substance. When we give to the soul the names of mind, life, or substance, we regard it in itself; but when we call it the memory, the intellect, or the will, we consider it in its relation to something. These three faculties make but one, inasmuch as the life, the mind, the substance, form one. They make three, inasmuch as they are considered in their external relations; for the memory is the recollection of something; the intellect is the understanding of something; the will is the will of something, and in this they are distinguished. And still there is in these three faculties a certain unity. I think that I think, that I will, and that I remember; I will to think, and to recollect, and to will; I remember that I have thought and willed, and that I have remembered, and thus these three faculties are combined in one."[1]

In other respects, there are in this treatise nothing but scattered ideas, and no systematic character.

After these two moral essays, come four treatises; 1. On grammar; 2. On orthography: 3. On rhetoric; 4. On logic, which I shall only mention; for to make known the contents and merits of them would render it necessary to enter too far into detail. The two last are in the form of a dialogue between Alcuin and Charlemagne, the object of which is evidently to instruct Charlemagne in the methods of the ancient sophists and rhetoricians, especially in what concerns logic and judicial eloquence.

3. The historical works of Alcuin are of little importance; they are confined to four lives of the saints, Saint Waast, Saint Martin, Saint Riquier, and Saint Willibrod. The latter, however, contains some rather curious details for a history of manners. It is said that Alcuin wrote a history of Charlemagne, in particular of his wars with the Saxons, but this, if it ever existed, is now lost.

4. His poetical works, although numerous, are also but of little value; there are two hundred and eighty pieces of verse, upon all kinds of subjects, most of them upon the incidents of the day. The principal is a poem upon the bishops and

[1] Vol. ii. p. 147.

saints of the church of York; it is worth reading, as an indication of the intellectual state of the age.

I regret that I am unable to enter more fully into these monuments of a mind so active and distinguished. Some will, perhaps, think I have dwelt too long upon them as it is: for myself, I fear that I have scarcely thrown a glance at them; and if we were to make a profound study of them, we should unquestionably find both profit and pleasure in it: but we must restrict ourselves. To sum up, the following seems to me to be the general character, the intellectual physiognomy of Alcuin and of his works. He is a theologian by profession, the atmosphere in which he lived, in which the public to whom he addresses himself lived, is essentially theological; and yet the theological spirit does not reign alone in him, his works and his thoughts also tend towards philosophy and ancient literature; it is that which he also delights in studying, teaching, and which he wished to revive. Saint Jerome and Saint Augustin are very familiar to him; but Pythagoras, Aristotle, Aristippus, Diogenes, Plato, Homer, Virgil, Seneca, Pliny, also occur to his memory. The greater part of his writings are theological; but mathematics, astronomy, logic, rhetoric, habitually occupy him. He is a monk, a deacon, the light of the contemporaneous church; but he is at the same time a scholar, a classical man of letters. In him, at length, commenced the alliance of these two elements of which the modern mind had so long borne the incoherent impress, antiquity, and the church, the admiration, the taste, the regret, shall I call it, for pagan literature, and the sincerity of Christian faith, the zeal to sound its mysteries, and to defend its power.

TWENTY-THIRD LECTURE.

Classification of celebrated men of the age of Charlemagne: 1. Leidrade, archbishop of Lyons—His letter to Charlemagne upon what he has done in his diocese—2. Theodulph, archbishop of Orleans—His measures for the instruction of the people—His poem entitled *Exhortation to Judges*—3. Smaragde, abbot of Saint Michael—His treatise of morality for kings, entitled *Via Regia*—4. Eginhard—His alleged marriage with a daughter of Charlemagne—Their relations—Of what happened after the death of this prince—His letters—His *Life of Charlemagne*—Recapitulation.

When I placed before you the view of the celebrated men of the age of Charlemagne, I comprehended therein those who died and those who were born in his reign, his contemporaries, properly so called, and those who long survived him; the former discovered, as it were, and employed by him, the second, formed under his influence: an important distinction if we would justly estimate an epoch and the influence of a man. A sovereign arrives at power in the midst of circumstances, and under the influence of causes, anterior to, and independent of his own will; and which have planted around distinguished men; he gathers them, but he has not made them: his merit consists in knowing how to recognise them, to accept them, to make use of them; but they are not the result of his action; we must not judge of this by them. We have in modern times a striking example of this distinction. Most of the men who constituted the glory of the reign of Louis XIV. were formed entirely independently of him, while the religious struggles still resounded in France, amidst the troubles of the Fronde, and in a liberty which soon vanished. The true fruit of the influence of Louis

XIV. belongs to the last period of his reign; it is the manners and the men of that time which are necessary to be considered in order to judge properly of the effects of his government, and the direction which it impressed upon mind. The distinction is great, and should be well observed.

We shall find no such difference among the men whom Charlemagne found, and those who were formed under him. The latter were in no way inferior to their predecessors, but they were different, and the truth of the distinction which I have pointed out is equally evident.

I spoke in our last lecture of the chief, and, without contradiction, the most distinguished cotemporary of Charlemagne. The men of whom I am about to speak, at least almost all of them, belong to the same epoch, to the same class; like Alcuin, they were not formed by Charlemagne; he discovered and made use of them. Two among them, Leidrade and Theodolf, were, like Alcuin, foreigners; and without Charlemagne, would probably never have appeared in Frankish Gaul.

I. Leidrade was born in the province which the Romans called Norica, situated on the confines of Italy and Germany. He was first attached to Arnon, bishop of Salzburg, and made himself distinguished at an early age by his mind and knowledge. Charlemagne first engaged him as a librarian, and employed him in various missions. The *missi dominici*, the principal instruments, as you have seen, of his government, were almost all men of this kind, whom he had attracted from all parts, and whom he habitually retained near him, in order to send them, according to need, to inspect some portion of his states, until, sooner or later, he separated from them, conferring upon them some great ecclesiastical or civil charge. It thus happened to Leidrade. After numerous missions, the last of which, in Southern Gaul, prevented him for some time from being consecrated, he was nominated, in 798, archbishop of Lyons. The church of Lyons had always been one of the most considerable of the south of Gaul, and, at the same time, one of those in which disorder had been the greatest, and calculated to give the greatest trouble to repair. It was on this ground, and to satisfy this want, that Charlemagne confided it to Leidrade. A curious monument has come down to us of what the new archbishop did in his diocese. This is a letter in which he himself gives a detailed account to Charlemagne of his labours and their results. I will read it entire, despite its emphatic prolixities. It is necessary to bear with them in order to form a true idea of the turn of mind of the age, and the relations of an archbishop with the sovereign. The date of this letter is not exactly known, but it probably belongs to the early years of the ninth century.

"*To Charles the Great, Emperor.*

"To the powerful Charles, emperor, Leidrade, bishop of Lyons, health. Our lord, perpetual and sacred emperor, I supplicate the clemency of your highness, to hear read this short epistle with a favourable countenance, so that your pious prudence may know what it contains, and that your noble clemency may know the purport of my request. You deigned awhile ago to entrust the government of the church of Lyons to me, the most infirm of your servants, incapable and unworthy of that charge. But since you treat men far less according to their merit, than according to your accustomed bounty, you have acted with me as it has pleased your ineffable piety; and without any title thereto on my part, you have been pleased to charge me with the care of this church, and to act in such a manner that the abuses which have been committed in it may be for the future reformed and avoided. Many things were wanting to this church, both externally and internally, as much in what concerns the holy offices, as for the edifices and other ecclesiastical wants. Listen, therefore, to what I, your very humble servant, have effected in it, since my arrival, with God's aid and yours. The all powerful Lord, who sees into consciences, is my witness, that I do not expose these things in order to draw profit therefrom, and that I have in no way arranged, and communicate this to you in order to procure any advantage to myself, but because I expect each day to leave this life, that because of my infirmities I think myself very near death. I tell you these things to the end that, having attained your benign ear, and being weighed with indulgence, if you think that they have been effected suitably, and according to your will, they may not, after my death, be allowed to languish and perish.

"When, according to your order, I had taken possession of this church, I acted with all my power, with all the strength of my weakness to bring the ecclesiastical offices to the point at which, with the grace of God, they have nearly arrived. It pleased your piety to grant at my request the restitution of the revenues which formerly belonged to the church of Lyons; by means of which, with God's grace and yours, there has been established in the said church, a psalmody, where is followed, as far as we are able, the ceremonies of the sacred palace, in all that the divine office requires. I have schools of singers, many of whom are already sufficiently instructed to be able to teach others. Moreover, I have schools of readers, who not only acquit themselves of their functions in the church, but who, by meditation on the holy scriptures, assure themselves the fruits of understanding of spiritual things. Some can explain the spiritual sense of the Evangelists; others have understanding of the prophecies; others, of the books of Solomon, the Psalms, and even Job. I have also done in this church what lay in my power, as to copying books. I have likewise procured clothing for the priests, and what was necessary for the offices. I have omitted nothing which lay in my power for the restoration of the churches, so that I have roofed the great church of this town, dedicated to Saint John the Baptist, and I have reconstructed a portion of the walls; I have also repaired the roof of the church of Saint Etienne; I have rebuilt the church of Saint Nizier, and that of Saint Mary, without counting the monasteries and episcopal houses, of which one in particular was almost destroyed, and which I have repaired and re-roofed. I have also constructed another with a high platform. This I have prepared for you, in order that if you come into these parts you may be received there. For the priests, I have constructed a cloister in which they now live all united in one edifice. I have also repaired other churches in this diocese, one of them dedicated to Saint Eulalia, where there is a nunnery dedicated to Saint George; I have had it re-roofed, and part of the walls built up from the foundations; another house in honour of Saint Paul has also been re-roofed. I have entirely repaired the church and house of a nunnery dedicated to Saint Peter, where rests the body of Saint Annemond, martyr, and which was founded by that holy bishop himself. Thirty-two virgins of the Lord now live there under the monastic rule. I have also repaired, by renewing the roof and part of the walls, the royal monastery of l'Isle Barbe; ninety monks now live there under a regular monastic rule. We have given to its abbot the power to bind and unbind; the same as his predecessors had —Ambrose, Maximian, Licinius, illustrious men who have governed this place, and which Euchere, Loup, Genest, and the other bishops of Lyons, when they were absent and could not fulfil in person, delegated, in order to take care that the catholic faith was believed with sincerity, and that heretical feuds did not abound.

"These abbots were even charged, if the church of Lyons was without its chief, to serve it in all things as guides and counsellors, until, with the grace of God, it was provided with a worthy pastor. We have likewise given this power to their successors. Above all things, we have ordered that the decrees of the ancient kings of France should be executed, to the end that, as it was by them ordained in their statutes respecting sales and augmentations, these monks may for ever possess without dispute, that which they have at present, that which by the grace of God they may one day acquire."[1]

I shall spare all commentary: the letter is sufficiently detailed to show what an archbishop did at that time, who wished to re-establish religion, society, and learning, in his diocese. Leidrade passed his life in works of this kind; we find him quitting his church but twice to go into Spain, by the order of Charlemagne, to discuss and preach against the heresy of the Adoptians. His eloquence, it is said, gained for him there brilliant triumphs, and thousands of heretics were converted by him. However this may have been, in 814, almost immediately after the death of Charlemagne, whether from sorrow or prudence, he resigned his bishopric, and shut himself up in the monastery of Saint Medard at Soissons. He was taken thence for awhile, by Louis le Debonnaire, who charged him with re-establishing order in the church of Macon. No chronicler pronounces his name after this epoch, and with the exception of the letter which I have just read, there only remain of his writings two or three short and very insignificant theological pieces.

II. We are better acquainted with a friend of Leidrade, his companion in the great mission entrusted to him by Charlemagne, in Narbonnese Gaul; I mean Theodulf, bishop of

[1] *Sanct. Agobardi Opera*, vol. ii. p. 125—129, ed. of Baluze, Paris, 1665.

Orleans. Like Alcuin and Leidrade, he was a foreigner, a Goth by nation, and an Italian by birth. Charlemagne sent for him, it is unknown at what epoch; we find him established in Gaul in 781, and between 786 and 796, he was bishop of Orleans. He took especial care to re-establish schools in his diocese. We have by him, concerning the duties of priests, a capitulary in forty-one articles, which displays rather elevated views of order and morality, and contains, among others, the two following articles:

"If any priest wishes to send his nephew or any other of his relations to school, we allow him to be sent to the church of Saint Croix, or to the monastery of Saint Aignan, or of Saint Benedict, or of Saint Lifard, or to any other monastery confided to our government.

"Let priests hold schools in villages and districts, and if any of the faithful wish to confide their young children to them, in order to have them study letters, let them not refuse to receive and to instruct them; but, on the contrary, teach them in perfect charity, remembering that it is written: 'And they that be wise, shall shine as the brightness of the firmament, and they that turn many to righteousness, as the stars for ever and ever.'[1] And while instructing children, let them exact no price therefore, and receive nothing, except when the parents shall offer it them, willingly, and out of affection."[2]

This last article is almost the only monument of this epoch which positively institutes a teaching destined for others than priests. All the measures, whether of Alcuin, or of Charlemagne, which I have hitherto spoken of, have the literary education of priests for their object; here are included the faithful in general, the people; and not only the people of towns, but of the country districts, which were far more neglected as regards instruction. There is nothing to show us the results of the recommendations of Theodulf in his diocese, and they were probably almost null; but the attempt deserves remark.

About the year 798, Theodulf was sent by Charlemagne, with Leidrade, into the two Narbonnese, to observe and reform the administration of those provinces. On his return

[1] Daniel, xii. 3. [2] Theod. cap. § 19, 20.

he composed a poem of 956 verses, entitled, *Parænesis ad Judices* (Exhortation to Judges), and destined to instruct magistrates in their duties in such missions. The course of the work is simple. After a religious preamble, which terminates with an eulogy on Charlemagne, Theodulf describes the route followed by Leidrade and himself, and the principal towns through which they passed, Vienne, Orange, Avignon, Nîmes, Agde, Beziers, Narbonne, Carcassonne, Arles, Marseilles, and Aix. To this enumeration succeeds a view of the dangers which assail the probity of magistrates, and of all the attempts which were made to corrupt Leidrade and himself. Then come his exhortations to the judges, exhortations over which he takes pleasure in dwelling at length, as a man who has seen the evil, and as a bishop accustomed to give everything the form of a sermon. The poem abruptly finishes with this general exhortation to the great men of the world:

"Mortal, always be prepared to treat mortals with mildness; the law of nature is the same for them and for thee. However different may be thy course here below, thou and they start from the same point; it is to the same point that you tend. One sacred spring runs for them as for thee, and throws upon them, as upon thee, the same paternal blot. . . . The Author of life died for them as well as for thee, and he will extend his gifts to each according to his merits. Let us here fold the sails of my book, and let the anchor retain my ship on this shore." [1]

There is, in all this, you see, very little invention or art: but, as an historical and moral monument, the poem is devoid neither of merit nor interest. The most curious passage, in my opinion, is that where Theodulf describes all the attempts at corruption which he had to resist:

"A large crowd," says he,[2] "pressed around us, of both sexes and of every age: the child, the old man, the young man, the young woman, the girl, the boy, he who had attained his majority, he who had reached puberty, the old woman, the full grown man, the married woman, she who

[1] *Paræneris ad Judices*, v. 947—956, in the *Opera Varia* of P. Germand, vol. ii. p 1046.

[2] Ibid. v. 163—290; vol. ii. p. 1032—1034.

was still a minor. But why did I stay? The entire nation earnestly promise us gifts, and think that at that price whatever they desire is as good as done. This is the machine by which all endeavour to throw down the wall of the soul, the battering-ram with which they wish to strike in order to seize it. Here one offered me crystals and precious stones of the east, if I would make him master of the domains of another; a second brings me a quantity of gold money, impressed with the tongue and character of the Arabians, or upon whose brilliantly white silver surface a Latin style has engraved words, with which he wished to acquire lands, fields, and houses; another secretly called one of our servants, and said to him with a low voice the following words, which were to be repeated to me: 'I possess a vase remarkable for its chasing and its antiquity; it is of a pure metal and of considerable weight; on it is engraved the history of the crimes of Cacus, the faces of the shepherds bruised by the blows from clubs of iron, and soiled with blood, the signs of his numerous robberies, a field inundated with the blood of men and herds; we see Hercules who in fury breaks the bones of the son of Vulcan, and the latter with his ferocious mouth vomiting the terrible fires of his father; but Alcides presses his knee upon the stomach of Cacus, his sides with his feet, and with his club shatters his face and throat, whence issue torrents of smoke. You next see Alcides bringing out of the cavern the stolen oxen, which seem to fear being dragged a second time backward. All this is on the hollow part of the vase, with a circle around it; the other side, covered with smaller designs, shows the child of Tyrinthus strangling the two serpents, and his ten famous labours are there placed in their order. But frequent use has so polished the exterior, that, effaced by time, the figures which represent Hercules, the river Chalydon and Nessus fighting for thy beauty, Dejanira, have almost completely disappeared. We see also the fatal mantle, poisoned with the blood of Nessus, and the horrible fate of the unhappy Lychas, and Antæus, who could not be conquered or fought upon earth, like other mortals, strangled in the formidable arms of Hercules. This, then, will I offer to the lord (for he even called me lord), if he will favour my wishes. There is a great number of men, women, young people, children of both sexes, to whom my father and mother have granted the honour or liberty, and this numerous group find themselves enfranchised; but, by altering their charters, we shall enjoy, thy master the possession of this antique vase; I, of all this people; and thou, of my gifts.'"

"Another says: 'I have mantles died in various colours, which came, as I believe, from the ferocious Arabians. We see there the calf following its mother, and the heifer the bull, the colour of the calf and that of the heifer exact to nature, as are those of the bull and the cow. See how brilliant they are, how pure are the colours, and with what art the larger parts are joined to the smaller. I have a quarrel with some one about some beautiful herds, and I offer on this occasion a fitting present, since I offer bull for bull, cow for cow, ox for ox.'

"Here one promises me beautiful cups, if by that means he can obtain what I ought not to give him: the inside of one of them gilt, the outside black, the colour of the silver having the dye of sulphur. Another says: 'I have cloths fit to cover splendid beds and beautiful vases; I will give them if my desires are granted.' 'A well watered estate, ornamented with vines, olives, meadows, and gardens, was left by my father,' says one; "my brothers and sisters claim from me a share, but I wish to possess it without partition; I shall obtain the accomplishment of this wish, if it find favour before thee; and if thou acceptest what I give thee, I shall reckon upon thy giving me that which I request.' One wishes to seize the house of his parent, another his estates; of these two, one had already taken, the other wished to take what did not belong to him; both burned with the desire, that to keep, this to acquire: one offered me a sword and casque, the other bucklers; one brother is in possession of the inheritance of his father, his brother likewise lays claim to it; one offers me mules, the other horses.

"Thus do the rich act; the poor are not less pressing, and the will to give is not more wanting. With various means, the conduct is alike: as the great offer great presents, the lower offer small. Here behold some who display prepared skins which take their name from thee, Cordova; one brings white, the other, red; this offers fine linen, that woollen stuffs, to cover my head, my feet, or my hands. Such a one offers as a gift one of those cloths which are used to wash, with a little water, our face and hands; others bring boxes. There was even one, who, with an air of triumph, presented round wax candles. How can we enumerate all these things? all were confident in their gifts, and no one supposed that he could obtain anything without presents. Oh wicked pest spread over all places! oh, crime, oh, fury! oh, vice, worthy of horror, which may boast of its having subdued the universe! nowhere is there wanting people who give and people who receive wrongfully. They hastened to gain me; and they would not have thought to find me susceptible of corruption, if they had not found my predecessors susceptible. No one seeks wild boars in the water, fish in the forest, a wood house in the sea, water in fire. . . . They expect to find each thing where they have been accustomed to find it, and mortals think that what has happened will always happen. When they see that the darts of their words are broken, and that the arms of their promises in no degree avail them, when they see that I remain firm as a fortress after an ineffectual siege, and that I do not allow myself to be deceived by any of their artifices, every one forthwith occupies himself only with his own business; every one receives what he is entitled to, and no more; thus, a man who sees closed up a passage, through which he has been accustomed to go for the purposes of robbery, turns aside, and proceeds hopelessly elsewhere. But, in order not to show myself deficient in moderation and discreet judgment, to manifest that I acted openly and frankly, to guard against my conduct exciting too much astonishment by its entire novelty, and that the so recent evil might not bring good into hatred, I did not refuse that which was offered to me by real benevolence, by that noble feeling which, joining souls together, causes them readily to take and receive from each other. I accepted with thanks the little presents made me, not by the hand of anger, but by that of friendship—fruit, vegetables, eggs, wine, bread, hay. I took the young fowls, and birds, smaller in size than they, but good to eat. Happy the virtue which is tempered, adorned, and maintained by discretion, the nurse of all virtues."

The invasions and their disasters, so often renewed, had not destroyed, as you see, in the cities of southern Gaul, all the wealth, and there still remained abundance wherewith to tempt the avidity of magistrates.

Independently of these details concerning the state of society, the poem of Theodulph is remarkable for the gentleness of the sentiments which pervade it; one is astonished to find, amidst barbarous disorders and tyrannies, that delicate goodness which seems to belong only to times of great civilization and peace. He exhorts the judges to treat considerately all who present themselves before them :

"If one," says he, "has lost his father, another his mother, another her husband, take particular care with their cause; be their protector, their advocate; be to the one her husband, to the other his mother. If any ever come to thee weak, infirm, or ill, infantine, or aged, bear towards him a charitable help; cause him who cannot stand erect, to sit; take by the hand him who cannot raise himself; sustain and encourage him whose heart, voice, hand, or legs, are about to fail him; with thy words raise him who is cast down; appease him who is irritated; give strength to him who trembles, recal to order him who is excited."[1]

I will cite the original text of this passage; the style, although very faulty, is of a remarkable conciseness and energy :

> "Qui patre seuue matre orbatur, vel si qua marito
> Istorum causas sit tua cura sequi
> Horum causiloquus, horum tutela maneto;
> Pars hæc te matrem noverit, illa virum,
> Debilis, invalidus, puer, aeger, anusve, senexve,
> Si veniant, fer opem his miserando piam ;
> Fac sedeat qui stare nequit, qui surgere prende ;
> Cui cor, voxque tremit, pesque, manusque juva ;
> Dejectum verbis releva, sedato minacem ;
> Qui timet, huic vires, qui furit, adde metum."

Independently of this poem, there are seventy-one various pieces of Theodulph remaining, divided into five books, but they are of little value. Two small theological treatises, and some fragments of sermons by him have also been collected.

After the death of Charlemagne, Louis le Debonnaire still employed Theodulph in various missions; but in 817, compromised in the conspiracy of Bernard, king of Italy, against

[1] Verse 621.

the emperor his uncle, he was exiled from his diocese, and banished to the town of Angers, where he died in 821.

III. Smaragde, abbot of Saint Mihiel, in the diocese of Verdun, was a man of the same character and the same position as the two bishops of whom I have just spoken. It is neither known in what country he was born, nor at what epoch Charlemagne took him into his service; but we find him abbot of Saint Mihiel before 805, and employed, in 809, in various negotiations with Rome. In the diocese of Verdun he took particular care of schools, and in the schools with the teaching of grammar. To expound and discuss the precepts of Donatus, a grammarian of the fourteenth century, who was preceptor of Saint Jerome, Smaragde wrote a large Latin grammar, which was celebrated in his time, and of which many manuscripts still exist. It has never been printed. We have two other works by him: the first, entitled *Via Regia*, is a treatise of morality for the use of princes, divided into thirty-two chapters, and addressed either to Charlemagne, or to Louis le Debonnaire; it is not exactly known which. The ideas are wise and benevolent, but common; one fact alone merits remark: this is the far more moral than religious character of the work. The church occupies but little place therein, and, with the exception of some general recommendations, the author only speaks of it in a cursory manner, and to exhort the prince to watch over it. If the book was addressed to Louis le Debonnaire, the emperor was far more of a monk than the abbot of Saint Mihiel.

The second work of Smaragde, entitled the *Diadem of the Monks*, is purely religious, and has no other object but that of giving to the monks advice on the means of sustaining or reanimating their fervour. The abbot of Saint Mihiel took an active part, among others, in the council of Aix-la-Chapelle in 817, in all measures for the reform of monastic orders. He died, it would appear, shortly after 819.

These were the most remarkable men among priests whom Charlemagne employed. Their origin is clear; their knowledge made their fortune; it was in their character of literary men that Charlemagne distinguished them, and called them near him. By the side of these, we meet men of another nature, of another origin; politicians, military men, who acquired a taste for learning, and ended by devoting themselves to it, after having been engaged at first in an entirely different career. Charlemagne employed literary men in affairs of state, and inspired statesmen with an esteem for letters. Among these last, three especially merit our attention, all three unconnected in the early part of their life, both with the church and with learning, soldiers or counsellors of Charlemagne, occupied in the business of civil government, taking part in warlike expeditions, and who, however, all three ended by study and by a religious life, and have left us monuments of their intellectual activity. These are Angilbert, Saint Benedict d'Aniane, and Eginhard.

I shall merely mention the names of the first two: they wrote but very little; of Angilbert we have only some poems, and some documents concerning the abbey of Saint Riquier, to which he retired; and when we shall especially occupy ourselves with the history of the church at this epoch, we shall again find Saint Benedict d'Aniane, who, after having led a life of war in his youth, became the second reformer of monastic orders. Eginhard alone fills an important place in the literature of this time, and we shall at present occupy ourselves with him.

He was of the Frankish race, born, perhaps, beyond the Rhine, and calls himself "a barbarian, but little versed in the language of the Romans." [1] Charlemagne took him into his service while very young, caused him to be brought up with his children in that school of the palace of which Alcuin was the head; and when Eginhard arrived at the age of manhood, he not only made him superintendent of all those works which we in the present day call public works, roads, canals, buildings of all kinds, but his councillor and private secretary.

Traditions go further; they attribute to Eginhard the honour of having married Emma, the daughter of Charlemagne; and the adventure which they say led to this marriage is one of the most popular traditions of our old history. Here it is as we have it in the chronicle of the monastery of Lauresheim,[2]

[1] *Preface* to his *Life of Charlemagne*, in my *Collection*, vol. iii. p. 121.

[2] Lauresheim, or Lorch, in the diocese of Worms, and four leagues from Heidelberg. This chronicle extends from the year 763 or 764, the period of the foundation of the monastery, to the year 1179.

the only ancient monument which makes any mention of it:

"Eginhard, arch-chaplain and secretary of the emperor, Charles, acquitted himself very honourably of his office in the court of the king, was welcomed by all, and especially loved with very lively ardour by the daughter of the emperor, herself named Emma, and who was promised to the king of the Greeks; each day love increased between them; fear restrained them, and, out of apprehension of the royal displeasure, they dared not incur the grave danger of seeing each other. But love, ever on the alert, conquered everything: at last this excellent young man, burning with irremediable fire, and not daring to address himself through a messenger to the ear of the princess, suddenly took confidence in himself, and secretly, in the middle of the night, repaired to where she lodged. Having knocked softly, and as if to speak with the young girl by order of the king, he obtained permission to enter, and then alone with her, they yielded to the tender impulses of love. But when at the approach of the light of day, he wished to return through the last shadows of night, to the place whence he came, he perceived that a great deal of snow had suddenly fallen, and dared not go out, for fear that the traces of a man's feet should betray his secret. They were both full of anguish at what they had done, and seized with fear, remained within; at length, as in that trouble, they deliberated upon what to do, the charming young girl, whom love rendered daring, gave her advice, and said that, stooping she would take him on her shoulders, that she would carry him before day close to his dwelling, and that having deposited him there, she would return, carefully following the same steps.

"Now, the emperor, by the Divine will, as it is believed, had passed the night without sleep, and rising before day, was looking from the tower of his palace. He saw his daughter walking slowly, and with steps tottering under the weight which she bore, and when she had deposited it in a convenient place, quickly retracing her steps. After having long looked at them, the emperor, seized at once with admiration and grief, but thinking that it could not have happened thus without a providential interposition, restrained himself, and preserved silence upon what he had seen.

"In the meantime, Eginhard, tormented with what he had done, and quite sure, in some way or other, the thing could not long remain unknown to the king, his lord, at last resolved in his anguish to seek the emperor, and on his knees demand a mission of him, saying that his services, already great and numerous, had received no suitable recompence. At these words, the king discovering nothing of what he knew, held silence for some time, and then assuring Eginhard that he would shortly give him an answer, he named a day for doing so. He immediately convoked his councillors, the chief of the kingdom, and his other familiar adherents, ordering them to repair to him. This magnificent assembly of various lords thus met, he commenced, saying that the imperial majesty had been insolently outraged by the guilty love of his daughter for his secretary, and that he was greatly troubled at it. Those present remaining struck with stupor, and some of them still appearing to doubt, the thing was so unheard of and daring, the king satisfied them by evidence, recounting matters exactly as he had seen them with his own eyes, and asked them their advice upon the subject. They pronounced various sentences against the presumptuous author of the deed; some wished him to be punished with chastisement hitherto without example, others that he should be exiled, others again that he should be subjected to such or such a penalty, each speaking according to the sentiment which animated him. Some, however, as much more benevolent as they were more wise, after having deliberated among themselves, earnestly implored the king to examine this affair himself, and to decide according to the wisdom which he had received from God. When the king had well observed the affection which each bore him, and amongst the various opinions offered had selected that which he had determined to follow, he spoke thus to them; 'You know that men are subject to various accidents, and that it often happens that things which commence with a misfortune have a more favourable issue; we must not grieve for this affair, which, by its novelty and gravity, has surpassed our foresight, but far rather piously seek for and respect the intentions of Providence, who is never deceived, and who knows how to turn evil to good. I shall not therefore subject my secretary, for this deplorable affair, to a chastisement which will increase instead of effacing the dishonour of my daughter. I think that it is more wise, and that it better becomes the dignity of our empire, to pardon their youth, and unite them in legitimate marriage, and thus give to their disgraceful fault a colour of honour.' Having listened to this advice of the king, all loudly rejoiced, and loaded with praises the grandeur and benevolence of his soul. Eginhard was ordered to enter; the king saluting him as had been resolved, said to him with a tranquil countenance: 'You have laid before us your complaints that our royal munificence has not worthily rewarded your services. To speak truly, it is your own negligence which should be accused, for despite so many and so great affairs of which I alone have borne the burden, if I had known anything of your desire, I would have accorded to your services the honours which are due to them. Not to detain you with a long discourse, I shall, however, put an end to your complaints by a magnificent gift; as I wish always to see you faithful to me as heretofore, and attached to my person, I will give you my daughter in marriage, your *bearer*, she who, girding up her robe, has shown herself so docile in carrying you.' Immediately, according to the orders of the king, and amidst a numerous suite, his daughter entered, her face covered with a charming blush, and the father put her hands within the hands of Eginhard, with a rich dowry, many domains, much gold and silver, and other valuable property. After the death of his father, the most pious emperor Louis likewise gave Eginhard the domain of Michlenstadt and that of Mühlenheim, which is now called Seligestadt."[1]

This is the graceful narrative upon which all the tales, all the poems, all the dramas of which this adventure has been the subject, are founded. The chronicler wrote at an epoch near to the event in an abbey which Eginhard endowed, and the monks of which might have been well acquainted with the incidents of his life. Still this is the only monument of the time in which the event is stated. Moreover, it seems denied by the silence of Eginhard himself, and by some passages in his Life of Charlemagne. Among the children of this prince, whose names he enumerates, we do not find Emma or Imma: he names seven boys and eight girls, whom Charlemagne had

[1] *Recueil des Historiens des Gaules et de la France*, vol. v. p. 383.

by his wives or his mistresses; none of his daughters is called Imma;[1] and in none of the other lists which have come down to us of the history of Charlemagne do we meet with this name. Moreover, we read in the *Life of Charlemagne:*

"His daughters were very beautiful, and he passionately loved them. Accordingly, to the astonishment of all, he would never consent to any of them ever marrying either to his own people, or to a foreigner; he kept them all about him, and with him, until his death, saying that he could not deprive himself of their society. Although happy in all else, he experienced the malignity of fortune with regard to his daughters; but he concealed his vexation, and conducted himself as if they had never given rise to injurious suspicions, and as if no reports went about concerning them."[2]

If the adventure which I have just read were true, how could such a passage be found in the work of Eginhard? How would he himself have spoken of the report which went abroad concerning the conduct of the daughters of Charlemagne, when his own wife would have been the principal object of them? It is impossible to resolve this little historical problem; but if I must give an opinion, I should strongly doubt the recital of the chronicle of Lauresheim.

However this may be, the affection of Charlemagne for his secretary was great, and they lived together in close intimacy. It was especially out of gratitude that Eginhard wrote the life of the emperor.

"Another motive," says he, "which seems to me not unreasonable, would moreover suffice in deciding me to compose this work: brought up by this monarch, from the time

[1] According to Eginhard, Charlemagne had:—

1. By Hildegarde, three sons, Charles, Pepin, Louis; three daughters, Rotrude, Bertha, Gisla.
2. By Fastrade, two daughters, Thebrade, Hildrade.
3. By a concubine, (Himiltrude,) one daughter, Rothaide.
4. By Mathalgarde, (a concubine,) one daughter, Rothilde.
5. By Gersuinthe (id.) one daughter, Adelrude.
6. By Regina, (id.) two sons, Drogon, Hugo.
7. By Adalinde (id.) one son, Theodoric.
8. By a concubine, one son, Pepin.—In all, seven sons and eight daughters.—*Life of Charlemagne*, p. 142—145.

[2] Life of Charlemagne, p. 145.

when I began to be admitted to his court, I lived with him and his children in constant friendship, which imposed upon me after his death, as during his life, all the ties of gratitude towards him. People would therefore be justly authorised to believe and declare me to be an ingrate if I retained no recollection of the benefits heaped upon me, and should say not a word of the high and magnificent actions of a prince who has acquired so many titles to my gratitude, and if I were to consent that his life should remain the same as if he had never existed, without a written memorial, and without the tribute of eulogy which is his due."[1]

Charlemagne never separated himself from his secretary; he did not employ him in any extraordinary missions: once only, in 806, he sent him to Rome to get his will confirmed by the pope; with this exception, he constantly kept him near him.

After the death of Charlemagne, Eginhard enjoyed the same favour with Louis le Debonnaire; but he soon became full of a distaste for that prince, and only desired to retire from the court. Among the sixty-three of his letters which have come down to us, many are curious monuments of the situation and despondency of the companions of Charlemagne, when they found themselves separated from that prince, and forced to live under the deplorable government of his son.

"I do not ask thee," writes Eginhard to one of his friends, "to write me anything concerning the affairs of the palace, for nothing done there can please me to know: I only desire to learn where my friends are, and what they do, if there remain there any of them but thou."[2]

Elsewhere he conjures one of the officers of the palace to excuse him to the emperor for not coming to court:

"The queen, in quitting Aix, ordered me to rejoin her at Compiégne, for I could not set out with her. To obey her orders, I proceeded with great difficulty, and in ten days, to Valenciennes. Thence, not in a state to mount my horse, I came by water to Saint Bavon. But I am alternately attacked with pains in the kidneys, and with relaxed bowels,

[1] Preface to the *Life of Charlemagne*, by Eginhard, vol. iii. p. 120, in my *Collection*.

[2] Letter 47, in the *Recueil des Historiens de France*, vol. ii. p. 382.

in such a manner that since my departure from Aix I have not passed a single day without suffering from one or other of these evils. I am likewise struck with that which cast me down last year, with a continual numbness in the right thigh, and an almost intolerable pain in the liver. Amidst these sufferings, I had a very sad life, and almost devoid of every enjoyment; but what most afflicts me is, that I fear I shall not die where I wish, and that I shall have to occupy myself with something other than the service of the holy martyrs of Christ."[1]

Domestic troubles were soon combined with political annoyances. Whether or not she was a daughter of Charlemagne, Eginhard had married an Imma, of whom he speaks several times in his letters, and whom he tenderly loved. In their old age, as it very often happened at this epoch, she separated from him to devote herself to a religious life. She died in 836, in the nunnery, whither she had retired; and Eginhard wrote to his friend Loup, abbot of Ferrieres:

"All my labours, all my cares for the affairs of my friends or for my own, are nothing to me; all is effaced, all sinks before the cruel sorrow with which the death of her who was formerly my faithful wife has struck me, who was also my sister and my cherished companion. It is a misery which cannot end, for her merits are so deeply engraven in my memory, that nothing can tear them thence. What redoubles my grief, and each day aggravates my wound, is, to thus see that all my wishes have been without effect, and that the hopes which I have placed in the intervention of the holy martyrs are deceived. Accordingly, the words of those who attempt to console me, and which have often succeeded with other men, do nothing but re-open and cruelly envenom the wound of my heart; for they call upon me to support with courage sorrows which they do not feel, and ask me to congratulate myself upon a trial wherein they are incapable ot pointing out to me the slightest subject for contentment."[2]

The language of sorrow, infected, in most of the monuments of this age, with a cold and dry religious jargon, which reduces it to monotonous common-place, is here frank and

[1] Letter 41, *Recueil des Historiens de France*, vol. vi. p. 380.
[2] Letter from Eginhard to Loup, abbot of Ferrieres, *Recueil des Historiens de France*, vol. vi. p. 402.

simple, and proves that Eginhard had not imprisoned his soul as well as his life in the monastic habit.

He did not long survive his wife: he died in 839, in the monastery of Sligestadt, which he founded.

Independently of these letters, we have remaining of his: —1, the *Life of Charlemagne;* 2, *Annals of his times.* Of these two works, the first is, without comparison, the most distinguished piece of history from the sixth to the eighth century—indeed, the only one which can be called a history, for it is the only one in which we recognise any traces of composition, any political and literary pretension. I have as yet only had occasion, for the most part, to speak to you of miserable chroniclers. The *Life of Charlemagne* is not a chronicle: it is a genuine political biography, written by a man who was present at the events he narrates, and who understood them. Eginhard commences by describing the state of Frankish Gaul under the last Merovingians. We see that their dethronement by Pepin was still a subject of discussion with a certain number of men, and caused some disquietude to the race of Charlemagne. Eginhard took care to explain how it could not be otherwise; he minutely describes the humiliation and powerlessness into which the Merovingians had fallen; proceeds from this exposition to recount the natural accessions of the Carlovingians; says a few words upon the reign of Pepin, upon the beginning of that of Charlemagne, and his relations with his brother Carloman; and enters at last into the account of the reign of Charlemagne alone. The first part of the account is devoted to the wars of that prince, and especially his wars against the Saxons. From wars and conquests, the author passes to the internal government, to the administration of Charlemagne; lastly, he comes to his domestic life, his personal character.

It is evident that this is not written at hazard, without plan or aim; we here recognise intention, a systematic composition—there is art, in a word; and since the great productions of Latin literature, no historical work had borne such characteristics. The work of Gregory of Tours itself, without comparison the most curious which we have encountered on our road, is a chronicle, like the others. The *Life of Charlemagne* is, on the contrary, a true literary composition, conceived and executed by a reflecting and cultivated mind.

With regard to the *Annals* of Eginhard, they have no value beyond that of a chronicle. His title to them has been disputed, and they have been attributed to other writers, but everything leads us to believe that they are by him.

It is said that he composed a detailed history of the wars against the Saxons. Nothing of it has come down to us.

Alcuin and Eginhard are, without doubt, the two most distinguished men of the reign of Charlemagne. Alcuin, a man of letters, employed in government affairs; Eginhard, a statesman, who became a man of letters. We are about to see this momentary splendour of the reign of Charlemagne disappear; we are about to be present at the dismemberment of his empire. The intellectual movement, of which we have observed the first steps, will not perish; we shall see it perpetuated as it began; on the one hand, in men who direct the affairs of the world; and on the other, in those who devote themselves to solitary study and learning. Society will often change its state and forms; intellect, reanimated, will now, without stopping, traverse all its revolutions.

TWENTY-FOURTH LECTURE.

The progress and causes of the dismemberment of the empire of Charlemagne—1. State of this empire in 843, after the treaty of Verdun—Inferior state of the kingdom of France at this epoch—2. In 888, after the death of Charles le Gros—Seven kingdoms—Definitive establishment of the inheritance of fiefs in France—Twenty-nine small states, or important fiefs, founded at the end of the ninth century—3. In 987, at the fall of the Carlovingians—Four kingdoms—In France, fifty-five important fiefs—Explanation of this dismemberment—Their insufficiency—One only, the diversity of races, developed by M. Thierry, is probable, but incomplete—The true cause is the impossibility of a great state at that epoch, and the progressive rise of the local societies which formed the feudal confederation.

We read in a chronicle of the century in which Charlemagne died:

"Charles, who was always travelling, arrived by chance unexpectedly at a certain maritime town of Narbonnese Gaul. Whilst he was dining, and was as yet unknown by any one, Norman corsairs came to execute their piracies even in the port. When the people saw the vessels, they supposed that they were merchants; according to these, Jews; according to those, Africans; according to others, Britons; but the able monarch, perceiving by the construction and speed of the vessels that they carried not merchants, but enemies, said to his people: 'These vessels are not filled with merchandise but with cruel enemies.' At these words, all his Franks, in emulation of one another, ran to their vessels, but in vain. The Normans, learning that he whom they used to call Charles le Marteau, was there, feared least their whole fleet should be taken in his port, or perish by wreck; and they avoided, by an inconceivably rapid flight, not only the sword, but even the eyes of those who followed them. Still the religious Charles, seized with a just awe, rising from the table, went to the window which looked towards the east, and long remained, with a countenance covered with tears. No one daring to interrogate him, this valiant prince, explaining to the great men who surrounded him the cause of his action and his tears, said to them: 'Know you, my friends, why I weep so bitterly? Truly, I fear not that these men should succeed in harming me by their miserable piracies; but I am deeply affected that, I living, they have dared to touch this shore; and I am troubled with a violent sorrow when I foresee with what evils they will overwhelm my successors and their people.'"[1]

By a singular chance, we know the precise date of this anecdote: it was written about the month of June 884—that is to say, seventy years after the death of Charlemagne, from the account of a man who had taken part in many of his expeditions against the Saxons, the Slaves, the Avares, &c. Omitting the emphasis and tears, which the chronicler doubtless added, we see therein that at the end of his life Charlemagne was occupied with the perils which menaced his kingdom on all sides. Many other texts, less precise, indicate the same uneasiness in him. He was still, surely, very far from foreseeing how brief a space this empire would survive him, and to what a degree the dissolution would be carried.

I do not propose recounting to you the events of this dissolution, but I wish to place before you the principal crises, and to point out their causes.

It took place between the death of Charlemagne in 814, and the accession of Hugh Capet in 987. All this epoch was employed in the accomplishment of this great work. It was by the fall of the race of the Carlovingians, and the accession of the Capetians, that it was definitively consummated.

At the death of Charlemagne, his empire extended from the north-east to the south-west, from the Elbe in Germany

[1] *Faits et Gestes de Charles le Grand*, by a monk of Saint Loup, in my *Collection des Memoires relatifs à l'Histoire de France*, vol. iii. p. 251.

to the Ebro in Spain; from north to south, it extended from the North Sea to Calabria, almost at the extremity of Italy. His power was, doubtless, exercised very unequally in this vast territory; upon many points he was not obeyed,—people did not even hear him spoken of, and he cared not for this: that was still his empire.

At the end of twenty-nine years, in 843, after the treaty of Verdun, by which the sons of Louis le Debonnaire, Lothaire, Charles le Chauve, and Louis le Germanique, shared this empire, this was its arrangement: it formed three kingdoms, divided according to this table:—

Table of the Dismemberment of the Empire of Charlemagne, in 843.

1. *Kingdom of France.* Charles le Chauve, 840—877.	2. *Kingdom of Germany.* Louis le Germanique, 840—876.	3. *Kingdom of Italy.* Lothaire I., emperor, 840—855.
It comprehended the countries situated between the Scheldt, the Meuse, the Saone, the Rhone, the Mediterranean, the Ebro, and the Ocean.	It comprehended the countries situated between the Rhine, the north sea, the Elbe, and the Alps.	It comprehended, 1. Italy, with the exception of Calabria; 2. The countries situated between the Rhone, the Saone, and the Meuse, to the West, the Rhine and the Alps to the East, that is, Provence, Dauphiné, Savoy, Switzerland, la Franche-Comté, a part of Burgundy, Lorraine, Alsace, and a part of the Netherlands.

Let it not be supposed that each of these kingdoms was compact unity; in that of France, the only one concerning which we have especially to occupy ourselves, two princes, Pepin II., in Aquitaine, (from the year 835), and Nomenoé in Brittany, (from the year 840), likewise assumed the title of king, and took from Charles le Chauve the sovereignty of a considerable portion of his territory.

The dismemberment followed its course: forty-five years after this epoch, in 888, on the death of Charles le Gros, the last of the Carlovingians, who seemed to unite for a moment all the states of Charlemagne, this was the point to which it had come. Instead of three kingdoms, we find seven:

Table of the Dismemberment of the Empire of Charlemagne, about the end of the Ninth Century.

Kingdoms.	Reigning kings.	Accession and death.	Extent.
1. Kingdom of France.	Charles le Simple.	893—929	The countries included between the Scheldt, the Meuse, the Saone, the Rhone, the Pyrenees, and the Ocean, and a portion of the north of Spain beyond the Pyrenees, formerly the county of Barcelona.
2. Kingdom of Navarre.	Fortun le Moine.	880—905	Almost all the north of Spain, between the Pyrenees and the Ebro.
3. Kingdom of Provence, or cis-Juran Burgundy	Louis l'Aveugle.	890—928	The countries included between the Saone, the Rhone. the Alps, the Jura, and the Mediterranean.
4. Kingdom of trans-Juran Burgundy	Raoul I.	888—912	The countries between the Jura, the Peninne Alps, and the Reuss, that is, Switzerland, Valais, the country of Geneva, Chablais, and Bugey.
5. Kingdom of Lorraine.	Zwentebold.	895—900	The countries between the Rhine, the Meuse, and the Scheldt.
6. Kingdom of Germany.	Arnoul.	888—899	The countries between the Rhine, the North Sea, the Elbe, the Oder, and the Alps.
7. Kingdom of Italy.	Bérenger I.	888—924	All Italy to the frontier of the kingdom of Naples, then the principality of Bénévento, and Calabria.

I return to the internal state of the kingdom of France. In 843, two princes only, a king of Aquitaine, and a duke of Brittany, shared his territories with Charles le Chauve. In 888, the dismemberment was carried still further, and by a cause which was not destined to stop. Every one knows that the possessors of domains and royal offices, that is to say, the beneficiaries and the dukes, counts, viscounts, centeniers, and other governors of provinces or districts, were constantly bent upon rendering themselves independent and hereditary, and assuring themselves the perpetual possession of their lands and governments. In 877, we find a capitulary of Charles le Chauve conceived in the following terms:

"If, after our death, any of our faithful subjects, seized with the love of God and our person, desire to renounce the world, and if he have a son or any other relation capable of serving the public, let him be at liberty to transmit his fees and honours as he pleases." [1]

And, in another article:

"If a count of this kingdom be about to die, and if his son be near us, we desire that our son, with those of our subjects who are most nearly related to the defunct count, as well as the other officers of the said county, and the bishop of the diocese in which it shall be situated, shall provide for his administration, until the death of the said count be announced to us, and we have been able to confer upon his son, present at our court, the honours with which he was invested. If the son of the defunct count be a child, let the same son, the bishop, and the other officers of the place, in like manner see to the administration of the county, until, informed of the death of the father, we have accorded the same honours to the son." [2]

Here we find the inheritance of benefices and of royal offices legally consecrated: and it is written in the manners, as in the laws; for numerous monuments attest that at this epoch, when, on the death of the governor of a province, the king attempted to give his county to any other than to his descendants, not only was he resisted therein by personal interest, but that such a measure was considered as a violation of right, a veritable injustice. Wilhelm and Engelschalk occupied two countships on the confines of Bavaria, under Louis le Begue: on their death, their offices were given to count Arbo, to the exclusion of their sons: "Their children and their relations, looking upon this as a great injustice, said that things should be otherwise, and that they would die by the sword, or that Arbo should quit the county of their family."[3]

This principle bore its fruits: About the end of the ninth

[1] *Cap. Car. Calv.*, a. 877, tit. 53, § 10; Bal., vol. ii., p. 264.

[2] Id. § 9 and 3; Bal., vol ii., p. 263—269.

[3] *Aune, Fuld*, a. 877, *Recueil des Historiens de France*, vol. viii. p. 48.

century, twenty-nine provinces, or fragments of provinces, were already erected into small states, the ancient governors of which, under the names of duke, count, viscount, had become their true sovereigns. Twenty-nine fiefs, in fact, which have played an eminent part in our history, are traceable to this period.

Table of the Feudal Dismemberment of the Kingdom of France, about the end of the Ninth Century.

Nos.	Title of the fief.	Date of becoming hereditary.	Name of the possessor at the end of the ninth century.	Date of his accession & of his death.
1	Duchy of Gascony.	872	Sanche Mittarra II.	
2	Viscounty of Bearn.	819	A son of Centulf II.	
3	County of Toulouse.	850	Eudes.	875—918
4	Marquisate of Septimanie	878	William le Pieux.	886—918
5	County of Barcelona.	864	Wifred le Velu.	864—906
6	County of Carcassonne.	819	Acfred I.	904
7	Viscounty of Narbonne.	...	Mayeul.	911
8	County of Roussilion.	...	Raoul.	About 905
9	County of Urgel.	884	Suinifred.	884—950
10	County of Poictiers.	880	Eble le Batard.	892—932
11	County of Auvergne.	864	William le Pieux.	886—918
12	Duchy of Aquitaine.	id.	The same.	id.
13	County of Angoulême.	866	Alduin I.	886—916
14	County of Perigord.	id.	William.	886—920
15	Viscounty of Limoges.	887	Adelbert.	914
16	Lordship of Bourbon.	...	Adhemar.	About 921
17	County of the Lyonnese.	890	William II.	890—920
18	Lordship of Beaujolais.	id.	Berauld I.	
19	Duchy of Burgundy.	887	Richard le Justicier.	877—921
20	County of Châlons.	886	Manasses de Vergy	
21	Duchy of France.	830	Robert II.	898—923
22	County of Vexin.	878	Aledran.	
23	County of Verman.	Abt. 880	Herbert I.	902
24	County of Valois.	id.	Pepin.	
25	County of Ponthieu.	859	Helgaud II.	878—926
26	County of Boulogne.	Abt. 860	Regniel.	882
27	County of Anjou.	870	Foulque le Roux.	888—938
28	County of Maine.	853	Gottfried.	
29	County of Britany.		Alain III.	877—907

The importance of these states is not equal, nor their independence absolutely alike; some still keep up frequent relations with the king of France; others are under the protection of a powerful neighbour; certain ties unite them, and hence certain reciprocal obligations result which will become the constitution of the feudal society. But the dominant feature is not any the less isolation, independence; they are evidently as many small states, born of the dismemberment of a great territory—local governments, formed at the expense of the central power.

From the end of the ninth century I pass at once to the end of the tenth, to the termination of the epoch which occupies us, to the complete fall of the Carlovingians, who give place to the Capetiens.

Instead of seven kingdoms, the ancient kingdom of Charlemagne then could number only four.

1. The kingdoms of Provence and Transjuran Burgundy were united, in 933, by Raoul II., king of Transjuran Burgundy, and formed the kingdom of Aries, governed, from 937 to 993, by Conrad le Pacifique.

2. The kingdom of Lorraine, from which many great fiefs were detached, was nothing more than a duchy, possessed, from 984 to 1026, by Thierry I.

3. Otho the Great, in 964, united the kingdom of Italy to the empire of Germany.

In the interior of the kingdom of France, the dismemberment was continued: instead of 29 small states or fiefs which we encountered at the end of the ninth century, we find therein, at the end of the tenth, fifty-five fully established.

Table of the Feudal Dismemberment of the Kingdom of France, about the end of the Tenth Century.

Nos.	Title of the Fief.	Date of the hereditary foundation.	Name of the possessor in 987.	Date of his accession and of his death.
1	Duchy of Gascony.	872	Bernard William.	984—1010
2	Viscounty of Bearn.	819	Centulf Gaston II.	984—1004
3	Viscounty of Bigorre.	End of 9th century.	Garcia Arnould I.	
4	County of Fezenzac.	920	Aimery I.	983—1032
5	County of Armagnac.	960	Gerard Trancalion.	

Table of the Feudal Dismemberment of the Kingdom of France, &c.—continue

Nos.	Title of the Fief.	Date of the hereditary foundation.	Name of the possessor in 987.	D ac of
6	County of Lectoure and Lomagne.	End of 10th century.	Raymond Arnaud.	
7	County of Astarac.	About 930	Arnaud II.	
8	County of Toulouse.	850	William Taillefer.	950—1037
9	County of Barcelona.	864	Borrel, count of Urgel.	967—993
10	County of Rouergue.	820	Raymond III.	961—1010
11	County of Carcassonne	819	Roger I.	957—1012
12	Viscounty of Narbonne	End of 9th century.	Raymond I.	966—1023
13	County of Melgueil.	Commencement of 10th century.	Bernard II.	
14	Lordship of Montpelier.	975	William I.	975—1019
15	County of Rousillon.	Middle of 9th century.	Gauffred I.	
16	County of Urgel.	884	Borrel.	950—993
17	County of Poictiers.	880	William Fier-a-Bras.	963—997
18	Duchy of Aquitaine.	864	The same.	
19	County of Auvergne.	Id.	Guij I.	979—989
20	County of Angoulême.	866	Arnaud le Bâtard.	975—1001
21	County of Perigord and of La Haute-Marche.	Id.	Adalbert I.	968—99
22	County of La Basse-Marche.	Id.	Bosson II.	968—103
23	Viscounty of Limoges.	887	Gerard.	963—100
24	Viscounty of Turenne.	Middle of 9th century.	Archambaud Jambe-Pourri.	
25	Viscounty of Bourges.	927	Geoffry II.	102
26	Lordship of Bourbon.	End of 9th century.	Archambaud II.	
27	County of Macon.	920	Alberic II.	979—99
28	Duchy of Burgundy.	877	Henry le Grand.	965—100
29	County of Chalons.	886	Hugues I.	987—103
30	Lordship of Salius.	920	Humbert II.	
31	County of Nevers.	987	Othon William.	987—102
32	County of Tonnerre.	End of 10th century.	Gui	987—99
33	County of Sens.	941	Renaud le Vieux.	951—99
34	County of Champagne.	End of 9th century.	Herbert II.	968—99
35	County of Blois.	834	Eudes I.	978—99
36	County of Rethel.	Middle of 10th century.	Manasses I.	

Table of the Feudal Dismemberment of the Kingdom of France, &c.—continued.

Nos.	Title of the Fief.	Date of the hereditary foundation.	Name of the possessor in 987.	Date of his accession and of his death.
37	County of Corbeil.	Mid. 10th cent.	Bouchard I.	1012
38	Barony of Montmorency.	Id.	Bouchard II.	1020
39	County of Vexin.	878	Gauthier I.	
40	County of Meulent.	959	Robert I.	
41	County of Vermandois.	880	Herbert III.	987—1000
42	County of Valois.	Id.	Gauthier I.	
43	County of Soissons.	End of 10th century.	Gui, Count of Vexin.	
44	County of Reucy and Rheims.	940	Gilbert.	739
45	County of Ponthieu.	859	Hugues.	
46	County of Boulogne.	860	Guy Barbe Blanche.	
47	County of Guines.	965	Adolphe.	966
48	County of Vendôme.	End of 10th century.	Bouchard I.	1007
49	Duchy of Normandy.	912	Richard-sans-Peur.	943—996
50	County of Anjou.	870	Foulques Nerra.	987—1040
51	County of Maine.	853	Hugues I.	955—1015
52	Lordship of Bellême.	940	Ives I.	997
53	County of Brittany.	...	Conan I.	987—992
54	Barony of Fougeres.	End of 10th century.	Meen I.	1020
55	County of Flanders.	862	Arnauld II. the younger	965—989

And these were not, as was the case under the Merovingians, accidental momentary dismemberments, the fruit of the general uncertainty of property and power; they were permanent, consummated results. These fifty-five duchies, counties, viscounties, lordships, had a long political existence; sovereigns hereditarily succeeded sovereigns; laws, customs, were regularly established therein. Men might write, indeed have written, their separate histories; for a long period they formed the history of France.

Such is the actual picture of the progressive dismemberment of the empire of Charlemagne, which commenced before the middle of the ninth century, and was accomplished at the end of the 10th. This dissolution was a subject of great sorrow and fear to some contemporaries, as, in the fall of the Roman empire, elevated minds thought they saw in it a new invasion of barbarism and of chaos. A talented man, Florus, deacon of the church of Lyons, under the reign of Louis le Debonnaire and of Charles le Chauve, has deplored it in a kind of lament, of which the following is the literal translation:—

"A beautiful empire flourished under a brilliant diadem; there was but one prince and one people; every town had judges and laws. The zeal of the priests was sustained by frequent councils; young people repeatedly read the holy scriptures, and the minds of children were formed to the study of letters. Love, on the one hand, on the other, fear, everywhere kept up good order. Thus the Frankish nation shone in the eyes of the whole world. Foreign kingdoms, the Greeks, the barbarians, and the senate of Latium, sent embassies to it. The race of Romulus, Rome herself, the mother of kingdoms, was subject to this nation; it was there that its chief, sustained by the help of Christ, received the diadem by apostolic gift. Happy if it had known its good fortune, the empire which had Rome as a citadel, and the door-keeper of heaven as a founder! Now fallen, this great power has lost at once its splendour and the name of empire; the kingdom lately so well united is divided into three parts; there is no one who can be looked upon as emperor; instead of a king, we see a kinglet; instead of a kingdom, a piece of a kingdom. The general good is annulled; each occupies himself with his own interests; they think of nothing else; God is forgotten. The pastors of the Lord, accustomed to meet, can no longer hold their synods amidst such division. There is no longer any assembly of the people, no longer any laws; an embassy arrives in vain there where there is no court. What will the neighbouring nations of the Danube, the Rhine, the Rhone, the Loire, and the Po, become? Anciently united by the ties of concord, now that the alliance is broken, they will be troubled by unhappy dissensions. To what end will the wrath of God bring all these evils? Scarcely is there one who thinks thereon with fear. Who meditates on what is passing, and is afflicted? men rather rejoice at the breaking up of the empire, and they call an order of things peace, which offers none of the benefits of peace."[1]

[1] *Recueil des Historiens des Gaules et de la France*, vol. vii. p. 302, and following pages.

Two facts clearly appear in this poem: on the one hand, the sorrow which the dismemberment of the empire caused to enlightened men; on the other, the popular satisfaction; the people felt as if restored to themselves, and disencumbered of a burden. The dissolution was evidently brought about by general, necessary causes. The bond which the will and conquests of Charlemagne had established between so many different nations, so many distant and separate territories, the unity of country and power, were factitious, and could not subsist.

What, upon regarding more nearly, were the causes of the phenomenon, whose principal crises we have just followed? How was the dismemberment effected? What internal transformation did society in the end then undergo?

A crowd of solutions, all equally unsatisfactory, have been given of this problem. Some people have assigned the decay of the empire of Charlemagne to the incapacity of his successors; of Louis le Debonnaire, of Charles le Chauve, Charles le Gros, and Charles the Simple; if they had had the genius and the character of the founder of the empire, the empire, say they, would gloriously have subsisted. Others have imputed its fall to the avidity of the dukes, counts, viscounts, beneficiaries, and other royal officers of all kinds; they sought to render themselves independent; they usurped the power, dismembered the state. According to others, it is the Normans who should answer for its ruin: the continuity of their invasions, and the misery into which the people had fallen, brought about all the evil. The explanations are evidently narrow and puerile. One only has more value, and merits a serious inquiry: this is that which M. Augustin Thierry has recently developed, in his *Lettres sur l'Histoire de France*, and especially in the second edition.[1] I do not entirely agree with it; I do not think that it is sufficient to account for the facts; but it is ingenious, lofty, and, without doubt, contains much truth.

According to M. Thierry, the dismemberment of the empire of Charlemagne was brought about by the diversity of races. On the death of Charles, when the terrible hand which forcibly held together so many different nations had

[1] Letters xi. and xii., p 191—247

lost its hold, they first separated, and then grouped themselves according to their true nature, that is to say, according to origin, language, manners; and under this influence was accomplished the formation of the new states. Such is the general physiognomy and explanation which M. Thierry assigns to this great event. Let us see how he applies the particular facts, and in what successive crises he supposes he can recognise the development of this cause. I shall perhap give a more precise, more systematic form to his ideas, tha they have in the letters themselves; but, at bottom, I sha neither add nor retrench anything.

Between the death of Charlemagne, and the accession of Hugues Capet, M. Thierry distinguishes two great epochs. The first extends from the death of Charlemagne to that of Charles le Gros, after which seven kingdoms, (M. Thierry reckons nine), shared the territory of the empire. The second extends from the end of the ninth century to the end of the tenth, to the accession of Hugues Capet. To these two epochs correspond two phases of the dismemberment, two revolutions different in object and character, although arising from the same causes, and tending to the same end.

To the first epoch belongs the national struggle of races, by which the great events which fill it are naturally explained. The two principal are incontestably the quarrel between Louis le Debonnaire and his sons, and that of the sons of Louis le Debonnaire among themselves. What is the true meaning of these two crises? Let us hear M. Thierry himself:

"From the commencement of the civil wars between t e emperor Louis I. and his children. . . . a great divergency of political opinion became visible between the Franks living in the midst of the Gaulish population, and those who remained upon the ancient German territory. The first, connect d, despite their descent, with the interest of the people conquered by their ancestors, in general took part against the emperor, that is, against the empire, which, for the Gaulish aborigines, was a government of conquest. The others united in the contrary party, with all the Teutonic colonies, the ancient enemies of the Franks. Thus all the Teutonic nations, leagued apparently for the rights of a single man, defended their national cause by maintaining against the Gallo-Franks and the Welskes, a power which was the result of the German victories. . . . According to the testimony of a cotemporary, the emperor Lodewig mistrusted the Gallo-Franks, and put confidence only in the Germans. When, in 830, the partisans of a reconciliation between father and son proposed, as a means of attaining it, a general assembly, the evil-disposed laboured to procure that this assembly might be held in a town in Roman France. "But the emperor," says the same historian, "was not of this opinion, and he obtained, according to his desires, that the people should be convoked at Nimeguen: all Germany repaired thither in great numbers, in order to aid him."[1]

"Shortly afterwards, Germany herself, hitherto so faithful to the empire, separated her national cause from that of the new Cæsars. When Lodewig I. at his death, left the Frankish dominion shared between his three sons, Lother, Lodewig, and Karle; although the first had the title of emperor, the Teutonic nations attached themselves to the second, who was only king. The question of the preeminence of the empire over the kingdoms was soon discussed between the brothers at the point of the sword; and from the commencement of the war, the eastern Franks, the Almanni, the Saxons, and the Thuringians took part against the *keisar*, (emperor.)

"Reduced to the government of Italy, Helvetia, Provence, and a small portion of Belgian Gaul, the emperor Lother also had as few partisans on the borders of the Rhine and the Elbe, as upon those of the Seine and the Loire: "Know," he wrote to his brothers, who prayed him to leave them in peace each in his kingdom, "know, that the title of emperor was given to me by superior authority, and consider what extent of power and what magnificence should accompany such a title." This haughty answer was, properly speaking, a manifesto against the national independence of which the people felt the want; they answered to it, in a terrible manner, by that famous battle of Fontanet, near Auxerre, where the sons of the *Welkses* and the *Teutskes*, fought under the same banner for the overthrow of the political system founded by Charles the Great."[2]

Despite the diversity of combination, both quarrels have, then, the same character: and, in this continued effort against

[1] *Recueil des Historiens des Gaules et de la France*, vol. vi. p. 8.
[2] Letter xi. p. 195—199.

unity and empire, it was always according to races that the dismemberment tended to operate.

In all the events comprehended between 814 and 888, as in these two, M. Thierry thinks the action of the same cause may be recognised, and he comes thus to the formation of the nine kingdoms that it raised upon the ruins of the empire. He reckons nine, for he looks upon Aquitaine and Brittany as kingdoms, although at the end of the ninth century the count of Brittany and the dukes of Aquitaine did not bear the title of king. Then commenced the second epoch, and the second revolution.

In this epoch it is no longer the breaking up of states according to the difference of race that is in question; this work was already consummated. But Frankish Gaul remains under the empire of foreign sovereigns: the population which inhabits it is mixed; even Gauls dominate in it; and the descendants of Charlemagne are pure Germans. To expel them, to put in their place princes of a more national origin, such according to M. Thierry, was the constant effort of France, properly so called, from 888 to 987; such is the secret of all the vicissitudes, of all the struggles of the 10th century, and especially, 1st, of the struggle of the elective king Eudes against the legitimate king, Charles le Simple; 2, of that of Hugues the Great, duke of France, against Louis d'Outre Mer; 3, of the definitive fall of Louis V. and of the succession of Hugues Capet.

"The race of Charles the Great," says M. Thierry, "entirely German, and attaching themselves by the ties of tradition and the affections of parentage, to the countries of the Teutonic language, could only be looked upon by the Franks as an obstacle to that separation upon which their independent existence had just been founded. The idiom of the conquest, fallen into disuse in the castles of the lords, was preserved in the royal house. The descendants of the Frank emperors deemed it an honour to understand this language of their ancestors, and collected pieces of verse composed by the poets beyond the Rhine. . . . Doubtless, in the events which followed 987, the premature death of Lodewig, son of Lother, we must attribute a large share to the ambition and character of the founder of the third dynasty. . . . Nevertheless it may be affirmed that this ambition, hereditary in the family of

Robert le Fort, for a whole century was maintained and aided by the movement of national opinion. Even the expressions of the Chronicles, dry as they are at this epoch of our history, lead us to suppose that the question of the change of dynasty was not then looked upon as a personal affair. According to them, the matter in hand was an inveterate hostility, an enterprise undertaken long since with the view of rooting up tho posterity of the Frank kings from the kingdom of France. . . . . The accession of the third race was the accomplishment of this enterprise ; it was, properly speaking, the end of the kingdom of the Franks, and the substitution of a national royalty instead of the government founded by the conquest."[1]

From Charlemagne to Hugh Capet, the history of France reduces itself into two great facts: 1, the separation of nations according to the diversity of races; 2, the expulsion of the sovereigns of a purely German race, in order to give place to sovereigns of Gallo-Frankish, that is to say, national origin.

Such is the system of M. Thierry ; a rare knowledge of events, a lively feeling of the situation and of manners are displayed therein, at each step. But a few observations will suffice, if I do not deceive myself, to show that it is incomplete, and too exclusive.

1. In the various alliances and combinations which took place under Louis le Debonnaire, and his children, the nations were far from being always connected or separated according to races; many other causes determined their movements, and the consideration of race often appears very subordinate therein. I desire for proof only, the facts of which M. Thierry himself has spoken. In the wars of Louis against his children, the nations of purely German race seem to defend the emperor and the empire; in the wars of the sons of Louis, it is they who combat him; and among those who defend it in the train of Lothaire, there are Romans, Gauls, Goths, Burgundians, Franks; nor are all the kingdoms ranged against the imperial pretensions of Lothaire, for the king of Aquitaine, Pepin II. allied himself with him against Louis le Germanique and Charles le Chauve. The geographical position, personal interests, numerous changing and special causes evidently exer-

[1] Letter xii. pp. 228, 235, 287.

cised an influence over their alliance which was often more decisive than the origin and relationship of nations.

2. This relationship is not more decisive as to the formation of kingdoms: those of Cis-Juran and Trans-Juran Burgundy clearly show this; all the races are there mixed, and there the demarcation is determined by entirely other motives.

3. The consideration of race is still more foreign to the formation of three small states, duchies, counties, lordships, &c., into which each kingdom was subdivided. There was here no struggle of origin or nationality, and yet there was separation, dismemberment, the same as among the great masses of populations of which kingdoms are formed.

Other causes than the diversity of races presided, then, at the dissolution of the empire of Charlemagne, and at the formation of the new states. That, doubtless, contributed to it: but it should not be looked upon as a general, dominant cause: for the same facts are brought about when it did not act, as when it did act. Now it is the general and dominant cause which we seek. Since the diversity of races does not furnish us with it, let us endeavour to find it elsewhere.

You will recollect that, in exhibiting the state of Roman Gaul and its inhabitants, ancient and modern, after the great invasion,[1] I established that the two primitive associations of the German nations—the tribes, administered according to the principles of liberty; and the warrior-band, in which military and aristocratic patronage prevailed—were equally broken up in passing to the Roman soil, for their institutions no longer suited the new situation of the conquerors, at once proprietors, and dispersed over a vast territory.

You have also seen the Roman society, its general organization, at least, as to the force which presided over it, the imperial administration, dissolve after the invasion: so that at the commencement of the eighth century, Roman society and German society had alike perished in Frankish Gaul, now abandoned to the most heterogeneous anarchy.

The attempt of Charlemagne was to entirely resuscitate it; to restore the empire and its unity, by re-establishing on the

[1] Lecture viii. vol. i.

one hand the Roman administration, on the other, national German assemblies, and military patronage. He in some sort renewed all the modes of association, all the means of government which the empire and Germany had known, and which lay disorganized and powerless, in order to replace them in vigour for his own good. He was at once chief of the warriors, president of the national assemblies, and emperor. He succeeded for a moment, and on his own account. But this was, as it were, a galvanic resurrection; applied to a great society, the principles of the imperial administration, those of the wandering band, and those of the free tribes of Germany, were equally impracticable. No great society could be maintained. It is necessary to find its elements, on one hand in the minds of men, on the other in social relations. Now the moral and the social state of the people at this epoch equally resisted all association, all government of a single and extended character. Mankind had few ideas, and did not look far around. Social relations were rare and restricted. The horizon of thought and of life was exceedingly limited. Under such conditions, a great society is impossible. What are the natural and necessary bonds of political union? on the one hand, the number and extent of the social relations; on the other, of the ideas whereby men communicate, and are held together. Where neither of these are numerous or extensive, the bonds of a great society or state are non-existent. Such was the case in the times of which we now speak. Small societies, local governments, cut, as it were, to the measure of existing ideas and relations, were alone possible; and these alone succeeded in establishing themselves.

The elements of these petty societies, and petty local governments were ready at hand. The possessors of benefices by grant from the king, or of domains occupied by conquest, the counts, dukes, governors of provinces, were disseminated throughout the country. These became the natural centres of corresponding associations. Round them was agglomerated, voluntarily, or by force, the neighbouring population, whether free or in bondage. Thus were formed the petty states called fiefs; and this was the real cause of the dissolution of the empire of Charlemagne. Power and the nation were dismembered, because unity of power and of the nation was impossible; all became local, because all generality was banished from interests, existences, and minds. Laws, judgments, the regulations for order, wars, tyrannies, liberties, all were compressed in small territories, because nothing could be regulated or maintained in a larger circle. When this great fermentation of the various social conditions, and of the various powers which covered France was accomplished, when the small societies which had arisen from it had invested with a more or less regular and determinate form, the hierarchical relations which united them, that result of the conquest and of the reviving civilization took the name of the feudal system. It is at about the end of the tenth century, and when the Carlovingian race disappeared, that this revolution may be looked upon as consummated. We have just followed it in the historical monuments; in the next lecture we shall study the legislative monuments of the same epoch, and if I do not deceive myself, we shall equally recognise it there.

TWENTY-FIFTH LECTURE.

History of legislation from the death of Charlemagne to the accession of Hugh Capet—Necessity of precisely determining the general characteristics of the legislation at the two terms of this epoch, in order to understand properly its progress during its course—1. State of the legislation under Charlemagne—It is personal, and varies according to races—The church and the imperial power give it some unity—2. State of the legislation after Hugh Capet—It is territorial; local customs have replaced national laws—All central legislative power has disappeared—3. History of legislation in Frankish Gaul between these two terms—Analytical tables of the capitularies of Louis le Debonnaire, Charles le Chauve, Louis le Begue, Carloman, Eudes, and Charles le Simple—Comparison of these tables according to the figures only—Comparison of the provisions of the capitularies—General results of this inquiry.

I HAVE sought the progress and the causes of the dismemberment of the empire of Charlemagne, in events, in history, properly so called. I have endeavoured to distinguish what transformation Gallo-Frankish society underwent, and why. I have shown that, of the various explanations which people have attempted to give of it, none is satisfactory; that that even which contains the most truth, the diversity of races, is exclusive, incomplete, does not account for all the facts. It seemed to me that the impossibility of a sole and extensive society, in the state in which social relations and minds then were, alone fully explains this great and so rapid metamorphosis; that the formation of a multitude of small societies, that is to say, the establishment of the feudal system, was the necessary consequence, the natural course of events; that since their meeting, Roman and German society had tended towards this end, and that they had, in fact, attained it at the end of the tenth century, when the dismemberment of the empire of Charlemagne was definitively accomplished.

If this explanation is established, if such was the progress of facts from Charlemagne to Hugh Capet, we ought to find it in the history of laws as in the history of events. Between the development of legislation and that of society, there is an intimate correspondence; the same revolutions are accomplished therein, and in an analogous order. Let us now study the history of the laws during the same epoch, and let us see if they will lead us to the same result, if we shall see the same explanation arise from it.

The history of laws is more difficult to understand thoroughly than that of events, properly so called. Laws, from their very nature, are monuments more incomplete, less explicit, and consequently more obscure. Besides, nothing is more difficult, and yet more indispensable, than to take fast hold of and never lose the chronological thread. When we give an account of external facts, wars, negotiations, invasions, &c., their chronological concatenation is simple, palpable; each event bears, as it were, its date written on its face. The actual date of laws is often correctly known; it is often known at what epoch they were decreed; but the facts which they were designed to regulate, the causes which made them to be written in one year rather than another, the necessities and social revolutions to which the legislation corresponds, this is what is almost always unknown, at least, not understood, and which it is still necessary to follow step by step. It is from this study having been neglected, from the not having rigorously observed the chronological progress of laws in their relation with that of society, that confusion and falsehood have so often been thrown into their history. For example, you constantly hear speak of the feudal laws as already in vigour at the sixth century, immediately after the conquest, and of barbarous laws as being still in vigour at the eleventh century, under the feudal system. The resemblance of certain facts, of certain words, which are equally met with in the two epochs, causes this mistake: a little more attention to the chronological development of laws and of the social state, would have prevented it. Numerous errors in this matter, some of them the result of mere ignorance, many systematic and learned, have no other origin.

In order to prevent falling into it in the study with which we have now to occupy ourselves, one means only seems to me efficacious, that is, to determine precisely the two terms between which this study is comprised, that is, the general state of Gallo-Frankish society, first at the death of Charlemagne, and then at the accession of Hugh Capet. When we correctly know these two facts, when we know what the legislation was throughout its progress, we shall not be so liable to deceive ourselves concerning the route which it had followed in the interval; and if the study which we make of its history, between the two terms, gives a clear account of its transition from one to the other, we shall be justified in confiding in it.

It will be understood that I only intend here to point out the general characteristics of legislation under Charlemagne and under Hugh Capet; but that will suffice for our purpose.

At the first epoch, at the commencement of the ninth century, the essential characteristic feature of the legislation is that it is personal and not territorial; that is to say, that each people, each race, has its law, and that wherever men, of such or such a race, live, they follow its law, and not that of the territory which they inhabit. The Romans are governed by the Roman law; the Franks by the Salic or the Ripuarian law; the Burgundians by the Burgundian law; the Lombards by the Lombard law; the Saxons by the Saxon law, &c. Nationality is inherent in the legislation; in the diversity of races, and not in that of places, resides the principle of the variety of laws.

Above this variety hover certain principles of unity. And first, the canonical legislation is one, the same for all people, whatever their origin or name. The religious society is essentially one; unity is the standard of the church; hence the unity of the ecclesiastical legislation, in the midst of the most various national laws.

Civil legislation itself, taking this word in its most extensive sense, and as opposed to religious legislation, is not devoid of all unity. The king, the emperor, with or without the concurrence of the national assemblies, decrees certain laws applicable to all the inhabitants of his empire, Romans, Franks, Lombards, Burgundians, &c. There is evidently universality in many of the capitularies of Charlemagne; they are addressed to the whole territory, and are obligatory upon all.

To speak in a general way, and leaving aside exceptions, it is more especially in respect to civil and penal law that diversity according to races pervades the legislation of this period. Unity is complete in the religious legislation, and tends to prevail in the political legislation, which comes under the influence of the central power.

Such are the general characteristics of legislation at the commencement of the ninth century. I pass at once to the commencement of the eleventh, the term at which the epoch which we are studying stops, and when the feudal system had taken her definitive consistency in France, and truly possessed society. What metamorphosis is brought about in the laws?

Their diversity, according to races, has disappeared. There still remain some traces of it; we still find the Saxon, Salic, Lombard law spoken of ; but these are only rare instances, the faint echo of an order of things becoming extinct. The laws vary, not according to races, but, on the one hand, according to conditions; on the other, according to places. The social legislation, from being personal, has become territorial. There are different laws for different kinds of property, different degrees of liberty. Accordingly, in each small state formed by the feudal subdivision of the territory, arise peculiar laws. The diversity of races has been replaced by that of classes and of places. To the national laws have succeeded privileges and customs. This is the first characteristic, the essential feature of the new physiognomy that legislation has taken.

Another great change also took place. You have just seen that in the beginning of the ninth century, the unity of the imperial power was, notwithstanding the variety of the national laws, a principle of unity in the laws. In the commencement of the eleventh century, nothing of the kind existed; there was no longer any central, general legislative power; the variety of laws established according to places, to circumstances—that is to say, the variety of privileges and customs was no longer combated or modified by any principle of unity derived from a higher sphere. There was no unity existing but in the legislation of the church, which alone remained superior to all diversities.

The great revolutions, then, which occurred in the legislation from the ninth to the tenth century, may be thus stated: 1. Legislation, according to races, had given way to legislation according to social conditions, to local circumstances. 2. Central legislative power, and the unity thence resulting to certain branches of legislation, more especially in political legislation, had disappeared.

This is the transformation which the history of legislation from the ninth to the eleventh century has to describe. Let us exhibit its course.

I have already spoken to you of the legislative monuments which remain of this period, the capitularies of the Carlovingian kings. You remember the analysis to which I subjected those of Charlemagne, and the results I derived from that analysis. I classed them, as you recollect, under eight principal heads: 1. Moral legislation; 2. Political legislation; 3. Penal legislation; 4. Civil legislation; 5. Religious legislation; 6. Canonical legislation; 7. Domestic legislation; 8. Occasional legislation. I have applied the same method to the capitularies of Charlemagne's successors, with these results:

Analytical Table of the Capitularies of Louis le Debonnaire.

Date.	Articles.	Moral Legislation.	Political Legislation.	Penal Legislation.	Civil Legislation.	Religious Legislation.	Canonical Legislation.	Domestic Legislation.	Occasional Legislation.
815	7	...	...	...	...	...	...	...	7
816	1	...	...	...	...	...	1		
Id.	29	...	...	4	...	1	24	...	1
Id.	1								
817	18	...	18						
Id.	80	...	...	...	...	...	80		
Id.	3	..	3						
Id.	1	. .	1						
819	21	1	4	12	4				
Id.	9	...	9						
Id.	12	...	...	6	6				
Id.	8	. .	6	...	2				

Analytical Table of the Capitularies of Louis le Debonnaire—continued.

Date.	Articles.	Moral Legislation.	Political Legislation.	Penal Legislation.	Civil Legislation.	Religious Legislation.	Canonical Legislation.	Domestic Legislation.	Occasional Legislation.
819	29	2	24	...	...	...	3		
Id.	11	2	3	...	...	...	6		
821	5	...	5						
822	6	...	6						
Id.	8	...	...	...	...	...	...	. .	8
823	28	11	16	...	...	...	1		
826	7	...	...	5	...	...	2		
827	1	...	...	...	...	...	...	...	1
828	10	...	4	...	...	...	6		
829	46	...	20	9	10	...	6	...	1
832	1	...	...	...	...	...	...	...	1
834	1	...	...	...	...	...	...	...	1
837	14	...	14						
Id.	5	...	3	...	2				
26	362	16	136	36	24	1	129		20

Analytical Table of the Capitularies of Charles le Chauve.

Date.	Articles.	Moral Legislation.	Political Legislation.	Penal Legislation.	Civil Legislation.	Religious Legislation.	Canonical Legislation.	Domestic Legislation.	Occasional Legislation.
844	6	...	6						
Id.	9	...	...	...	...	...	9		
845	6	...	6						
Id.	12	...	4	...	...	...	5	...	3
Id.	8	...	8						
844	10	...	...	...	...	...	...	...	10
846	19	...	10	...	...	...	9		
847	11	...	7	...	...	...	...	...	4
Id.	12	...	8	...	...	...	...	...	4
851	8	...	8						
853	19	...	6	...	...	...	6	...	7
Id.	3	...	...	...	...	...	...	...	3
Id.	15	...	12	...	...	...	3		
Id.	13	...	7	5	...	...	...	...	1
854	13	...	10	1	...	...	1	...	1
Id.	7	...	1	...	...	...	...	...	6
Id.	1	...	...	...	...	...	...	...	1

Analytical Table of the Capitularies of Charles le Chauve—continued

Date.	Articles.	Moral Legislation.	Political Legislation.	Penal Legislation.	Civil Legislation.	Religious Legislation.	Canonical Legislation.	Domestic Legislation.	Occasional Legislation.
856	1	...	1						
Id.	15	...	6	...	...	..	...	..	9
Id.	5	1	...	...	...	..	..	...	4
Id.	6	1	...	...	...	...	...	...	5
Id.	1	...	...	...	...	...	...	...	1
857	10	...	9	...	...	1			
Id.	8	...	4	4					
Id.	5	...	...	...	...	...	...	..	5
858	15		15						
859	12	...	8	...	...	...	...	...	4
Id.	13	...	...	...	...	...	...	...	13
Id.	13	...	...	...	...	...	...	...	13
860	19	...	19						
Id.	18	...	18						
861	1	...	1						
862	4	...	...	...	...	...	...	...	4
Id.	20	...	...	...	...	...	...	...	20
864	43	...	32	3	4	...	...	1	3
865	23	...	5	...	...	...	4	...	14
868	12	...	8	...	...	...	4		
Id.	1	...	...	...	...	...	...	...	1
869	17	...	12	...	...	...	5		
Id.	7	...	...	...	...	...	...	...	7
870	1	...	...	...	...	...	...	...	1
Id.	2	...	...	...	...	...	...	...	2
872	3	...	...	...	...	...	...	...	3
873	12	...	8	4			...		
874	3	...	...	...	...	...	...	...	3
876	15	...	9	...	...	1	5		
Id.	9	...	...	...	...	...	...	...	9
Id.	4	...	...	...	...	...	...	...	4
877	1	...	...	...	...	...	...	...	1
Id.	1	...	...	...	...	...	...	...	1
Id.	37	...	11	...	...	...	...	...	26
51	529	2	259	17	4	2	51	1	193

Analytical Table of the Capitularies of Louis le Begue—877-9.

Date.	Articles.	Moral Legislation.	Political Legislation.	Penal Legislation.	Civil Legislation.	Religious Legislation.	Canonical Legislation.	Domestic Legislation.	Occasional Legislation.
877	5	...	...	...	...	...	...	...	5
878	8	...	3	1	...	...	4		
879	9	...	3	...	...	...	...	...	6
3	22	...	6	1	...	...	4	...	11

Analytical Table of the Capitularies of Carloman, son of Louis le Begue, (879—884.)

Date.	Articles.	Moral Legislation.	Political Legislation.	Penal Legislation.	Civil Legislation.	Religious Legislation.	Canonical Legislation.	Domestic Legislation.	Occasional Legislation.
882	1	...	...	...	...	...	...	...	1
Ib.	14	...	12	2					
883	3	...	...	3					
3	18	...	12	5	...	...	...	...	1

Capitulary Table of Eudes, King of France, (887—898.)

Date.	Articles.	Moral Legislation.	Political Legislation.	Penal Legislation.	Civil Legislation.	Religious Legislation.	[illegible]al Legislation.	Domestic Legislation.	Occasional Legislation.
888	...	...	...	...	...	...	...	...	1

Analytical Table of the Capitularies of Charles le Simple, (893—929.)

Date.	Articles.	Moral Legislation.	Political Legislation.	Penal Legislation.	Civil Legislation.	Religious Legislation.	Canonical Legislation.	Domestic Legislation.	Occasional Legislation.
907	1	...	...	...	...	...	...	...	1
921	8	...	...	...	...	...	...	...	8
926	1	...	...	...	...	...	...	...	1
3	10	...	...	...	...	...	...	...	10

Comparative Analytical Table of the Capitularies of Charlemagne, Louis le Debonnaire, Charles le Chauve, Louis le Begue, Carloman, Eudes, and Charles le Simple.

Date.	Articles.	Moral Legislation.	Political Legislation.	Penal Legislation.	Civil Legislation.	Religious Legislation.	Canonical Legislation.	Domestic Legislation.	Occasional Legislation.	
65	1151	87	293	130	110	85	305	73	12	Charlemagne. (768—814.)
26	362	16	136	36	24	1	129	...	20	Louis le Debonnaire. (814—840.)
51	529	2	259	17	4	2	51	1	193	Charles le Chauve. (840—877.)
3	22	...	6	1	...	...	4	...	11	Louis le Begue. (877—879.)
3	19	...	12	5	...	...	...	...	2	Carloman. (879—884.)
1	1	...	...	...	...	...	...	...	1	Eudes. (887—898.)
3	10	...	...	...	...	...	...	...	10	Charles le Simple. (893—929.)
152	2094	105	706	289	138	88	489	74	249	

Before we enter into an examination of the provisions themselves, thus classified under these different heads, let us consider their numeral aspect: the mere comparison of figures will develop important facts.

Between the reign of Charlemagne and that of Louis le Debonnaire, if we merely look to the number of articles in moral, political, penal, religious, &c., legislations, we shall notice very little difference; the various classes of capitulalaries are, as to mere figures, in very nearly the same respective proportions. The occasional legislation is somewhat fuller in the latter reign, but not sufficiently so to arrest our attention. We must penetrate quite into the interior of the legislation to discover that it has become changed in its character, that it is no longer the work of the same government in the latter as in the former case.

We perceive a further distinction under Charles le Chauve; here the numerical proportion of the various classes of legislation is changed. Under the heads of moral, penal, civil, religious, canonical, and domestic legislation, we find very few articles, while, on the other hand, the list of political and occasional measures is much fuller; a certain indication of a great change in the state of society and of power. To what interests does moral, penal, civil, religious legislation address itself. To interests which affect society far more nearly than they do power; important, doubtless, for power itself, but of an importance which has nothing direct or selfish about it, which has relation to the public functions of government, and not to distinct and personal existence. Political and occasional legislation, on the contrary, affects power in its personality; it is power which such measures serve or impede; it is power, more especially, and often power alone which they contemplate in their effects. Accordingly, whenever, in whatever epoch, or under whatever form, you see political and occasional laws multiply, be assured that the government is in danger, that it has enemies against whom it is defending itself, that it is not simply and solely occupied in fulfilling its public character, that it is not principally intent upon social interests, but that it is its personal interests which guide and rule its action. In the course of the Revolution of England, and of our own, in all similar crises, what classes of legislation fill the statute books? Political and occasional laws.

The name and character of law is given formally to all the measures of government; but, in point of fact, they are merely acts of government, acts framed in the view above all to the interest of power, and for its service, rather than for the public service. This fact manifests itself clearly in a simple numerical comparison of the different classes of capitularies under Charlemagne and under Charles le Chauve. Under Charlemagne, occasional legislation is very limited; it is evidently a tranquil government, having full confidence in itself, occupied solely with the idea of accomplishing its task and conducting the affairs of the society. Under Charles le Chauve, it is to political and occasional measures that legislation applies itself; this, assuredly, is a tottering government, desperately endeavouring to regain the force and order which are abandoning it. Weakness and disorganization in the central power are manifested in the very fact.

How stands the matter under the successors of Charles le Chauve? What do the figures tell us here?

Political and occasional legislation still predominate in the capitularies, but even that is more and more limited; even the legislative measures in which power is personally interested, become fewer and fewer. It is clear that, not only as under Charles le Chauve, the central government is in peril, but that it is disappearing altogether; before, it defended itself; now, it makes no attempt to do so; it abandons itself, it takes no heed to itself; it has, indeed, no self to take heed to, for it is non-existent.

Thus, without any examination of the contents of the capitularies, by a simple comparison of the figures which indicate the various classes of laws, we identify the same progress, we are present at the same spectacle that has been exhibited to us by the history of events. Legislation is stamped with the impress of the revolutions which the country underwent. The government of Charlemagne, like his Empire, is dismembered and dissolved.

Let us examine the interior of this legislation, the contents of the capitularies: we shall arrive at precisely the same results.

This examination is susceptible of great extension, and might be made the topic of a vast number of curious observations; but I am compelled to limit myself to general facts. Of these, the most important are as follow:

1. In describing to you the capitularies of Charlemagne, I pointed out their extreme diversity; they are not, as you will remember, merely laws, but comprise acts of every kind; ancient laws re-enacted, fragments of ancient laws, applied specially to particular portions of the empire; additions to the ancient laws; new laws of the emperor, decreed sometimes with the concurrence of the laity and ecclesiastics together; sometimes with that of the ecclesiastics alone, sometimes, again, of the emperor in person, independently of any assembly at all; instructions given to the *missi dominici;* questions addressed to the *missi;* answers by the emperor to questions from the *missi;* notes made by the emperor for his own use; memoranda of questions that he proposed to put, in the next general assembly, to such and such persons, bishops, counts, &c. In a word, the prodigious variety of the acts comprehended under the general title of capitularies was one of the facts upon which I particularly dwelt.

But, however great their variety, it was always from Charlemagne himself that these acts emanated; he was on all occasions the author and centre of the legislation. Whether old or new laws were in question, whether instructions or private memoranda, whether questions or answers, his presence and his power were everywhere felt; he was everywhere active and sovereign.

Under Charles le Chauve, the case was altogether different. The diversity of the acts comprised under the title of capitularies still subsisted, but a far different diversity had introduced itself: that of legislators. It is no longer the emperor alone who speaks and ordains; it is no longer from him alone that all things emanate. Among the capitularies which go under the name of Charles le Chauve, there are several acts with which he had nothing to do.[1] 1. Petitions from certain bishops to the king, requiring him, and that sometimes in a very imperious tone, to establish order, and to protect the church. 2. Counsels addressed by bishops to the king respecting the government of his states, and even as to that of the interior of his palace;[2] 3. Acts of bishops regulating the administration of their affairs in the different kingdoms among themselves, entirely without any reference to the king him-

[1] Cap. Car. Calv. a. 845, 856; Baluze, ii. 7, 14. [2] Ib. a. 808; ii., 101.

self.[1] 4. Acts of the pope, with respect to the affairs of the king and of the kingdom.[2] Finally, treaties, conventions entered into between the king and his brothers, or his nephews, or his *fideles*. So that the sources of the acts constituting this collection are as various as the nature of the acts themselves. A most significant fact, which a glance at the title and first two or three lines of each capitulary fully enables us to recognise.

2. There is another no less deserving of attention. Not only does political legislation, under Charles le Chauve, occupy a larger space than under Charlemagne; it is wholly different in itself, has no longer the same object in view. The political laws of Charlemagne have almost always reference to truly public interests, to the business of general government, sometimes relating to the conduct of the imperial delegates, the dukes, counts, centeniers, *missi dominici*, *scabini*, &c.; sometimes to the holding of the assemblies, local or general, in which justice was administered. The relations of Charlemagne with his beneficiaries and with the church, make their appearances indeed, but more occasionally and more briefly. Under Charles le Chauve the case is reversed: provisions bearing upon administration, properly so called, upon the conduct of the royal officers, on the holding of assemblies, on really public business, are rare; the predominant feature, that, in fact, which constitutes the political legislation of this reign, is provisions having for their object the arrangements of the king with his beneficiaries, and with the church, that is to say, with the portion of the government, further removed from the public, nearer to the king himself, whether the other parties in these cases are ecclesiastics or laymen, it is always class or personal interests that we find in question; it is always some personal or class grievance for which redress is sought at the hands of the king, or some extension of privileges solicited. The representations made are more or less powerful, more or less legitimate, but it is no longer the body of the people that is in question, nor the government of the people; political legislation is no longer a public legislation; it has changed its character; its object is wholly private interests.

1. It has, at the same time, changed its tone. The legislation of Charlemagne is, in general, concise and imperious; it

[1] Cap. Car. Carlo. a. 859; ii. 121. [2] Ib. a. 877; ii. 251.

commands or prohibits summarily, without taking up the time in roundabout phrases and dissertations, and such is the proper method. Laws are not theses of philosophy nor specimens of eloquence; it is not their business to maintain doctrines nor to move the passions; to command, to forbid, is their purpose, and they always suffer when they deviate in any way from it. The legislation of Charlemagne, for the most part, went straightforward to this object. Such was by no means the case with the legislation of Charles le Chauve. However closely we examine that legislation, you can scarce detect either command or prohibition, amid the heaps of ratiocination, exhortation, advice, entreaty. The capitularies of Charles le Chauve are not regular laws, but either sermons addressed to minds sought to be brought over to particular views, or negotiations with men whose obedience was only to be hoped for by a certain degree of obedience in return.

This leads us to the greatest legislative change which is seen between these two epochs, to the really new character of the legislation of Charles le Chauve, and of his successors, the character in which the approach of the feudal system is clearly shown.

I have just said that in the capitularies of the last Carlovingians, we find many acts which do not emanate from the king only, from the central legislative power, and especially many treaties; between Charles le Chauve, for example, and his brothers, his nephews, or other princes, in possession of some portion of the territory of the empire of Charlemagne. Out of the fifty-one capitularies of Charles le Chauve, there are nine treaties of this kind. But this is not all; almost the entire legislation at this epoch is a series of negotiations between separate and independent powers. Under Charlemagne, however various they may have been, whether they were addressed to the agents of power or to its subjects, all the acts bore the character of a superior who commands inferiors. Social and political unity was strongly marked on it. Under Charles le Chauve, the unity disappeared; it is evidently no longer a general power which commands; it is a special power which treats with other powers, a government which defends its territory and rights against other governments. Out of the 529 articles which the capitularies of Charles le Chauve contain, more than a hundred have this appearance; legislation has become diplomacy. Now what is the dominant characteristic of the feudal society? Precisely the facts which we here observe; petty states, petty governments, considering themselves each independent in its territory, or nearly so, quarrel, dispute, reciprocally send ambassadors, hold conferences, form conventions. During a long period the relations of royalty with the feudal lords dispersed throughout the French territory are nothing else; its laws, its charters, are treaties; its progress is concession or acquisition. This is what distinguishes, what characterises feudal society when considered in its whole. Now, under the last Carlovingians, this characteristic already appears in the laws : there is no longer any legislation, properly so called: there is diplomacy between independent states.

You see the history of legislation leads us to the same results to which history, properly so called, conducted us. We have just put to laws the corresponding question to that which we have addressed to events; the answer is the same: we have discovered not only the same tendency, but the same progression in the development of facts so different. This, if I do not deceive myself, is the best confirmation of our view of the dismemberment of the empire of the Carlovingians. We have had reason to lay aside as incomplete that which is drawn from the diversity of races, for you see it is contradictory to the history of legislation; from the ninth to the eleventh century, the diversity of races, instead of exercising any more empire over laws, ceased to be a dominant principle, and the source of variety: the laws vary not according to races, but according to classes and to places.

The diversity of races, then, will never explain the history of the legislation at this epoch, whilst the progressive development of the feudal society, the necessary formation of a multitude of petty states and petty powers,—one sole state and one sole power having become impossible—alike accounts for the vicissitudes of legislation and the vicissitudes of society

I will go no further into the history of the laws under the Carlovingians. I should find there the texts for many curious observations; but they would require too much detail, and would carry us further than we have time to go. In our next lecture we will examine the history of the church, of religious society at the same epoch; and then see if it will give us results analogous to those which have been furnished us by the history of civil society. Before, however, I close this lecture, I will place before you a particular fact which did not come naturally within the scope of the considerations I have been suggesting to you, but which yet it is desirable that you should be acquainted with. This is the distribution of the *missi dominici*, sent throughout the kingdom by Charles lĕ Chauve in 853, the only year in reference to which the details of this distribution have come down to us. France was then divided into eighty-six districts or territorial circumscriptions. The coincidence of this number with that of our present department, though very singular, is pure matter of chance; some of these eighty-six districts are described as comprehending several counties. They were divided among twelve companies of *missi*, whose total number was forty-three. We have their names and their quality. Of the forty-three, thirteen were bishops, five abbots, and twenty-five laymen, without any particular title; at the head of each mission was a bishop; at least a bishop occurs first in each list.

The consequences to be deduced from this table are unimportant, but the document is a curious one in itself.

TWENTY-SIXTH LECTURE.

Object of the lecture—Internal history of the Gallo-Frankish church, from the middle of the 8th century to the end of the 10th—Anarchy which pervaded it in the first half of the 8th century—Twofold principle of reform—The reformation is actually undertaken by the first Carlovingians: 1. By the civil power; 2. By the ecclesiastical power—Special reforms—Order of canons—Its origin and progress—Reformation of the monastic orders by Saint Benedict d'Aniane—They change character—Preponderance of the temporal power in the Gallo-Frankish church at this epoch—Proofs—Still the church progresses towards its future preponderance—But it is not to the profit of its own government, of the bishops of France, that this progress is to turn.

I HAVE already given the history of the Gallo-Frankish church up to the accession of the Carlovingians, towards the middle of the eighth century. I then considered it under the two points of view to which all questions which may arise with regard to a religious society attach themselves; on the one hand, without, in its relations with the civil society, with the state; on the other, within, in its organization and internal government. And not only the church in general, but those two distinct elements, the priests and the monks, the secular clergy and the regular clergy, have been the subject of a twofold inquiry.[1]

It conducted us, you will remember, to this result—that at the commencement of the eighth century, the Gallo-Frankish church was a prey to an ever-increasing anarchy. Externally, far from simplifying and fixing itself, its relations with the state became more and more confused, disordered,

[1] See the 10th Lecture.

uncertain; the spiritual power and the temporal power "lived from day to day without principles, without fixed conditions; they encountered everywhere, running against each other, confounding, disputing the means of action, struggling and meeting in darkness and at chance."[1] Internally, in its own government, the situation of the church was no better — episcopacy had entirely usurped it; the inferior clergy in vain struggled to maintain some rights, to assure themselves some guarantees. And, after having usurped everything, the episcopal aristocracy itself fell into a powerless anarchy: scarcely were there any more councils, scarcely any more metropolitan power; egoism penetrated there as in civil society; each bishop governed his diocese at his will—despotic towards his inferiors, independent of his superiors and his equals. The monasteries presented almost the same phenomena. So that, taking all things together, a little before the middle of the eighth century, that which dominated in the heart of the church, as in the state, in Frankish-Gaul, was disorganization.

Still, at the same time that we recognised this fact, we caught a glimpse on the two banks of the Rhine, both for church and for state, of the first glimmering of another destiny. There were growing up together, on the one hand, that race of the Pepins which was to give Frankish-Gaul new masters; on the other, that Germanic church which, regularly and strongly organised under the influence of papacy, might serve for the reform of the other churches in the west, as a fulcrum and model.

It so, in fact, happened. You have seen, under the first Carlovingians, order and life re-enter into civil government: we are about to be present at the same fact in the church, at the same epoch, and from the same causes.

There is no need of demonstration; it breaks forth on all sides. From Pepin le Bref to Louis le Debonnaire, it is impossible not to be struck with the movement of reform which speaks out and propagates itself in the Gallo-Frankish church. Activity and rule appear in it at the same time. The temporal government labours with all its strength to introduce them. Pepin and Charlemagne commenced by drawing the episcopacy out of the anarchy and indolence into which it had fallen; they

[1] See the 12th Lecture

restored the power of the metropolitans, frequently assembled the bishops, occupied themselves with giving back to ecclesiastical government its entirety and regularity. Towards 747, at the request of Pepin, pope Zachary sends a collection of canons to him. In 774, Adrian I. sends a second, much more complete, to Charlemagne: and Charlemagne does not confine himself to circulating these codes of ecclesiastical discipline; he carefully watches over their observation; he causes new canons to be decreed; religious administration is evidently one of the principal affairs of his government. He succeeded in reawaking in the church that general, regular activity which so long since had almost died away. Twenty councils only were held in the seventh century, and only seven in the first half of the eighth. Dating from Pepin, they once more became frequent. The following is a table of those which met under the Carlovingian race:

Kings.	Date of accession and death.	Number of Councils.	
Pepin le Bref	752—768	14	in 16 years.
Charlemagne	768—814	33	in 46 years.
Louis le Debonnaire ...	814—840	29	in 26 years.
Charles le Chauve ...	840—877	69	in 37 years.
From the death of Charles le Chauve, to the accession of Hugh Capet ...	877—987	56	in 110 years.
		201	in 235 years.

This fact alone attests the return of activity and life into ecclesiastical society; and this activity did not content itself with holding councils, with regulating the immediate and special affairs of the clergy; it extended itself to the wants of religious society in general; of all the Christian people, in the future as in the present. This was the time of the definitive improvement of the liturgy; writings upon the ecclesiastical offices, their celebration, their history abound; and rules establish themselves in the train of these treatises. It is also the time when the greater part of the *penitentials*, or codes of ecclesiastical punishment, were drawn up, which regulated the relation between sins and penances; they often vary from diocese to diocese, and appear in great number before any had acquired the least extended authority. Then, also, homiliaries or collections of sermons for the use of priests and the faithful, were multiplied. In a word, everything at this epoch gives testimony of a great ardour for labour and reform, a reform which, whether pursued by the civil power, which concurred very actively in the government of the church, or by the church itself, was applied to re-establish rule and progress in its own bosom.

Two special reformations, undertaken and accomplished by solated individuals, the formation of the order of canons, and the re-establishment of rule among the monks, attest the same movement, and powerfully contributed to accelerate it.

About the year 760, Chrodegand, bishop of Metz, struck with the disorder which pervaded the secular clergy, and with the difficulty of governing the scattered priests, living isolately and each in his own fashion, undertook to subject those living in his episcopal diocese to an uniform rule, to make them live in common—in fact, to constitute of them a society analogous to that of monasteries. Thus arose the constitution of canons; the institutions of the times were its occasion, the monastic order its model. Chrodegand applied himself to render the assimilation as complete as he could. The rule, in thirty-four articles, which he gave to the first canons is almost literally borrowed from the rule of Saint Benedict. Labours, relaxations, duties, the whole employment of the time of the canons, are regulated in it; meals are to be taken in common, clothing to be uniform. It is true, a fundamental difference exists between the two orders; the canons may possess private property, while, with the monks, the monastery alone is possessed. But in the details of life the resemblance is minute, and it has evidently been sought.

The institution must have answered to the wants of the age, for it was rapidly propagated. Many bishops imitated Chrodegand; the organization of the clergy of episcopal churches into chapters became general; in 785, 789, 802, 813, we find the civil and ecclesiastical power eagerly sanctioning it. At length, in 826, Louis le Debonnaire, in a council held at Aix-la-Chapelle, had a rule of canons drawn up in 145 articles, which reproduced and extended that of Chrodegand, and he sent it to all the metropolitans of his kingdom, in order that it should everywhere be applied, and become the uniform discipline of churches.

It seems that this discipline encountered much resistance in the secular clergy; it deprived them of the disorderly liberty which they had so long enjoyed; it imposed an uniform and rather rough yoke upon them. But a circumstance to which most historians have paid but too little attention, almost everywhere removed these obstacles, and powerfully favoured the extension of the new order.

I have already observed,[1] that the possessions of the church in each diocese were at the disposition of the bishop, who administered and distributed her revenues almost alone and arbitrarily; so that the simple priests, and not only the priests dispersed through the country districts, but those of the episcopal city, of the cathedral church itself, depended entirely on the bishop for their support, for the first and most imperious wants of life. And as a great number of bishops gave themselves up to infinite disorders, and spent, on their own account, the revenues of the church, the existence of the priests was very miserable and precarious; poverty, even distress, was often their condition.

The evil was so real, that when many bishops wished to imitate what had been done by the bishop of Metz to unite the priests of their cathedral in the same edifice, and make them live in common, the temporal and spiritual powers thought it their duty to interfere, in order to prevent this being done, unless there were means of subsistence, a secured livelihood for the new establishment. The council of Mayence ordered, in 813, that the reform should be carried out, "where there were the means;" and that of Aix-la-Chapelle, in 816, enjoined bishops in the admission of canons to regulate themselves according to the revenues of the church.

But this difficulty did not last long. When the people saw priests thus confined, disciplined, and leading a life as regular and severe as the monks, it felt a redoubled respect

[1] 13th Lecture

and fervour for them. Gifts flowed to chapters as well as to monasteries. Never, perhaps, had so many and so well-endowed churches been founded; most of the cathedrals were rapidly enriched, and many donations were especially addressed to the canons, now become an object of edification and admiration. Simple priests thus escaped, in many places, from the state of distress and dependence into which they had been cast; the secular clergy became favourable to the new order, although it bore its yoke; and the order of canons soon played a very important part in the movement of reformation of the church at this epoch.

At the same time, a new reformation of monks was accomplished, by the influence of a man who took the name of their first reformer in the west, Saint Benedict d'Aniane.

Benedict was not his original name; it is not known what that was; he was a Goth by race, and was born in 751, in the diocese of Maguelonne, in Septimania, of which his father was count. Sent in his childhood to the court of Pepin-le-Bref, he was page, cup-bearer, warrior, and took part in many expeditions of Charlemagne. In 774, without any details remaining to us concerning the adventures of his lay life, we find he has renounced it, become a monk in the abbey of Saint Seine, the foundation of which I have already recounted.[1] There he soon became the most respected of the monks; so much was he respected, that the abbot being dead, they wished to confer the title upon him: a singular resemblance, you perceive, between his destiny and that of the great reformer, whom he had adopted as a model. As Saint Benedict of Nursia at first opposed the wishes of the monks of Vicovaro, Benedict d'Aniane repelled those of the monks of Saint Seine: they were not, he said, capable of supporting the severe rule which he wished to establish; they would not be long before they rose up against him. The monks insisted; but Benedict, more obstinate than his patron, resolved to quit the abbey. About the year 780 he returned into southern Gaul, and, still faithful to the example of Saint Benedict, he became a hermit on the borders of a small stream, the Aniane, in the diocese of Maguelonne. His celebrity accompanied him, increased even, in his hermitage; a crowd of companions, already

[1] 17th Lecture.

monks, or eager to become so, assembled around him, and he soon found himself obliged to build a large monastery, where he put in force the reformation which he proposed, in all its rigour.

This reformation was, at bottom, but a return to the primitive rule of Saint Benedict, concerning which I spoke to you in detail,[1] and which the relaxation of discipline, in most monasteries, had caused to be abandoned. Benedict d'Aniane published it anew, at the same time collecting the various rules given to monasteries from that up to his own day; he formed of them the *codex regularum*, a regular body of law for the monastic society, and circulated it in Frankish Gaul. Not content with thus placing the law before the eyes of those who were to obey it, he undertook the practical reform of monasteries; and, either in his own person, or by disciples of his choice, in point of fact, accomplished it in those of Gellon in Languedoc, of l'Isle Barbe, near Lyons, of Saint Savin in Poitou, of Cormery in Touraine, of Massay in Berry, of Saint Mesmin near Orleans, of Marmunster in Alsace, and many others.

So great a work soon attracted the consideration of the people and of Charlemagne to its author. In 794, we see Benedict seated at the council of Francfort, and there taking part in the condemnation of the heresy of the Adoptians, in the person of Felix, bishop of Urgel. In 799, by order of Charlemagne, he repaired to Urgel, with archbishop Leidrade, to preach to the heretics. Lastly, in 815, Louis le Debonnaire called him near his person, made him abbot of a large monastery, which he had just founded at Inde, in the vicinity of Aix-la-Chapelle, and in 817, Benedict presided at the special assembly, held at Aix-la-Chapelle, for the reformation of monastic orders, an assembly entirely composed of monks and abbots, and the convocation of which he probably brought about.

From this assembly there went forth a great capitulary, destined to accomplish, in a general manner, and by the instrumentality of the public power, that reformation which Benedict followed in detail so long ago; it contains eighty articles, and should be looked upon as the completion and

[1] 14th Lecture.

commentary of the rule of Saint Benedict. But the commentary differs greatly from the text, and here is shown, in the monastic mind, a revolution which it is necessary for us to characterize.

It will be recollected how, in analysing the rule of Saint Benedict, we found it, despite the severe enthusiasm of which it is the fruit, to be feeling, even liberal—that is to say, foreign to all minute details, to all narrow views; humane and moderate with regard to practical life, in the heart of a very rigid general thought. Utterly different is the character of the additional rule which the capitulary of 817 contains. It seems, at first, to have no other object than that of again putting the primitive rule in vigour. The three first articles impose upon every abbot the obligation of re-perusing it upon re-entering his monastery, and of penetrating thoroughly into its purpose; upon every monk, that of learning it by heart. But to this succeeds a legislation most foreign to the text and spirit of the ancient law; a legislation overcharged with puerile details, with minute forms and vain observances; the following are some examples:

"Let the monks not shave during Lent, unless it be Holy Saturday. During the rest of the year, let them shave once a fortnight, and at the octave of Easter."[1]

"Let the bath be used according to the directions of the prior."[2]

"Let them not eat poultry either within or without the monastery, except by reason of sickness; let no bishops order monks to eat poultry. At Christmas and at Easter let them eat poultry for four days, if there be any; if not, they shall not demand it as their due."[3]

"Let them eat no fruit nor salad, except with their other food."[4]

"Let the length of the hood be two cubits."[5]

"Let his portion of meat and drink be given separately to each brother, and let no one give any of his own share to another."[6]

"Let no fixed time be observed for bleeding, but let every one be bled according as he needs it; and at such times have some especial indulgence as to eating and drinking."[7]

[1] Art. 6. [2] Art. 7. [3] 8, 9, 78. [4] Art. 10.
[5] Art. 21. [6] Art. 66. [7] Art. 11.

And so on, of eighty-one articles, twenty-one are of a kind entirely foreign to all religious sentiment, to all moral tendency; and contain nothing but miserable prescriptions of this kind. Assuredly, nothing less resembled that enthusiasm, that gravity, with which the primitive rule is marked; nothing more clearly attests the decay of the monastic mind, and its rapid tendency towards a miserable superstition. Benedict d'Aniane, like Benedict of Nursia, wished to reform the monasteries; but the reformation of the sixth century was at once extensive and sublime; it addressed itself to what was strong in human nature: that of the ninth century was puerile, inferior, and addressed itself to what was weak and servile in man. Such, in point of fact, is the general character of the monastic order from this epoch, despite numerous attempts to lead it back towards its source; it lost its grandeur, its first ardour, and remained laden with those puerilities, those ridiculous details, which humiliate men, even when they submit to them with a good intention.

Puerile or grave, monastic or secular, all this reformation of the Gallo-Frankish church was accomplished under the inspection and with the concurrence of the temporal power. In truth, from Pepin le Bref to Louis le Debonnaire, it is the temporal power, king or emperor, which governs the church, and effects all that I have just placed before you. The proofs of this are evident.

1. All the canons, all the measures relative to the church at this epoch, are published under the name of the temporal power; it is that which speaks, which orders, which acts. To be convinced of this, one need only open the acts of the councils.

2. These acts, and many other monuments, even formally proclaim that it is to the civil power that the ordering of such things belongs, and that the church lives and acts under its authority. The canons of the council of Arles, held under Charlemagne, in 813, terminate as follows :—

" We have briefly enumerated the things which seem to us to require reformation, and we have decided that we shall present them to the lord emperor, invoking his clemency, to the end that if anything be wanting to his work, his prudence may supply it; that if there be anything contrary to reason, is judgment may correct it; that if anything be wisely ordered, his support, with the aid of the Divine goodness, may cause it to be carried into effect."[1]

We likewise read in the preface of the acts of the council of Mayence, also held in 813:

"Above all things, we have need of your aid, and of your holy doctrine, to warn us, and instruct us with benevolence; and if what we have drawn up below in some articles, appear worthy to you, let your authority confirm them; if anything appear to you to require correction, let your imperial grandeur order its correction."[2]

What texts can be clearer?

3. The capitularies of Charlemagne likewise prove at every step, that the government of the church was one of his principal affairs; a few articles, taken promiscuously, will show with what attention he occupied himself with it.

"Our *missi* are to inquire whether there be any cause of complaint against a bishop, an abbot, an abbess, a count, or any other magistrate whatsoever, and inform us thereof."[3]

"Let them examine if the bishops and the other priests live according to the canonical institution, and whether they know and properly observe the canons; whether the abbots live according to rule and canonically, and whether they thoroughly know the canons; if in monasteries the monks live according to rule; if in nunneries they live according to rule, and what is the extent of the establishment."[4]

"Let them examine the monasteries and nunneries in each city; let them see how the churches are kept up or repaired, both as regards the edifices themselves and their ornaments; let them carefully inform themselves of the manners of each, and of what has been done with regard to what is ordered concerning readings, the chaunting, and all which concerns the ecclesiastical discipline."[5]

"If any of the abbots, priests, deacons, &c., do not obey his bishop, let them go before the metropolitan, and let him decide the business with his suffragans; and if there is anything which the metropolitan bishop cannot reform or settle, let the accusers and the accused come to us with the letters

[1] Con. Labbe, vol. vii., col. 1238. [2] Ibid. 1241.
[3] 3rd Cap. a. 789, § 11; Bal. vol. i. col. 244.
[4] 2nd Cap. a. 802, § 2—5; vol. i. col. 375.
[5] 5th Cap. a. 806. § 4, vol i. col. 453.

of the metropolitan, that we may know the truth of the thing."[1]

"Let the bishops, abbots, counts, and all the powerful men, if they have between them any dispute and cannot reconcile themselves, come into our presence."[2]

This is assuredly a very direct and active intervention. Charlemagne did not govern civil affairs more immediately.

4. He exercised, besides, a very efficacious influence, although indirect; he nominated bishops. We read, indeed, in his capitularies, the re-establishment of the election of bishops by the clergy and the people, according to the primitive custom and the legal right of the church:

"Not being ignorant of the sacred canons, " says he, " and to the end that in the name of God the holy church may freely enjoy her privileges, we have given our assent that the bishops be elected, according to the canonical statutes, by the choice of the clergy and the people, in the diocese itself, without any regard to persons or presents, by the merit only of their life and wisdom; and to the end that they may be completely able to direct those who are subject to them."[3]

But the fact continued to be but little in accordance with this right; both after and before this capitulary, Charlemagne almost always nominated the bishops; and even after his death, under his feeblest successors, the intervention of royalty in such matters was allowed by the most jealous of its rivals. In 853, pope Leo IV. wrote to the emperor Lothaire:

"We supplicate your mansuetude to give the government of this church to Colonna, an humble deacon, to the end, that having received your permission, we may, with the aid of God, consecrate him bishop. If it do not seem well to you that he be bishop of this church, let your serenity confer upon him that of Tusculum, which is now without a shepherd."[4]

In 879, pope John VIII. made a similar request to Carloman, in reference to the church of Verceil.[5]

The chronicles of the time are, besides, full of particular facts which can leave no doubt upon the subject, and prove

[1] Cap. a. 794, § 4, vol. i. col. 264.

[2] 3rd Cap. a. 812, § 2. [3] 1st Cap. a. 803, § 2, vol. i. col. 379.

[4] Gratian. *Decret.* p. ii. dist. 63, c. 16.

[5] Gieseler, Manual of Eccles. Hist., vol. ii. p. 44, note 9.

that the choice of bishops was the occasion, on the part of the candidates, of a multitude of intrigues; on the part of the prince himself, of partiality, or a singular indifference. Two anecdotes, derived from the chronicle of the monk of Saint Gall, (a monument more important and more instructive than the pedantry of scholars is willing to believe), are remarkable examples of it: I shall give them literally.

"It is known that Charlemagne brought up, in the school of the palace, many young men whose learning and talent he afterwards employed.

"He made one of these pupils, who was poor, the chief and writer of his chapel. . . . . One day, when they announced the death of a certain bishop to the most prudent Charles, he asked if this prelate had sent before him into the other world any of his property and of the fruit of his labours.

"'Not more than two pounds of silver, sire,' answered the messenger. The young man in question, unable to contain within his breast the vivacity of his spirit, cried, in spite of himself, in the presence of the king: 'What a light viaticum for a journey so great, and of so long duration.'

"After deliberating some minutes within himself, Charles, the most prudent of men, said to the young priest: 'What sayst thou? were I to give thee this bishopric, wouldst thou be careful to make more considerable provision for this long journey?' The other hastening to devour these wise words, as grapes ripe before their time falling into his half-open mouth, threw himself at the feet of his master, and answered: 'Lord, it is for the will of God and your power to decide.'

"'Conceal thyself,' said the king, 'behind the curtain, and thou shalt learn what rivals thou hast for this honourable post.' When the death of the bishop was known, the officers of the palace, always ready to watch the misfortune, or, at all events, the death of another, impatient of all delay, and each with the other, set to work the favourites of the emperor in order to obtain the bishopric. But he, firm in his design, refused them all, saying that he would not break his word to the young man. At last queen Hildegarde sent first the great men of the kingdom, and then came herself, to solicit the bishopric for her own chaplain. The king received her request with the most gracious air, assured her he could not, and wished not to refuse her anything, but added, that he could not pardon himself, if he were to deceive his young priest. In the manner of all women, when they think to make their desires and ideas predominant over the will of their husbands, the queen, dissimulating her rage, softened her naturally strong voice, and endeavouring to mollify, by caressing manners, the immovable soul of Charles, said to him: 'Dear prince, sire, why throw away this bishopric by giving it to such a child? I conjure you, my amiable master—you, my glory and my support, grant it to my chaplain, your devoted servant.' At these words the young man, whom Charles had enjoined to place himself behind the curtain, near which he himself was seated, and to hear the prayers which each made, cried in a lamentable tone, but without quitting the curtain which surrounded him: "Lord king, hold firm; suffer no one to tear from thy hands the power given thee by God.' Then this prince, the courageous lover and friend of truth, ordered his priest to show himself, and said to him: 'Receive this bishopric, but take the utmost care to send before me, and before thyself, into the other world, great alms, and a good viaticum, for the long journey, from which no one returns.'"

This is the second.

"Another prelate was dead. Charles gave the succession to a certain young man. He, all content, prepared to set out. His servants brought him, as suited the episcopal gravity, a horse of a very quiet sort, and placed a stool for him to get into his saddle. Indignant that they should treat him as he were infirm, he sprang from the ground on to the horse so energetically, that it was with difficulty he could keep his seat, and not fall over the other side. The king, who saw what passed from the balustrade of the palace, had this man called to him and said: "My brave man, thou art lively, agile, quick, and thou hast a strong foot. The tranquillity of our empire is, as thou knowest, incessantly troubled by a multitude of wars; we have need of such a priest as thou in our suite: remain, then, to be the companion of our fatigues, since thou canst mount thy horse so freely."[1]

I might cite many facts of this kind. This was assuredly treating the episcopacy and the church without ceremony.

[1] *Deeds and Exploits of Charlemagne the Great*, by a Monk of Saint Gall; vol. iii. p. 181, of my *Collection.*

5. Not only did the Carlovingians thus dispose of the bishoprics, but they often appropriated a portion of their domains to themselves. Every one knows what Charles Martel did in this way. But it is less generally known that this fact was repeated many times under the princes of his race, even the most devoted and submissive to the church. In 743, Carloman, brother of Pepin le Bref, decreed the following capitulary:

"We have resolved, with the counsel of the servants of God and the Christian people, because of the wars and the invasions of other neighbouring nations which menace us, to take for a while, and by way of usufruct, some portion of the ecclesiastical domains, and to keep them, with the permission of God, for the maintenance of our army, on the condition that every year there shall be paid to the proprietary church or monastery, a sol—that is to say, twelve deniers, for each farm; and that if he to whom the capital belongs dies, the church is to retake possession of it; and if necessity requires, or the prince orders it, this possession shall be renewed."[1]

We read also in a capitulary of Louis le Debonnaire, in 823:

"We order the abbots and *laymen* to have observed *in the monasteries which they hold from our gift*, and according to the counsels of the bishops, all which relates to the religious life of monks, canons, &c."[2]

There were, then, laymen who received from the emperor certain monasteries in the way of benefices. Abbots of this kind were still more numerous under Charles le Chauve; they had the name of *Abbacomites*.

Doubtless the church was constantly protesting; and, upon the whole this fact passed, and properly passed, for an attack on her rights, a violent usurpation. Yet it was so frequent, so open, that an idea of some kind of royal right was almost attached to it; and the church more than once seemed to acknowledge, that in extreme need, a portion of her property might be thus temporarily applied to the service of the state.

6. It was not only with ecclesiastical administration and

[1] 2 Cap. Carlom. a. 743; Bal. vol. i. col. 149.
[2] Cap. Lud. p. a. 823, § 8; vol. i. col. 635.

discipline that the temporal power occupied itself at this period. It interfered even in matters of dogma, and they were governed in its name. Three questions of this kind were raised in the reign of Charlemagne. I shall merely point them out. 1. The question of the worship of images, raised in the west by a canon of the second council of Nice, in 787. The Gallo-Frankish church rejected this worship, and all that seemed to tend to it. A special work, drawn up by order of Charlemagne, probably by Alcuin, entitled, *Libri Carolini*, was published against it. The favour given by the popes to this doctrine did not operate upon the Frankish bishops nor their master, and, in 794, the council of Frankfort formally condemned it. 2. The heresy of the Adoptians concerning the nature of Jesus Christ, of which I have already spoken, and which Charlemagne also formally condemned in three successive councils, at Ratisbon, in 792, at Frankfort in 794, and at Aix-la-Chapelle, in 799. 3. The question of an addition to the symbol as to the procession of the host. These, assuredly, are matters entirely foreign to the external government of the church—they are purely dogmatical. They were not the less regulated, if not by the civil power itself, at least under its authority, and with its intervention.

It may, therefore, be affirmed, without discussing the question of right, without examining whether it be good or ill that it should be thus, that at this epoch, directly or indirectly, the temporal power governed the church. The situation of Charlemagne in this respect was almost exactly the same as that of the king of England in the English church. In England, also, the civil assembly, or parliament, and the ecclesiastical assembly, or convocation, were long distinct; and neither one nor the other decided upon, or could do anything without the sanction of royalty. Whether the matter in hand was a council or a *champ de mai*, a dogma or a proclamation of war, Charlemagne equally presided at it: in neither case did they think of dispensing with him.

But at the same time that they governed the church, and for the very reason that they did not in any way fear her independence, the first Carlovingians conferred immense advantages on her, and provided the most solid foundations for her future power.

1. It was by their support that the tithe was definitively

and generally established. You have seen that the church, relying upon the Hebrew customs, had at various different times, but without any great success, attempted to appropriate this rich revenue to herself. Charlemagne gave to the tithe the aid not only of his laws but of his indefatigable will. It was under his reign that it truly took root in the legislation and practice of the west.

2. He also extended the jurisdiction of the clergy. We read in one of his capitulations:—

"We will that neither abbots, priests, deacons, nor under-deacons, nor any priests, be cited or taken before public or regular judges, for deeds concerning their person: let them be judged by their bishop, and so let justice be done them. If any complaint be carried against them before the judge concerning the domains of the church or their own property, let the judge send the complaint with one of his own messengers to the bishop, in order that he may do justice by the intervention of his advocate; and if there arise between them any dispute which they cannot or will not settle themselves, let the cause be carried before the court or the judge by the advocate whom the law gives the bishop, and let it there be decided according to the law, respect being always paid to what has just been said with reference to the person of the priest."[1]

Whenever he had any purpose in interfering in the disputes of the bishops, whether among themselves or between them and the laymen, he made no hesitation in doing so. But in general, as the ecclesiastical jurisdiction was more enlightened and regular, he was more inclined to extend than to restrict it; and despite the submission of the bishops during his reign, they drew from it at a later period many useful precedents in favour of their independence.

3. In the civil order also, especially in reference to marriages and wills, the power of the clergy greatly increased at this period. I have already pointed out the cause from which it drew this important attribute. I have shown how, among the barbarians, the family was unfixed, unstable, and how it was the interest of a regular government to introduce more order and fixedness into it. It was more especially for this

[1] Cap. Car. M. A. 801, § 39, vol. i cap. 355.

reason that all questions of parentage, marriage, or wills, came under the ecclesiastical jurisdiction; and the church, by penetrating into the interior of families, acquired an enormous power.

4. Lastly, Charlemagne gave up to each church, under the name of *mansus ecclesiasticus,* a farm free from all kinds of charges and taxes; an important concession at an epoch when rural property furnished almost all the public expenditure.

Despite her momentary servitude, the church assuredly had here numerous fertile principles of independence and power. These were not long in developing themselves. During the early years of the reign of Louis le Debonnaire, the order of things established by Charlemagne continues, or nearly so: it is still the emperor who governs, who, at least, appears to govern the church. But everything soon changes, and the church in her turn governs the emperor. I shall not enter with any detail into this subject. Every one knows that the usurpation of power by the clergy is the dominant characteristic of the reigns of Louis le Debonnaire and Charles le Chauve, up to the time when all general society, all central government, disappeared to give place to the feudal system. The facts are present to all minds. I shall quote but one text, possibly more clear than all the facts put together. This is Art. 2 of the accusation brought the 14th of June, 859, before the council of Toul, by Charles le Chauve, against Wenilon, archbishop of Sens, who had separated from him to ally himself with his enemies. This denunciation of a bishop by a king seems an act of the resistance and independence of royalty; it is expressed in the following terms:

"By his election, and that of the other bishops, and with the will, consent, and acclamations of all the faithful of our kingdom, Wenilon, in his own diocese, in the city of Orleans, in the cathedral of Saint Croix, in presence of the other archbishops and bishops, consecrated me king, according to the ecclesiastical custom; and in calling me to reign, he anointed me with the holy oil, gave me the royal diadem and sceptre, and led me to the throne. After this consecration, I could not be cast from the throne, nor supplanted by any one—at least, not without having been heard and judged by the bishops, by whose ministry I was consecrated king, and who have been named the throne of God. God rests upon them, and it is through them that he decrees his judgments. I have always been, and am at present ready to submit myself to their paternal corrections, and to their castigatory judgments."[1]

Truly the revolution which, in Frankish Gaul, had raised the priesthood above the empire, cannot be proved by a less suspicious and more formal testimony.

It was to the profit of the Gallo-Frankish episcopacy that this revolution seemed to be brought about; it was by the bishops that the temporal power was thus acquired and thus treated. But this sovereignty of the national church was not to subsist long, and it was not to the profit of the bishops that the church had overcome the state. It will be recollected that in seeking amidst the dissolution which invaded Gaul under the last Morovingians, what principles of civil and ecclesiastical regeneration became visible—that it was beyond the Alps, at Rome, that the principle of ecclesiastical regeneration appeared to us.[2] There, in fact, was developed the power called upon to rule the church in general, and the Gallo-Frankish church in particular. It was in the hands of the papacy, not of the episcopacy, that the empire definitively fell. In the next lecture I shall place before you the history of the relations between the Gallo-Frankish church and papacy during this epoch, and you will see that it was papacy that took possession of the sovereignty on the decay of the Carlovingians.

Bal., vol. ii. col. 133.

[2] 19th Lecture.

TWENTY-SEVENTH LECTURE.

History of papacy—Peculiar situation of the city of Rome—Relations of the popes about the middle of the eighth century, with the Italian, Spanish, Anglo-Saxon, Gallo-Frankish, and Germanic churches—Their alliance with the early Carlovingians—Advantages which they drew from it—Donation of Pepin and of Charlemagne—Sovereignty of the Carlovingian emperors over the popes—Uncertainty of the ideas, and incoherency of the facts concerning the rights of papacy—It increases more and more in minds—It apparently acquires a legal title—False decretals—Nicholas I.—His character—Affair of the marriage of Lothaire and of Teutberge Affair of Rhotarde, bishop of Soissons—Triumph of papacy: 1. Over temporal sovereigns; 2. Over national churches—Its decided preponderance in the west.

I HAVE shown that the Gallo-Frankish church was raised by the first Carlovingians, from the state of impotence and anarchy into which it had fallen. We have seen it re-enter into order and activity; we have seen this revolution brought about by the concurrence and under the authority of the temporal power. Pepin, Charlemagne, and even Louis le Debonnaire, on his accession, actually governed the Gallo-Frankish church. This state of things was of short duration. I have pointed out with what rapidity the spiritual power passed from docility to independence, from independence to sovereignty; I have shown its pretensions already acknowledged by the temporal power itself, particularly by Charles le Chauve. It was to the profit of the Gallo-Frankish episcopacy that this change was brought about. I announced that it would not long enjoy it, that a third power, the papacy, would soon take their scarcely acquired supremacy from the national bishops. It is with this fact—that is to say, with the history of papacy, from the eighth to the tenth century, especially in its relations with the Gallo-Frankish church, that we have to occupy ourselves at present.

There is a primitive fact with regard to the development of papacy in Europe, which, I think, has never been taken sufficiently into account. Not only was Rome always the most important city in the west; not only did the recollections of its ancient grandeur tend to the good of the bishop, who, without as yet reigning, was already the chief of its people; but Rome also had a particular advantage in the west, that of never remaining in the hands of the Barbarians, Heruli, Goths, Vandals, or others: they had many times taken and pillaged it—they never long retained possession of it. Alone, among all the great western cities, and whether as united to the empire of the west, or as independent, it never passed under the German yoke: alone it remained Roman, after the ruin of the Roman empire.

It happened, without premeditation, without labour, by the sole nature of its situation, that Rome found herself, morally at least, at the head of the ancient population disseminated throughout the new Western States. In this struggle, at first public, afterwards secret, but for a long period so active—this struggle of the conquered against the conquerors—the attention of the Gallo-Romans, of the Hispano-Romans, of all the cities desolated by their barbarous conquerors, naturally turned towards Rome, so long their sovereign, and now the only living wreck of the ancient society, alone exempt from new masters, alone capable of still preserving the respected traditions of the people that they still governed. For this reason, Rome was a name dear to the whole mass of the population in the west, the centre of recollections and ideas, the image of all which remained of the Roman world. It was under the influence of this fact that papacy took rise; it was, so to speak, its cradle; it placed it in its very origin at the head of nations; it rendered it a kind of national power for the race of the conquered.

Let us now see what was its situation with regard to the principal churches of the west, at the middle of the eighth century.

At this epoch, there were in the west five great national churches: the Italian church, or rather the Lombard—for I only speak of the north of Italy, then in the power of the

Lombards—the Spanish church; the Anglo-Saxon church; the Gallo-Frankish church, and the rising Germanic church.

1. It was in Italy, in the Lombard church, that papacy was the least powerful. The bishop of Rome had never been, either as metropolitan or by any other title, the superior of the bishops of the north of Italy: the Lombard kings, who had long been Arians, and incessantly applied themselves to drive their conquests into the territory which they administered, were its natural enemies. "The perfidy of the Lombards," wrote pope Pelagius I., in 584, "has caused us, despite their own oaths, so many tribulations and evils, that no one can recount them." The correspondence between the Lombard bishops and the popes, became, therefore, difficult and rare; and that church, which reached almost to the gates of Rome, was stranger to them than any other.

2. For a long time, on the contrary, their influence over the Spanish church was great and progressive. Under the domination of the Arian Visigoths, the catholic and persecuted clergy of Spain maintained frequent and intimate relations with the bishop of Rome, who, in the name of the catholic church, supported it in its resistance. It happened, moreover, that in the course of the fifth and sixth centuries, two illustrious Spanish bishops, Torribius, bishop of Astorga, and Leandro, bishop of Seville, were the secretaries and friends—the one of Leo the Great, (440-461,) the other of Gregory the Great, (590-604,) and established habitual relations between their church and that of Rome. Accordingly, it is on the subject of the Spanish church that the pretensions of papacy are the most openly manifested at this epoch. In 538. pope Vigilius writes to Profuturus, bishop of Braga:

"As the holy Roman church possesses the primacy over all churches, it is to her, as the chief of the church, that all important affairs are to be sent, the judgments and complaints of bishops, as well as great questions of ecclesiastical matters. For that church, which is the first, in confiding her functions to the other churches, called upon them to share in her labours, not in her plenitude of power."[1]

There was, at that time, no other church in the west to which the bishop of Rome addressed language like this.

[1] Baluze, *Nov. Coll. Conc.*, vol. i., coll. 1468.

Accordingly, some doubts have been raised as to the authenticity of this letter; still it seems to me probable. The power of the papacy in Spain was so real, that in 603 two Spanish bishops, Januario of Malaga, and Stephen, having been irregularly deposed, Gregory the Great sent an envoy, named John, with orders to inquire into the affair: and without convoking any council, without seeking the adhesion of the Spanish clergy, John declared that the deposition was illegal, annulled it, and reinstated the two bishops, thus exercising the rights of the most extended ecclesiastical supremacy.

It was not, however, so well established as one would suppose. The Visigoth kings, dating from Ricared (586—601), had become catholics. At first, the papacy profited by it; the fact which I have related proves it. But the struggle between the national clergy and the temporal government having ceased, the clergy grew more closely connected with the government, and less so with the foreign bishop, whom they had taken for a chief. Accordingly, we see the power of papacy a little weakened in Spain during the course of the seventh century, and the national church acting with more independence. At the commencement of the eighth century king Witiza quarrelled with the pope, interdicted all recourse to Rome, rejected the Roman discipline, and, it is said, even authorized the marriage of priests. Some years afterwards, the invasion of the Arabs took place, and the greater part of Spain was lost both for papacy as well as for Christianity. In the middle of the eighth century, it preserved power only among the Christian refugees in the north of the Peninsula, or at the foot of the Pyrenees; and there even the disorder was such, and society so agitated or weak, that there was scarcely anything for a distant and systematic influence to do.

3. With regard to the Anglo-Saxon church, you know, that, founded by the popes themselves, it was placed, from its very origin, under their most direct influence; it was still in the middle of the eighth century in the same situation.[1]

4. The situation of the Gallo-Frankish church was different. You have seen that during the course of the seventh century her relations with Rome had become very rare.[2] It was

[1] 19th Lecture. [2] Ibid.

in the middle of the eighth century, precisely at the opening of the epoch with which we are about to occupy ourselves, that they again became more frequent and efficacious. I will resume this history presently.

5. The Germanic church, as you know, owed its success to the labours of the Anglo-Saxon missionaries, of Saint Boniface, more especially; and her founders, in creating her, gave her, as it were, to the papacy.[1]

Such was the situation of the popes with regard to the great national churches in the West, when, about the middle of the eighth century, the first Carlovingians closely allied themselves with them. It is easy to recognise the happy effects upon the papacy of this alliance.

And, first, it acquired an ascendancy in the Italian church which it had never before possessed. After the defeat of the Lombards by the Franks, the bishop of Rome did not become the metropolitan of the Lombard bishops; he did not receive the title of patriarch; but he was invested with a superiority without example, indefinite, and so much the greater.

The Lombard clergy saw him respected by the Frank-conquerors, who in general looked upon him as their representative and minister beyond the Alps, and it was through him accordingly that the clergy treated with the conquerors. No one in the Lombard church could think of equalling it; and the church itself rapidly fell under his authority.

He also acquired fresh authority in the Gallo-Frankish church. It was with his aid, and by supporting themselves with his name and opinions, that the first Carlovingians laboured to reform her. Even before their elevation, Saint Boniface wrote to pope Zachary, that Carloman, brother of Pepin le Bref, asked him to repair to Gaul: "Protesting that he wished to amend and reform the state of religion and the church, which, for at least seventy or eighty years, had been abandoned to disorder, and crushed under foot."[2]

It was under the presidence and influence of Saint Boniface, in his character as legate of the pope, that councils were held, formerly so rare, but now again become frequent. The acts of the council of 742, called *Germanicum*, commence in the following terms:

[1] 19th Lecture. [2] S. Bon., ep. 51, p. 107.

"I, Carloman, duke and prince of the Franks, with the counsel of the servants of God and our great men, have convoked the bishops of my kingdom, and Boniface, who is sent from Saint Peter, that they may give me counsel," &c.

The same fact reappears in the council held the following year at Lestines or Leptines, in the diocese of Cambray, and at the assembly of Soissons (752), where Pepin was consecrated king. Not content with thus serving as mediator between the temporal sovereigns and the popes, Saint Boniface undertook to unite closely to the see of Rome the metropolitans, or archbishops, whose power he was establishing; he induced those of Rouen, of Sens, and of Reims, at the time of their nomination, to demand the *pallium*—the sign of their new dignity—from the pope, and thus to claim of him a sort of investiture. Only one among them followed his counsel, and the pope testified to Boniface his disappointment that the other two had not done the same. Lastly, it was not the sovereigns or the clergy only who were reconciled to papacy, and contracted a more intimate alliance with it. The same movement was manifested among the faithful, the people: the number of pilgrims who repaired to Rome with pious intentions rapidly increased. We read in a capitulary of Pepin le Bref:

"As regards pilgrims who make a pilgrimage in the service of God, let no one demand toll of them."[1]

And it is evidently to the pilgrimage of Rome that this provision relates.

Though we had no other proof of the ascendant movement of papacy in the Gallo-Frankish church, but the tone in which it is there spoken of, this were sufficient: not only the language of the clergy, but of writers in general, the temporal sovereigns themselves, becomes extremely pompous—magnificent and respectful epithets increase. The pope was no longer simply the bishop of Rome, the brother of other bishops; titles were given to him, and expressions employed towards him which were not employed towards or given to any other. Certain phrases of Alcuin, who, in his capacity of favourite to Charlemagne, cannot be suspected of wishing to sacrifice the power of his

[1] Cap. Pipp. a. 755, p. 22 · Bal. vol. i. col. 175.

master to a foreign power, will say more concerning those titles and expressions than any generalities. In 796, he addresses pope Leo III. (695—816) in these words:

"Most holy father, elected pontiff of God, vicar of the apostles, heir of the fathers, prince of the church, guardian of the only dove without stain."[1]

And in another place, in 794, to Adrian I. (761—795):

"Very excellent father, even as I recognise thee for the vicar of the blessed Peter, the prince of the apostles, so do I regard thee as the heir of his miraculous power."[2]

Again, in writing to Charlemagne, in 799:

"Hitherto there have been in the world three persons of supreme rank: the sublimity of the apostolical vicar who occupies the seat of the blessed Peter, the prince of the apostles; the dignity of the emperor who exercises the secular power in the second Rome; the third is the royal dignity with which the will of our Lord Jesus Christ has invested you, that you may govern the Christian people."[3]

It is true that it would be improper to accept these expressions literally; we must not believe that the pope possessed, in its whole extent, the power which they attribute to him; but they show what moral and religious supremacy he already possessed in the mind of the people. His intellectual dominion, the source of all other species of his dominion, really dates from this period.

His temporal power received at the same time a notable accretion. When Pepin had conquered the Lombards, he compelled them to restore to the bishop of Rome the lands which they had taken from him, and he, moreover, added a part of those which he had himself conquered, especially in the exarchy of Ravenna. After the complete ruin of the Lombard kings, Charlemagne, in appropriating these states, made new and considerable donations of the same kind to Adrian the First. The authenticity of these two gifts has been called into question, and it is true that the original act is, in neither ease, extant. Nevertheless, they are, directly or indirectly, mentioned by contemporary writers; and numerous chronicles and monuments of various kinds

[1] Letter 20, vol. i, p. 30. [2] Letter 15, vol. i., p. 25.
[3] Letter 80, vol. i, p. 117.

attest, or suppose their existence. The extent of the lands thus conceded may be disputed: in the succeeding centuries the pope greatly exaggerated it, no doubt; but I conceive that it is impossible reasonably to question the reality of these donations. They present nothing which is not perfectly natural, and in harmony with the entire history of the eighth century. We ought rather to have been surprised had they not occurred.

It is more difficult to determine the true meaning and political bearing of such concessions. Two hypotheses have been maintained upon this point. According to some, Pepin and Charlemagne gave to the pope no more than the civil proprietorship, the *dominium utile*, the revenue of the lands, and of the slaves and labourers who inhabited them—not the sovereignty, the government of the territory. According to others, political sovereignty was attached to the concession; the popes exercised all the rights of political sovereignty, as had been done before them by the exarch of Ravenna, and the other delegates of the emperor of the East, who, even after the donations had been made, preserved, for a while, some shadow of supremacy over these lands, but soon completely lost it, leaving the pope as their only successor.

In my opinion, neither one nor the other of these hypotheses can be maintained; each of them depends upon an oblivion of the condition of minds in the time which it relates to. In those days, people did not acquire such clear and precise ideas of sovereignty, power, and rights, as are formed of them by us, in the present day. They did not distinguish with such strictness between the *dominium utile* and political government, between property and sovereignty. All this science of modern civilians was foreign to men's minds and to facts, in the middle of the eighth century. The proprietor, as proprietor, exercised in his domains a portion of those rights which are at present ascribed to the sovereign alone. He maintained order, did justice or caused it to be done, led or sent to war the men upon his lands, not in virtue of a special power, called political, but in virtue of his proprietorship itself, in the idea of which the most various powers were confounded. Thus, on the one hand, when, in the ninth century, we see the popes exercising the greater part of those rights which we name political, in the domains which they had received from Pepin and Charlemagne, we must not therefore conclude that real, complete, and independent sovereignty had been conferred upon them; and, on the other hand, neither must we any more believe that Charlemagne, in retaining a certain sovereignty over the territory which he had given to the popes, thought that he ought to and, in fact, did, reserve to himself all the rights which, in the present day, appear to us to be attached to the word. At the same time that the pope, in the name of proprietor, had ministers, judges, and even military chiefs, chosen by and dependent upon himself, on his domains, Charlemagne received taxes from them, and sent them, as to the rest of his states, *missi dominici*, charged with the inspection of all matters, the suppression of abuses, &c. In a word, complete sovereignty was attributed neither to the pope nor to the emperor; it fluctuated between the two, in a divided and uncertain state; and from this fact arises all the difficulties of a question which does not exist in the eyes of any one who is acquainted with and understands the period of which we are speaking.

Whether or no he possessed such sovereignty, there can be no doubt but that the acquisition of such vast domains, and of all the rights of proprietorship, was a great increase of temporal power for the bishop of Rome. He found himself, from that time, beyond any comparison, the richest bishop in Christendom, and without a peer materially as well as morally.

Thus, the early Carlovingians, and especially Charlemagne, were the most useful allies to the papacy: 1st, in ensuring to the pope a power over the Italian church, which they had not hitherto possessed; 2ndly, in giving them a very active influence in the affairs of the Gallo-Frankish church; 3rdly, in recognising in these, by language and all demonstrations which strike the imagination of nations, a majesty and supremacy which had not yet been admitted by princes; 4thly, and finally, in increasing, whether by wealth, or by its indirect consequences, their temporal power.

Nevertheless, you must not believe that, in their relations with the papacy, they had abdicated their empire. As you have seen that Charlemagne favoured the influence of the clergy within the Gallo-Frankish church, and yet subjected em to his own power, so he ruled the popes even while he prepared for them the means of ruling his successors. In the first place, their election was not complete until it had received the approbation of the emperor. Facts and texts abound in proof of this. In 796, Charlemagne wrote to Pope Leo III. who had just been elected :

"After having read your excellency's letter, and noticed the decree, we were greatly rejoiced both with the unanimity of the election and with the humility of your obedience, and with the promise of fidelity which you have made to us."[1]

In 816, the election of Stephen IV. took place in the presence of the commissaries of Louis le Debonnaire, to whom the decree was sent in order that it should receive his confirmation. In 817, Pascal I. excuses himself for the precipitation of his ordination. In 825, at the time of the election of Eugenius II., Louis le Debonnaire sent his son Lothaire to Rome, and it was determined that commissaries of the emperor should always be present at the ordination of the pope.

This consent of the emperor has sometimes been represented as a nomination; it has been pretended that he named the pope like the other bishops. Nothing is less founded than this assertion. The pope was elected at Rome by the clergy, and sometimes, too, with the concurrence of the people of Rome; but in order to his consecration, the approbation of the emperor was necessary. The concurrence of the temporal power went no further than this.

The language of many popes at this period expressly witnesses their dependence, and the positive superiority of the imperial power. Leo III. wrote to the emperor :

"If we have done anything incompetently, and if, in the affairs which have been submitted to us, we have not rightly followed the path of the true law, we are ready to reform what we have done, according to your judgment and that of your commissaries."[2]

Leo IV. wrote to Lothaire the First:

"We promise that we will always do all that shall be in our power to keep and observe inviolably the statutes and decrees as well of yourself, as of your predecessors."[3]

[1] Cap., vol. i., col. 271.

[2] Gratian. Decret., p. 11, caus. 2, quot. 7, col. 41.

[3] Gratian. Decret., Distinct. 10, c. 9

Moreover, in France, within the Gallo-Frankish church, the emperors governed alone, without, in any respect, sharing the power with the papacy. That influence upon the Gallo-Frankish church which I have just exhibited to you as being in the hands of the popes, was only indirect. They did not convoke the councils; the emperor alone called them. The decisions of these assemblies did not require their approbation. All ecclesiastical supervision or administration belonged either to the national bishops or to the delegates of the emperor, and the pope only interfered indirectly, by way of advice.

There existed, moreover, with the public, both laity and clergy, a certain idea of an ancient and general legislation of the church, to which the popes were bound to submit, as well as the other bishops. People made no precise estimate of its source and its authority; they were not fully aware from what power it ought always to emanate; the question was not, as it afterwards was, very clearly laid down between the councils and the popes; but it was the firm impression of the public that, above the popes, were the canons, discipline, and general law of the church, and that of themselves they had no right to change them.

Such was the situation of the papacy, more especially in its relations with the Gallo-Frankish church, at the commencement of the ninth century, and the end of the reign of Charlemagne. You see that much incoherence and confusion reigned in it. We thus meet with a multitude of contradictory facts; some bear witness to the independence of the national churches; others exhibit the papal power above the national churches. Here appears the superiority of the temporal power; there, that of the spiritual power enthroned at Rome. In 833, Gregory IV. interfered to reconcile Louis le Debonnaire and his sons, reproaching the bishops of Frankish Gaul with their conduct: they protested against his interference, and contested with him the rights which he assumed, declaring that "they would by no means submit to his will, and that if he came to excommunicate, he should depart excommunicated; for the authority of the ancient canons permitted nothing of this kind." Nevertheless, in his answer, Gregory reproaches them with having employed, in writing to him, the titles *frater* and *pater*, by turns, "whereas it would have been much more becoming to have exhibited towards him nothing but a filial respect;" and, upon this, not only did they not expostulate again, but the word *frater* gradually disappeared from their language. In 844, the bishops of Frankish Gaul refused to acknowledge Drogon, archbishop of Metz, the natural son of Charlemagne, as vicar of pope Sergius II., who had given him his diploma; and, in 849, they menaced Nomenoe, king of Brittany, with excommunication, because he received with disdain a letter of pope Leo IV., "to whom God had given the primacy of the entire world." I might multiply examples; I might exhibit temporal sovereigns, popes, and national churches, turn by turn, conquerors or conquered, arrogant or humble. Nevertheless, through all these contradictions, we plainly perceive that the papacy was making progress; it reigned, if not in fact, at least in the minds of men. The conviction that the pope was the interpreter of the faith, the chief of the universal church, that he was above all other bishops, above national councils, and above temporal governments, in matters of religion, and even in temporal affairs, when they related to religion; this conviction, I say, became more and more established in the minds of men. In the middle of the ninth century, we may regard it as definitively formed; the conquest of the intellectual order was then completed for the profit of the papacy.

It had also to make the conquest of the legal order; the mind of nations attributed to it the sovereignty of law, but there were wanting titles in which its laws should be written, and in the name of which it might assert their historical antiquity, as well as their national legitimacy. These it soon found.

Collections had been making, for a long time, of the canons of the church. The first collection of this kind, in the west, had been compiled in the sixth century by a Roman monk, named Denis le Petit. It soon became a kind of ecclesiastical code, and the object of general emulation. Many similar collections were written in the different states of the west. Spain, in particular, had one of them, to which the name of *Isidore* was given, although St. Isidore, bishop of Seville, had evidently no hand in it. It was more extensive than that of Denis le Petit, and contained a greater number of letters of the popes, as well as of canons of councils, and particularly of the Spanish councils. It spread itself beyond Spain, and very soon obtained great credit, particularly in Gaul.

In the first half of the ninth century, between the years 820 and 849, there suddenly appeared, still under the name of Saint Isidore, a new collection of canons, much more important than that which I have already mentioned. It is in the north and east of Frankish Gaul, in the dioceses of Mayence, Trèves, Metz, Reims, &c. &c., that we first meet with it; there it had no obstacle opposed to its circulation; very few were the doubts which arose here and there concerning its authenticity, and in a short time it acquired a sovereign authority. This is the collection which is called The False Decretals. It has received this name because it contains numerous pieces which are manifestly false, and because it bears all the characters of a lying fabrication. It begins with sixty letters of the most ancient bishops of Rome, from Saint Clement (91—100) to Melchiades (311—314); letters of which no monument had yet made mention, and of which the falsehood appears at the first glance. The popes of the three first centuries are therein continually made to employ Saint Jerome's translation of the bible, which was not produced until the end of the fourth century; they also allude to facts and to works of the sixth and seventh centuries. In short, the fabrication cannot in the present day be called into question by a man of any sense or information.

The author of this fabrication is not known. Since we meet with it first of all in the dioceses of Treves and Mayence, and on account of other minor indications with which I will not occupy your time, it has been attributed to Benedict, deacon of Mayence, whom I have already named to you, and who made the second collection of the statutes of Charlemagne. Whoever he may have been, his work spread rapidly: many took it for the ancient collection already known by the name of Saint Isidore: others, believing it to be new, neglected even to examine its contents. It had for patrons, not alone the popes and their partisans, but also nearly all the bishops; for, in fact, it was not written exclusively in the interest of the papacy. It even seems, all things considered, in its primitive intention to have been more especially destined to serve the bishops against the metropolitans and the temporal sovereigns. The greater portion of the fabricated pieces, even whilst displaying with pomp the power of the popes, have for their principal object the establishing of the independence of the bishops, and it is above all against the metropolitans and the temporal princes that the power of the pope is invoked.

The false decretals had, therefore, from the first, the support of the bishops; and, far from calling them into question, they eagerly adopted them, pre-occupied, as has so often happened, with the interest of the moment, and not troubling themselves to perceive that one day the fraud would turn to the profit of the pretensions of the papacy, rather than to their own advantage.

About the middle of the ninth century the pope had thus triumphed both in the intellectual and in the legal orders; they were in possession of rational right and a written title; this sovereignty reposed not only upon public belief, but also upon traditions.

Thus founded, and invested with such forces, their power was naturally not slow to display itself practically. About the same period, in fact, all the consequences of the principles set down, either in the general opinions of the time, or in the false decretals, made their appearance in certain particular events.

In 856, a nephew of Charles le Chauve, and great-grandson of Charlemagne, Lothaire, king of Lorraine, had married Teutberge, daughter of Boson, a Burgundian count. In 857 she displeased him, and he put her away; he accused her of all kinds of crimes, among others, of incest with Hubert, her brother. He lived openly with another woman, Waldrade, sister of Gunther, archbishop of Cologne, and niece to Teutgaud, archbishop of Trèves, whom he had loved, it is said, for a long time, and to whom he had even promised marriage.

In 858, Teutberge, with the assistance of a champion, justified herself by the proof of boiling water, and Lothaire found himself forced to take her back again, but he never ceased in his efforts to get rid of her. Whether truly, or through fear, she permitted herself to avow the crime of which she was accused; and between 860 and 862, three councils held at Aix-la-Chapelle solemnly condemned her, annulled the marriage, and allowed Lothaire to wed Waldrade.

But, pretty nearly about the same time, in 858, the holy see was assumed by a monk of severe manners, ardent character, and inflexible spirit, who had not, without great difficulty, determined upon leaving his cloister to become pope, and who, once pope, desired to reign over Christianity indeed. Hear how a contemporary chronicler speaks of Nicholas the First:

"Since the blessed Gregory, no bishop exalted, in the city of Rome, to the pontifical see, may be compared with him; he reigned over kings and tyrants, and subjected them to his authority, as if he had been the master of the world. He showed himself humble, benign, pious, and benevolent towards religious bishops and priests, and those who observed the precepts of the Lord — terrible and extremely severe towards the impious, and those who wandered from the right way; so that he might be taken for another Elias, resuscitated in our days by the voice of God, if not in body, at least in spirit and in virtue."[1]

In the year 859, it appears that Teutberge addressed herself to Nicholas I., and claimed his interference. He made her wait for some time. It was not till 862, and after the holding of the three councils of Aix-la-Chapelle, that he sent two legates to Lorraine, with orders to investigate the matter anew. For this purpose a council was convoked at Metz, in 863. Whether the facts with which Teutberge was charged appeared sufficiently proved, or whether Lothaire (which seems the most probable) succeeded in winning over the two legates, the council at which they assisted sanctioned the conclusions of former councils, and the matter appeared to be terminated, with the accord of all judges and all powers.

But when the news of this decision came to Rome, whether with or without reason, (and, for my part, I believe that it was with reason,) Nicholas perceived in it nothing more than the effect of obsequiousness, or, to speak plainly, of servility and corruption, whether upon the part of the bishops of Lorraine, or upon that of his own legates. The general voice accused them; the two archbishops who had directed the council were relations of Waldrade. Nicholas resolved to take no half

[1] Chron. de Reginon, ad a. 868

measures; and, without convoking any council at Rome, he, with his single authority, not only annulled the acts of the council of M·tz, but deposed the archbishops of Trèves and Cologne, and commanded Lothaire to receive his wife again. He had, to excuse him in adopting this bold and despotic conduct, upon one hand, public opinion, which was strongly pronounced against Lothaire and Waldrade; on the other hand, as far as we can judge at this distance of time, truth and justice: against him were the rights of the bishops and councils, and all the ancient discipline of the church; but the text of the false decretals furnished him with a point of support against these last objeetions. Strong in the austerity of his conscience and the approbation of the people, he persisted in his resolution, and not content with avenging morality, called also to his aid the spirit of liberty. In 863, he wrote to Adventius, bishop of Metz:

"Examine well whether these kings and princes, to whom you profess yourself subjected, are really kings and princes. Examine whether they govern well, first, themselves—next, their people: for he who is worth nothing for himself, how can he be good for another? Examine whether they reign according to justice; for, otherwise, they should be regarded as tyrants rather than as kings; and, in such case, we ought to resist and oppose, instead of submitting to them. Were we to submit to them, were we not to rise up against them, we should be obliged to encourage their vices."[1]

Against such arms, the temporal princes, aided even by their own clergy, as Lothaire was upon this occasion, were too weak. Nicholas I. triumphed at the same time over Lothaire and over the clergy of Lorraine; both one and the other submitted to, whilst they expostulated against, his decision.

Nearly at the same moment, a second matter presented itself which furnished him with the occasion of a second victory. Hincmar, archbishop of Reims, with whom I shall occupy you now in detail, by and bye, desired to reign almost as despotically in the Gallo-Frankish church, as Nicholas reigned in the church universal. One of his suffragans, Rothade, bishop of Soissons, had deprived a priest of his diocese of his rank, on account of misconduct; three years after this

[1] Mansi.

condemnation, under the pretext that it was unjust, and rather, as it appears, from ill-humour against Rothade, than from any other motive, Hincmar re-established the priest in his parish, against the will of his bishop, and excommunicated the latter for his disobedience. A dispute was thus established between the bishop of Soissons, and the archbishop of Reims. The bishop deposed in 862, by the council of Soissons, appealed from it to the pope; Hincmar, by means of stratagems and violence, eluded, for some time, the effects of their appeal, and even prevented its arrival at Rome; but Nicholas I. received it at last, and in 865, having called a council upon this subject, he said, in his opening discourse:

"The bishops of Gaul, having convoked a general council, (which it is permitted to none to do,) without the order of the apostolic see, have there cited Rothade .... Even though the council had not been called, he ought not to have been deposed without our knowledge, for the sacred statutes and the canonical decrees have remitted to our decision the trials of bishops, together with all other important matters."[1]

This was to misunderstand and to brave all canonical rules, all the examples of the past, all the customs of the church. But upon this particular occasion, as upon the former, Nicholas had right and the public voice on his side; and he upheld justice and the popular opinion. He triumphed again; Rothade was re-established, and the national churches were conquered in the person of Hincmar, as the temporal sovereigns had been in the person of Lothaire.

This double victory was not undisputed: more than once, in the course of the tenth century, resistance reappeared; and the successors of Nicholas I., among others, Adrian II., were not all of them so skilful or so fortunate in their enterprises as he had been. Nevertheless, on the whole, their power and the maxims which supported it, were making progress in external things, as well as in the minds of men; and it is from the reign of Nicholas I. that the sovereignty of the papacy really dates.

I approach my limits. I have occupied you with the internal history of the Gallo-Frankish church, from the eighth to the tenth century, as regards its relation with the temporal

[1] Mansi, t. xv., p. 686.

sovereign. I have placed before you its external history, its relations with its foreign sovereign. And to this I confine my picture of the Carlovingian ecclesiastical society. It remains for us to study intellectual development in the same period. You have already seen what this was under Charlemagne, and up to the time of Louis le Debonnaire. The study of it, from the reign of Louis le Debonnaire to the accession of Hugh Capet, will be the object of our next meetings.

TWENTY-EIGHTH LECTURE.

Of the intellectual condition of Frankish Gaul, from the death of Charlemagne to the accession of Hugh Capet—Sketch of the celebrated men of this period—The theological mind—The philosophical mind—Hincmar and John Erigena are respectively their representatives—Life of Hincmar—His activity and influence as archbishop of Reims—1. Concerning his relations with kings and popes—2. Concerning his administration in the interior of the Gallo-Frankish church and of his diocese —3. Concerning his disputes and theological works—Origin of the theology of the middle ages—Quarrel between Hincmar and the monk Gottschalk upon predestination—Numerous writings upon this subject—Councils of Kiersy, Valence, and Langres—Recapitulation.

In exhibiting the intellectual revival of Frankish Gaul under Charlemagne,[1] I affirmed that the movement which was then given to mind, did not cease under his successors. It is to the progress of this movement, in the ninth and tenth centuries, that I purpose to direct your attention to-day.

When I arranged the table of the celebrated men of the times of Charlemagne,[2] I included in it, you remember, those alike, whom he found, and those whom he formed, his contemporaries, properly so called, and their immediate disciples. I have treated in detail only of the first, confining myself, as regards the last, to the indications of their names and their works. The majority of these—for instance, the historians Thegan, Nithard the astronomer, the theologians Raban, Florus, Walfrid Strabo, Paschase Radbirt, Ratramne, and many other erudite and literary men, and poets, who were comprised in the last part of the table which I have placed before you, belong to the epoch whereupon we are now to be

[1] Lecture 23rd. [2] Lecture 20th.

engaged; and in adding to this table that of the celebrated men who appeared towards the end of the ninth, and in the course of the tenth century, I complete a summary of the intellectual activity of Frankish Gaul under the Carlovingian line. Here is this supplement:

ame.	Country.	Born.	Died.	Condition.	Works.
. Remi.	Gaul.	Beginning of the ninth century.	878	Archbishop of Lyons.	Theological writings; amongst others, writings upon predestination and free-will.
. Ado.	Diocese of Sens.	800	875	Archbishop of Vienna.	1. Theological writings; 2. An universal chronicle.
ncmar.	Gaul.	806	882	Archbishop of Reims.	1. Theological writings; among others, writings on predestination; 2. Political writings and decrees; 3. Letters.
mi.	Burgundy.	About the middle of the ninth century.	About 908	Monk of St. Germain d'Auxerre.	1. Commentaries upon the scriptures; 2. Theological writings; 3. Commentaries upon the ancient grammarians and rhetoricians.
bo.	Gaul.	Idem.	About 924	Monk of St Germain des Prés.	1. A poem upon the siege of Paris by the Normans, in 885; 2. Manuscript sermons.
cbald.	Flanders.	About 840	930	Monk of St. Amand.	1. Poems; 2. Lives of the Saints.
Odo.	Maine.	879	942	Abbot of Cluny.	1. Theological writings; 2. Lives of the Saints, particularly Gregory of Tours; 3. Sermons.
doard.	Epernay.	894	966	Canon of Reims.	1. Poems; 2. History of the church of Reims: 3. A chronicle from 919 to 966.
rbert. . II.)	Aurillac.	In the first half of the tenth century.	1003	Pope.	1. Works on mathematics; 2. On philosophy; 3. On theology; 4. Poems; 5. Letters.

Now, in endeavouring to go further than this series of names, dates, and titles, of works, I experience the same embarrassment which I experienced when I desired to depict the intellectual condition of France under Charlemagne. The works of all those men whom I have just named form no united whole, do not connect themselves with any great idea, or with any general and fruitful system, around which we may group them, or which may be employed as a thread of connection in this study. Their works are detached, partial, little varied, and more remarkable for the activity they manifest than for the results they have produced. In the absence of a systematic summary, shall I take these men one by one, relating the life, and describing the writings of each? Such biographies would be uninteresting and uninstructive unless they were very minute; but we have little time to devote to them. I will solve the question as I solved it in the case of the reign of Charlemagne. I referred the intellectual picture of his epoch to the life of one man, of a man who seemed to me its most faithful representative: I traced, in the destiny and works of Alcuin, the delineation of the condition and general movement of mind. I shall adopt the same method for the following epoch: I shall seek for some man who is the image of it, in whom the intellectual life of his contemporaries is reflected: and I shall endeavour to make him thoroughly understood, well assured that, considering the shortness of the time to which I am limited, this will be the best way of making you acquainted with the entire period. Two men will enable us to arrive at this result.

In studying the life and writings of Alcuin, we were led to recognise therein a double tendency, a double character: "Alcuin," I said, "was a theologian by profession; the atmosphere in which he lived was essentially theological; but nevertheless the theological spirit did not reign in him alone; his labours and his thoughts also tended towards philosophy and ancient literature. He was familiar with St. Jerome and St. Augustin; but Pythagoras, Aristotle, Aristippus, Diogenes, Plato, Homer, Virgil, Seneca, and Pliny, lived also in his memory. He was a monk, a deacon, the light of the contemporary church, but he was also a man of learning and classical literature. In him, in fact, commences the alliance of the two elements of which the modern mind has so long carried the discordant impress: antiquity and the church; admiration, love—shall I say regret?—for pagan literature; with sincerity of Christian faith, and eagerness to fathom its mysteries and defend its power."[1]

The same fact is the predominant character of the epoch with which we now occupy ourselves; but it is no longer in any one man that we find its image; the Christian and the Roman mind, the new theology and the ancient philosophy manifest themselves equally, but in a separate and even hostile state. We met with two men who may be considered as the distinct representations of these two elements. One, Hincmar, archbishop of Reims, is the centre of the theological movement; the other, Scotus or Erigena, is the philosopher of the time. With the life of Hincmar the events and labours of contemporaneous theology connect themselves; in that of Erigena, the modes of ancient philosophy are revealed. In the history of these two men appear the two forces of which the struggle for a long time constituted all the intellectual history of modern Europe; I mean the doctrinal church, and free thought. I shall endeavour to make you acquainted both with one and with the other. It is with Hincmar that I shall begin.

He was born about the year 806, in Frankish-Gaul, properly so called, that is to say, in the north-east of present France. His family was one of the most considerable of the time: the famous Bernard II., count of Toulouse, and another Bernard, count of Vermandois, were his relations. He was brought up from his childhood in the monastery of St. Denis, under the abbot Hilduin. Louis le Debonnaire, when he ascended the throne, whether it was that he already knew Hincmar, or whether he took an interest in his family, caused him to come to his court, and retained him near him. You know the efforts that were made by this prince, from 816 to 830, to reform the church, and particularly the monasteries. The monastery of St. Denis, like many others, greatly required reform; discipline and knowledge were there equally declining. Hincmar, young as

[1] Lecture 22.

he was, laboured and powerfully assisted, in 829, to enforce their regeneration. He did more: he himself entered the monastery, and led the most rigid life there; but he was not permitted to remain in peace long; the abbot Hilduin took part, about 830, in the quarrels of Louis le Debonnaire with his sons; he declared himself against the emperor; and when Louis recovered power, Hilduin was dispossessed of his monastery and banished to Saxony. Whether from affection to his abbot, or from other considerations with which we cannot now become acquainted, Hincmar followed him there, and nevertheless retained sufficient credit, not only to allow of his son returning to the court himself, but to enable him to cause Hilduin to be recalled and reinstated.

To begin from this epoch, we see him sometimes with the emperor, sometimes in his monastery, leading, by turns, the life of a favourite priest, and that of an austere monk. It is difficult, at this distance of time, to decide upon what were the parts taken in his actions by worldly ambition and by religious fervour. What appears certain is, that neither one nor the other was ever wholly absent from him, and that, in the entire course of his life, as at this epoch, he was almost equally taken up with his fortune and his salvation.

At the death of Louis le Debonnaire, in 840, Charles le Chauve took Hincmar into the same favour. From 840 to 844, he lived at the court of this prince as his most intimate confident, and his principal agent in all ecclesiastical affairs. Charles gave him many abbeys. In 844, he assisted at the council of Verneuil. The archbishopric of Reims had been vacant for nine years, in consequence of the deposition of the archbishop Ebbo—a complicated and obscure business, into the details of which I will not enter. The clergy demanded, at last, that this important see should be filled, and the following year, in 845, at the council of Beauvais, Hincmar, then thirty-nine years old, was elected archbishop of Reims.

His activity and influence in the Gallo-Frankish church date from this epoch. He was archbishop of Reims for thirty-nine years, from the year 845 to the 23rd of December, 882. In this long space of time we find his signature below the acts of thirty-nine councils, not to speak of many minor ecclesiastical assemblies, of which there remain no records.

In the greater part of these councils he **presided and directed** affairs.[1]

The historian of the church of Reims, Frodoard, who had the archives of the church at his disposal, especially mentions four hundred and twenty-three of his letters, and, at almost every page, indicates the existence of a great many others. These letters are directed to kings, queens, popes, archbishops, bishops, abbots, priests, dukes, counts, &c. He was evidently in habitual and familiar correspondence with all the considerable men of the time. Finally, there remain to us sixty-six of his works, great or small, religious or political, collected by father Sirmond, in two folio volumes, to which another jesuit, father Cellot, afterwards added a third volume; and we know with certainty that there are many other writings of Hincmar which have not reached us.

Assuredly we have here an active and powerful life. In order to appreciate it well, and to draw from it much light concerning the general history of the time, we must classify, to some degree, the facts which filled it, considering Hincmar under three principal points of view:

I. Without the Gallo-Frankish church and his own diocese, in his relations whether with the national civil power, the kings of France, or with the foreign ecclesiastical power, the

[1] Hincmar assisted,

In 844, at the council	of Verneuil.
845,	of Beauvais.
id.	of Meaux.
847,	of Paris.
849,	of Kiersy.
id.	of Paris.
850,	of Moret.
851,	of Soissons.
853,	*id.*
id.	of Kiersy.
id.	of Verberie.
857,	of Kiersy.
858,	*id.*
859,	of Metz.
id.	of Toul.
860,	Place uncert^{n}.
id.	of Toul.
861,	of Soissons.
862,	of Sens.
id.	of Sablonniere.
id.	of Pistes.

In 862, at the council	of Soissons.
id.	of Pistes (transferred to Soissons.)
863,	of Senlis.
id.	of Verberie.
866,	of Soissons.
867,	of Troyes.
869,	of Verberie.
id.	of Metz.
id.	of Pistes.
870,	of Attigy.
871,	of Douzy.
873,	of Senlis.
874,	of Douzy.
875,	of Châlons.
876,	of Pontion.
878,	of Neustria.
id.	of Troyes.
881,	of Fismes.

pope. II. Within the Gallo-Frankish church and his ow diocese, in his ecclesiastical influence and his episcopal administration. III. In his scientific and literary activity as theologian and writer. All the important and instructive facts of Hincmar's life come under one or other of these three aspects.

I. Considered in his relations with the national civil power, Hincmar appeared, throughout his entire life, as the bishop of the court of France, the director of two kings. It is advisedly that I say the bishop of the court of France. We find him, indeed, at the head of all the events of the court, of all official ceremonies. Four coronations, four consecrations of kings and queens took place in this epoch, and Hincmar presided at them all. In 856, at Verberie, he crowned Judith, daughter of Charles le Chauve, who married Ethelwolf, king of the Anglo-Saxons. In 866, at the council of Soissons, he crowned Hermentrude, wife of Charles le Chauve. In 869, at the council of Metz, he crowned Charles le Chauve himself king of Lorraine. In 877, he crowned Louis le Begue, king of France. In a word, it was always Hincmar who, upon all great occasions, within or without his diocese, in ecclesiastical or civil assemblies, represented the church amidst the court, and presided at the alliance of religion with royalty.

In matters of a graver nature than ceremonies, in politics properly so called, the remarkable characteristic of the life of Hincmar was his constant fidelity to the direct line—to the legitimate descendants of Charlemagne; a difficult task in his time, amidst all the vicissitudes of the throne, and the dissensions of the reigning family. Whether by attachment, principle, foresight, or skill, the faith of Hincmar never lost itself in this labryrinth; he always kept himself at a distance from the party which history has qualified as the rebellious; and those princes who are recognised as having formed the series of true kings of France ever counted him among their defenders. We find him, nevertheless, keeping himself, at the same time, on good terms with their enemies and rivals. It would be unjust to say that, in history, Hincmar bears the appearance of an intriguer; there is nothing to indicate that he sought out intrigue, that he pursued, at all cost, opportunities of acting, influencing, and prevailing; but everything shows that, when need was, he knew how to employ intrigue with activity and dexterity, and that he excelled in acquiring or preserving influence wherever the interest of his position, in the state or in the church, made it necessary to him. He, in consequence, possessed great credit with all kings and contemporary powers during the long period of his life. We see his intervention not only in the relations of princes with the church, but in civil government itself; he was employed upon difficult missions, consulted in delicate questions. And not only does this political activity appear in his history, but there are written monuments remaining of it. We have five works by him, either upon government in general, or upon the events and affairs wherein he took part, which abound in valuable information upon the ideas and political condition of France at that epoch. These works are:

I. A treatise, in thirty-three chapters, addressed to Charles le Chauve, and entitled: *De regis persona et de regio ministerio*;[1] a work upon morality rather than upon politics, judging according to our present ideas, but which, in the ninth century, was truly political, for it was in the name of morality, and in developing its precepts, that the ecclesiastics influenced governments. In the treatise of Hincmar, morality is moreover mingled with a great number of maxims of prudence and practical wisdom, very like those which, in the fifteenth century, constituted all political science, and of which the book of the *Prince* is the type.

II. A letter addressed to Louis le Begue, after his coronation, at the end of the year 877, containing advice upon the government of his states, and terminating with this remarkably sensible paragraph:

"I address to your majesty, by letter, what I would say in words if I were near you. As to the affairs properly so called of the church and of the kingdom, I ought not to give counsel upon this subject without the general concurrence and advice of the great, and I cannot, and dare not, decide concerning it of myself. If, in the interim, there should befal any cause of trouble, (from which may God preserve us,) and if it should please your majesty to inform me of it, I will endeavour to assist you with my advice and services, according to my knowledge and my power."[2]

[1] Hincm. Op., vol. ii. p. 184. [2] Ibid.

III. A letter to the emperor Charles le Gros, engaging him to superintend the education of the two young kings of France, Louis III. and Carloman, and to provide them with good councillors.

IV. A long letter, addressed to the grandees of western France, who had consulted Hincmar concerning the government of king Carloman, in which he transmits to them long extracts from, perhaps an entire copy of, the work of Adalhard, *de ordine palatii*, in which is exhibited Charlemagne's method of government, and of which I have already treated.[1]

V. Finally, advice upon the government of Carloman, addressed to the bishops of his kingdom in 882, the year of Hincmar's death, and written at Epernay, where he had just fled from his episcopal town, besieged by the Normans; so much did the affairs of the states, in the government of which he had assisted, continue to engage him.

We must not believe that this desire of political importance, this court popularity which Hincmar constantly enjoyed, cost nothing to the independence, say, rather, to the pride of the bishop. He was not, as you have seen, of the number of those insolent and shuffling prelates who, under Louis le Debonnaire and Charles le Chauve, delighted in humiliating royalty before them; but he professed, as a general position, the principles upon which their pretensions were founded, and, more than once, he opposed to the desires of the temporal power, language very similar to theirs. We read, in his treatise upon the divorce of Lothaire and Teutberge, a quarrel of which I have already spoken:

"Some wise men say that their prince, being king, is not subject to the laws or to the judgments of any one, unless it be God himself.... who made him king.... and that, as he must not, whatever he may have done, be excommunicated by his bishops, so he cannot be judged by other bishops; for God alone has a right to command him.... Such is not the language of a catholic Christian; it is full of blasphemy and of the spirit of evil.... The authority of the apostles says that kings ought to be subject to those whom it establishes in the name of the Lord, and who watch over their soul, in order that this task may not be a source of trouble to them. The

[1] Lecture 20.

blessed pope Gelasius wrote to the emperor Anastasius: 'There are two principal powers by which this world is governed: the pontifical authority and the royal dignity; and the authority of pontiffs is so much the greater, inasmuch as they must account to the Lord for the souls of kings themselves.' .... When it is said that the king is not subject to the laws or judgments of any one, save God alone, no more than the truth is said, if he be indeed king as his name indicates him to be. He is called king because he rules and governs; if he governs himself according to the will of God, if he directs the good in the right way, and corrects the wicked, in order to lead them from the bad way into the good, then he is king, and is subject to no judgment save that of God alone ....; for laws are made, not for the just, but for the unjust, ... but if he be an adulterer, a murderer, partial, or avaricious, then ought he to be judged, in secret or in public, by the bishops, who are the throne of God."[1]

Assuredly, the maxims of ecclesiastical sovereignty were never more formally set forth.

In fact, the life of Hincmar was full of acts of resistance to the very sovereigns whom he served with most zeal, and his language towards them was that of the most inflexible haughtiness. I will cite but one example:

In 881, under the reign of Louis III., a dispute had occurred between this prince and the council of Fismes, touching the election of a bishop of Beauvais; the king had protected and obstinately supported a clergyman, named Odacre, whom the council thought unworthy. Hincmar wrote to Louis:

"As regards what you have written to us, saying that you will do nothing other than what you have already done, know that, if you do it not, God will himself do that which is pleasing to him. The emperor Louis (le Debonnaire) did not live so many years as his father Charles. King Charles (le Chauve), your grandfather, did not live so many years as his father; your own father (Louis le Begue) did not live so many years as his father; and, even while living amidst that pomp in which your father and grandfather lived at Compiegne, cast your eyes where your father rests; and,

[1] Hincm. Op., de Divort. Loth. et Teuth., vol. i., p. 693—695

if you do not know, ask where your grandfather died and reposes; and do not let your heart swell before the face of Him who died for you and for us all, and who afterwards rose from the dead, to die no more. And be sure that you must die: you know not at what day, nor at what hour; and you have therefore need, as we all have, of being ever ready for the call of the Lord. . . . You will pass away soon; but the holy church, with its heads, under Christ, its sovereign head, according to his promise, shall never pass away."[1]

I might multiply these quotations: the writings, like the entire life of Hincmar, prove that, without carrying them as far as rebellion and usurpation of the civil power, he professed, concerning the relations of the two powers, all the maxims which, since the death of Charlemagne, had developed themselves in the Gallo-Frankish church, and that he knew, when need was, to take advantage of them as means of resistance.

As regards his relations with another power, with the foreign sovereign of the church, the pope, they are more difficult to determine, as also are the ideas which he entertained upon this subject; there is much contradiction and uncertainty touching this matter. Hincmar appears often to have been in high favour at Rome: Leo IV., upon sending him the *pallium*, gave him the right, which, (said he,) had scarcely ever been given to other archbishops, of wearing it every day. Adrian II., John VIII., shaped their conduct by his advice, and accorded to him all that he asked of them. In the great struggle of Nicholas I. against king Lothaire, concerning Waldrade and Teutberge, Hincmar took the part of the court of Rome, supported its cause, and received from it many marks of esteem and good will. Upon other occasions, on the contrary, we find him not only opposing but combating the court of Rome, by which, on such occasions, he is very ill-treated. I have already spoken to you of the check he met with in the affair of Rothade, bishop of Soissons.[2] I will instance another matter in which Nicholas the First was not more favourable to him. Ebbo, the predecessor of Hincmar in the see of Reims, had appointed a certain number of priests or deacons, among others, one called

[1] Hincm. Op., vol. ii., p. 199.

[2] Lecture 27.

Wulfad: it was maintained that this appointment was not canonical; that Ebbo, not having been legitimate archbishop of Reims, had not possessed the right of conferring orders, and that they ought to be withdrawn from these pretended clergymen. In 853, the question was carried before the council of Soissons, and after a long and curious process, whether it was by the influence of Hincmar, or by the real opinion of the council, the priests and deacons ordained by Ebbo were dismissed. They appealed to Rome; and, in 866, Nicholas the First commanded the revision of the matter: a new council took place at Soissons; and the pope addressed to the assembled bishops a long letter, in which the conduct of Hincmar, in that of 853, was harshly censured:

"There," said he, "we saw the archbishop sometimes laying aside, sometimes reassuming his rights; sometimes submitting himself to the council, sometimes presiding over it; by turns, the accused, accuser, and judge; ruling all things after his own fancy, changing his part unceasingly, and thus taking the semblance of a certain animal, which is not always of one and the same colour."[1]

Opposed by such reproaches and by the influence of Charles le Chauve himself, who, this time, showed favour to his adversaries, the predominance of Hincmar in the Gallo-Frankish church failed; the dismissed clergymen were re-established in their canonical rank; and, notwithstanding the discretion which the pope recommended them to observe towards Hincmar in their conquest, the defeat was a marked one for him.

The same struggle with the same result was renewed upon other occasions, with the detail of which I will not occupy your time. Upon such occasions, we find Nicholas the First sometimes keeping fair with, sometimes severely reprimanding Hincmar; and the latter, upon his part, in his correspondence with the pope, appears singularly embarrassed and fluctuating in his maxims and language. Sometimes he himself recognises, and, in magnificent terms, proclaims the sovereignty of the pope; sometimes he defends the rights of archbishops and of bishops, and seems even to lay the foundations of a

[1] Labbe, Concil., vol. viii., col. 834.

national independent church; and then he presently abandons all that he has said upon the subject, as if he feared to be accused of maxims and intentions, which, nevertheless, he could not suppress, which, haply, he wished to become apparent. His letters to the pope, inserted by Frodoard in his *Histoire de l'Eglise de Reims*, betray, at every word, this uncertainty of ideas and desires.

All things considered, and remembering the vast difference of mind and times, there was, in the situation and conduct of Hincmar, whether towards the civil power or the papacy, some analogy with the situation and conduct of Bossuet, in nearly similar questions, in the seventeenth century. Not that these two great bishops bear the least resemblance to one another as writers: a talent for writing, a genius for expression, brilliancy of imagination and style were wholly wanting to Hincmar; and, looking merely to his works, the idea would never arise of tracing any relation between him and Bossuet. But when we look deeper, the analogy becomes substantial, and the two men are explained and elucidated one by the other. Through all the fluctuations, all the changes of his language, we recognise in Hincmar a firm and bold mind, a powerful logician, who, when he had once conceived a principle or a system, unfolded its consequences skilfully, and, in the freedom of his thought, followed them without hesitation to their last results. But he was, at the same time, a man of strong common sense, and of great practical understanding, who saw what obstacles were opposed to his ideas by external circumstances, and did not allow himself to be deceived by the seduction of logic, concerning the possibility or expediency of their application. In writing, he laid down or deduced maxims with that loftiness of thought which seems to delight in its own bold and free development. In acting, no fact, no detail of the true situation escaped him; he comprehended all that ought to influence the conduct of the matter, all that was required in order to succeed; he wisely measured the possible, and attempted that and no more. Hence the embarrassment which sometimes appears in his ideas and words; sometimes it is the logician, sometimes the man of business that predominates; he fluctuates, so to speak, unceasingly between the strict stedfastness of his thought and the practical impartiality of his reason.

Thus it was with Bossuet, placed in very different society and circumstances. That lofty genius, that simple and irresistible reasoner, who arrived, by a glance, at the last consequences of a principle, and grasped them, like a club, to let them fall at a single blow, upon the head of his adversaries, more than once exhibited himself, in practice, uncertain, dilatory, anything but logically strict, inclined to cautious and to middle courses. Was this mere weakness of soul, compliance, and a tendency to yield? Sometimes perhaps, but, assuredly, not always. Another cause led to this contrast. When the mind of Bossuet was free and in the presence only of its ideas, whatever might be the system upon which he was engaged, whether it concerned the pontifical power or a national church, authority or free inquiry, and whether he wished to attack or to defend it, he boldly embarked, as M. Turgot expresses himself, upon the faith of an idea, and voyaged at full sail as far as it would carry him ; but when it became necessary to act, when he was called upon actually to regulate the relations of different powers, of different rights, then all the considerations, all the difficulties of action presented themselves to him; he saw what was required by his times, by the state of society and of mind; the clear perception and impartiality of his good sense suppressed the boldness of his thought; and a prudence and caution, which seemed like servile compliance, took the place of that intractable dialectic and of that haughty eloquence which lately characterized him. It is a difficult problem to ally the height and rational consequence of philosophy with the flexibility of mind and the common sense of the practical man. Hincmar and Bossuet did not solve it; but they knew how to place themselves, by turns, under the two different points of view : they deemed themselves capable, if not of reconciling, at least of playing the two parts, and it is precisely this superiority that casts their deficiencies into relief.

You will pardon me for having paused awhile upon this analogy, which seems like a digression; but to be just towards great men, we must understand them well; and in order to understand them, we must turn for a long time around them, for they have a thousand different faces to show us.

II. Within his diocese, in ecclesiastical administration properly so called, Hincmar had no such difficulties to surmount; he was alone, and master; he could, at least almost always, regulate facts according to his ideas; he governed despotically, sometimes even tyrannically, but generally with wisdom, and to the true interest of the clergy, and of the faithful who were under him. We have written monuments of his government; that is to say, capitularies, addressed to his priests, as those of kings are addressed to their courts, *missi dominici*, or other agents. The capitularies of Hincmar which remain to us, are of four different epochs. The first, addressed in 852, to the clergy of his diocese, after an assembly of the same clergy, held at Reims, under his presidency, contain forty-three articles, of which seventeen are in the form of precepts upon the conduct of priests, and twenty-six in that of interrogations and inquiries upon the same subject. The second, in three articles, are of the year 857; the third, in five articles, of 874; the fourth, in thirteen articles, of 877.[1] These capitularies are generally very judicious; their object is either to recommend to the clergy regularity of behaviour, knowledge, and a gentle and legal administration, or to prevent the vexations of the archdeacons, who were placed between the simple priest and the bishop, and who often oppressed those who were under them, or, finally, to protect the diocese against the invasions of the civil magistrate, the disorders and the depredations of the laity, &c. They bear witness to an active, provident, and skilful government, one that was taken up with the advancement of the moral and material welfare of its objects.

III. Hitherto, I have endeavoured to show you in Hincmar, the spiritual or temporal governor, the bishop or councillor of kings. It remains for us to consider him in his intellectual activity as theologian; and this is the point of view which in the present day, at least, and in the questions upon which we are now occupied, is the most important to us.

Christian theology suffered, at this epoch, that is to say, in the course of the ninth century, a revolution which has not generally been recognised. From the sixth to the eighth century it had been dormant, as, indeed, had been every department of human thought. We do not find that any great religious questions were discussed in this period: there were bishops, priests, and monks, but no theologians. It was under

[1] Hincm. Op., vol. i., p. 710—741.

Charlemagne that theological discussions recommenced; you remember that we then met with discussions upon the worship of images, the nature of Jesus Christ, the procession of the Holy Ghost; and intellectual activity, once set in motion in this direction, ceased not to advance in it. But it soon changed its character. Created in the first five centuries by the Greek and Roman fathers, Christian theology, even in combating, received the impress of that ancient civilization, in the bosom of which it had been born. The system of dogmas, put forth and arranged by St. Basil, St. Athanasius, St. Jerome, St. Hilary, St. Augustin, &c., differed essentially from all the systems of the stoics, platonists, peripatetics, neoplatonists, &c., and yet it connected itself with them; it was a philosophy, a doctrine, of which the decisions of the church were not the only source, nor its authority the only support. When, after a sleep of a hundred and fifty years, the theological movement recommenced in the west, the fathers of the first centuries, especially St. Augustin, were regarded as irrefragable authorities, as masters of the faith. They were to the theologians who then began to arise, what the apostles and the holy books had been to themselves. But the condition of society, both civil and religious, was completely changed; and the new theologians, in adopting the fathers as masters, found it impossible to reproduce or even to imitate them. There was an abyss between the theology of the first five centuries, which was born in the bosom of Roman society, and the theology of the middle ages, which was born in the bosom of the Christian church, and truly commenced in the ninth century. I cannot pretend to treat in this place of the new and important question of their difference and its causes; I can do no more than indicate its existence, by the way, and in one particular subject.

Two kinds of religious questions re-appeared at this period; 1st, questions purely Christian, that is to say, which belonged especially to Christianity, and which do not necessarily arise in all religious philosophies, because they are not connected, or are, at least, very remotely connected, with the general nature of man; such, for instance, are the questions relating to the nature of Jesus Christ, the Trinity, transubstantiation, &c. 2nd, general questions which are met with in all religions and in all philosophies, because they arise from the very essence of human nature, as for instance, the question of the origin of good and evil, that of atonement, that of free-will and predestination, &c.

I have nothing to say to the first; they belong to pure Christian theology; the second come within the general domain of thought. I will select from the latter the questions of free-will and predestination, to which I have already called your attention, that arose in the ninth century, and upon which Hincmar and all the great minds of that epoch were long and intensely occupied.

I pray you call to mind, as accurately as you can, the state in which we left this question at the beginning of the ninth century, after the struggle of St. Augustin and his disciples against Pelagius and his successors. Two great heresies present themselves to our view: 1st, that of the Pelagians and of the anti-Pelagians, who attributed to the free choice and free-will of man the principal part in his moral life, and greatly abridged the action of God upon the human soul, over which they yet endeavoured to preserve it; 2nd, that of the predestinarians, who well nigh annul human freedom, and attribute the moral life and destiny of man to the direct action of the Divinity. We have seen the predestinarians pretending to be alone the faithful disciples of St. Augustin, and deducing their principles from his works. We have seen St. Augustin disowning them, refusing to abolish human freedom; and we have seen the church, after his example, placing herself, with more good sense than philosophical consequence, between the two parties, condemning, on the one hand, the predestinarians, on the other, the Pelagians or semi-Pelagians, and at once maintaining, without reconciling, the freedom of man and the all-powerful action of divine grace upon his soul. It was at this point we left the discussion.[1]

When it was recommenced in the ninth century, minds were much changed; the fathers of the first centuries, St. Augustin among others, had regarded all questions, and especially this, under a triple aspect: 1st, as philosophers examining things in themselves: 2nd, as heads of the church charged with governing it; 3rd, as teachers of the faith, and called upon to maintain orthodoxy—that is to say, to harmonize the solution of all questions with the essential principles

[1] Lecture 5

of Christianity. I have endeavoured to show how the combination of these various characters was calculated to exert, and, in fact, did exert the greatest influence upon the quarrel originated by Pelagius. In the ninth century, nothing of the kind existed; minds had no longer so much freedom and greatness; no one was any longer like St. Augustin, at once a philosopher, head of the church, and teacher of the faith; the theologians, above all, had become total strangers to the philosophical point of view. Their doctrine reposed exclusively upon the texts of the fathers who had preceded them, and applied itself only to the deduction of consequences from rules of belief already laid down. From the epoch at which we are now, the essential character of the theological spirit is, never to examine things in themselves, but to judge of all ideas by their relations to certain determined principles. The theologians in this respect have played the same part in modern Europe as was played by the jurisconsults in the Roman world. The Roman jurisconsults did not examine what we call the general principles of law, or natural law; they had for their point of departure, certain axioms, certain legal precedents; and their skill consisted in subtilly unravelling the consequences, in order to apply them to particular cases, as they presented themselves. Thus the Roman jurisconsults were logicians of admirable ingenuity and accuracy, but they were never philosophers. The theologians of the middle ages were similarly constituted; they applied themselves to the same kind of work, and attained the same excellences—namely, accuracy and logical subtlety—and fell into the same faults—namely, want of attention to facts themselves, and of any feeling for reality.

Now, in the question of free-will and grace, in particular, St. Augustin had laid down all the principles. His doctrines were made the obligatory point of departure, from which no one dared to confess that he deviated. Whatever opinion a man desired to maintain, whether human freedom or predestination, it was only by reasoning upon texts of St. Augustin, and taking them for his rule, that he was allowed to defend his system. The discussion, in short, became a matter of logic; it was no longer a question of philosophy. It was under this banner and these conditions that the dispute recommenced. I will tell you how, and upon what occasion.

A monk, Saxon by birth, named Gottschalk, lived in the abbey of Fulda, under the discipline of the abbot Raban, whom I have already mentioned, and who was afterwards archbishop of Mayence, and one of the most celebrated theologians of the time. Gottschalk, we know not for what reasons, did not wish any longer to remain as monk in this abbey, and he succeeded in annulling his monastic engagement. Raban conceived a strong antipathy to him on this account. Gottschalk quitted the abbey of Fulda, and retired into that of Orbais, situated in the diocese of Soissons, and, consequently, under the jurisdiction of Hincmar, as archbishop. About the year 847, Gottschalk (it is not known upon what occasion) went upon a pilgrimage to Rome. In returning, he stopped in a valley of Piedmont, at the house of a count of the place, named Eberhard. There he had, either with count Eberhard, or with Noting, bishop of Verona, who was also staying there, long theological conversations, and he maintained that the good and the bad, the elect and the reprobate, were equally and from all time predestinated by the divine omnipotence and omniscience to their present and future fate. The bishop of Verona, shocked at this opinion, whether because it was new to him, or because it had long been repugnant to him, denounced it to Raban, now become archbishop of Mayence, and prevailed upon him to combat it. Raban, already prepossessed against Gottschalk, wrote to count Eberhard, informing him that he harboured a heretic in his house. Gottschalk, accused, departed immediately, in order to defend himself. We find him at Mayence, in 848, addressing to Raban a justification of his conduct. But it was condemned by the council which assembled the same year at Mayence; and, by order of the council, Raban wrote to Hincmar:

"Know, your Dilection, that a certain wandering monk, named Gottschalk, who affirms that he was ordained priest in your diocese, is come from Italy to Mayence, disseminating new superstitions, and a pernicious opinion concerning the predestination of God, seducing people into error; for he says that there is a predestination of God, as regards the good as well as the wicked, and that, in this world, there are certain men whom the predestination of God forces to pursue the path of death, not being able to correct their error and their sin, as if God in the beginning had created them incorrigible. . . . . Having lately heard this opinion from his own mouth, at a council held at Mayence, and having found him incorrigible, by the consent and order of our very pious king Louis, we have decided, after having condemned him, as well as his pernicious doctrine, to send him to you, in order that you may retain him in your diocese, from whence he irregularly went forth, and that you may not permit him any longer to teach error, and seduce the Christian people. According to report, he has already seduced many persons, and has rendered them less devoted to the work of their salvation; for they say: 'To what purpose shall I labour in the service of God? If I am predestinated to death, I shall never escape from it; and if I am predestinated to life, even though I do wickedly, I shall, no doubt, arrive at eternal rest.' "

Hincmar was at bottom little of a theologian; the spirit of government and practical dexterity predominated in him, and he had not made a very attentive study of the fathers. When the letter of Raban reached him, he judged of Gottschalk and his opinions according to the instinct of common sense, rather than according to any profound and extensive acquaintance with theology. He was, moreover, haughty and despotic. Gottschalk agitated the faithful, and resisted his superiors. Hincmar forthwith (in 849) condemned him by a council held at Kiersy-sur-Oise, and, thinking to subdue him by force, ordered him to be publicly scourged, and summoned to retract his opinions and to cast his writings into the fire. But the arrogance of despotism can never force the obstinacy of conscience. Gottschalk resisted all, and was shut up in the prison of the monastery of Hautvilliers, where he was treated with extreme severity.

The matter soon became noised about. Hincmar was not well acquainted with the spirit of his contemporary theologians, nor with the power which an argument, drawn from St. Augustin, could exercise over them. Whether from pity for Gottschalk, who had been so barbarously treated, or rather through the prevalence of the theological spirit, a loud clamour was raised against the conduct of the archbishop of Reims. Some very influential men in the Gallo-Frankish church, Prudence, bishop of Troyes, Loup, abbot of Ferrieres, Ratramne, monk of Corbie, and many others, attacked him nearly all at the same time. They did not positively take the part of Gottschalk, but they declared against the treatment which he had suffered, protested against the meaning that was attributed to his words, and maintained the doctrine of predestination, rejecting only so much of it as seemed contrary to divine justice.

Hincmar was not prepared for such a storm. He wrote to Raban, who had drawn it upon him, to persuade him to defend what they had thought and done in common; Raban, intimidated, did not write, and left Hincmar exposed to the danger alone. Seeking upon all sides for champions, the archbishop of Reims addressed himself first of all to a priest of Metz, named Amalaise. who, at his request, wrote a work against Gottschalk, which is now lost. A man of much talent and learning, Scotus Erigena, concerning whom I shall soon speak more in detail, was at that time in great favour at the court of Charles le Chauve. Hincmar persuaded him to write against predestination, and he readily consented; but Erigena was a philosopher and a free thinker; he made the fact of human liberty much greater than any other had represented it, mingled in his defence a number of opinions repugnant to the theological world, and compromised Hincmar instead of serving him. The explosion was far more violent against him than it had been against the archbishop of Reims; controversial writings became multiplied; triumphant theologians discovered a thousand heresies in the work of Scotus Erigena. The church of Lyons, in particular, under its archbishop Remi, took a very active part in this war. An ill-suppressed struggle had always existed between the south and north of Gaul. The south of Gaul had preserved more considerable remains of Roman civilization; the character of the north was much more German. The archbishop of Lyons was the most important prelate of southern Gaul, as the archbishop of Reims was the most important of northern Gaul. The rivalry of sees became coupled with the opposition of doctrines. Compromised by his writers, Hincmar, in order to defend himself, had recourse to the arms of authority. A council, held at Kiersy, in 853, laid down, in four articles, the opinions which it pronounced orthodox upon this matter, and Gottschalk found himself condemned thereby for the second time. But the archbishop of Lyons was also able to invoke councils and to cause articles to be written; and he summoned one at Valence, in 855, and the articles of Kiersy were condemned by it in their turn. Hincmar again invoked the aid of learning and argument; but this time he determined to entrust the task to no one, and he himself, in 857 and 859, wrote two works upon predestination, of which one is lost; the other, which remains to us, is addressed to Charles le Chauve, and is divided into forty-four chapters, including six chapters of epilogue. The whole course of the controversy is herein reproduced, with a great display of theological erudition; but, in reality, the theological spirit is wanting; there is more of good sense exhibited in the general ideas than of subtlety in the argumentation; and, as theologians, properly so called, the adversaries of Hincmar had the advantage over him.

His works failed, therefore, in putting a stop to the quarrel; and the matter ended by its being carried to Rome, like all other great questions of the time. It is difficult to affirm that Nicholas the First took any positive part, or that he declared either one or other of the opinions to have been the doctrine of the church. Nevertheless, we see plainly that he inclined to the ideas of Gottschalk, and to the canons of the councils of Valence, confirmed, in 859, by the council of Langres. His correspondence and his conduct in this matter are unfavourable to Hincmar.

The dispute was thus prolonged, becoming, however, cooler, until the death of Gottschalk, which happened suddenly on the 30th of October, 868 or 869. A little while before, when they saw him very ill, the monks of Hautvilliers, where he was in prison, consulted Hincmar as to what they were to do in his case: the inflexible bishop replied that it was absolutely necessary that he should retract his opinions, and that otherwise they must refuse him confession and the sacrament. Not less inflexible than his persecutor, Gottschalk again refused to retract, and died beneath the severities which he was suffering. Hincmar survived him only three years. He died, in his turn, on the 21st of December, 882, driven from his episcopal city by an incursion of the Normans, and still engaged in writing, at Epernay, where he had taken refuge.

It is time for me to pause; one remark will conclude my account of this great controversy. You may see three elements appearing in it; the three spirits, so to speak, of which the coexistence and the struggle for a long while constituted the intellectual history of modern Europe: 1. the logical spirit which predominated among theologians by profession, engaged exclusively in arguing, in deducing consequences from principles, which were never called into question; 2. the political spirit, peculiar, in general, to the heads of the church, who were, above all, charged with the duties of government, and were much more engaged with the practical than the logical point of view, with business than discussion; 3. finally, the philosophical spirit, existing in certain free-thinkers, who yet endeavoured to regard things in themselves, and to seek for truth, independently both of practical aim and predetermined principle. The theological spirit, the political spirit, and the philosophical spirit, were all openly at work in this affair; Hincmar represented the politicians, Gottschalk the theologians, Scotus Erigena the philosophers. The last I have scarcely more than named to you; I shall treat of him at full in my next lecture.

TWENTY-NINTH LECTURE.

Object of the lecture—Of the philosophical spirit in the 9th century—Scotus or Erigena—His country—Date of his birth—Tradition respecting his travels in Greece—He settles in France, at the court of Charles le Chauve — Of the School of the Palace under Charles — Ancient philosophy studied there—Encouragement of Scotus Erigena—His learning—Relations of Christianity with the Neoplatonism of Alexandria—Their struggle—Attempt at amalgamation—History and pretended works of Dionysius the Areopagite—Fundamental differences of the two doctrines: 1, in the point of departure and the method; 2, in the bases of the questions — These differences occur between Scotus Erigena and the Christian theologians of the 9th century—Examination of his works: 1, De Prædestinatione; 2, De Divisione Naturæ—His celebrity and his death—Recapitulation.

I REMINDED you, in the last lecture, of the two fundamental elements to which we may ascribe the intellectual development of modern Europe: Christianity, on the one part, and ancient literature on the other; Christian theology and pagan philosophy, religious polemics and classical learning; already, at the end of the eighth century, at the moment of the intellectual revival of Frankish Gaul, under Charlemagne, we have recognised the presence of these two elements in Alcuin, whom we considered as the most faithful image of the state of the mind at this epoch. In proportion as this influence developed itself, they became distinct and separate: about the middle of the ninth century, two men appeared to us as the representatives, one of the theological, the other of the philosophical element. I named to you Hincmar and John Erigena; I led you to a consideration, in the history of Hincmar, of the theological life of his time: let us now try to ascertain if any philosophical life corresponded to it; it is from the history of John Erigena that we shall learn it.

There exists amongst scholars much uncertainty respecting the date of his birth and his country. The uncertainty respecting his country appears to me not well founded: his double name indicates it clearly. John Erigena, or John Scotus, means John of Ireland. Ireland was anciently called *Erin*, and its people were of the same race as the population of the highlands of Scotland, the Scots. The name Erigena points out therefore his country, that of Scotus his race and nation. All the little difficulties, all the elaborate conjectures of the learned, fall to the ground before this simple fact.

With respect to the date of the birth of John, it is more difficult to determine anything, and I will not enter upon a minute and purposeless discussion of this subject. All that can be affirmed, is that he was born in the early part of the ninth century, from the year 800 to 815. We do not know where he passed his childhood, or where he followed his first studies. The peculiarities of his knowledge, however, agreeing with natural probabilities, give rise to the belief that it was in Ireland. Of all the western countries, Ireland was, as you know, that wherein letters maintained themselves and prospered, amidst the general confusion of Europe.

A tradition which we find prevailing at an early period, attributes to John Scotus travels in the east, in Greece particularly; we read, in a manuscript deposited in the library of Oxford, a passage of his which seems to point at them:

"I quitted," said he, "no place or temple where the philosophers were accustomed to compose or deposit their secret works, without inspecting it; and there was not one amongst such scholars, as might be supposed to possess any knowledge of philosophical writings, whom I did not question."[1]

He does not indicate, you see, any place or period; yet his words seem to relate to a country where the ancient philosophers lived and laboured. No other document sheds further light upon these travels; and the knowledge possessed by John Erigena of Greek literature does not appear to me a conclusive proof. However the case may have been, about

[1] Wood's *Hist.* and *Antiquit. Univers. Oxon.*, in fol. 1674, vol. i. p '15.

the middle of the ninth century, we find him settled for life at the court of Charles le Chauve. There has also been much dispute about the date of his arrival; it has been placed as far forward as the year 870; but the error of this appears evident to me. Many documents indicate that John was connected with Saint Prudence before the latter became bishop of Troyes in 847. It was probably, therefore, between the years 840 and 847 that John Erigena went into France, perhaps attracted thither by a formal invitation from Charles le Chauve.

History gives a very false idea of this prince and his court—not certainly under the political point of view; all that it says of the weakness of the government and the falling condition of France is well founded; but under the intellectual point of view there was much more activity and liberty of spirit, much more taste for letters than is commonly supposed. The School of the Palace, so flourishing under Charlemagne, and under the teaching of Alcuin, had greatly fallen away under Louis le Debonnaire. Louis had been engaged much more with the church than with science, and much more with the religious reform of the monasteries than with the progress of study. The School of the Palace was thus a subject little considered, a sure proof of its decay; for the social state was not then such that it could subsist by itself, and without powerful protection. Charles le Chauve revived it; he summoned thither foreign scholars, especially Irish and Anglo-Saxons; he treated them with marked favour; he appreciated their works and their conversation, and lived on familiar terms with them. The School of the Palace resumed such a splendour that contemporaries were struck with it as with a novelty. To judge by the words of Herric, a monk of Saint Germain l'Auxerrois, and of Wandalbert, a monk of Prum, in the diocese of Trèves, the prosperity of the studies at those places became such that Greece might have envied the fortune of France, and that France had nothing for which to envy antiquity. There is, no doubt, great monastic emphasis in the phrase; but, at all events, the public at the time were so struck with the revival of letters in the court of Charles le Chauve, that instead of saying *the School of the Palace* (*Schola Palatii*) they said, *the Palace of the School* (*Palatium Scholæ*). What, then, was the direction of mind in this flourishing school? what studies were preferred? We may, I think, affirm, that ancient philosophy and literature held a high place there. Of this we have abundant and apparently undeniable proofs.

The first are deducible from the works of John Erigena himself, chief of the School of the Palace, and teacher there. Of these works, ancient philosophy, as you will presently see, is generally the object. Not only did the original works which he has left emanate from this source; not only did he translate many treatises of the Neoplatonic school of Alexandria; but it appears certain that there exist in manuscript in many libraries, especially in that of Oxford, commentaries by him on several works of Aristotle; and in the twelfth century, at the very moment when the peripatetic philosophy resumed in the west a despotic empire, Roger Bacon lauded Scotus Erigena as a very faithful and clear-sighted interpreter of Aristotle, and awarded him the merit of having preserved, pure and authentical, certain of his writings.

It is said, also, that Scotus Erigena applied himself to the study of the works of Plato; and in some sentences of his on these two masters of antiquity, he has passed so strong and precise a judgment upon them, as to negative the supposition that he knew them merely from the writings of certain of their disciples, or from vague traditions. He calls Plato "the greatest philosopher in the world," and Aristotle "the most subtle investigator, among the Greeks, of the differences of natural things."[1]

It is not to be doubted that he understood Greek well, since he translated the treatises attributed to Dionysius the Areopagite, and gave a Greek title to his principal work. There is also reason to think that he understood Hebrew, by far the most unusual accomplishment of his time; for, in citing a verse of Genesis, he corrects the Vulgate; and instead of saying, as St. Jerome, "*Terra autem erat invisibilis et incomposita,*" he says, "*Terra erat inanis et vacua;*" a translation far more exact, and nearer the original.[2]

Lastly, a celebrated scholar of his time, named Mannon,

[1] Scot. Erig., *De Divisione Naturæ*, vol. i. c. 33, c. 16.
[2] Ibid., vol. ii., chap. 20.

succeeded Scotus Erigena as director of the School of the Palace, and held that office, until the death of Louis le Begue; and Mannon, like Erigena, made ancient philosophy his principal study. Many contemporaries praised the learned lectures which he gave on this subject; there exists, we are assured, in some libraries of Holland, commentaries by him on Plato's discourses on *Laws*, and on *the Republic*, and also on Aristotle's *Ethics.*

Were all these indications wanting, or were they to prove unworthy of credit—were we to possess no direct and positive assertion concerning the study which Scotus Erigena made of the Greek philosophers, the language of his contemporaries would reveal clearly the tendency and character of his works. I have told you what an uproar was created amongst theologians by his treatise on predestination, written at the request of Hincmar, against Gottschalk. The following are the terms in which Florus, a priest of the church of Lyons, immediately attacked him:

" In the name of our Lord Jesus Christ," commences the book of Florus, " against the follies and errors of a certain presumptuous man named John, on predestination and divine prescience, and the true liberty of human thought.

" There have reached us, that is, the church of Lyons, the writings of a certain vain and ostentatious man, who, disputing upon divine prescience and predestination by means of arguments of a purely human, and, as he himself boasts, philosophical kind, has dared, without assigning any reason, and without alleging any authority from the scriptures and holy fathers, to affirm certain things, as though they ought to be received and adopted on his sole and presumptuous assertion. By the assistance of God, readers, who are faithful and well exercised in the sacred doctrine, easily judge and reject these writings, which are so full of vanity, falsehood, and error, and which offend the faith and divine truth, and are to them an object of contempt and derision. Nevertheless, from what we have heard say, this same man is much admired by many persons, for being learned and versed in the knowledge of the schools: whether by speaking or writing, he casts some in doubt, and others he draws away with him in his error, as though he uttered something remarkable; and, by the vain and pernicious flow of his words, he so takes possession of his hearers and admirers, that they no longer yield themselves to the divine scriptures, nor the authority of the fathers, but prefer following his fantastic reveries. We have, therefore, judged it necessary, through charitable zeal, and for the sake of our city and our order, to reply to his insolence," &c.[1]

You observe that the character of the writings and ideas of Scotus Erigena is clearly portrayed in the accusation here put forth against him; he is denounced for *purely human*, and, according to his own words, *philosophical arguments*, and as being *learned and versed in the knowledge of the schools.* It was, in short, as a philosopher that he was condemned. In 855, the council of Valence decreed as follows:

"We banish absolutely from the pious ears of the faithful, as useless, nay, even as hurtful and contrary to the truth, the four articles (*capitula*) adopted with so little foresight by the council of our brethren,[2] and the nineteen other *capitula*[3] very foolishly set down in syllogisms, wherein no ability, though they are lauded in this respect, shines in the secular point of view, and wherein we find an invention of the devil, rather than any argument for the faith. By the authority of the Holy Spirit, we interdict them everywhere, and we think that those who introduce novelties ought to be punished, in order to prevent the necessity of having afterwards to strike harder." [4]

Some years after, in 859, the council of Langres renewed the same sentence of condemnation against Scotus Erigena. Both accusers and judges, the simple clergy and the assemblies of the church, were then unanimous in their judgment of Scotus Erigena, and the character of his works. Let us see what he says himself; he describes and paints himself as his enemies have painted him.

His treatise on predestination begins thus:—

"Since, in earnestly investigating and attempting to discover surely the reasons of all things, every means of attaining to a pious and perfect doctrine, lies in that science

[1] *Veterum Auctorum qui* ix. *sæculo de Prædestinatione et Gratiâ scripserunt Opera et Fragmenta*, published by the president Mauguin; 2 vol. in 4to, v. i., p. 585. Paris, 1650.

[2] The council of Kiersy.

[3] The nineteen chapters of Scotus Erigena's treatise on *Predestination.*

[4] Council of Valence in 855, can. 4.

and discipline which the Greeks call *philosophy*, we think it necessary to speak in a few words of its divisions and classifications. 'It is believed and taught,' says St. Augustin, 'that philosophy, that is, the love of wisdom, is no other than religion; and what proves it is, that we do not receive the sacraments in common with those whereof we do not approve the doctrine.' What, then, is the object of philosophy but to set forth the rules of true religion, whereby we rationally seek and humbly adore God, the first cause and sovereign of all things? From thence it follows that true philosophy is true religion, and conversely, that true religion is true philosophy."[1]

Is not this evidently the language of a man who is much more a philosopher than a theologian, and who takes his point of departure in philosophy, attempting to mix, or at least to reconcile it with religion, either because he considers them as one and the same science, or because he has need of the shield of religion to protect himself against the attacks of which he is the object?

Again, in his work *On the Division of Nature*:—

"We must follow in all things the authority of the holy scriptures, for the truth is there enclosed as in a secret sanctuary; but we must not think that, in order to endow us with the divine nature, the holy scripture always employs precise and literal words and signs; it makes use of similitudes, strained and figurative expressions, adapts itself to our weakness, and raises, by a simple mode of teaching, our dull and immature spirits."[2]

Who does not recognise here an effort, very often made, to avoid the strict interpretation of texts or dogmas, and to introduce into the study of religion some liberty of thought, under the veil of explanation and allegory?

We cannot doubt it: even before examining deeply into the ideas of Scotus Erigena, and judging only by the traditions which remain to us respecting his works, by the language of the church and of his enemies, and by his own, the philosophical character appears vividly in the life and spirit of this man; he differs from theologians essentially; it is to

[1] *Divina. Prædest.* c. i., col. of Maug., v. i. p. 221.

[2] *De Nat. Divis.*, v. i., c. 66.

antiquity that he belongs, it is of ancient knowledge that he discourses to his contemporaries.

His character was by no means a cause of disfavour with Charles le Chauve. It is well attested, on the contrary, that Charles often attended his lectures, took a lively interest in them, and consulted him upon all the affairs, upon all the intellectual difficulties, so to speak, which arose in his kingdom. An anecdote in a manuscript of William of Malmesbury, a chronicler of the thirteenth century, will show you to what an extent the familiarity of the king with the philosopher was carried:

"John," says he, "was seated at table in front of the king, who sat at the other side of the table; when the viands had disappeared, and jokes began to circulate, in a light humour and after some other pleasantries, seeing John do something which shocked the Gallic politeness, the king rebuked him mildly, saying, '*Quid distat inter sottum et Scotum?*' (what separates a sot from a Scot?) 'Nothing but the table,' replied John, returning the quip to its author."[1]

Are not these the liberties of a licensed *bel-esprit*, who believes all things are permitted to him because he amuses and pleases.

It was, I am much disposed to think, this encouragement of Scotus Erigena by Charles le Chauve, that suggested to Hincmar the idea of gaining his interference in his quarrel with Gottschalk, by engaging him to write on his behalf. Hincmar (as I have already remarked) was more of a politician than theologian, more filled with the idea of governing than reasoning, and rather aiming at success than truth. He found himself in a difficult position; most of the theologians of Frankish Gaul were rising against him; the celebrated Raban, after having compromised him, refused to support him. He applied to Scotus Erigena, wishing, doubtless, to profit at once by his interest and by his knowledge, and hoping to find in him an able and influential defender.

But Hincmar knew not what an ally he was calling to his assistance, and in what a strife he was again about to engage. In order to make clearly understood the turn which the question then took, and the part which Scotus Erigena played in it, I am obliged to ascend a step higher.

[1] *William of Malmesbury*, in his unpublished work, *De Pontificibus.*

Christianity, in order to establish itself, had had to vanquish all sorts of enemies, governments, nations, priests, and pagans, civil, as well as religious power, and laws as well as customs. But in the intellectual order, the Alexandrine neoplatonism had been its sole adversary.

Properly speaking, it was between the Neoplatonists of Alexandria, and the Christians, that the question lay. From the second century, some attempts had been made by the rival schools at conciliating, or rather at amalgamating the two doctrines. St. Clement of Alexandria, who died in 220, and Origen, from 185 to 254, were disciples of the Alexandrine philosophy, Neoplatonists become Christians, and who endeavoured to accommodate their philosophical doctrines to the Christian creeds which were developing themselves and taking the form of a system. In the course of the third or fourth centuries, these attempts were once more renewed: but it was in the middle of the sixth, that they became most vigorous. The victory was then completely on the side of Christianity; the Alexandrian Neoplatonism, abandoned by princes, and decried, and persecuted, had no alternative but to lose itself in the bosom of its enemy, preserving of itself only so much as Christianity would consent to receive. We see, indeed, at that time most of the philosophers of this school, become or near becoming Christians, blending their old opinions with their new faith, by endeavouring to make them agree. To this epoch belongs, for example, the dialogue of Æneas of Gaza, a disciple of Hierocles, entitled, "*Theophrastus; or on the immortality of the soul and the resurrection of the body,*" and that of Zacharius the Scholastic, entitled, '*Ammonius; or on the construction of the world, against the philosophers;*" writings, the design of which was evidently to introduce into the theology of St. Athanasius, St. Jerome, and St. Augustin, such ideas and forms of the expiring philosophy, as would accommodate themselves with it. There were then, assuredly, many more works of this kind than are now remaining to us; the proof of which is, that they were composed with a view to being ascribed to the ancient philosophers, in the hope of thereby enforcing upon them more authority. In the middle of this fifth century, there appeared, under the name of Dionysius the Areopagite, several treatises bearing the character which I have just described. Dionysius the Areopagite, was one of the most illustrious names in Christian traditions, one of the most glorious conquests of nascent Christianity. He is mentioned for the first time in the 17th chapter of the *Acts of the Apostles*. This chapter is so remarkable, and carries in itself, independently of all external evidence, such indications of authenticity, that I beg your permission to read the text of the principal passages. Nowhere is the preaching of Christianity in the midst of ancient society painted with so much truth and clearness : the sacred chronicler relates the sojourn of St. Paul at Athens:

"Now while Paul waited for them at Athens, his spirit was stirred in him, when he saw the city wholly given to idolatry. Therefore disputed he in the synagogue with the Jews, and with the devout persons, and in the market daily with them that met with him. Then certain philosophers of the epicureans and of the stoics, encountered him. And some said, 'What will this babbler say?' other some, 'He seemeth to be a setter forth of strange gods:' because he preached unto them Jesus, and the resurrection.

"And they took him, and brought him unto Areopagus, saying, 'May we know what this new doctrine whereof thou speakest is? For thou bringest certain strange things to our ears: we would know, therefore, what these things mean.'" (For all the Athenians and strangers which were there, spent their time in nothing else, but either to tell or hear some new thing.)

"Then Paul stood in the midst of Mars' Hill, and said,—'Ye men of Athens, I perceive that in all things ye are too superstitious. For as I passed by and beheld your devotions, I found an altar with this inscription—*To the unknown God.* Whom, therefore, ye ignorantly worship, him declare I unto you. God that made the world and all things therein, seeing that he is Lord of heaven and earth, dwelleth not in temples made with hands; neither is worshipped with men's hands, as though he needed anything, seeing he giveth to all life, and breath, and all things. That they should seek the Lord, if haply they might feel after him, and find him, though he be not far from every one of us: for in him we live, and move, and have our being; as certain also of your own poets have said, For we are also his offspring. Forasmuch, then, as we are the offspring of God, we ought not to think that the godhead is like unto gold, or silver, or stone, graven by art and man's device. And the times of this ignorance God winked at; but now commandeth all men everywhere to repent: because he hath appointed a day, in the which he will judge the world in righteousness, by that man whom he hath ordained; whereof he hath given assurance unto all men, in that he hath raised him from the dead.

"And when they heard of the resurrection of the dead, some mocked: and others said—'We will hear thee again of this matter.' So Paul departed from among them.

"Howbeit, certain men clave unto him, and believed: among the which was Dionysius the Areopagite."[1]

Such a convert would naturally have been cherished by the new society: accordingly, since that epoch, the name of Dionysius the Areopagite frequently occurs in Christian narrations. In the second century, particularly, Saint Justin, one of the earliest and most able defenders of Christianity, mentions him on several occasions with honour. Tradition relates that, towards the end of the first century, in 95, Dionysius being burnt alive at Athens, obtained the honours of martyrdom. The fact is possible, but does not rest on any sure proofs.

Whatever may have been the truth of the case, towards the end of the fifth century, there appeared under the name of Dionysius the Areopagite, several works designed to effect the amalgamation of the Alexandrian Neoplatonism with Christian theology; they are entitled: 1. *On the Celestial Hierarchy*; 2. *On the Ecclesiastical Hierarchy*; 3. *On Divine Names*; 4. *Mystical Theology*; lastly, to the dogmatic writings are subjoined ten letters. The forgery is evident: the books and letters could not have been written before the middle of the fifth century: facts and customs which did not belong to the Christian church before that epoch, are therein mentioned; and at every step we meet with ideas and forms of style, of which Dionysius the Areopagite could not have had the least notion. Accordingly, in the first half of the sixth century, about the year 532, at Constantinople itself, Hypatius, a rhetorician, attacked the authenticity of these pretended works of the Athenian senator. But they agreed very well

[1] Acts of the Apostles, chap. 17, ver. 16—34.

with the nature of an attempt, at that time very actively prosecuted, and very important in the then state of society; their object was to effect that reconciliation, that amalgamation of Christian dogmas with Neoplatonic ideas which formed the intellectual problem of the age. Public credulity was great, true criticism almost dormant; the writings of which I speak, easily passed into circulation. Several scholars, amongst others Maximus the Confessor, (in 622,) added commentaries to them; and they continued to bear the name of the illustrious Christian to whom they had been attributed.

At the commencement of the ninth century, a particular circumstance gave them immense popularity in the west, and especially in Frankish Gaul. A Saint Denis passed for having been, about the middle of the third century, the apostle of the Gauls and the first bishop of Paris. It entered the heads of some monks to maintain that this Denis and Dionysius the Areopagite, were one and the same man. The Christianity of the Gauls was thus referred to an antiquity far more remote, and might thus boast of a far more illustrious founder. In 814, Hilduinus, abbot of Saint Denis, the same by whom Hincmar was educated, wrote a book, entitled *Areopagetica*, to uphold the opinion in point. It rapidly gained credit, and became in Gaul a sort of national creed. The works of Dionysius the Areopagite were from that time forward the object of eager curiosity, and in 824, Michael the Stammerer sent a copy of one of them to Louis le Debonnaire. The precious MS. was deposited and preserved in the abbey of Saint Denis; but it was in Greek, and few persons could understand it. Charles le Chauve engaged Scotus Erigena to translate it. He undertook this translation, which was probably the work that, of all others, most extended the fame of his learning in Gaul.

Historically, then, the character of the works of Scotus Erigena is incontestable. He was in the ninth century the representative and interpreter of that attempt, commenced in the second century, and so active in the fifth, at an amalgamation of the Alexandrine Neoplatonism and Christian theology. It is under this aspect that he presents himself in the succession of facts and proper names. He was the last link of that chain whose first link, a pious delusion had attempted to trace to Athens herself, to the bosom of the schools of ancient philosophy.

Let us now quit history, and let us penetrate into the ideas themselves: let us judge from the works of Scotus Erigena, by comparing them, on the one hand, with those of the Neoplatonists of Alexandria—on the other, with those of the Christian theologians of his time, whether they indeed connect themselves with Neoplatonian doctrines, and vainly attempt to reproduce them and infuse them into Christianity.

I cannot, as you may easily understand, think of here offering any very extensive or strict comparison between Alexandrine Neoplatonism and Christianity. I am forced to limit myself to a few broad features, to the most general characteristics of the two doctrines; they will suffice, I hope, to distinguish them, and to show clearly to which Scotus Erigena properly belonged.

At first sight, and neglecting minor questions, two essential differences are remarkable between the Alexandrine Neoplatonism and Christianity. 1st. Neoplatonism is a philosophy, Christianity a religion. The first has human reason for its point of departure; it is to her that it addresses itself, her that it interrogates, in her that it confides. The point of departure of the second is, on the contrary, a fact exterior to human reason; it dictates to, instead of interrogating her. From thence it follows, that free inquiry predominates in Neoplatonism; it is its fundamental method and habitual practice; whereas Christianity proclaims authority for its principle, and proceeds by means of authority. From thence it again follows that, although the Alexandrine Neoplatonism, to judge of it by the language and character of its writings, presents itself under a profoundly mystical aspect; its principle at the bottom is rational; whilst primitive Christianity, the character of which is in no degree mystical, which is, on the contrary, very positive and simple, has, nevertheless, a supernatural principle. There is, then, in the starting points of these two doctrines, a radical difference.

2nd. If we pass over this question of the point of departure, and of the preliminary method of every philosophy, and examine ideas to the very bottom, a second essential difference will strike us. The main doctrine of Alexandrine Neoplatonism is pantheism, the identity of substance and being, individuality reduced to the condition of a simple phenomenon, of a transitory fact. Individuality, on the contrary, is the fundamental belief of Christian theology. The God of the Christians is a distinct being, who communicates and treats with other beings, to whom the latter address themselves, who replies to them, whose existence is sovereign, but not sole. Among many other indications, the diversity of the two doctrines reveals itself clearly in the idea which they respectively involve concerning man's future state beyond his present one of actual existence. How does Neoplatonism view the condition of human beings at the moment of their death? As being absorbed in the bosom of the great all; all individuality having been abolished. How, on the other hand, does Christianity view them? It regards individuality as perpetuated even to infinity; and an eternity of punishments and rewards is substituted for the absorption of individual beings; so that, casting but a rapid glance at the two doctrines, we notice a radical difference both in the foundation and in the point of departure of the ideas—a difference which especially appears in the two essential features to which I have now drawn your attention.

Is it not true, then, that if we find these very same differences between the philosophy of John Scotus Erigena, and the Christian theology of his time; the filiation of his ideas and their affinity with Alexandrine Neoplatonism will be as certain by the very essence of the ideas, as it has appeared to us by historical traditions?

Independently of his translation of the pretended works of Dionysius the Areopagite, and of some treatises now lost, or still in manuscript,[1] there remains to us two great works of Scotus Erigena: 1st, his treatise, *De Prædestinatione*, of which I have already spoken to you; 2nd, a treatise entitled, Περὶ Φύσεως Μερισμοῦ, *Concerning the Division of Nature*, which contains the systematic exposition of his ideas on man and the universe.

From these two works alone I shall select the quotations to be presently offered to your view. The first is found in the collection of writings relative to the quarrel between Hincmar and Gottschalk, published by the president Mau-

[1] Among others, a treatise on the *Vision of God*, of which Mabillon had seen the MS. in the library of Clairmarest, near St. Omer, and which commenced with these words: *Omnes sensus corporei nascuntur ex conjunctione animæ et corporis.*

guin. But, by an ill fortune, which I have attempted in vain to remedy, I shall be unable to present you with an analysis, whose accuracy I could guarantee, of the second, which is of most importance, for I could discover it in none of the libraries of Paris. It was published in Oxford in 1681, by Thomas Gale, in one volume, folio. Great kindness has been shown towards me, at the different public libraries, in the efforts that have been made to find it; but, unfortunately, none of them contain it. I have also made inquiries for it in England, but have not yet obtained it. I have therefore been obliged to content myself with the extracts and numerous quotations which I have found in several histories of philosophy, and particularly in two German dissertations, whereof Scotus Erigena is the special object.[1] I should say also, by the way, that it has been demonstrated to me, by the attentive examination which I have made of them, that many foreign writers who have spoken of this work have not had it before them, any more than myself, in its entire state. Of this they ought to have made their readers aware.

I begin with the first question, the preliminary question of every doctrine, that of the point of departure and the method. I have just shown you what, with respect to this, was the radical difference between Alexandrine Neoplatonism and Christian theology, and how one had reason for its principle, —the other, authority. The following are some of the passages wherein Scotus Erigena expresses his thoughts on this subject:

I.

"Nature" (by nature he means the universe, all created things,) "and time were created together, but authority does not date from the origin of time and nature. Reason is born at the commencement of things, with time and nature. Reason itself demonstrates it. Authority is derived from reason, and not reason from authority. An authority which is not acknowledged by reason seems valueless. Reason, on the contrary, invincibly resting on its own strength, has no need of the confirmation of any authority. Legitimate

[1] One is entitled, *John Scotus Erigena; or, On the Origin of a Christian Philosophy and its Holy Mission*, by P. Hiort, Copenhagen, 1823; the other, *The Mysticism of the Middle Ages in their Infancy*, by H. Schmid, Jena, 1824.

authority appears to me to be but truth unfolded by the force of reason, and transmitted by the holy fathers, for the use of future generations."[1]

II.

"We should not allege the opinions of the holy fathers, especially if they are known to most people, unless it be necessary thereby to strengthen arguments in the eyes of men, who, unskilful in reasoning, yield rather to authority than to reason."[2]

III.

"The salvation of faithful souls consists in believing what we have reason to affirm concerning the sole principle of all things, and in comprehending what we have reason to believe."[3]

IV.

"Faith is nothing more, in my opinion, than a certain principle from which the knowledge of the Creator takes its derivation in a reasonable nature."[4]

V.

"The soul in itself is unknown; but it begins to manifest itself to itself and to others in its form, which is reason."[5]

VI.

"I am not so fearful of authority, and I do not so dread the rage of minds of small intelligence, as to hesitate to proclaim aloud the things which reason clearly unfolds and with certainty demonstrates; there are, moreover, subjects of which we need only discourse with the learned, for whom nothing is more sweet to hear than the truth, and nothing more delightful to investigate, or more beautiful to contemplate, when found."[6]

Assuredly, no philosopher has ever more clearly expressed the rational character of his point of departure, which is that of all philosophy. The last passage also clearly indicates that the contest was then being waged between this principle and that of authority, and that Scotus Erigena hesitated not to engage in it. Devotion to truth and liberty is thus in a few words indicated with striking power:—

[1] *De Divisione Naturæ*, v. i. p. 39.
[2] Ibid. v. iv p. 81.
[3] *De Divisione Naturæ*, v. ii. p. 81.
[4] Ibid. v. i. p. 41.
[5] *De Divisione Naturæ*, v. ii. p. 74.
[6] Ibid. v. i. p. 39.

He goes further, and points out here and there in the course of his work some of the principles of philosophical method, with a precision so much the more remarkable that he often violates it himself, and like the rest of the Neoplatonic school, does often the very reverse of proceeding from the known to the unknown, and by the path of observation. The following are a few of these passages:—

VII.

"The true course of reasoning may be from the natural study of things sensible, to the pure contemplation of things spiritual." [1]

VIII.

"If we do not desire to study and to know ourselves, it is because we do not desire to raise ourselves up to what is above us, that is to our cause; for there is no other way of attaining to the most pure contemplation of the sovereign model than to well regard his image, which is nigh unto us."[2]

IX.

"Far from being of little importance, the knowledge of things sensible is greatly useful to the understanding of things intellectual. For, in the same manner as, by the senses, we arrive at intelligence, so, by the creature, we return to God." [3]

Are not the scientific spirit, and the method of observation and induction, clearly opposed, in these places, to the theological spirit, to the method of authority and deduction?

Let us pass the vestibule of the philosophy: let us go into the interior of the temple. There, the affinity of Scotus Erigena with the Alexandrine Neoplatonism will not be less apparent. He is likewise essentially a pantheist, and he hesitates not to say so, with all that confusion, it is true, which is inherent in this doctrine, and dooms it to incoherency and absurdity in the very terms by which it attempts to declare itself, yet he does so as openly and as consequently (if the word *consequence* may be here used) as his more illustrious predecessors.

X.

"The cause of all things, which is God, is at the same

[1] *De Divisione Naturæ*, v. v. p. 227. [2] Ibid. p. 268.
[3] *De Divisione Naturæ*, v. iii. p. 149.

time simple and multiple. The divine goodness (essence) spreads itself, that is, multiplies itself in all things which exist.... and lastly, by the same paths, disengaging itself from the infinite variety of things which exist, again returns and concentrates itself in the simple unity which comprehends all things, which is in God and is God. Thus, all is God and God is all.[1]

XI.

"In the same manner that, originally, the river flows entire from its source; and as the water which first gushes out from the spring, spreads itself constantly and without ceasing in the bed of the river, whatever be the length of its course, in the same manner the goodness, essence, wisdom, divine life, and all which is in the source of all things, spreads itself first in the first causes, and makes them to subsist; then passes from the first causes into their effects, according to an ineffable mode, and thus circulates by uninterrupted degrees from things superior to things inferior, and finally returns to its source by the most subtle and secret ways of nature."[2]

XII.

"God, who alone truly exists, is the essence of all things, as Dionysius the Areopagite says: 'The existence of all things is what remains in them of divinity.'"[3]

XIII.

"God is the beginning, the middle, and the end: the beginning, because all things come from him and participate in his essence; the middle, because all things subsist in him and by him; the end, because all things move towards him in order to attain repose, the limit of their motion, and the stability of his perfection."[4]

XIV.

"All things which are said to be, are images of God (*Theophaniæ*).... all that we perceive and comprehend is but an apparition of what we see not, a manifestation of what is hidden.... opened a way towards the apprehension of that which we have no comprehension of, a name of that which is

[1] *De Divis. Nat.*, v. iii. c. 4.
[2] Ibid. v. i. c. 3.
[3] Ibid. c. 12.
[4] Ibid. v. iii. c. 4.

ineffable, a step towards that which we cannot attain .... a form of that which does not possess form, &c."[1]

XV.

"We can conceive nothing in the creature which is not the Creator, who alone truly *is*. Nothing out of himself can be called really essential; for all things, coming from him, are nothing more, inasmuch as they exist, than a certain participation in the existence of him who alone comes from no other and subsists of himself."[2]

XVI.

"We ought not to conceive the Lord and the creature as two beings distinct one from the other, but as one and the same being. For the creature subsists in God, and God, in a marvellous and ineffable manner, creates himself, so to say, in the creature in whom he manifests himself, and thus renders the invisible visible, and the incomprehensible comprehensible."[3]

XVII.

"All that the human soul, by its intelligence and its reason, knows of God and the principles of things, under the form of unity, it perceives under the multiple form, and by the senses, in the effects of causes."[4]

Although I have not the complete work before me, it would be an easy matter for me to continue these quotations; but I have given enough, doubtless, to establish the Pantheism of Scotus Erigena, and to show that he was really, with respect to the ground of his ideas, as also indeed of his method, the representative, in the ninth century, of that Alexandrian philosophy, which was for a long time the intellectual adversary of Christianity, and which from the second century had sought, if not to reconcile itself, at least to amalgamate itself with the nascent theology.

Since the attempt had not succeeded from the second to the fifth century, when Alexandrine Neoplatonism was still popular and powerful, far more reason was there for its failing in the ninth, when it had only for its organ and defender a wandering philosopher, favoured by a king without power. I will not return to what I told you in the last lecture, about the clamour which was raised against Scotus Erigena; it was as general as it was violent, and greatly injured the cause of

[1] *Dedic. ad S. Maximi Schol. in Gregorium Nazianz.*
[2] *De Divis. Nat.*, v. ii. c. 2. [3] Ibid. v. ii. p. 74. Ibid.

Hincmar, who had chosen him for his defender. Scotus Erigena had foreseen this, and was obliged to protect himself by all the precautions in his power. We read at the head of his treatise on predestination, dedicated to Hincmar:—

"Of this opuscule, then, which we have written at your command, and in proof of your orthodox faith, adopt and assign so much to the catholic church as you shall judge true —reject what appears to you false; and, simply human as we are, pardon us for it. As regards what seems doubtful, believe it, until authority teaches you that it must be rejected, or taken for truth, and believed always."[1]

But the precaution was in vain: we cannot deceive or lull to sleep intellectual adversaries. Not only did a crowd of theologians write against the philosopher—not only was he condemned by councils, but the rumours of his opinions soon arrived at Rome, and pope Nicholas I. addressed to Charles le Chauve—probably between 865 and 867—a letter conceived in these terms:

"It has been reported to our apostleship that a certain John, of Scotch origin, has lately translated into Latin the work which the blessed Dionysius wrote in the Greek language, on divine names and celestial orders. This book ought to have been sent us, according to custom, and approved by our judgment; the more so, that this John, though he is cried up as possessed of great knowledge, has not always, it is everywhere said, been sound in his views upon certain subjects. We recommend, therefore, very strongly, that you cause the said John to appear before our apostleship, or at least that you do not permit him any longer to reside at Paris, in the school of which he is stated for a long time to have been the chief, in order that he may no longer mingle his tares with the wheat of the holy word, giving poison to those who seek for bread."[2]

There is much difference of opinion amongst scholars as to the consequences which this formidable attack produced with regard to Scotus Erigena. According to some, Charles le Chauve, after having for a long time supported him, was at last obliged to abandon him; and Erigena fled to England, where

[1] *De Div. Præd. Præf.*, Col. of Maug., v. i. p. 110.

[2] Collection of P. Mauguin, v. i. p. 105; Boulaz., *Univ. Hist.*, Paris, v. i. p. 184.

king Alfred then reigned, who gave him a favourable reception, and placed him at the head of the university ot Oxford. This opinion is founded on a passage of Matthew of Westminster, an English chronicler of the thirteenth century. We there read, under the date 883—

"This year came to England, Master John, of Scottish origin, a man of a very penetrating mind, and of singular elo quence. A long while before, having quitted his native country, he went to Gaul, to the court of Charles le Chauve, and, being received by him with great honour, became his boon companion and bedfellow. . . At the request of this same king, he translated from the Greek into Latin, the Hierarchy of Dionysius, the Areopagite, and gave to the world another book, which he entitled περὶ φύσεως Μεριςμοῦ, that is, *Concerning the Di vision of Nature*,—'very useful,' says he, 'for resolving divers questions scarcely soluble;' we must excuse him on certain occasions, whereupon he has strayed from the path pursued by the Latins, for he had his eyes especially directed towards the Greeks. He has accordingly by some been judged heretical. A certain Florus has written against him: we are ignorant who this man was, who condemned the writings of John by perverting them. There are indeed many things in this book which, if we do not examine them with care, appear contrary to the catholic faith. (He then speaks of the letter of Pope Nicholas I.) . . . In consequence of this reproach, this same John quitted France and came into England, where, some years after, he was stabbed to death by his own pupils with their styles, and died in great agony. For some time he had only a humble grave in the church of St. Laurence: but a ray of celestial light having fallen upon that place, the monks, encouraged by such signs, transported him to the cathedral, and honourably deposited him on the left of the altar."[1]

A mass of objections are raised against this narrative of a chronicler who lived more than three centuries after the occurrence of the facts which he relates. He appears to have confounded Scotus Erigena with another of the same name, whom king Alfred in effect summoned from the continent about the year 884, with the view of entrusting to him the

[1] *Collection* of Mauguin, v. i. p. 106

direction of the university of Oxford. Such is the account of Asser, a biographer contemporary with Alfred, who adds, that in 895, John the Saxon, having become abbot of Ethelingay, was slain by strokes of the style in a commotion of monks, and that, being a very strong man, he defended himself a long while. But, in 895, Scotus Erigena must have been eighty years old; he could not, therefore, have been *very strong*, nor have *defended himself a long while* against his assassins. Thus the details given by his contemporaries are absolutely inapplicable to him, and the whole story of his return to England becomes very doubtful. Most French scholars contend that he remained in France, and even that he died there before Charles le Chauve, that is, before 877; and independently of the circumstances which I have just noticed, their opinion seems confirmed by a letter of Anastasius, librarian of Rome, to king Charles, written about 876, wherein he speaks to him of Scotus Erigena, as of a man deceased. Contemporary testimony has, in my opinion, more authority than that of Matthew of Westminster, and I am disposed to side with this latter opinion.

However that was, the philosophical movement which Erigena had prolonged or re-animated declined with him. His history is nearly the last glimmer which marks the presence and activity of the Alexandrian Neoplatonism in the bosom of Christianity. With him ended all the attempts whether at warfare or at amalgamation between these two great intellectual adversaries. Dating from this epoch, Christian theology became more and more a stranger to ancient philosophy, and the tenth century witnessed the birth of the theology of the middle age, the true ecclesiastical theology, that which was to bring forth the creeds and the Christian church, alone and free in their development.

Scotus Erigena, however, preserved to himself a great reputation, and I meet with a fact, in the thirteenth century, which loudly attests it. It appears that at this epoch, when the great heresy of the Albigenses burst forth, his works, particularly his treatise *De Divisione Naturæ*, and his translation of Dionysius the Areopagite were known and much esteemed in southern France; to such an extent was this the case that Pope Honorius III. ordered that a search should be made for the manuscripts of them in all libraries, and that they should be sent to Rome to be there burnt. No document, no narration attaches this fact to the history of Scotus Erigena himself, and I am not in a condition to follow, from the ninth to the thirteenth century, the traces of his writings and of their influence; but the fact, though isolated, is the no less certain and curious.

I have detained you a long time upon the life and writings of a man much forgotten in the present day. But, in the first place, it was but justice to restore to his proper rank this strong and great intellect, which appeared as a phenomenon in the middle of his age; on the other, I desired to show you that this phenomenon had in it nothing strange, and that, in the case of philosophy as of legislation, ancient society, the Greco-Roman society, had not so completely or so hastily perished as we have been accustomed to think. I will here conclude my description of Frankish Gaul from the eighth to the tenth century; and in our next lecture, which will be the last—I shall endeavour to sum up all the facts which I have placed before your notice, and to trace rapidly that course of French civilization, under the two first races, which we have now been considering.

THIRTIETH LECTURE.

General summary of the course — Extent and variety of subjects — The history of civilization, its price—It is the result of all partial histories—Unity and variety of the existence of a people—Three essential elements in French civilization, Greco-Roman antiquity, Christianity, Germany—1. Of the Roman element, from the 5th to the 10th century—Under a social point of view—Under an intellectual point of view—2. Of the Christian element, from the 5th to the 10th century—Under a social point of view—Under an intellectual point of view—3. Of the Germanic element, from the 5th to the 10th century—Under a social point of view—Under an intellectual point of view—Two principal facts characterize this epoch: 1. The prolongation, more or less apparent, but everywhere real, of Roman society and its influence—2. The disorderly and indeterminate fermentation of the different elements of modern civilization—Conclusion.

We are come to the termination of this course. I would now take a review of the whole, noticing the chief and predominant facts, which appear to me to result from it, and which characterize, during that long period, the history of our civilization.

I gave at the commencement a description of Gaul prior to the German invasion, at the end of the fourth and the beginning of the 5th century, under the Roman administration. We considered its social and intellectual state in civil and in religious society.[1]

After I had thus made you acquainted with Roman-Gaul, I took you across the Rhine. I directed your view towards Germany, prior to the invasion also, and in the infancy of its institutions and manners.[2]

[1] Lect. 2—6. [2] Lect. 7.

The Germans having invaded Gaul, we examined what were the consequences, whether immediate or probable, of this first contact of Roman with barbarous society. I drew your attention to their abrupt and violent collision.[1]

From the sixth century to the middle of the eighth, we followed the progressive amalgamation of the two societies. In the civil order, we saw barbarous laws arise, and the Roman law perpetuated. I laboured to explain the character, generally misunderstood, in my opinion, of these first rudiments of modern legislation.[2] We passed from thence to religious society; and considering it in its double element, priests and monks, the secular and regular clergy, we gave an account both of its relations with civil society, and of its own internal organization.[3]

Such has been our progress, from the sixth to the eighth century, in the history of the social state; but we had also to consider the intellectual state of Frankish-Gaul at the same period; we searched both in sacred and profane literature, and we endeavoured to ascertain their distinctive character and reciprocal influence.[4]

We thus arrived at the great crisis which signalized the middle of the eighth century, the fall of the Merovingian kings and the accession of the Carlovingians; I attempted to characterise this revolution, and to assign its real causes.[5]

The Carlovingian revolution being comprehended, the reign of Charlemagne specially occupied us; I considered it in its events, properly so called, in its laws, in its action on mind. I desired particularly to distinguish that which he attempted, and that which he effectually accomplished, that which perished with him, and that which survived him.[6]

After the death of Charlemagne, the rapid dissolution of his vast empire struck our attention; we endeavoured to take an account of it, and to make known to ourselves the progress as well as the causes of that phenomenon; we pursued it, on the one hand, in its events, on the other, in its laws; we inquired into the political and the legislative revolution, which, from the death of Charlemagne to the accession of Hugh Capet, led to the feudal system.[7]

[1] Lect. 8. [2] Lect. 9—11. [3] Lect. 12—15. [4] Lect. 16, 18.
[5] Lect. 19. [6] Lect. 20—23. [7] Lect. 24—25.

To this history of civil society, from the middle of the eighth to the end of the tenth century, succeeded the history of religious society at the same period, that is to say, the history of the Gallo-Frankish church, considered firstly in itself, that is, in its national existence; secondly, externally, in its relations with the government of the universal church, that is, the popedom.

Lastly, always remaining true to the essential idea of civilization, and always mindful to consider it under its double aspect, with respect to society and the human soul, the intellectual state of Frankish-Gaul, from the eighth to the tenth century, was our concluding study. We saw ancient philosophy expire, and ecclesiastical theology arise: and we determined with some precision the profane and the sacred elements which have contributed to the modern development of the human mind.[1]

Such is the vast career, the steps of which we have followed; such is the immense variety of objects which have passed under your view. Certainly, I have not arbitrarily or from mere fancy led you into this vast expanse, causing you continually to be changing the point of view of subject. The very nature of our study rigidly exacted it: the history of civilization can only be given at this expense.

This history is a new work, scarcely more than sketched. The idea of it has been first conceived in the eighteenth century, and it is in our own times, under our own eyes, that we see its true fulfilment begin. It is not, however, only in the present day that history is made a study of; not only facts, but their connexion and their causes, have been studied; philosophers and scholars have equally laboured in this field. But up to the present times, we may say, the study of history, both philosophical and scholastic, has been partial and limited; political, legislative, religious, and literary histories have been written; learned researches have been made, brilliant reflections have been presented on the destination and development of laws, manners, sciences, letters, arts, of all the works of human activity; but they have never been regarded together, at one view, in their intimate and fertile

[1] Lect. 28, 29.

union. And wherever there has been an attempt to grasp at general results, or a desire to form a complete idea of the development of human nature, it is altogether on a partial foundation that the edifice has been raised. The *Discours sur l'Histoire Universelle*, and the *Esprit des Lois*, are glorious essays on the history of civilization; but who cannot see that Bossuet has almost exclusively confined his search to religious creeds, and Montesquieu to political institutions? These two geniuses have thus narrowed the horizon of their view. What are we to say concerning minds of an inferior order? It is evident that, scholastic or philosophical, history up to the present day has never really been general; it has never at one time followed man in all the careers wherein his activity exhibits itself. And yet the history of civilization is possible only under this condition; it is a summary of all histories; it requires them all for materials, for the fact which it relates is the summary of all other facts. An immense variety, without doubt; yet do not think that unity is destroyed thereby. There is unity in the life of a people, in the life of the human race, just as there is in that of an individual; but, as in fact all the circumstances of destiny and activity in an individual contribute to form his character, which is one and the same, so the unity and history of a people must have for its basis all the variety of its entire existence.

It is, then, wholly of necessity, and driven by the very nature of our subject, that we have gone over the political, ecclesiastical, legislative, philosophical, and literary history of Frankish Gaul, from the fifth to the tenth century: if we have arrived at any precise and positive results, we owe them to this method. You may have observed, especially, how much we have been enlightened by placing civil and religious society continually in juxta-position, both of which are incomprehensible if we leave them separate. Let us now endeavour to understand clearly these results, which we have obtained, I think, with some certainty; let us endeavour to determine the point of departure of Gaulish civilization in the fifth century, and the point at which it had arrived at the end of the tenth.

You are aware that the essential, fundamental elements of modern civilization in general, and of French civilization in particular, reduce themselves to three: the Roman world, the Christian world, and the Germanic world; antiquity, Christianity, and barbarism. Let us see what transformation these three elements underwent between the fifth and tenth centuries, what they became in this last period, and what remained of them in the civilization of that period.

I. I commence with the Roman element. I wish to cast a slight glance at what the Roman world has furnished to France, under a social and an intellectual point of view; and we must discover what remained of it in the tenth century, in society and in mind.

Under the first point of view—that is to say, the influence of Roman on Gallo-Frankish society, from the fifth to the tenth century, the result of our inquiries is, that the Roman world, when it broke up, bequeathed to the future the wrecks of three great facts — 1st, central sole power, empire, and absolute royalty; 2nd, imperial administration, government of provinces by the delegates of the central power; 3rd, the municipal system, the primitive mode of existence of Rome and most of the countries which had successively formed the Roman empire.

What are the changes which these three facts underwent between the fifth and tenth centuries?

1. With respect to the central power, sole and sovereign, it perished, as you know, in the invasion; in vain some of the first barbarous kings tried to restore it, and to exercise it to their advantage; they were baffled in the attempt; imperial despotism was too complex an instrument for their rude hands. At the fall of the Merovingians, Charlemagne attempted to revive it, and to use it; the attempt had a momentary success; central power re-appeared: but, after Charlemagne, as after the first invasion, it broke asunder, and was lost in the chaos. Nothing, surely, less resembled imperial power than the royalty of Hugh Capet. Some remembrance of it, nevertheless, lay in the minds of men: Empire had left behind it profound traces. The names of emperor, imperial authority, sovereign majesty, had still a certain virtue, and recalled a certain type of government; these were now only words, yet words still powerful, and sufficient to produce deeds if the occasion offered. Such was the state in which, at about the end of the tenth century, this first legacy of the Roman world manifested itself.

2. The imperial administration underwent very nearly the same vicissitudes; the barbarous chiefs tried to use it, but with no better success. This mode of governing the several parts of a state was too complicated, too exact; it required the concurrence of too many agents, and intelligence of too developed a kind; the administrative machine of the empire was speedily deranged, if I may so speak, in the hands of its new masters. Charlemagne attempted to give it regularity and motion; it was a necessary consequence of the restoration of central power; and, by an analogous consequence, together with the central power of Charlemagne, perished also the provincial administration, which he had, as well as he could, reconstructed. After the complete dissolution of the new empire, however, when the feudal system had prevailed, and when the holders of fiefs had succeeded the ancient delegates of the sovereign, there remained, in the thoughts of the people and of the possessors of fiefs themselves, some recollection of their origin. That origin, I have been careful to point out to you, was of a double kind; the fiefs originated on the one hand in benefices, or lands conceded, whether by the sovereign or by other chiefs; on the other hand, in offices or appointments of dukes, counts, viscounts, centeniers, &c., that is, of officers, invested by the sovereign with local administration. This second origin was not, therefore, absolutely effaced from memory: it was vaguely remembered that these lords—now sovereigns, or nearly so—had formerly been delegates of a greater sovereign: that they had been the representatives of a general and superior power; and that instead of being then proprietors of the sovereignty on their own account, they were only magistrates or administrators in the name of another, and that the portion of that sovereignty which they possessed might have been usurped from this sole and remote monarch, who was now lost sight of. This idea, which pervades the course of our history, and which has been the favourite theory of jurisconsults, and other writers upon public laws, is clearly a wreck of the ancient Roman administration—an echo which had survived the ruin of that vast and learned hierarchy. Such is all that we discern of it towards the end of the tenth century; but a potent germ of life lay buried under this remembrance.

3. The third fact bequeathed by the Roman to the modern world is the municipal system. You know what the state of towns was, at the end of the tenth century, into what depopulation, decay, and distress they had fallen. Nevertheless, so much as still remained of internal administration, especially in southern Gaul, was Roman in its origin; here was still some shadow of the curia, of consuls, duumvirs, and other ancient municipal magistrates. The Roman law presided over the acts of civil life, donations, contracts, &c. Municipal magistrates, deprived of their political importance, were become in a manner simple notaries who registered civil acts, and preserved records of them. A new municipal system, of a different principle and character, the system of the commons of the middle age, was about to raise itself upon the ruins of the Roman municipality; but as yet it had scarcely begun to dawn; and, in general, all that we can discern as existing in the tenth century, of distinct administration in towns, is Roman. Let us now see what remained of Greco-Roman antiquity under an intellectual point of view, what the mind of the tenth century still retained of it. I cannot here enter into detail; I do not mean to search, in the theological tenets and popular opinions of that time, for those which were allied to Roman philosophy and opinions; I merely wish to characterize, in its most general features, the intellectual heritage which ancient society has bequeathed to us, and the condition of it at the end of the tenth century. An important fact, and far too little noticed, in my opinion, first strikes me; it is that the principle of liberty of thought, the principle of all philosophy, reason being its own point of departure and guide, is an idea essentially the daughter of antiquity, an idea which modern society holds from Greece and Rome. We have received it evidently neither from Christianity nor from Germany; for it was included in neither of those elements of our civilization. It strongly prevailed on the contrary in Greco-Roman civilization: there is its true origin; there the most valuable legacy which antiquity has left to the modern world: the legacy which has never been absolutely set aside and without value; for you have seen the idea which is the mother of philosophy, namely, the right of reason to act from itself, animating the works and life of Scotus Erigena, and the

principle of liberty of thought still prevailing in the ninth century, in face of the principle of authority. A second intellectual legacy of Roman civilization to ours, is the body of beautiful works of antiquity. In spite of the general ignorance, in spite of the corruption of language, ancient literature has always been presented to the mind as a worthy object of study, of imitation, and of admiration, and as the type of the beautiful. The influence of this idea was very great, you are aware, from the fourteenth to the sixteenth century; it has never been lost completely, and in the eighth, ninth, and tenth centuries, we have encountered it at every step.

The philosophical and the classical spirit, the principle of liberty of thought and the model of the beautiful, are the gifts which the Roman has transmitted to the modern world, and which still survived to it in the intellectual order at the end of the tenth century.

II. I pass to the Christian element; I desire to ascertain what was its condition at this epoch, and what effects it had produced.

You have followed the changes of Christian society from the fifth to the tenth century; in its birth you have seen the origin and model of all the modes of organization, of all the systems which subsequently appeared; therein you have recognised the democratical, aristocratical, and monarchical principles: you have seen the lay community one while associated with the ecclesiastical community, and at another, excluded from all participation in power: all the combinations, in short, of religious social organization offered themselves to your view. During the period which we have considered, the aristocratic system prevailed; episcopacy became soon the ruling and almost the sole power. At the end of the tenth century, the popedom raised itself above episcopacy, the monarchical overcame the aristocratic principle. Under a social point of view, therefore, the state of the church at that time reduced itself to two facts:—the preponderance of the church in the state, and the preponderance of papacy in the church. Such are the results which at this epoch we may regard as established.

Under an intellectual point of view, it is more difficult, and still more important, to render to ourselves an account of what the Christian element had at that time furnished to modern civilization. Let me here ascend a step higher, and compare for a moment what has passed in antiquity with that which passed in Christian society.

Spiritual and temporal order, human thought and human society, developed themselves amongst the ancients parallel rather than together, not without an intimate correspondence, but without exercising a prompt and direct influence one upon the other. I will explain myself: without speaking of the earlier times of philosophy, but taking it at the epoch of its highest glory, Plato, Aristotle, and most of the philosophers, whether of Grecian, or more latterly of Greco-Roman antiquity, had full liberty of thought, or nearly so. The State, public policy interfered but little with their labours to cramp them and give them a particular tendency. They, on their part, concerned themselves little about politics, nor cared much to influence immediately and decisively the society in which they lived: undoubtedly they exerted that indirect and remote influence which belongs to all great human thought cast into the midst of mankind; but the ancient philosophers made few pretensions to the action or direct influence of thought over exterior facts, of pure knowledge over society; they were not essentially reformers; they aspired to govern neither the private conduct of individuals, nor society in general. The ruling character, in one word, of intellectual development in antiquity, is liberty of thought and its practical disinterestedness; it is a development essentially rational and scientific. Upon the triumph of Christianity in the Roman world, the character of intellectual development changed: that which was philosophy became religion; philosophy was enfeebled more and more; religion usurped the understanding; the form of thought was essentially religious. It aspired from that time to much more power over human affairs; the end of thought, in religion, is essentially practical; it aspires to govern individuals, frequently even society. The spiritual order, it is true, continued to be separate from the temporal order; the government of nations was not directly and completely committed to the clergy; its lay society and ecclesiastic society developed themselves independently. Nevertheless, the spiritual penetrated much further into the temporal order than it had done in ancient times; and whereas liberty of thought, and its purely scientific activity, had been, in Greece and Rome, the ruling character of the intellectual development; its practical activity and pretension to power, was the distinguishing trait of intellectual development amongst Christian nations.

From this there resulted another change, which was not of less importance. In proportion as human thought, under the religious form, aspired to more power over the conduct of mankind, and the fate of states, it lost its liberty. Instead of remaining open and free to competition, as amongst the ancients, intellectual society was organized and governed; instead of philosophical schools, there was a church. It was at the cost of its independence that thought purchased empire; it no longer developed itself in all directions, and according to its simple impulse; but it acted forcibly and immediately on mankind and on societies.

This fact is important; it has exercised a decisive influence on the history of modern Europe, so decisive, as still to subsist and to manifest itself around us in our own days. The religious form has ceased to hold exclusive dominion in human thought; scientific and rational development has recommenced; and yet what is come to pass? Have philosophers thought, have they wished to treat pure knowledge in the same manner as those of antiquity have done? No: human reason aspires in the present day to govern and reform societies after its own conceptions, to rule the exterior world according to general principles; that is to say, the thought, again become philosophical, has preserved the pretensions it held under the religious form; with this immense difference, it is true, that it would unite the liberty of thought with its power, and that even whilst it tries to take possession of societies, to govern them, and place the power in the hands of intelligence, it does not wish intelligence to be organized nor subjected to forms and a legal yoke. It is in the alliance of intellectual liberty, as it shone in antiquity, with the intellectual power, as it showed itself in Christian societies, that we find the great and original character of modern civilization; and it is without doubt, in the bosom of the revolution effected by Christianity in the relations of the spiritual and temporal orders of thought and of the exterior world, that this new revolution has taken its origin and its first point of support.

At the epoch to which we are now come, at the end of the

tenth century, the double fact which characterizes the first revolution, I mean the abdication of the liberty of the human intellect, and the increase of its social power, was already consummated. From the tenth century, you observe spiritual society pretending to the government of temporal society, that is, announcing that thought has a right to govern the world; and, at the same time, you observe thought subjected to the rules, the yoke of the church, and organized according to certain laws. These are the two most considerable results of the vicissitudes which intellectual order has suffered from the fifth to the tenth century, the two principal facts which the Christian element has thrown into modern civilization.

III. We come to the third primitive element of this civilization, the Germanic world or barbarism. Let us see what modern society had already received from it in the tenth century.

When we considered the condition of the Germans prior to the invasion, two facts especially, two forms of social organization, struck us:

1. The tribe formed of all the proprietary chiefs of family, governing itself by an assembly, where justice was rendered, and where public business was transacted—in one word, by the common deliberation of free men; a system very incomplete and precarious, without doubt, in such a state of social relations and manners, but of which, however, glimpses may be caught of the principal rudiments.

2. Side by side with the tribe, we have met with the warlike band, a society where the individual lived in so free a manner, that he could adopt it or reject it, according to his taste, and where the social principle was not equality of free men, and common deliberation, but the patronage of a chief towards his companions, who served him, and lived at his expense, that is to say, aristocratic and military subordination; words which ill answer to the idea which must be formed of a band of barbarians, but which describes the system of social organization which was about to issue from it.

Such are the two principles, or rather the two germs of principles, which Germany has furnished in the earliest times, to modern society in its nascent state. The principle of common deliberation of free men no more existed in the Roman world, unless in the bosoms of the municipal system; it was the Germans who restored it to the political order. The principle of aristocratic patronage, combined with a large portion of liberty, was become equally foreign to Roman society. Both the one and the other of these elements of our social organization are of German origin.

From the fifth to the tenth century they underwent great changes. At the end of this period, the assemblies, or government, by the voice of common deliberation, had disappeared; in fact, there remained scarcely any trace of the ancient *mâls*, fields of Mars and May, or Germanic courts. The remembrance, however, of national assemblies, the right of free men to join together, to deliberate and transact their business together, resided in the minds of men as a primitive tradition and a thing which might again come about. It was with the ancient German assemblies as with imperial sovereignty: neither the one nor the other any longer existed; government by the voice of free deliberation and absolute power had equally fallen, yet without absolutely perishing. They were germs buried under immense heaps of ruins, but which yet might one day reappear and be fruitful. Such was, in fact, what really happened.

With respect to the patronage of the chief towards his companions, the acquisition of large domains and the territorial life had much changed this relation of the ancient Germans. We can no more find, in any degree worth mentioning, the same liberty which used to reign in the wandering band. Some had received benefices, and were settled in them; others had continued to live around their chief in his house and at his table. The chief was become eminently powerful; there was introduced into this little society much more inequality and fixedness. Nevertheless, although the aristocratic principle and the inequality which accompanies it, and which constitutes even it, had assumed a great development, they had not destroyed all the ancient relation between the chief and his companions. The inequality did not draw servility after it; and the society which resulted therefrom, and with which we will occupy ourselves more in detail hereafter, the feudal society reposed, for those at least who composed part of it, that is, the proprietors of fiefs, upon the principles of right and liberty.

In the tenth century, and under the social point of view, the

Germanic element then had furnished to modern civilization in its nascent state, on the one hand, the remembrance of national assemblies, and of the right of free men to govern themselves in common; on the other hand, certain ideas, certain sentiments of right and liberty implanted in the bosom of an entirely aristocratic organization.

Under the moral point of view, although eminent writers have strongly insisted upon what modern Europe holds from the Germans, their assertions seem to me vague and too general; they make no distinction of epoch or country; and I think that, in western Europe, especially in France, the energetic sentiment of individual independence is the most important, I would willingly say the only great moral legacy which ancient Germany has transmitted to us.

There was, in the tenth century, a national German literature, consisting of songs and popular traditions, which hold a high place in the literary history of Germany, and which have exerted a great influence on its manners. But the part played by these traditions, and by all primitive German literature, in the intellectual development of France, has been very limited and fugitive; this is the reason why I have not entered upon it with you, though this literature is positively full of originality and interest.

Such was the state of the three great elements of modern civilization in the tenth century; such are the changes, social and moral, which Roman antiquity, Christianity, and barbarism have experienced on our soil.

From thence flow, if I mistake not, two general facts, two great results, which it is necessary to exhibit.

The work of M. de Savigny on the History of Roman Law, after the fall of the Empire, has changed the face of the science; he has proved that the Roman law had not perished; that, notwithstanding great modifications, without doubt, it was transmitted from the fifth to the fifteenth century, and had always continued to form a considerable part of the legislation of the west.

If I am not mistaken, the facts which I have laid before your view, in this course, have generalized this result. It follows, I think, evidently, that not only in municipal institutions and civil laws, as M. de Savigny has proved, but in political order and philosophy, in literature and all departments, in a word, of social and intellectual life, Roman civilization was transmitted far beyond the date of the Empire; that we may everywhere discern a trace of it; that no abyss separates the Roman from the modern world; that the thread is nowhere broken; that we may recognise everywhere the transition of Roman society into our own; in a word, that the part played by ancients in modern civilization is greater and more continuous than is commonly thought. A second result equally arises out of our labours, and characterizes the period which is the object of them. During all this period, from the fifth to the tenth century, we have nowhere been able to pause; we have been unable to find, either in social or intellectual order, any system, any fact, which became fixed, which took a firm, general, and regular hold on society or mind. The general fact with which we have been struck is a continual and universal fluctuation, a constant state of uncertainty and of transformation. It was, then, from the fifth to the tenth century, that the work of fermentation and amalgamation of the three elements of modern civilization, namely, the Roman element, the Christian element, and the German element, was in operation; and it was only at the end of the tenth century that the ferment ceased, and the amalgamation became nearly accomplished, and that the development of the new order and truly modern society commenced.

The history which we have just concluded, then, is the history of its very conception and creation. All things rise out of the chaos, modern society among the rest. That which we have studied now is the chaos, the cradle of France: what we shall have to study hereafter is France itself. Dating only from the end of the tenth century, the social being which bears that name, if I may thus speak, has been formed and exists; we might attend it in its proper and exterior development. This development will merit, for the first time, the name of French civilization. Until now, we have spoken of Gaulish-Roman, Frankish, Gallo-Roman, and Gallo-Frankish civilization; we have been obliged to combine foreign names in order to characterize, with any justice, a society without unity and certainty. When we again enter upon our labours, it will be to speak of French civilization; we shall date therefrom; the question will no longer be concerning Gauls, Franks, and Romans, but of Frenchmen, of ourselves.

ILLUSTRATIONS AND HISTORICAL TABLES.

ON authorising the publication of these lectures, I promised to add to them a number of tables and documents intended to prove or to explain the ideas which I might have occasion to express. I have inserted some of these tables in the lectures themselves. There are some others for which I could not find a place there, and which seem to me no less necessary. I give them here. It would have been both easy and useful to multiply illustrations of this kind; but I have been obliged to limit myself. The object of those which I have selected is both to show in their development facts which I have been merely able to point out, and to place before the reader those events, the knowledge of which I took for granted. They are seven in number:—

I. Table of the organization of the court, and of the central government of the Roman empire at the commencement of the fifth century—that is to say, at the epoch which I took as the starting point of the course.

II. Table of the hierarchy of ranks and titles in Roman society at the same epoch.

III. Narrative of the embassy sent in 449 by Theodosius the Younger, emperor of the west, to Attila, established on the banks of the Danube.

IV. Chronological table of the principal events of the political history of Gaul, from the fifth to the tenth century.

V. Chronological table of the principal events of the ecclesiastical history of Gaul, from the fifth to the tenth century.

VI. Chronological table of the principal events of the literary history of Gaul, from the fifth to the tenth century.

VII. Table of the councils and canonical legislation of Gaul, from the fifth to the tenth century.

Unless I am much deceived, there is no occasion for me to insist upon the utility of these documents—it will speak for itself; and for persons who weigh and study them attentively, the history of our civilization, so obscure and so vague in its cradle, will appear, I think, under more clear and precise forms. This is my aim and hope in publishing them.

I.

Table of the Organization of the Court and of the Central Government of the Roman Empire, at the commencement of the Fifth Century.

It was under the reigns of Diocletian and of Constantine that the court and the central government of the Roman emperors gained that systematic and definitive organization, whose image the *notitia imperii Romani* has preserved to us. It was the same both in the empire of the east and in that of the west, with the exception of some unimportant differences occasioned by that of localities. For the basis of this table I have adopted the empire of the east, the most complete and the best known of the two, taking care to point out here and there facts which distinguish the empire of the west.

IMPERIAL COURT.

I.—*Præpositus sacri cubiculi,* (grand chamberlain.)

He had under his orders a large number of officers, divided into six classes, *scholæ*, and all named *palatini;* their duty in the palace was called *in palatio militare.* The principal were:—

1.—*Primicerius sacri cubiculi* (first chamberlain.)—He was at the head of all those who served the emperor in his apartments, and accompanied him everywhere for this purpose; they were named *cubicularii* (chamberlains or valets de chambre); they were divided into parties of ten men, at the head of each of which was a *decanus.*

2.—*Comes castrensis* (count of the palace.)—The chief of those who served the emperor at table, and took care of the interior of the palace this was a kind of steward, or maître-d'hotel. He had under his orders:—

(1.) *Primicerius mensorum,* the chief of those who, when the emperor travelled, went before to get everything prepared upon his road, and in the places where he was to stop.

(2.) *Primicerius cellariorum,* chief of all those employed in the kitchens and offices.

(3.) *Primicerius pædagogiorum,* the chief of the young pages. brought up for service in the interior of the palace.

(4.) *Primicerius lampadariorum,* the chief of those who overlooked the lighting of the palace. There was in this class a number of subdivisions and subaltern officers.

3.—*Comes sacræ vestis* (count of the sacred wardrobe.)—He was charged with the imperial wardrobe, and commanded many officers.

4.—*Chartularii cubiculi* (secretaries of the chamber.)—They were generally three in number, and were the private secretaries of the emperor; and although occupied with public affairs, they were under the direction of the *præpositus sacri cubiculi*, because their service was personal.

5.—*Decurionus III. silentiariorum.*—The *silentiarii* were charged with preventing all noise in the palace: the thirty principal were subdivided into three parties of ten, each commanded by a decurion.

6.—*Comes domorum per Cappadociam.*—This was the steward of the property which the emperor of the east possessed in Cappadocia: these patrimonial estates were very considerable; the *comes domorum* directed their administration and collected the revenues: he held office as a magistrate.

II.—*Comites domesticorum equitum peditumque* (counts of the cavalry and infantry of the palace.)

These were the two commanders of the select bands of cavalry and infantry who guarded the person of the emperor. These bands, who were called *protectores domestici*, were drawn from the seven schools of Armenian soldiers, called *palatini*, and destined for the military service of the palace. The seven schools formed a body of 3500 men, from among whom were taken the *protectores domestici*, who enjoyed great privileges. The counts of the domestic infantry and cavalry also had under their orders *deputati*, charged with executing their commands in the provinces.

The empress also had her court, organised in nearly the same manner as that of the emperor.

CENTRAL GOVERNMENT.

I.—*Magister officiorum* (master of the offices.)

This was a sort of universal minister, whose functions were very extensive; he administered justice to almost all the officers of the palace (*palatini*), received the appeals of private citizens, presented senators to the princes, &c. His jurisdiction also extended over the officers belonging to other departments, such as the *mensores*, the *lampadarii*, and those who were in the department of the *præpositus sacri cubiculi.* He had under his jurisdiction:—

1.—The seven schools of the *milites palatini.* (1.) Schola scutariorum prima; (2.) Schola scutariorum secunda; (3) Gentilium seniorum; (4.) Scutariorum sagittairorum; (5.) Armaturaıum juniorum; (7.) Gentilium juniorum.

2.—The school of the *agentes in rebus:* these were the messengers and spies of the princes in the provinces: before Constantine they were called *frumentarii.*

3.—The *mensores* and the *lampadarii*, of whom we have already spoken; also, the *admissionales*, or the gentlemen ushers of the palace, and the *invitatores*, who were charged with transmitting invitations.

4.—Four *scrinia* or officers, where the affairs of the prince with his subjects were immediately managed.

(1.) *Scrinium memoriæ.* Here were kept registers of employments and grades; hence, for the most part, issued the nominations.

(2.) *Scrinium epistolarum:* here were received the deputations and requests from cities, and hence were dispatched the answers of the prince.

(3.) *Scrinium libellorum:* hither were addressed the requests and appeals of subjects.

(4.) *Scrinium dispositionum:* the functions of this last office resembled those of the two preceding ones; it is omitted in the *notitia*, but the laws make mention of it.

Each of these offices had its own chief, *magister scrinii memoriæ, epistolarum*, &c.; the last was called *comes dispositionum;* there were numerous officers in it.

5.—The armourers of the empire. The master of the offices of the east had fifteen under his direction: Damascus, Antioch, 2; Edessa, Irenopolis, Cæsarea in Cappadocia, Nicomedia, 2; Sardis, Adrianople, 2; Thessalonica, Naissus, Ratiaria, Margus. The master of the offices of the west had nineteen: Sirmium, Acincum, Cornutum, Lauriacum, Salona, Concordia, Verona, Mantua, Cremona, Pavia, Lucca, Strasburg, Macon, Autun, Besançon, Reims, Trèves, 2; Amiens.

II—*Quæstor* (the questor.)

He judged, in concert with the pretorian prefect, and sometimes alone, affairs referred to the prince; he composed the laws and edicts which the prince was to publish; he signed the rescripts; he had the superintendence of the register (*laterculum minus*), in which were enumerated the tribunes and the prefects of the camps and frontiers. He was a kind of high chancellor. He sent his edicts to the *scrinium dispositionum*, where they were kept, and copies distributed throughout the empire. He had no officers attached to his post, but he had twelve secretaries in the *scrinium memoriæ*, seven in the *scrinium epistolarum*, and seven in the *scrinium libellorum.*

III. *Comes sacrarum largitionum*, (count of the sacred largesses.)

This was the high treasurer of the empire; he collected and administered all the public revenues; all the payments issued from his office; Constantine put him in the place of the questors, the *præfecti ærarii*, &c.

His administration was divided into two offices, *scrinia*, at the head of which was a *primicerius*, or *magister scrinii*, (chief of the office.)

1. *Scrinium canonum.*—This, it seems, was the office in which was prepared the account of what each province, each town, &c., was to send to the public chest, *arcæ largitionum.*

2. *Scrinium tabulariorum*,
3. *Scrinium numerariorum*, } These two offices kept an account of the moneys received and expended by the treasury.

4. *Scrinium aureæ massæ.*—This office was occupied in keeping accounts of the bullion which was sent to the treasury, and of the use made of it in coining money, in the decoration of public monuments, in crown jewels, &c.

5. *Scrinium auri ad responsum.*—They here regulated and furnished the sums of money, whether intended to supply the expenses of the officers whom the prince sent into the provinces, of the armies, &c., or whether to be sent into the different parts of the empire, or for tribute paid to allies, barbarians, &c.

6. *Scrinium ab argento.*—This was the office where were deposited silver in ingots, the imperial plate, vases, &c.

7. *Scrinium vestiarii sacri.*—This was the office from whence issued the funds for the clothing of troops, the monarch, the imperial family, the people of his court, to whom he furnished clothing.

8. *Scrinium annularense vel miliarense.*—According to the first reading, this office would be intended to preserve the rings and jewels of the emperor; according to the second, which seems to me the most probable, its intention was to strike and distribute the small silver money, called *miliarensium*, of which the value was the tenth part of an *aureus.*

9. *Scrinium à pecuniis.*—Pancirollus thinks that it was this office which directed the coining of money throughout the empire.

10. *Scrinium exceptorum.*—The clerks of this office wrote out the account of the cases which had been judged by the count of the sacred largesses.

The attributes of these various offices were very uncertain; their names are obscure, and we can only conjecture their object. It seems that they afterwards added an eleventh office, called *scrinium mittendariorum*, and composed of officers who were sent into the provinces to get the payment of taxes hastened and completed.

Besides these offices attached to his service, the count of the largesses had a great number of subordinates in the provinces, charged with directing the affairs of his department. The principal were:

1. Six *comites largitionum*, in the east, in Egypt, in Asia Minor, in Pontus, in Thrace, and in Illyria; there were five of these in the west. They were charged with paying the salaries of the generals, soldiers, and other officers, and to overlook the collection of taxes.

2. Four *comites commerciorum*, charged with buying the stuffs and jewels necessary for the imperial household, with overlooking the operations of the merchants, and watching that the duties levied upon the commodities should be correctly paid. There was but one in the west.

3. *Præfecti thesaurorum*; they received and kept, in each province, the money proceeding from taxes, until it was sent to the count of the sacred largesses.

4. *Comes metallorum*, charged with deducting, from the produce of the mines of gold, silver, or other metals, the portion which went to the prince.

5. *Comes vel rationalis summarum Ægypti*, charged with collecting the property which fell to the prince in that province, whether by escheat, or any other cause; he also superintended the great commerce in Indian merchandise, which passed through Egypt; there were eleven *rationales* of this kind in the west.

6. *Magistri lineæ vel tinteæ vestis*; they directed all the labourers who worked in flax for the wardrobe, or furniture of the emperor. Their office was filled in the west by a *comes vestiarii*.

7. *Privatæ magistri*; they directed the workmen in silk, linen, &c., for the royal household.

8. *Procuratores gynæciorum*; charged with the superintending of spun and wove fabrics.

9. *Procuratores baphiorum*; inspectors of the dying of stuffs in purple, &c. There were nine in the west.

10. *Procuratores monetarum*; mint inspectors. There were six of them in the west.

11. *Præpositi bartagarum*, charged with superintending the transport of goods intended for the public service, or that of the emperor, corn, commodities, merchandise, silver, &c.

12. *Procuratores linificiorum*, charged with procuring the flax necessary for the imperial fabrics. There were two in the west, at Vienna and at Ravenna.

IV. *Comes rerum privatarum*, (the crown treasurer.)

The public treasury was called *ærarium*; the private treasure of the emperor was called *fiscus*. Although he equally disposed of both one and the other, yet there was a distinction, and they were administered separately.

The *comes sacrarum largitionum* had the administration of the *ærarium*, and the *comes rerum privatarum* had that of the *fiscus*, whose revenues were the property which devolved upon the emperor in any manner whatsoever, the produce of certain taxes, &c. He had under his orders:

1. A department directed by the *primicerius officii*, and divided into four offices.

 (1.) *Scrinium beneficiorum.*—Here were managed all affairs relative to gifts of property, real or personal, to the concession of privileges, &c., which the emperor made to such or such of his subjects.

 (2.) *Scrinium canonum.*—This office received the rents of the farms on the imperial property, and kept the accounts of them. The rent was paid in money or in kind.

 (3.) *Scrinium securitatum.*—In this office were deposited the receipts of those who had received the money of the fisc; and the duplicates of those which had been given to people who had paid anything to the fisc.

 (4.) *Scrinium largitionum privatarum.*—Here were kept the accounts of money given by the emperor to individuals, and the salaries which he paid to the people attached to his personal service.

2. *Rationales vel procuratores rerum privatarum.*—These were officers charged with collecting the revenues of the fisc, in the provinces. They were often judges in cases where the fisc was concerned.

3. *Præpositi bastagarum rei privatæ*, inspectors of transports made for the service of the prince. There were two of these in the west.

4. *Præpositi stabulorum, gregum et armentorum*, inspectors of the studs and herds of the emperor throughout the empire. There was also a *comes stabuli*, answering to our master of the horse.

5. *Procuratores saltuum*, inspector of the woods and pasturages where the herds of the emperor were taken to graze.

There were, doubtless, many other petty officers, mention of whom has not come down to us.

V. *Primicerius notariorum*, (first secretary of state.)

This was a magistrate charged with keeping the register in which were inscribed all the public functionaries, their duties, salaries, warrants of nomination, &c. This register was called *laterculum majus*. The people nominated to the places, paid certain fees to this *primicerius notariorum*, who thus kept the list of all the dignities which we have just enumerated. There were three classes of *notarii*.

In each province there was a provincial chest, in all one hundred and eighteen chests. The receivers of taxes transmitted the money to these chests, under the superintendence of the *præfecti thesaurorum*. These latter gave to the *comites largitionum* the sums necessary for the expenses of the province, the salary of the officers, &c. They transmitted the balance to the governor of the province, who sent it to the chest of the sacred bounty. The carriages intended to transport it, were furnished by men kept on purpose, and formed part of the public post, (*cursus publicus*,) which the government alone, or those whom it authorised, had to make use of.

II.

Table of the Hierarchy of Ranks and Titles in the Roman Empire at the commencement of the Fifth Century.

Rank and titles multiplied in the Roman empire, at the same epoch in which the court and central government received their definitive form, as given in the preceding table. These ranks and titles conferred important privileges upon the possessors, with reference to the other citizens, but in no degree rendered them independent of power. They were mere personal distinctions attached to certain offices, and which even the holders of these offices did not enjoy, until they had been authorized to assume them by letters patent from the prince. There were six principal ranks or titles, the rights of precedence among which were minutely regulated.

I. *Nobilissimi.*

This was the highest of the titles; it came close to the throne, and conferred, to a certain extent, the dignity of Cæsar. It was bestowed upon the members and allies of the imperial family.

II. *Illustres.*

The persons decorated with this title, were twenty-seven in number—viz.,

1. The pretorian prefect of the East.
2. The pretorian prefect of Illyria.
3. The pretorian prefect of Italy.
4. The pretorian prefect of Gaul.
5. The prefect of Constantinople.
6. The prefect of Rome.

7—11. The five generals, commanders of the army in the East.
12. The general of the horse in the West.
13. The general of the infantry in the West.
14, 15. The two grand chamberlains of the East and West.
16, 17. The two masters of the offices in the East and West.
18, 19. The two questors of the palace in the East and West.
20, 21. The two counts of the sacred largesses in the East and West.
22, 23. The two counts of the privy purse in the East and West.
24, 25. The two counts commanding the body-guard, cavalry, in the East and West.
26, 27. The two counts commanding the body-guard, infantry, in the East and West.

The consuls were also *illustres.* The date of the introduction of this title is not known. Augustus used to select, every month, at first fifteen, and afterwards twenty, members of the senate, to form his privy council; their decisions were held as having emanated from the entire body of the senate; they were called *patricii,* while the other senators were only entitled *clarissimi.* They, in concurrence with the sovereign, discussed and directed public affairs. Constantine formed of them his *consistorium principes* (council of state,) and entitled the members *comites consistoriani.* They were, with the consuls, the first honoured with the title of *illustres,* which was afterwards extended, probably also under Constantine, to the magistrates above mentioned. The *illustres* were addressed thus,—*vestra tua*, or *tua, magnificentia, celsitudo, sublimitas, magnitudo, eminentia, excellentia*, &c. Those who neglected to observe the etiquette in this respect, had to pay a fine of three pounds in gold.

The *illustres* could only be tried for any offence, by the prince in person, or his immediate delegates; they were entitled to have their sentences read by the registrar; they were prohibited from making a traffic of their power and influence, and from marrying women of an inferior rank; this latter prohibition, however, was recalled at a later period; neither they nor their families could be put to the torture, nor be subjected to any of the capital punishments inflicted upon plebeians; they were exempt from being summoned to any court as witnesses, &c.

III. *Spectabiles.*

Of these there were sixty-two.

1, 2. The two first chamberlains in the East and West. (*Primicerii sacri cubiculi.*)

3, 4. The two counts of the palace, in the East and West. (*Comites castrenses.*)

5, 6. The two chief secretaries of the emperor, in the East and West. (*Primicerii notariorum.*)

7—13. The seven heads of the principal departments of the central government in the East and West. (*Magistri scriniorum.*)

14—16. The three proconsuls (governors of dioceses or provinces) of Asia, Achaia, and Africa.

17. The count of the East.

18. The prefect of Egypt. (*Præfectus Augustalis.*)

19—29. Eleven vicars, or governors of dioceses; five in the empire of the East, and six in the empire of the West.

30—37. Eight counts, or generals of armies; two in the East, and six in the West.

38—62. Twenty-five dukes, or generals of armies; thirteen in the East, and twelve in the West.

The title of *spectabiles* was also given to the senators, probably under Constantine. It seems to have had no other origin than the mania for the classification of ranks. It was very uncertain in its application; we find it given to men who are called elsewhere *clarissimi*, or *perfectissimi*, or even *egregii;* thus the *duces*, the *silentiarii* (ushers in law courts), the *notarii* (secretaries), are designated sometimes by the one, sometimes by the other of these appellations.

IV. *Clarissimi.*

We find this title already, under Tiberius, in possession of the senators and senatorial families. After a certain number of senators had become *illustres*, the rest continued to assume the title of *clarissimi*, and by degrees it became extended to all the inferior officers employed in the provinces. At the commencement of the fifth century there were, it would appear, 115 persons addressed by this title—viz.,

Thirty-seven consular personages, governors of provinces; fifteen in the East, and twenty-two in the West.

Five *correctores*, governors of provinces; two in the East, and three in the West.

Seventy-three *præsides*, governors of provinces; forty-two in the East, and three in the West.

V. *Perfectissimi.*

This title was invented by Constantine; we find it, indeed, made use of in a law of Diocletian, but it was Constantine who introduced it into his classification of ranks, and divided the *perfectissimi* into three grades. The title was given,

To the *præsides*, or governors, of Arabia, Isauria, and Dalmatia.

To the *rationales*, collectors of the public revenues in the provinces.

To the *magistri scriniorum*, heads of the offices of the court of the sacred largesses.

To the counts of the sacred largesses, or imperial collectors and paymasters in the provinces.

And to many other persons in the public service.

VI. *Egregii.*

This last title was very common; it appertained to all the imperial secretaries, to all the persons employed in the offices of the various governors of the provinces, to priests, to the crown lawyers, and to a whole host of other persons.

III.

Narrative of the Embassy sent in 449 to Attila, by Theodosius the Younger, Emperor of the East.

Introduction.

There is scarcely any feature of the history of this period which it were more interesting to be thoroughly acquainted with, than the relations of the Roman emperors with the barbarians, the Germans, Huns, Slavonians, &c., who pressed upon their frontiers. A knowledge of this can alone enable us to form anything like a precise and accurate idea of the comparative state of Roman and of barbarian civilization. Unfortunately, the materials of this knowledge are very deficient; we have upon the subject little more than mere sentences, paragraphs, scattered throughout the Latin chroniclers, the confused traditions of the German tribes, or some old poems which, in their present form, are evidently greatly posterior to the fourth and fifth century. The narrative of the embassy sent in 449 by Theodosius the Younger to Attila, at that time master of the whole of Germany, and himself established on the Danube, is, unquestionably, the fullest and most instructive of the monuments remaining to us of this branch of history; the only one, in fact, which shows us the interior of the states, and the life of a barbarian chief, and enables us to examine closely, and, as it were, in person, his relations with the Romans: the narrative itself is of the highest authenticity; it formed part of the history of the war against Attila, in seven books, written by the sophist Priscus, of Panium in Thrace, a member of the embassy; it has come down to us among the *Excerpta legationum*, inserted in the first volume of the Collection of Byzantine historians, and which formed the 53rd book of a great historical collection made by one Theodosius, by order of Constantine VI. Porphyrogenitus (911—959). I here present you with a literal translation of this interesting production. The narrative, it is true, relates to the empire of the east, not to that of the west, and to Hun barbarians, not to German barbarians: but the relative situation of the two empires and of the two classes of barbarians at this period was very nearly the same; the social state and manners of the Huns, notwithstanding the diversity of origin and of language, very closely resembled, in general outline, at all events, those of the Germans. We may, therefore, in the absence of documents specially relating to the Germans or to the west, regard the narrative before us, as a tolerably faithful image of the relations of the expiring empire with its future conquerors:

448—449.

Embassy of Attila to Theodosius. Plot of Chrysaphus the Eunuch to take away the life of Attila by means of Edeco and Vigilius. Embassy of Theodosius to Attila. Details as to the manners of the Huns; their mode of life, &c.

The Scythian Edeco, who had performed great military exploits, again came with Orestes, in quality of envoy; the latter, a Roman by birth, lived in Pæonia, a country situate on the Savus, and which, in virtue of the treaty with Ætius, general of the western Romans, was now subject to the barbarian.

This Edeco, on being admitted into the palace, presented to the emperor letters from Attila, in which the barbarian complained that the deserters from his camp had not been brought back to him, and threatened to resume hostilities unless they were forthwith restored; and, moreover, unless the Romans at once abstained from cultivating for themselves the territory which the fortune of war had added to his dominions. Now this territory extended along the Danube from Pæonia to Thrace; its breadth was fifteen days march. Moreover, the barbarian required that the great market should no longer be held, as heretofore, on the banks of the Danube, but at Naissus, which town, taken and sacked by him, and distant from the Danube five days rapid march, was situate, he said, at the limit of the Scythian and Roman states. Finally, he ordered that ambassadors should be sent to him, men not of common birth and dignity, but consular personages, to receive whom, he added, he would come as far as Sardica.

These letters having been read, Edeco quitted the presence in company with Vigilius, who had acted as interpreter of the words of Attila; and after having visited the other apartments, repaired to that of Chrysaphus, servant of the emperor, and in great favour and authority with him.

The barbarian had greatly admired the magnificence of the imperial abode. Vigilius, who still accompanied him as interpreter, repeated to Crysaphus his expressions of praise of the imperial palace, and his feeling that the Romans must be very happy by reason of their vast wealth. Chrysaphus hereupon told Edeco that he might himself have a similar abode, splendidly decorated, with gilded ceilings, and be placed in possession of every other advantage he might desire, if he would quit Scythia to reside at Rome. Edeco replied that it was not permissible to the servant of a foreign prince to take this step without his master's sanction. The eunuch asked him whether he had easy access to Attila, and what power he was invested with in his own country. Edeco replied, that he and Attila were upon terms of familiar intercourse, and that he was one of the guards who took it in turn to keep watch over that prince in his abode. The eunuch then said, that if Edeco would do a certain service for him, he would confer upon him very important advantages; but that, as the affair required deliberation, he would communicate it to him after he had taken supper, if he would then return to his apartment without Orestes and his other fellow ambassadors. The barbarian promised to do so; and, accordingly, after he had supped, again presented himself to Chrysaphus.

After they had, by means of the interpreter Vigilius, exchanged mutual oaths, the eunuch, not to propose anything to the detriment of Edeco, but solely what should be to his great advantage, the latter not to reveal what should be proposed to him, even though he should not execute it, the eunuch told Edeco that if on his return to Scythia, he would kill Attila, he should pass the rest of his life in affluence and luxury. Edeco consented to the proposition, and said that he should want some money to effect the business, about fifty pounds in gold, to divide among the soldiers under his orders, and in other ways to facilitate his proceedings. The eunuch offered to give him the amount he named at once; but the barbarian said that, in the first place, it would be advisable to send him back, accompanied by Vigilius, to give Attila the answer that should be determined upon respecting the deserters; that then he and Vigilius would consult further upon the best mode of executing the design, and that this being settled, Vigilius should come for the money; this, he said, would be better than for him to take the gold with him, seeing that, immediately upon his return, in the first instance, Attila would assuredly interrogate him and his fellows as to whether they had received any presents, and as to how much money the Romans had given them, and that in such case, were he to take the money at once, it would be impossible for him to keep the fact a secret, by reason of his companions. The eunuch admitted the soundness of the barbarian's view of the matter, and acted upon it.

After that Edeco had taken his leave, Chrysaphus repaired to the emperor's privy council, who immediately sent for Martial, the minister of the offices, and communicated to him the agreement entered into with the barbarian; for it was the very nature of his post that he should be made acquainted with the matter, he being on all occasions a confidential adviser of the emperor, and having under his orders all the couriers and interpreters, and all the troops entrusted with the guard of the palace. The emperor and Martial having considered the whole affair, it was determined to send to Attila not only Vigilius, but Maximin also, as ambassador. Vigilius, whose ostensible office was that of interpreter, was to fulfil the directions of Edeco; while Maximin, who knew nothing of the real affair in hand, was to deliver the emperor's letter to Attila.

The emperor's letter was to the effect, that he had sent Vigilius as interpreter, and had selected Maximin as his ambassador, who was superior to Vigilius in rank, being of illustrious birth, and employed about his own person in many affairs; that it was not fitting that Attila, violating treaties, should invade the Roman territory; that he had already sent back to him a great many deserters, and now forwarded seventeen more, being all that remained of those who had come over to him.

Besides these things which were set forth in the letter, Maximin has ordered to ask Attila, by word of mouth, not to request men of higher rank to be sent to him as ambassadors; adding, that the predecessors of the emperor had been accustomed to send to those who heretofore ruled in Scythia, merely one of their soldiers who had become a prisoner of Rome, or any other private messenger who was capable of repeating that which he was told to say. That with reference to the other matters which still kept up dissension between them, he would suggest that Attila should send him Onegeses as an envoy, that it was impossible Attila could properly receive a consular personage in a devastated place like Sardica.

Maximin having, at the earnest request of the emperor, undertaken the proposed embassy, asked me to accompany him, and we departed with the barbarians, and proceeded to Sardica, which is thirteen days rapid march from Constantinople. On our arrival, we invited Edeco and some other principal barbarians to dine with us. Several oxen and sheep furnished by the inhabitants of the place were slaughtered and prepared in various ways, and everything being ready, we sat down to our repast. During the banquet, the barbarians exalted Attila to the skies, and we the emperor. Vigilius imprudently went the length of saying that it was not fitting to compare a man with a god; that the emperor was a god, and Attila only a man. The Huns took this in very ill part, and by degrees became inflamed with the fiercest anger. We endeavoured to turn the conversation, and to appease them by soft words, which we at length succeeded in doing.

On rising from table, Maximin, desirous of conciliating by presents Edeco and Orestes, gave them silk garments and precious stones of India. Orestes, Edeco having withdrawn, said to Maximin that he was the wise and prudent man who took care not to do as so many others did, and who avoided anything that might be offensive to kings. We found out afterwards that some of our people, neglecting Orestes, had invited Edeco to supper, and loaded him with presents. At the time, ignorant of this circumstance, and not understanding what Orestes meant, we asked him how and in what he had been treated displeasingly; but he gave us no answer, and quitted us.

Next day, on continuing our journey, we related to Vigilius what Orestes had said. He observed that the latter had no right to complain of not obtaining the same honours with Edeco; that he was but a servant, a common secretary of Attila, whilst Edeco, a Hun by birth, and famous for his military exploits, far surpassed him in dignity. He then addressed Edeco in the native language of the latter, and afterwards told us, whether it was true or false I know not, that he had repeated to Edeco what we had mentioned. Edeco became so angry that we had great difficulty in tranquillizing him.

On arriving at the town of Naissus, which had been taken and destroyed by the enemy, we found no inhabitants there except a few invalids, who had taken refuge in the ruins of the temples. Proceeding thence into the desert plains at some distance from the river, the banks of which were covered with the bones of those who had been killed during the war, we arrived at the abode of Agintheus, chief of the soldiers of Illyria, who dwelt not far from Naissus. We had with us orders from the emperor for him to deliver up to us five deserters, who were to complete the number of seventeen, mentioned in the letter to Attila. We went to Agintheus and applied for them; and after he had addressed some words of consolation to them, he made them depart with us.

It was scarcely yet day when we crossed the mountains of Naissus towards the Danube. We arrived, after many turnings and windings, in a certain town which was still dark. We thought that our road should turn towards the west; but as soon as it was day, the rising sun presented itself before our eyes. Ignorant of the position of this place, we exclaimed, as if the sun, which we saw in front of us, was following another than its accustomed course, and thus indicated commotion in the regular course of things; but it was because of the inequalities of places that this part of the route turned towards the east.

From this place, by a steep and difficult road, we descended into the swampy plains. There the barbarian boatmen received us in canoes, made of a single piece, which they construct from the trunks of trees cut and scooped out, and they passed us over the river.[1] It was not for our passage that these canoes had been prepared, but for that of a multitude of barbarians whom we met upon the road, for Attila seemed marching to the invasion of the frontiers of the empire, as to a hunting party. Such were the preparations for war against the Romans, and the deserters not yet being given up, merely served as a pretext for commencing it.

After having passed the Danube, and having proceeded with the barbarians the distance of fifteen stadia, they made us stop in a plain, to wait while Edeco went to announce our arrival to Attila.[2] The barbarians who were to be our guides still remained with us. Towards night, while we were at supper, we heard the sound of approaching horses: two Scythian warriors soon appeared, who ordered us to repair to Attila. We invited them first to partake of our supper; they descended from their horses, supped with us, and the next day marched before us to show us the road. About the eighth hour of the day we arrived at the tent of Attila.[3] There were also a large number of others. As we wished to plant ours on a certain hill, the barbarians hastened to prevent us, because those of Attila were placed in a valley on the side. We left them to decide at their will where our tents were to be pitched.

There soon arrived Edeco, Scotta, Orestes, and some other principal Scythians, who demanded with what object we had undertaken this embassy. We mutually looked at each other, astonished at so ridiculous a question. They still insisted, and assembled in a crowd and tumult to force an answer from us. We answered that the emperor had commanded

---

[1] They probably passed the Danube near the small town of *Aquæ*, whose environs, situated between a chain of mountains and the river, must have been marshy; perhaps it was at the confluence of the Marcus with the Danube.

[2] This plain must be in the Bannat of Temeswar; the tents of Attila were, therefore, probably pitched between the Themes and the Danube.

[3] Reckoning an hour's march at a league, their tents would be about nine leagues from the Danube. The great number of boats already prepared upon the Danube for the passage of troops, and the multitude of barbarians whom the ambassadors had met, induce me to believe that they were not, in fact, more distant from it.

us to show our commission to Attila alone, and to none others. Scotta, offended at these words, said that for what he did he had received the order of his chief. "Greeks," cried he, "we well know your craft and your perfidy in affairs." We protested that the obligation had never been imposed upon ambassadors to display the object of their mission before being admitted into the presence of those to whom they were sent.

We added, that the Scythians must needs know it, since they had often sent deputies to the emperor, and that we ought in all respects to enjoy the same rights; that, otherwise, the privileges of ambassadors would be violated. They immediately went to seek Attila, and, returning soon after, but without Edeco, they openly told us all that our orders contained, and enjoined us to depart immediately, if we had nothing further to treat of with them.

These words threw us into great anxiety; we could not conceive how the projects of the emperor, which the gods themselves could not penetrate, had been discovered and revealed; but we thought it best not to show any of our orders until they had allowed us to see Attila. We answered; "Whatever may be the aim of our mission, whether we may have come to treat of what you have just said, or of any other matter, it concerns only your chief, and we are resolved to speak with none but him." They then renewed their order for us to depart immediately.

As we were making our preparations for departure, Vigilius reproached us for the answer which we had just made to the Scythians: "It would have been much better to have lied," said he, "than to return without having done anything. If I had spoken with Attila, I could easily have deterred him from making war against the Romans; I have formerly rendered him many services, and I was very useful to him at the time of the embassy of Anatolius. Edeco is of the same opinion as myself." Whether he spoke true or false, his only object was to profit by the embassy, to find an occasion to make Attila fall into the snare prepared for him, and to carry back the gold which Edeco had said he required to divide among certain warriors. But Vigilius was ignorant that he was betrayed: Edeco, in fact, whether he feared that Orestes would report to Attila what had been said at the supper of Sardica, or accuse him of having secret interviews with the emperor and Chrysaphus, had revealed to Attila the conspiracy against his life, and informed him of the quantity of gold which was to be provided for this design, as well as of all the subjects concerning which we were to treat in our embassy.

Forced, therefore, to return, despite the approach of night, we were getting ready our horses, when the barbarians came to tell me that Attila ordered we should remain, by reason of the night, which opposed our departure. Men immediately came leading an ox to us, and brought us fish of the Danube,[1] which Attila sent us. After having supped, we went to sleep. When day appeared, we hoped that Attila would be softened, and would make

---

[1] The carp of the Danube were celebrated at this epoch, and formed part of the luxury of the tables of the barbarians. Cassiodorus says: *Privati est habere quod locus continet; in principali convivio hoc decet exquiri quod visum debeat admirari. Destinet carpam Danubius, a Rheno veniat ancorago.* (Vari., l. xii. ep. 4.)

us some favourable answer; but the same barbarians came on his part to repeat the order for us to go, if we had no other business to speak of except that with which he was already acquainted. We answered that we had not, and we prepared to retreat, although Vigilius did all he could to get us to say that we had to speak with Attila of things which would much interest him.

As I saw that Maximin was afflicted, I took with me Rusticus, who understood the language of the barbarians: he had accompanied us into Scythia, not because of the embassy, but for some private business which be had with Constantius, an Italian by origin, whom Actius, the general of the western Romans, had sent to Attila as a secretary. I sought Scotta (Onegeses being absent,) and told him, through the medium of Rusticus, that he should receive rich presents from Maximin, if he would procure a safe interview with Attila. I added that the ambassador had to speak of things very advantageous, not only to the Romans, but to the Huns; that his embassy would be very profitable to Onegeses himself, for the emperor requested Attila to send him to his court, to terminate the differences of the two nations, and that he would return loaded with the most magnificent presents. I observed to him, that since Onegeses was absent, he could not do less than his brother would have done in so important an affair. "I know," said I, "that Attila also places great confidence in you; but we cannot reasonably believe all one has heard on this point, and it is for you to prove to us that Attila really bestows such favour upon you." "Rest content," said the barbarian immediately, "whether in speaking or acting, I have as much credit with Attila as my brother," and, mounting his horse, he departed for the camp of Attila.

I returned to Maximin, whom I found with Vigilius, very much troubled and uncertain as to the course he ought to take; I recounted to him the conversation I had just had with Scotta, and what answer he had given me; I then got him to prepare presents to make to this Hun, and to think what he should say to Attila. They immediately arose, (for I had found them lying on the turf,) thanked me for the trouble I had taken, and recalled those of their people who had already commenced their journey; they then discussed between them what Maximin should say to Attila, and how they should give him the presents which he brought for him on the part of the emperor.

While we were occupied with all these things, Attila sent for us by Scotta; we therefore set forward toward his tent, which we found surrounded by a multitude of barbarians, who formed a guard all round it.

When we were allowed to enter, and had been introduced, we saw Attila seated on a wooden chair: we remained at some distance from the throne; Maximin advanced, saluted the barbarian, and giving the letter of the emperor, said that the emperor wished him and all his people health and prosperity. "May that happen to the Romans which they desire for me!" answered the Barbarian; and immediately turning towards Vigilius, he called him an impudent animal, asked him how he dared present himself before him, when he must know what had been settled with reference to peace at the time when he accompanied the embassy of Anatolius, and added, that no other ambassador ought to have approached him until all the deserters had been sent back. Vigilius attempted to reply that they had all been given up, and that there no longer remained one among the Romans; but Attila, becoming more and more heated, loaded him with reproaches and abuse, and raising his voice in fury, told him, that but for his respect for the character of ambassador which restrained his rage, he would have crucified him, and abandoned him to the vultures, to punish him for his audacity and the insolence of his language. He added, there were still many deserters among the Romans; and having a list brought on which their names were written, he ordered his secretaries to read it aloud.

After this reading had made known all who were still wanting, Attila required that Vigilius should immediately set out with Esla to carry an order to the Romans to send him all the Scythian deserters who were still in their power, and who had gone over to them since the time when Carpilion, son of Aetius, general of the western Romans, had remained as hostage in his court. "I will not allow my slaves to bear arms against me," said he; "they shall not be any help to those who pretend to intrust to them the guard of lands which I have conquered. Where, throughout the whole Roman empire, is the city or fortress which can remain whole and erect, when I have decided that it shall be destroyed? After I have proclaimed my will concerning the deserters, let the envoys immediately return to me to announce whether their masters choose to return them, or whether they prefer war."

He had begun by ordering Maximin to await the answer which he should make to the letter of the emperor, but he demanded the presents forthwith. After having given them to him, we retired into our tent, where we conversed in our native tongue upon all that had just been said. As Vigilius was astonished at the abuse with which Attila had loaded him, he who had experienced so much benevolence and kindness from him in his first embassy, I told him I was very much afraid that some of the barbarians who had supped with us at Sardica had irritated Attila by telling him that Vigilius had called the emperor a god and Attila a man. This also appeared probable to Maximin, who was ignorant of the conspiracy formed against the king of the Huns: but Vigilius was in very great anxiety, and could not divine the cause of the abuse and rage of Attila; it was impossible to believe, as he afterwards said to us, that the conversation at the supper at Sardica had been reported to him, or that the conspiracy had been discovered. The fear which had overcome all hearts was such, that, with the exception of Edeco, none who surrounded Attila dare address a word to him; and Vigilius thought that Edeco would only be the more careful to keep everything a profound secret, both on account of the oath which he had taken, and by reason of the gravity of the affair. He would fear, in fact, that the crime of having been present at clandestine councils directed against Attila, would cause him to be treated as guilty, and very severely punished.

While we were a prey to this uneasiness, Edeco came in: he took Vigilius aside, (he indeed feigned a wish to execute seriously and sincerely the project which they had formed); he told him to bring the gold which he was to distribute among those whom he made use of in striking the blow, and then he left us. Curiosity caused us to ask Vigilius what Edeco had just said to him; but, deceived himself, he persisted in deceiving us, and concealing the true subject of their conversation. he pretended that Edeco had reported to him that it was because of the deserters that Attila was so enraged against him; the king of the Huns required, he added, either that they should be given up to him, or that they should send him ambassadors, drawn from among the richest and most powerful men of the empire.

Our conversation was interrupted by people who came, on the part of Attila, to forbid both us and Vigilius to buy any Roman captive, or barbarian slave, or anything whatever, except the necessaries of life, until the differences between the Huns and the Romans were terminated. This prohibition was not without intention: he wished to detect Vigilius in the fact, by leaving him no pretext upon which he could excuse himself for having brought a considerable number of money. He also ordered us to wait for Onegeses, to receive from him the answer to our embassy, and that we ourselves should give him the presents sent by the emperor, and what we wished to have. Onegeses had, in fact, been sent to the Acatzires, with Attila's eldest son. After this order had been given to us, he made Vigilius and Esla set out for Constantinople, under the pretext of again demanding the deserters, but, in fact, with the intention that Vigilius should bring the gold promised to Edeco.

After the departure of Vigilius, we did not remain more than one day in this place; we departed with Attila for more distant places, towards the north. We had proceeded but a very short distance with the barbarians, when we changed the direction, according to the order of the Scythians, our guides.[1] Attila, however, stopped at a certain village, where he took for wife his daughter Esca, although he already had several wives; the laws of the Scythians allow this.[2]

Thence we proceeded across a great plain, over a level and easy road, and

---

[1] Priscus does not say what their new direction was: everything leads to the supposition that it was towards the west, and that in general their route lay almost constantly towards the north-west.

[2] This passage has been the subject of great discussion: the following is the phrase of Priscus: Ἐν ᾗ γαμειν θυγατερα Εσκαμ ἐβουλετο. The sense which naturally presents itself is: "where he willed to espouse his daughter Esca." Still the *his* is wanting, and it would seem as though Priscus ought to have put ἑαυτου. Some learned men have inferred from this, that it was not his daughter whom Attila married, but that it was the daughter of Esca, and that it must be read, θυγατερα του Εσκαμ; they have remarked, and with reason, that the Greeks almost always made the proper names of barbarians, with which they were imperfectly acquainted, indeclinable; that if Attila had married his own daughter, Priscus would not have failed to insist upon the irregularity of such a marriage; and the desire to clear Attila from the crime of incest has made them regard this conjecture as certain. It is possibly well founded; still they cannot dispute that the following phrase of Priscus: "The laws of the Scythians allow this," relates to Attila having married his daughter, as well as to the plurality of his wives; and moreover, historical testimony does not allow us to doubt but that, among a large number of barbarous nations, it was allowable for a man to marry his daughter; that of Saint Jerome is positive: *Persæ, Medi, Indi, et Æthiopes, regna non modica, et Romano regno paria, cum matribus et aviis, cum filiabus et nepotibus copulantur.* (Lib. ii. *Adv. Jovinianum.*) Why should not the Huns have done the same?

we met with many navigable rivers; the largest, after the Danube, are called the Drecon, the Tigas, and the Tiphisas. We crossed the most considerable upon boats of a single piece, which those who inhabit the banks of the river make use of; the others we crossed in canoes which the barbarians always have with them; for they carry them on chariots, to make use of upon ponds and inundated places. They brought us provisions from the villages, *millet* instead of wheat; *mead* instead of wine; it is thus that the inhabitants call them. Those who accompanied us to serve us, brought *millet*, and gave us a kind of drink made from barley, which the barbarians call *cam*.

At the approach of night, after a rather long journey, we set up our tents upon the borders of a morass, whence the inhabitants of the neighbouring villages drew their water, which was very good to drink: but a violent hurricane, mixed with lightning, thunder, and rain, suddenly arising, our tent was overthrown, and our utensils thrown into the morass. Alarmed with this fall and with the storm, we abandoned the place; we dispersed ourselves, and each at hazard took the road which seemed best to him, amidst darkness and rain. Arrived at last, from different directions, at the huts of the village, we assembled and demanded with loud cries what we wanted. On this noise, the Scythians came out: they lighted the reeds which serve them for torches, and asked what we wanted, and why we raised such cries? the barbarians who accompanied us, answered that we had been dispersed and had lost our way in the tempest: they then granted us a generous hospitality, and made us a fire with dry reeds.

The mistress of the village, one of the wives of Bleda, sent us nourishment and beautiful women. This among the Scythians is looked upon as an honour. We thanked the women for the provisions which they had brought us, and we slept in our huts, without availing ourselves of the latter present of their queen. When it was day, we set about seeking for the moveables and travelling utensils which we had lost; we found part of them in the place where we had stopped in the evening, and a part on the borders of the morass or in the morass itself: the storm had ceased, the sun had risen brilliantly, and we passed the whole day in the village, drying our things. After having taken care of our horses and other beasts of burden, we went to salute the queen, and, not wishing to be inferior in generosity to the barbarians who had received us so well, we gave her silver cups, red woollen garments, Indian pepper, dates and other dry fruit: after wishing all kind of prosperity to the inhabitants of the village, in return for the hospitality which had been accorded us, we proceeded on our way.

After a march of six days, the Scythians, our guides, ordered us to stop at a certain village, in order that we might continue our route in the train of Attila, who was going to pass that way; we here met the ambassadors whom the western Romans had sent to him; the principal were: Romulus, invested with the title of count, Primutus, prefect of Norica, and Romanus, chief of a body of troops. With them were Constantius, whom Ætius had sent to Attila for a secretary, and Tatullus, father of Orestes, the colleague of Edeco; the latter had accompanied them not because of the embassy, but out of friendship, and by reason of their own affairs. Constantius had become united with them during his sojourn in Italy, and family reasons had determined Tatullus; his son, Orestes, had taken for wife the daughter of Romulus of Petovio, a city of Norica.

These ambassadors had been endeavouring to soften Attila, who had demanded that they should give him up Sylvanus, prefect of the imperial plate of Rome, because he had received some gold cups which had been sent to him by a certain Constantius. This Constantius, a native of western Gaul, had been given to Attila and to Bleda for a secretary, in the same way as, at a later period, another Constantius was. This man then, at the time when the town of Sirmium, in Pannonia, was besieged by the Scythians, had received some gold vases from the bishop of the city; the bishop wished, that if he survived the taking of the town, the value of these vases should be employed for his ransom, and that, if he died, this money should serve to deliver the captive citizens; but Constantius, after the ruin of the town, without troubling himself as to the results of the siege, repaired to Italy on business, gave the vases to Sylvanus, received the price of them, and it was arranged between them that if Constantius repaid the capital and interest of this money within a fixed time, the vases should be returned to him; that, in the contrary case, Sylvanus should keep and use them as his own. Attila and Bleda, suspecting this Constantius of treason, had him crucified; and Attila, informed of the affair of the cups of gold, demanded that they should give up Sylvanus to him, as having stolen property belonging to him. Aetius and the emperor of the western Romans sent deputies to him, to tell him that Sylvanus had not stolen these vases, that he was the creditor of Constantius, that he had received them in pledge for the sum lent, and had sold them to the first priest who wished to buy them, seeing that it was not permitted to laymen to make use of cups consecrated to God. They were to add, in case such good reasons and respect for God did not prevent Attila from persisting in again demanding the cups, that Sylvanus would send him the price of them, but they could not give up a man who had done no wrong.

Such was the object of the mission of these deputies, who were following the barbarian in order to obtain an answer and then return.

As we were to march by the same route as Attila, we waited for him to go before us, and we followed him at a short distance with the rest of the barbarians. After having crossed some rivers, we arrived at a large town; here was the house of Attila, much higher and more beautiful than any of the other houses of his empire; it was made of highly polished planks, and surrounded with a palisade of wood, not by way of fortification, but as an ornament.

The house nearest, to the king's was that of Onegeses, also surrounded with a palisade of wood, but it was neither so high nor furnished with towers like that of Attila. At some distance from the enclosure of the house was situated the bath which Onegeses, the richest and most powerful of the Scythians next to Attila, had had constructed with stones brought from Pannonia; there was, indeed, in this part of Scythia, neither stones nor large trees, and it was necessary to get materials elsewhere. The architect who had constructed this bath, made prisoner at Sirmium, had hoped that liberty would be the reward of his labour, but this sweet hope was utterly deceived; he was cast, on the contrary, into a far still harder servitude; Onegeses made him his bather, and he waited on him and all his family when they went to the bath.

When Attila arrived at this village, young girls came to meet him; they walked in a file, under pieces of fine white linen, held up on either side by many ranks of women, and so well held out, that, under each piece, walked six virgins, or even more: they sang barbarous songs.

We were already close to the house of Onegeses, past which the road leading to that of the king went, when his wife came out, followed by a multitude of women slaves, who brought meats and wine, which is regarded among the Scythians as the greatest honour. She saluted Attila, and prayed him to taste her meats, which she presented to him with the most lively protestations of her devotion. The king, to give a mark of his good-will towards the wife of his confidant, eat upon his horse. The barbarians who escorted him held the table, which was of silver, up to him. After having dipped his lips into the cup which they offered him, he entered his palace, which was much more conspicuous than any of the other houses, and stood upon an eminence.

As for us, we remained in the house of Onegeses, according to the orders of the latter, who had returned with the son of Attila; we were received by his wife and by the other illustrious chiefs of his family, and we supped there. Onegeses could not remain with us and enjoy himself at table, because he had to give an account to Attila of what he had done in his mission, and of the accident which had happened to his son, who had dislocated his right wrist; this was the first time he had presented himself before the king of the Huns since his return.

After supper, we quitted the house of Onegeses, and pitched our tents nearer to the palace of Attila, in order that Maximin, who was to have an interview with that prince, and to converse with those who acted as his council, might thus be as little distant as possible. There we passed the night.

When day appeared, Maximin sent me to Onegeses to carry him the presents which he himself offered and those which the emperor sent him, and to ask him when and where he could have a conversation. I therefore repaired to Onegeses, with the slaves who carried the presents; the doors were closed, and I was obliged to wait till they were opened, and until some came out who could inform him of my arrival.

While I passed the time in walking round the enclosure of the house of Onegeses, some one advanced whom I at first took for a barbarian of the Scythian army, and who saluted me in Greek, saying to me, Χαίρε. I was surprised that a Scythian should speak Greek, for the barbarians, shut up in their own manners, cultivate and speak none but barbarous languages, that of the Huns or that of the Goths; those who have much commercial intercourse with the Romans also speak Latin; none of them speak Greek, with the exception of the captive refugees in Thrace or in maritime Illyria; but when we meet with these latter, they are easily recognised by their wretched clothing and pale faces, signs of the ill fortune into which they have fallen. This man, on the contrary, had the air of a happy and rich Scythian; he was elegantly clothed, and had his head shaved round: saluting him in return, I asked him who he was, from whence he came into the country of the barbarians, and why he had adopted the customs of the Scythians? "You are, then, anxious to know?" said he. "My reason for asking," I answered, "is, that you spoke Greek." He then told me, smiling, that he was a Greek by birth, that he had established himself with a view to commerce, at Viminacium, a town of Mœsia on the Danube, that he had long remained there, and had there married a rich wife; but that, at the taking of the town, all his fortune vanished, and that in the subdivision of booty his goods and himself had fallen to Onegeses. It is, indeed, the custom among the Scythians, for the principal chiefs, after Attila, to put aside the richest captives and share them afterwards. My Greek had afterwards courageously fought against the Romans; he had assisted in subjecting the nation of the Acatzires to his barbarous master, and, according to the Scythian laws, he obtained liberty as a reward, with the possession of all which he had acquired in war; he had married a barbarian wife, by whom he had children; he was the companion of Onegeses, and his new mode of life appeared to him far preferable to the old. In fact, those who remain among the Scythians, after having supported the fatigues of war, pass their life without any trouble; each enjoys the property that fate has granted him, and no one interferes with or troubles him in any way whatever.....

While we thus conversed, one of the domestics of Onegeses opened the gates. I hastened towards him, and asked for Onegeses; I added, that I had to speak with him on the part of Maximin, the ambassador from the Romans: he answered, that if I waited a little, I might soon see him, for he was going out; shortly afterwards, indeed, I saw Onegeses advancing; I went towards him, saying, "The ambassador from the Romans salutes you, and I bring you presents on his part, as well as the gold sent you by the emperor." As I tried to ask him when and where he would converse with us, he ordered his people to take the gold and presents, and told me to inform Maximin that he would repair to him soon.

I therefore returned to tell Maximin that Onegeses was about to visit him; almost immediately afterwards he arrived at our tent, and, addressing himself to the ambassador, thanked him for the gifts of the emperor and his own, asking him what he wished, since he had required him to come Maximin answered him, that the time approached when he might acquire great glory, by repairing to the emperor, terminating the contentions of the Huns and the Romans, and by his wisdom establishing a solid peace between the two nations; a peace which would not only be very advantageous to them, but which would be of so much value to him and to all his people, as his family would then experience an eternal gratitude from the emperor and all the imperial race. Onegeses then asked how he could render himself agreeable to the emperor and terminate these contests: Maximin answered him that he had but to take part in the present affairs, go to thank the emperor, carefully study the causes of discord, and interpose his credit to arrange the differences, according to the conditions of treaties. "But," said Onegeses, "I long since informed the emperor and his councillors of the will of Attila concerning this affair: do the Romans think that their intreaties will induce me to betray my master, and to hold no reckoning of the advantages which I have found among the Scythians for my wives and children? Is it not better to serve with Attila, than to enjoy the greatest riches with the Romans? As to the rest, I shall be much more useful to them in remaining at home, in calming and softening the rage of my master, if he is forming any violent project against the empire, than by repairing to Constantinople, and exposing myself to suspicions, if I were to do anything which appears contrary to the interest of Attila." At these words, thinking that I should be charged to converse with him, upon what we desired to learn, (such an interview little suiting the dignity with which Maximin was invested,) he withdrew.

The next day, I went into the interior inclosure of the house of Attila, to carry presents to his wife, who was called Creca: he had three children by her; the eldest already reigned over the Acatzires, and the other nations which inhabited Scythia, around the Pontus Euxinus. Within this enclosure, there were many edifices, partly constructed of carved planks, elegantly arranged: partly of uncarved beams, well formed with the adze, and polished, with round pieces of wood mixed with them; the circles which united them, rising from the ground, were elevated and distributed, according to certain proportions. Here lived the wife of Attila. The barbarians who guarded the gates allowed me to enter, and I found her lying on a soft couch the floor was ornamented with carpet, upon which we walked: numerous slaves surrounded her in a circle; and opposite to her, maid servants, seated on the ground, were making piece work, composed of linen of various colours, which the barbarians wear over their dress as ornaments.

After having saluted Creca, and offered her the presents, I withdrew; and, while waiting for Onegeses to return from the palace, whither he had already repaired, I went through the other buildings of the enclosure where Attila dwelt. While I was there, with many other persons, (as I was known to the guards of Attila and the barbarians of his train, they allowed me to go everywhere,) I saw a numerous crowd advancing in tumult, and with a great noise. Attila came out with a grave air: all eyes were directed towards him; Onegeses accompanied him, and he seated himself before his house. Many people who had causes approached him, and he delivered judgments upon them. He then re-entered his palace, where he received deputies from barbarian nations, who had come to seek him.

While I waited for Onegeses, Romulus, Promutus, and Romanus, the deputies who came from Italy about the affair of the gold vases, Rusticus, who was in the train of Constantius, and Constantiolus, a native of Pannonia, then under Attila, spoke to me, and asked me if we had received our dismissal. "It is to know this of Onegeses," said I, "that I wait in this enclosure." I asked, in my turn, whether they had obtained any favourable answer concerning the object of their mission. "Not at all," answered they; "it is impossible to change Attila's determination; he threatens war, unless they give him up Sylvanus."

As we were expressing our mutual astonishment at the intractable pride of the barbarian, Romulus, a man of great experience, and who had been charged with many very honourable missions, said to us: "This pride arises from his happy fortune, which has placed him in a rank so elevated; his fortune gives him great power, and he is so inflated with it, that reason has no access to him, and he only thinks that just which he has once taken into his head; none of those who have reigned, whether in Scythia or elsewhere, have done such great things in so short a time; he has subdued all Scythia, he has extended his dominion to the islands of the ocean, he has made the Romans his tributaries; not content with this, he meditates still greater enterprises; he still wishes to drive back the frontiers of his empire, and he is preparing to attack the Persians."

One of us asked what road led from Scythia to Persia; Romulus answered that the country of the Medes was situated not very far from that of the Scythians, and that the Huns knew the road well, having often gone it. During the ravages made in their country by a famine, and the tranquillity in which the Romans, occupied elsewhere, left them, Basich and CurRich, warriors of the royal family of the Scythians, and chiefs of numerous troops, had penetrated into the country of the Medes; these chiefs, lately come to

Rome to treat for an alliance, related that they had journeyed across a desert country, that they had traversed a morass, which Romulus believed to be the Palus-Meotis, and that after fifteen days, after having ascended certain mountains, they descended into Medea; that there, while they were pillaging and making incursions in the country, there suddenly came a Persian army, which darkened the air with its arrows; that at the sight of such danger, they had retired, repassed the mountains, and brought but a small part of their booty, because the Medes had regained the greater portion; that to avoid the shock of the enemy, they had taken another route, had crossed places strewn with marine stones which burnt,[1] and at last arrived at their native country after a journey, the duration of which Romulus could not recollect: it was easy to see from this that Scythia was not very far from the country of the Medes.

Romulus added, that if, in consequence, the idea of attacking the Medes seized upon Attila, the invasion would cost him neither much care nor fatigue, and that he would not have a long road to take in order to fall upon the Medes, the Parthians, and the Persians, and oblige them to pay him tribute. He had such an immense number of troops, that no nation could resist him. We then set about forming the wish that Attila might attack the Persians and thus turn the weight of the war from us. "It is to be feared," said Constantiolus, "that the Persians once conquered, he will treat the Romans not as a friend but as a master. Now we send him gold, because of the dignity with which we ourselves have invested him; but if he subjugates the Medes, the Parthians, and the Persians, he will no longer spare the Romans, who form, on this side, the boundaries of his empire; he will regard them as his slaves, and will force them to obey his terrible and insupportable will."

The dignity of which Constantiolus spoke, was that of general of the Roman armies, an honour which Attila had received from the emperor, receiving at the same time the salary attached to this title. Constantiolus thought that Attila would without scruple violate the duties of this dignity, or of any other with which it might please the Romans to invest him, and that he would force them to give him the name of king instead of that of general. Already, when he was out of humour, he said that the generals of his armies were his slaves, and that his generals, in his eyes, were the equals of the Roman emperors.

The discovery of the sword of Mars had greatly added to his power. This sword, formerly worshipped by the kings of the Scythians, as being sacred to the god of war, had disappeared for many centuries, and had just been again found on the occasion of the wounding an ox. While we discussed the matter rather eagerly, Onegeses came out; we approached and asked him concerning the affairs with which we were charged. After conversing with some barbarians he told me to ask Maximin what consular personage the Romans proposed to send to Attila. I returned to our tent, and related to Maximin what Onegeses had just said to me; we deliberated upon what answer to make to the barbarians. I then returned to Onegeses

---

[1] These stones were the bitumen which abounds upon the borders of the sea of Azof and the Black Sea.

and told that the Romans eagerly desired that he should repair to Rome, and that he should be charged with arranging their differences with Attila; but that if they were deceived in this hope, the emperor would send whatever ambassador he pleased. He ordered me immediately to fetch Maximin; and directly he came he conducted him to Attila. Maximin returning soon after, told us that the barbarian declared that he positively willed the emperor to send him as an ambassador, Nomius or Anatolius, and that he would receive no other. Maximin observed to him that it was not proper to make the deputies who should be sent to him suspected of the emperor, by designating them, but Attila answered that if the Romans refused him he would terminate the quarrel by taking arms.

We had scarcely entered our tent when the father of Orestes came to say: "Attila invites you both to a banquet which is to take place about the ninth hour of the day." At the hour mentioned, we repaired to the invitation, and in company with the ambassadors of the western Romans we presented ourselves before the entry of the hall in front of Attila; there, the cup-bearers, according to the usage of the country, presented us a cup, in order that, before sitting down, we should offer libations; after having performed this, and having tasted of the cup, we occupied the seats upon which we were to sup.

Seats were prepared on each side the hall, along the walls; in the midst was Attila, upon a couch, opposite to which was another couch, and behind that the steps of a staircase which led to where this prince slept. This couch was ornamented with cloths of various colours, and resembled those which the Romans and the Greeks prepare for married people. It was then arranged that the first rank of guests should seat themselves on the right of Attila, and the second rank on the left; we were placed in the second rank with Berich, a very considerable warrior among the Scythians, but Berich was above us. Onegeses occupied the first seat on the right of the king, and opposite him were two of the sons of Attila; the eldest lay upon the same couch as his father, not by his side but below him, and he always kept his eyes cast down out of respect for his father.

Every one being seated, Attila's cup-bearer presented him a cup of wine; on receiving it, Attila saluted him who occupied the first place. At this honour the latter immediately arose: he was not allowed to re-seat himself until Attila, tasting the cup, or emptying the contents, had returned it to the cup-bearer. Attila, on the contrary, remained seated, while the guests, each receiving a cup in his turn, gave him homage, by saluting him and tasting the wine. Each guest had a cup-bearer, who took his place after Attila's had gone. All the guests were honoured in the same manner; Attila, when it came to our turn, saluted us in the manner of the Thracians. After these ceremonies of politeness, the cup-bearers retired.

By the side of Attila's table were prepared four other tables, made to receive three or four, or even more guests, each of whom, without disarranging the order of seats, could take upon plates with his knife whatever he pleased. In the middle, first the servant of Attila came forward, carrying a dish full of meat, then those who were to serve the other guests covered the tables with bread and meats. There had been prepared for the barbarians, and for us, meats and ragouts of all kinds, and they served them to us upon plates of silver, but Attila had only a wooden plate, and eat nothing but plain meat.

In all things he showed the same simplicity: the guests drank from cups of gold and silver; Attila had only a wooden cup; his clothes were very simple, and were only distinguished from the other barbarians because they were of one colour, and were without ornaments; his sword, the cords of his shoes, the reins of his horse, were not like those of the other Scythians, decorated with plates of gold or precious stones.

When the meats served in the first plates were eaten, we arose, and no one again sat down until he had drank a full cup of wine to the health and prosperity of Attila, according to the forms which I have just described. After rendering him this homage, we re-seated ourselves. They then brought to every table fresh plates with other meats; and when each was satisfied, we arose, again drank as at first, and again sat down

On the approach of night the meats were taken away; two Scythians advanced, and recited before Attila verses of their own composition, in which they sang of his victories and warlike virtues. The attention of all the guests was fixed upon them; some were charmed by the verses, others were excited by the description of battles; tears flowed down the cheeks of those whose strength had been worn away by age, and who could therefore no longer satisfy their thirst for war and glory. After these barbarian songs were ended, a buffoon came and went through all sorts of extravagances and ridiculous gesticulations and sayings, which made those present laugh heartily

The last person who came in was the Moor, Zercho: Edeco had told him to come to Attila, and promised to employ all his influence to have his wife brought to him; the Moor had married but some years before in Scythia, where he enjoyed great favour with Bleda, but on quitting that country had left her behind him. When Attila sent the woman as a gift to Aetius, Zercho at first hoped to see her again; but this hope had been frustrated by reason that Attila had been angry at his returning into his own country. Availing himself of the occasion of this festival, the Moor again sought permission to have his wife brought to him, and his face, his demeanour, his pronunciation, and his strange mixture of Hunnish, Latin, and Gothic words, excited such mirth and transports of joyousness, that the shouts of laughter on all sides appeared undistinguishable.[1]

Attila alone preserved an unaltered visage; he was grave and motionless; he neither said nor did anything indicating the slightest disposition to participate in the merriment around him; the only change that we observed in him was, that when his youngest son, named Irnach, was brought in, he looked at him with eyes of affection and pleasure, and patted him on the cheek. I was wondering why Attila paid so little attention to his other children, and seemed only to care for this one, when a barbarian, who sat next to me, and who spoke Latin, after having made me promise that I would not repeat what he was about to say to me, told me that the

[1] Is it not singular to find an harlequin at the court of Attila? yet such is the origin of these buffoons. The colour of the black slaves, the strangeness of their face and manners, caused them to be sought after by the barbarians as excellent ministers of mirth; to complete the singularity, Zercho asks his wife at the hands of Attila, closely paralleling harlequin demanding columbine.

diviners had predicted to Attila that all his race would perish except this boy, who would once more restore it.

As the banquet seemed likely to be extended to a late hour of the night, and as we did not wish to remain drinking any longer, we withdrew.

Next day we went to Onegeses, to tell him that we desired to be dismissed, not wishing to lose any more time; he replied, that such also was the intention of Attila, who had determined upon our departure. He then held a council of the principal chiefs upon the subject of the resolution which had been formed by Attila, and drew up the letter which we were to carry to the emperor. He had with him his corresponding secretaries, and among them Rusticus, a native of Upper Mœsia, who, having been made prisoner by the barbarians, had been raised to this post in consequence of his talent for composition.

After the council, we entreated Onegeses to restore to liberty the wife and children of Sylla, who had been reduced to slavery at the taking of Ratiaria; he was not indisposed to grant our request on our paying a considerable ransom. We earnestly supplicated him to be merciful, in consideration of their former condition, and of their present misery. At length, as he was taking his leave, Onegeses granted us the liberty of the woman for 500 *aurii*, and made the emperor a present of that of his sons.

Meantime Recca, the wife of Attila, who superintended his domestic affairs, had sent to invite us to supper.[1] We accordingly proceeded to her apartments, and found her surrounded by a great number of Scythian chiefs; she overwhelmed us with kindness, and gave us a magnificent banquet. Each of the guests rose, presented to us a cupful of wine, and kissed us on the forehead in taking it back, which among the Scythians is a mark of great good will. After supper, we retired to our tents for the night.

Next day Attila invited us to another banquet: the same ceremonies were observed as on the first occasion, and we diverted ourselves very much; this day it was not the eldest son of Attila who was seated on the same couch with the chief, but his uncle Ocbar, whom Attila regarded in the light of a father.

Throughout the banquet Attila conversed with us in the kindest manner; he ordered Maximin to induce the emperor to give to his secretary Constantius the wife he had promised him. This Constantius had gone to Constantinople with the deputies of Attila, and had offered his services in maintaining peace between the Romans and the Huns, in consideration of a rich wife being given him; the emperor had consented to this, and had promised him the daughter of Saturnillus, a man of noble family and large fortune; but Athenais, or Eudoxia (the empress went by both these names), put Saturnillus to death, and Zen, a consular personage, prevented the emperor from fulfilling his promise. This Zen, at the head of a numerous body of Isaurians, was at that time guarding the city of Constantinople, menaced by war, and had, besides, the general command of the armies of the east; he withdrew the young girl from the prison in which she had been placed, and gave her to one Rufus, a relative of his. Thus disappointed in his marriage,

---

[1] The learned have warmly discussed the question whether this Recca was the same with that wife of Attila of whom Priscus has already spoken, and whom he then named Creca.

Constantius had earnestly entreated Attila not to suffer the affront which had been put upon him, to pass, but to insist upon a wife being given him: either the one just snatched from him, or some other woman with a rich dowry: accordingly, during supper, the barbarian desired Maximin to tell the emperor that Constantius was not to be disappointed of his hopes, and that it was contrary to the dignity of an emperor to be a liar; Attila took this interest in the matter because Constantius had promised him a large sum of money in the event of his obtaining by the barbarian's influence a rich Roman wife.

On the approach of night we withdrew from the banquet.

Three days afterwards we were dismissed, after having received a present each of us. Attila sent with us, as his ambassador, Berich, one of the lead ing Scythian chiefs, lord of many villages in that country, and who, at the banquet, had been placed on the same side of the table with us, and, indeed, above us. Berich had before this been received as ambassador at Constantinople.

On our way, as we were entering a certain village, the barbarians who accompanied us part of the road, took prisoner a Scythian who was acting as spy for the Romans. Attila ordered him to be crucified. Next day, again, as we were passing through another village, there were brought to us, their hands tied behind their backs, two slaves, who had killed those whom the fortune of war had rendered masters of their life and death; their heads were fastened between two pieces of wood, and they were then cruci fied.

Berich, so long as we journeyed in Scythia, travelled with us, and treated us with kindness; but no sooner had we passed the Danube, than he became an enemy, upon some miserable pretexts furnished by our servants. He began by taking from Maximin the horse he had given him; Attila had required all the Scythian chiefs who accompanied him to make presents to Maximin, and they had all offered him horses, Berich among the rest: but Maximin, wishing to show his moderation, had refused most of these offers, accepting only two or three horses. Berich now took the one he had given him, and moreover, would no longer converse with us, nor even follow the same route. Thus, this pledge of an hospitality contracted in the country of the barbarians themselves, was withdrawn. We proceeded to Adrianopolis through Philippolis, and stopped for a while to repose ourselves; while there, we addressed Berich, who had also reached the city, and asked why he so pertinaciously observed silence towards men who had given him no offence. He was pacified by our words, accepted an invitation to supper, and we departed the next day from Adrianopolis in company together.

On our way, we met Vigilius, who was returning to Scythia, and after informing him of the manner in which Attila had received us, continued our journey. On arriving at Constantinople, we thought that Berich had altogether forgotten his anger, but our kindness and courtesy had not overcome his naturally fierce and vindictive disposition; he accused Maximin of having said that the generals Areobindus and Aspar enjoyed no credit with the emperor, and that since he had become acquainted with the frivolous and unstable character of the barbarians, he had no faith whatever in their alleged exploits.

IV.

Chronological Table of the Principal Events of the Political History of Gaul, from the Fifth to the Tenth Century.

A.D.	
406—412	General invasion of the Germans into the empire of the west, and especially into Gaul.
411—413	Establishment of the Burgundians in eastern Gaul.
412—419	Establishment of the Visigoths in southern Gaul.
418—430	Establishment of the Franks in Belgium and northern Gaul.
451	Invasion of Attila into Gaul. His defeat in the plains of Châlons in Champagne.
476	Definitive fall of the empire of the west.
481—511	Reign of Clovis. Establishment of the kingdom of the Franks. Their conquests in eastern, western, and southern Gaul.
27 Nov. 511	Death of Clovis. Division of his domains and states between his four sons.
523—534	Wars between the Franks and the Burgundians. Fall of the kingdom of the latter.
558—561	Clotaire I., fourth son of Clovis, sole king of the Franks.
587	Treaty of Andélot, between Goutran, king of Burgundy, and Childebert II., king of Metz.
613—628	Clotaire II., son of Chilperic I., and of Fredegonde, sole king of the Franks.
628—714	Progressive elevation of the family of the Pepins among the Austrasian Franks.
656—687	Struggle between the Franks of Neustria and the Franks of Austrasia.
687	Battle of Testry. Triumph of the Austrasian Franks.
715—741	Government of the Franks by Charles Martel.
714—732	Invasion and progress of the Arabs in southern and western Gaul.
Oct. 732	They are defeated near Tours, by Charles Martel.
1st Oct. 741	Death of Charles Martel. Division of Gaul between his sons, Pepin and Carloman.
747	Carloman enters a monastery. Pepin sole chief of the Franks.
752	Childeric III., last of the Merovingian kings, is deposed. Pepin, surnamed Le Bref, is declared king of the Franks, and crowned at Soissons by Winfried (Saint Boniface) archbishop of Mayence.
754	Pope Stephen II., who visits France, again crowns Pepin and his family.
754, 755	Pepin makes war in Italy against the Lombards. His alliance with the popes.
750—759	The wars of Pepin in southern Gaul against the Saracens. He makes himself master of Septimania.

A.D.	
745—768	The wars of Pepin in the south-west of Gaul, against the Aquitani. He seizes upon Aquitaine.
Sept. 768	Death of Pepin. Division of his states between his two sons, Charles and Carloman.
771	Death of Carloman. Charlemagne sole king of the Franks.
769	Expedition of Charlemagne against the Aquitani.
772 774—776 778—780 782—785 794—796 797—798 802 804	Expeditions of Charlemagne against the Saxons.
773—774	Expeditions of Charlemagne against the Lombards.
776	He defeats their kings, and possesses himself of their states.
787 801	Expeditions of Charlemagne against the Lombards of Benevento.
778 796—797 801 806, 807 809, 810 812	Expeditions of Charlemagne against the Arabs of Spain, Italy, Sardinia, &c.
788, 789 791 796 805 812	Expeditions of Charlemagne against the Slaves and the Avares in eastern Europe.
	Relations of Charlemagne with the emperors of the east.
24 Oct. 800	Charlemagne enters Rome.
25 Dec. 800	He is proclaimed emperor of the west.
801	Embassy of Haroun-al-Raschid to Charlemagne.
806	Charlemagne divides his states between his three sons, Charles, Pepin, and Louis.
808—814	The Normans begin to ravage the coasts of Frankish-Gaul.
21 Jan. 814	Death of Charlemagne.
816	Coronation of Louis le Debonnaire, at Reims, by Pope Stephen IV.
817	Louis associates with himself his son Lothaire, and gives to his two youngest sons, Pepin and Louis, the kingdoms of Aquitaine and Bavaria.
828—833	Intrigues and revolts of the sons of Louis le Debonnaire against their father.
1 Oct. 833	The assembly of Compiegne meet to degrade Louis.
2 Nov. 833	Public penance and degradation of Louis at Soissons.
835	The assembly of Thionville annuls the acts of that of Compiegne.
838	The assembly of Kiersy-sur-Oise, when Louis deprives his eldest sons, Lothaire and Louis, in favour of the youngest, Charles le Chauve.

A.D.	
30 May, 839	Louis le Debonnaire is reconciled with his son Lothaire. New division of the empire between Lothaire and Charles le Chauve.
20 June, 840	Death of Louis le Debonnaire.
840—843	War between the sons of Louis le Debonnaire.
29 June, 841	Battle of Fontenay.
843	Treaty of Verdun. Definitive division of the empire.
862—877	Charles le Chauve reunites successively a great part of the states of Charlemagne.
25 Dec 875	He is crowned emperor at Rome.
877	He acknowledges in the assembly of Kiersy-sur Oise, the right to the hereditary possession of fees and royal offices.
6 Oct. 877	Death of Charles le Chauve.
836—877	Continued and augmenting invasions of the Saracens, and of the Normans, in Frankish Gaul.
877—879	Reign of Louis le Begue, son of Charles le Chauve.
10 April, 879	Death of Louis le Begue.
879—882	Reigns of Louis III. and Carloman, sons of Louis le Begue.
5 Aug. 882	Death of Louis III.
882—884	Reign of Carloman.
6 Dec. 884	Death of Carloman.
884—888	Reign of Charles le Gros.
885—886	The Normans besiege Paris during one year.
12 Jan. 888	Death of Charles le Gros.
887—898	Reign of Eudes, count of Paris, son of Robert le Fort, elected king during the life of Charles.
877—888	Formation of a number of independent lordships.
28 Jan. 893	Coronation of Charles le Simple, son of Louis le Begue.
1 Jan. 898	Death of king Eudes.
893—929	Reign of Charles le Simple.
911	By the treaty of Clair-sur-Esste, he gives to Rollo, a Norman chief, that part of Neustria which has since taken the name of Normandy.
922	Robert, duke of France, brother to king Eudes, is elected king.
15 June, 923	He is killed near Soissons in a battle with Charles le Simple.
923	Raoul, or Rodolph, duke of Burgundy, is elected king of France.
923—929	Captivity of Charles le Simple in the hands of Herbert, count of Vermandois. He is set at liberty for a time, but soon imprisoned again.
7 Oct. 929	Death of Charles le Simple.
15 Jan. 936	Death of king Raoul.
936—954	Reign of Louis IV., surnamed d'Outre-Mer, son of Charles le Simple. He is sometimes friendly, sometimes hostile; on one hand with the emperor Otho I., master of eastern France, on the other with the independent lords of central and western France.
10 Sept. 954	Death of Louis d'Outre Mer.
954—986	Reign of Lothaire, son of Louis. His wars with Otho II.
2 Mar. 986	Death of Lothaire.

A.D.	
986, 987	Reign of Louis V., son of Lothaire.
21 May, 987	Death of Louis V.
3 July, 987	Hugh Capet, count of Paris, is crowned king of France, at Reims.

V.

Chronological Table of the Principal Events of the Religious History of Gaul, from the Fifth to the Tenth Century.

A.D.	
11 Nov. 400	Death of St. Martin, archbishop of Tours.
400—407	Writings of Vigilantius, priest, against the relics of the martyrs, and some other practices of the church. Answered by St. Jerome.
400—420	Foundation of monasteries in southern Gaul; amongst others, those of St. Victor, at Marseilles, and of Lerens.
418	St. Germain, bishop of Auxerre.
420	The Burgundians embrace arianism.
423	Birth of semi-Pelagianism in southern Gaul. St. Augustin combats it.
428	St. Loup, bishop of Troyes.
429	A numerous council. Place uncertain.[1]
—	St. Hilary, bishop of Arles.
441	Council of Orange.
450	Contest between the bishops of Arles and Vienna, upon the extent of their metropolitan jurisdiction.
452	Council of Arles.
455	Council of Arles.
462	Faust, bishop of Riez; his discussion with Claudienus Mamertius, upon the nature of the soul; he is accused of semi-Pelagianism; he writes against the predestinarians.
470	Institution of the Rogations by St. Mamertius, bishop of Vienne.
472	St. Sidonius Apollinaris, bishop of Clermont.
475	Council of Arles.
490	St. Avitus, bishop of Vienne.
496	Clovis embraces Christianity.
499	Conference held at Lyons, in the presence of Gondebaud, king of Burgundy, between the Catholic and Arian bishops.
501	St. Cesaire, bishop of Arles.
506	Council of Agde.
510	Sigismond, a Burgundian prince, abandons Arianism.

---

[1] I only indicate in this table the principal councils, without mentioning their object. The seventh table is especially devoted to the history of the councils and canonical legislation of Gaul at this period.

A.D.	
511	Council of Orleans.
517	Council of Epaone, in the diocese of Vienne.
529	Council of Orange.
—	Council of Vaison.
533	Council of Orleans.
538	Council of Orleans.
541	Council of Orleans.
543	Introduction of the rule of St. Benedict into Gaul. Reform and progress of monasteries. Monastic life receives the name of *religio*.
549	Council of Orleans.
554	Council of Arles.
555	St. Germain, bishop of Paris
557	Council of Paris.
573	St. Gregory, bishop of Tours
—	St. Senoch, and several other hermits, render themselves celebrated by their austerities.
576	Childebert II., king of Austrasia, obliges the Jews to receive baptism.
578	Council of Auxerre.
585	Council of Macon.
—	Arrival of St. Colomban in Gaul.
590	He founds the monastery of Luxeuil.
590—600	Disorder in the monasteries. Impostors overrun Gaul, and give themselves out to be Christ.
600—650	Progressive incorporation of the monks into the clergy.
615	Council of Paris.
—	Clotaire II. allows to the people and clergy the right of electing bishops, reserving to himself the confirmation of their choice.
625	Council of Reims.
626	St. Amand, a missionary bishop, labours at the conversion of the infidels in Belgium.
628	Dagobert I. obliges the Jews to receive baptism.
—	Foundation of the abbey of St. Denis.
638	Council of Paris.
639	St. Eloy, bishop of Noyon.
639	St. Ouen, bishop of Rouen.
640—660	Foundation of numerous monasteries.
650	Council of Châlons.
658	Saint Leger, bishop of Autun.
—	Progress of the temporal power of the bishops.
670—700	Preaching of Anglo-Saxon and other monks, sustained by the mayors of the palace of Austrasia, amongst the people beyond the Rhine, such as the Saxons, the Frisons, the Danes, &c.
—	Tyranny of the bishops over the monasteries—Charters obtained by the monasteries—Protection afforded them by the kings and popes.
715—755	Preaching and institutions of Saint Boniface in Germany—Foundation of the bishoprics of Salzburg, Freysingen, Ratisbon, Wurtzburg, Passau, Eichstædt, &c.
720—741	Charles Martel seizes a part of the domains of the clergy.

A.D.	
739—752	Relations of the popes with Charles Martel and Pepin le Bref.
743	Council of Leptines.
751—800	Progress of the papacy by means of its alliance with Pepin and Charlemagne.
752	Council of Wermerie.
755	Council of Verneuil.
—	Pepin le Bref gives to the church of Rome the dominions taken from the Lombards.
761	Recommencement of the dispute upon dogmatical questions—reform of the church by the civil power.
761—763	Establishment and rule of the canons by Chrodegaud bishop of Metz.
767	Council of Gentilly.
769	Charlemagne interdicts the abuse of the right of asylum in the churches.
772	Pope Adrian I. gives a collection of canons to Charlemagne.
774	Charlemagne extends Pepin's donation to the church of Rome.
780	Benedict d'Aniane undertakes the reform of monastic life.
785	Theodulf, bishop of Orleans.
786	Especial bishops established in certain monasteries.
790—794	Condemnation of the worshipping of images by the Gallo-Frankish church—Caroline works composed on this subject by Alcuin, and sent to the pope by the order of Charlemagne.
790—799	Heresy of the adoptians—Opposed by Alcuin, and condemned by the Gallo-Frankish church.
798	Leidrade, archbishop of Lyons.
809	The Gallo-Frankish church adopts the doctrine, that the Holy Ghost proceeds from the Father and the Son.
813	Five councils held the same year labour at the reform of ecclesiastical discipline.
816	Rules of canons and canonesses adopted at the council of Aix-la-Chapelle—Louis le Debonnaire gives the force of law to the treatise of ecclesiastical offices by Amalaire, priest of Metz.
817	Reform of the monasteries ordered by a council of abbots and monks held at Aix-la-Chapelle.
820—877	Progress of the independence and temporal power of the bishops—Decline of royalty.
823—824	Proofs of the right of the emperor of the west to interfere in the election of the popes.
826	Harold and his wife, Danish princes, with their suite, are baptised in the palace of Louis le Debonnaire.
About 830	Ideas and attempts of Agobard, archbishop of Lyons, after the example of Claude, bishop of Turin, to reform the abuses of the church, particularly the worship of relics and the adoration of images.
831—865	The writings of Paschase-Radbert give rise to a controversy upon transubstantiation and the immaculate conception.
833	Council of Compiegne.
835	Council of Thionville.
836	Council of Aix-la-Chapelle.

A.D.	
840—877	Progress of the papal power at the expense, 1st, of the power of temporal sovereigns; 2nd, of the power of the bishops and the national churches—Relations of Nicholas I. with the government of the Gallo-Frankish church.
About 843	Appearance of the False Decretals.
844	Council of Thionville.
845—882	Hincmar, archbishop of Reims.
847—861	Saint Prudentius, archbishop of Troyes.
849—869	Controversy upon predestination and grace—Contest between Gottschalk and Hincmar.
852—875	Saint Remy, archbishop of Lyons.
853	Council of Soissons.
853—866	Affair of Wulfad and the other priest ordained by Ebbo, archbishop of Reims.
856—869	Affair of the divorce of Lothair and Teutberge.
858	Letters of counsel and reproach from the bishop of Gaul to Louis le Germanique.
862—866	Affair of Rhotade, bishop of Soissons.
869—878	Affair of Hincmar, bishop of Laon.
876	Ansegise, archbishop of Sens, is instituted primate of Gaul and Germany by pope John VIII.
—	Council of Pontion.
887	Council of Mayence.
909	Council of Trosley.
910	Foundation of the abbey of Cluny by William the Pious, duke of Aquitaine.
912	Rollo and a great number of Normans embrace Christianity.
926—942	Saint Odo, bishop of Cluny, reforms his monastery and several others, which being authorised by the pope, unite in one congregation—First example of common government in a monastic order.
943	Struggle between the Christian Normans and the Normans that remained pagans.
991	Gerbert, archbishop of Reims, pope in 999.
993	Canonization of Ulrich, bishop of Augsburg, by Pope John XV.—First example of papal canonization—The bishops continue to declare saints in their diocese.
Towards the end of the century.	Odillo, abbot of Cluny, institutes the feast of All Souls.
	Institution of the office of the Virgin.
	Progress of simony, disorder in the manners of the clergy, and superstitions of all kinds amongst the people—Infinite number of saints and relics—Extension of penances and absolutions.
	The popes declare themselves more and more the adversaries of the disorder in the church, and attempt to put a stop to it.
	Private individuals rise against abuses and superstitions, amongst others, Leutard, in the environs of Châlons-sur-Saone.
	The monasteries labour to escape from the jurisdiction of the bishops.

VI.

Chronological Table of the principal Events of the Literary History of Gaul, from the Fifth to the Tenth Century.

Fifth Century.

Name.	Date.	Condition in Life.	Works.
Rutilius Numatianus, of Toulouse, or Poictiers.	Died after 418.	Civil magistrate.	A poem, entitled, *Itinerarium;* or, *De Reditu*, from Rome to Gaul.
Sulpicius Severus, of Aquitaine.	Died after 420.	Ecclesiastic.	1. The Life of St. Martin of Tours; 2. A Sacred History, from the Creation to 400; 3. Dialogues on the Monks of the East, and a Life of St. Martin.
Evagrius.	Beginning of the 5th century.	Idem.	1. Controversy between Theophilus, a Christian, and Simon, a Jew; 2. Dialogue between Zacheus, a Christian, and Apollonius, a philosopher.
Saint Paulin, of Bordeaux.	354—431.	Bishop of Nola.	1. Letters; 2. Short poems; 3. a sermon upon charity; 4. Several lost works.
Cassienus, (John) of Provence.	350—433	Bishop of Nola.	1. A treatise on monastic institutions; 2. Conferences on monastic life; 3. Several works on theology.
Palladius, of Poictiers.	Beginning of the 5th century.	Jurisconsult.	A poem upon agriculture.
Saint Prosper, of Aquitaine.	Died towards 463.	Ecclesiastic.	1. A poem upon the question of predestination and grace, entitled, *Of Ingrates;* 2. A chronicle from the creation of the world until 455; 3. Several theological writings and letters.
Mamertius Claudienus, of Vienne.	Died about 474.	Idem.	1. A treatise upon the nature of the soul; 2. hymn upon the passion, *pange lingua;* 3. Letters.

Name.	Date.	Condition in Life.	Works.
Salvienus, of the north of Gaul.	Died about the end of the 5th century.	Ecclesiastic.	1. A treatise upon avarice; 2. A treatise on the government of God, or Providence; 3. Letters; 4. Lost writings.
Sidonius Apollinaris, born at Lyons.	430—488.	Bishop of Clermont.	1. Nine books of letters; 2. Poetry; 3. Lost writings.
Faust, of Breton origin.	Died towards the end of the 5th century.	Idem.	1. A treatise upon grace; 2. Letters, wherein he treats of several philosophical and theological questions; 3. Sermons.
Gennade, of Provence.	Died at the end of the 5th century.	Idem.	1. A treatise, or catalogue of illustrious men, or ecclesiastical authors; 2. A treatise on ecclesiastical doctrines.
Pomerius, of African origin, resided at Arles.	End of the 5th century.	Idem.	1. A treatise on contemplative life; 2. A treatise on the nature of the soul; lost.
	Sixth Century.		
Saint Ernodius, of Arles.	473—521.	Bishop of Paris.	1. Panegyric of Theodoric, king of the Ostrogoths; 2. Life of Saint Epiphonius, bishop of Paris; 3. Letters; 4. Poems; 5. Theological writings.
Saint Avitus (Alcimus Ecdicius) of Auvergne.	Died in 525.	Bishop of Vienne.	1. Two religious poems; 2. Letters; 3. Lost Sermons; 4. Lost Poems.
Saint Cesaire, of Châlons-sur-Saône.	470—542.	Bishop of Arles.	1. Sermons; 2. A treatise upon grace and free will; lost.
Saint Cyprien, of Arles.	Died about 546.	Bishop of Toulon.	Life of Saint Cesaire.
Saint Gregory, of Auvergne.	544—595.	Bishop of Tours.	1. An ecclesiastical history of the Franks; 2. On the glory of martyrs; 3. On the glory of confessors; 4. Lives of the fathers; 5. The miracles of Saint Martin; 6. Several theological writings; lost.

Name.	Date.	Condition in Life.	Works.
Marius, of Autun.	532—596.	Bishop of Avenche.	A chronicle extending from 455 to the year 581.
Joseph of Touraine.	Towards the end of the 5th century.	A Jew.	A history of the Jews, in Hebrew
		Seventh Century.	
Saint Fortunatus, of Ceneda, in Italy.	530, Beginning of the 7th century.	Bishop of Poictiers.	1. Sacred and profane poems; 2. Lives of the saints.
Saint Colomban, of Irish origin.	Died in 615.	Abbot of Luxeuil.	1. Poems; 2. Homilies; 3. Letters; 4. Short theological writings.
Marculf.	Towards the middle of the 7th century.	A monk.	Collection of formula, or models of public and private acts.
Frédégaire, of Burgundy.	Towards the middle of the 7th century.	A monk.	A chronicle from the creation until the year 641.
Jonas, of Italian origin.	Idem.	Abbot of Saint Amand.	The life of Saint Colomban.
Saint Ouen, of Sanci, near Soissons.	609—683.	Archbishop of Rouen.	The life of Saint Eloy.
		Eighth Century.	
An anonymous historian.	Beginning of the 8th century.	... ...	Les Gestes des Francs, a chronicle extending to the year 584.
Saint Boniface, (Winfried,) Anglo-Saxon.	680—755.	Archbishop of Mayence.	1. Letters; 2. Sermons; 3. Theological writings; lost.
Ambroise Autbert, probably of Aquitaine.	Died in 778.	Abbot of Saint Vincent near Benevento.	1. A Commentary upon the Apocalypse; 2. Sermons; 3. A treatise on combating vice.
An anonymous historian.	Towards the end of the 8th century.	... ...	The Life of Dagobert I.
Turpin.	Died in 800.	Archbishop of Reims.	It is to him that has been attributed the fabulous chronicle entitled, Histoire de la Vie de Charlemagne et de Roland.

Ninth Century.

Name.	Date.	Condition in Life.	Works.
Alcuin in England, Yorkshire.	735—804.	Abbot of Saint Martin of Tours.	1. Commentaries upon the Scriptures; 2. Philosophical and literary writings; 3. Poems; 4. Letters.
Anonymous.	Beginning of 9th century.		Annales de l'Histoire des Francs.
Angilbert in Neustria.	Died in 814.	Counsellor of Charlemagne, abbot of St. Regnier.	1. Poems; 2, A relation of what he had done for his monastery.
Leidrade, originally from Norica.	Died towards 816.	Archbishop of Lyons.	1. Letters; 2. Theological writings.
Smaragde.	Died about 820.	Abbot of St. Mihiel.	1. Moral treatise; 2. Commentaries on the New Testament; 3. A Grammar.
Saint Benedict, of Aniane, in Septimania.	751—821.	Abbot of Aniane and Inde.	1. The Code of Monastic Rules; 2. The Concordance of the rules; 3. Writings on Theology.
Theodulf, an Italian Goth.	Died in 821.	Bishop of Orleans.	1. Instruction schools, 2. Theological writings, 3. Poems.
Adalhard, born in Austrasia.	753—826.	Counsellor to Charlemagne, abbot of Corbie.	1. Statutes for the abbey of Corbie; 2. Letters; 3. A treatise *De Ordine Palatii*, reproduced by Hincmar.
Dungal, of Irish origin.	Died about 834.	A hermit, near St. Denis.	1. A letter to Charlemagne on the pretended eclipses of the sun in the year 810; 2. A treatise in favour of the worship of images; 3. Poems.
Halitgaire.	Died in 831.	Bishop of Cambray.	1. A penitential; 2. A treatise on the lives and duties of priests.
Ansegise of Burgundy.	Died in 833.	Counsellor to Charlemagne, abbot of Fontenelle.	The first collection of the capitularies of Charlemagne and Louis Le Debonnaire, in four books.

Name.	Date.	Condition in Life.	Works.
Friedgies, an Anglo-Saxon by birth.	Died in 834.	Abbot of Saint Martin of Tours.	1. A philosophical treatise on Chaos and Darkness; 2. Poems.
Ermold le Noir, from Septimania.	Died towards the middle of the 9th century.	Abbot of Aniane.	A poem on the life and actions of Louis le Debonnaire.
Amalaire, in Austrasia.	Died in 837.	A priest at Metz.	1. The rule of the Canonesses; 2. A treatise on the ecclesiastical offices; 3. Letters.
Eginhard in Austrasia.	Died in 839.	Counsellor to Charlemagne, abbot of Seligenstadt.	1. The life of Charlemagne; 2. Annals; 3. Letters.
Agobard, originally of Spain.	779—840.	Archbishop of Lyons.	1. Theological writings; 2. Letters; 3. Poems.
Hilduin.	Died about 840.	Abbot of Saint Denis.	The Areopagites destined to prove that Denys the Areopagite is the same as St. Denis, first bishop of Paris.
Dodane.	Died in the middle of the 9th century.	Duchess of Septimania.	A manual containing counsels to her sons.
Jonas in Aquitaine.	Died in 842.	Bishop of Orleans.	1. A treatise on the institution of laymen; 2. On the institution of the king; 3. On Images.
Saint Ardon, Smaragde, in Septimania.	Died in 843.	A monk at Aniane.	The life of St. Benedict d'Aniane.
Benedict in Belgium.	Towards the middle of the 9th century.	Deacon at Mayence.	A collection of the capitularies of the kings of the Francs, in three books, added to the four books collected by Angesisc.
Thegan, in Austrasia.	Died in 846.	Chorepiscopus of Trèves.	The life of Louis le Debonnaire.
An anonymous writer called the Astronomer.	In the first half of the ninth century.	... ...	The life of Louis le Debonnaire.
Walfried Strabo, in Germany.	807—849.	Abbot of Reichenau.	1. A commentary on the whole of the Bible; 2. The life of Saint Gall; 3. Theological writings; 4. Poems; amongst others a descriptive poem, entitled *Hortulus*.

Name.	Date.	Condition in Life.	Works.
Freculf.	Died in 850.	Bishop of Lisieux.	An universal history from the creation of the world until the end of the sixth century.
Angelome, in Burgundy.	Died about 855.	A monk at Luxeuil.	Commentaries upon several parts of the Bible.
Raban-Maur, in Austrasia.	776—856.	Archbishop of Mayence.	Fifty-one works on theology, philosophy, philology, chronology; Letters, &c.
Nithard, in Austrasia.	Died in 859.	Duke of Maritime France, monk at Saint Riquier	The history of the dissensions of the sons of Louis le Debonnaire.
Florus, in Burgundy.	Died about 860.	A priest at Lyons.	1. Theological writings, amongst others, a refutation of the treatise on predestination, by John Scotus; 2. Poems; amongst others, a complaint on the division of the empire after Louis le Debonnaire.
Saint Prudentius, in Spain.	Died about 861.	Bishop of Troyes.	Theological writings; amongst others, on predestination, and against John Scotus.
Loup (Servat), in Burgundy.	Died about 862.	Abbot of Ferrieres in Gatinais.	1. Theological writings; amongst others, on predestination; 2. Letters; 3. A history of the emperors; lost.
Radbert (Paschase), in the diocese of Soissons.	Died in 865.	Abbot of Corbie.	1. Theological writings; amongst others, a treatise on the Eucharist; 2. The life of Wala, abbot of Corbie.
Ratramne.	Died in 868.	Monk at Corbie.	Theological writings; amongst others, on transubstantiation and predestination.
Gottschalk, of Saxon origin.	Died in 869.	Monk at Orbais.	Writings on predestination.
Otfried.	Died about 870.	Monk at Weissemburg.	A paraphrased translation of the Gospel, in German rhymed verse.

Name.	Date.	Condition in Life.	Works.
Milon.	Died in 872.	Monk at Saint Amand.	Poems; amongst others, a poem on sobriety, dedicated to Charles le Chauve; and a pastoral entitled, The Combat of Winter and Spring.
Jean, called the Scot, or Erigena, in Ireland.	Died between 872 and 877.	Layman.	Several philosophical works: 1. On divine predestination; 2. On the division of nature; 3. The translation of the pretended writings of Dionysius the Areopagite.
Usnard.	About the middle of the ninth century.	Monk at Saint Germain des Pres	A great martyrology.
Saint Remy.	Died in 875.	Archbishop of Lyons.	Theological works; amongst others, on predestination and free will.
Saint Adon, in the diocese of Sens.	800—875.	Archbishop of Vienne.	1. Theological writings; 2. A universal chronicle.
Isaac.	Died in 880.	Bishop of Langres.	An extensive collection of canons.
Henrie, at Hery, near Auxerre.	834—881.	Monk at St. Germain d'Auxerre.	The life of St. Germaine d'Auxerre, in verse, in six books.
Hincmar.	Died in 882.	Archbishop of Reims.	1. Theological writings; amongst others, on predestination; 2. Political writings and counsels; 3. Letters.
Anonymous.	... ...	... ...	The annals of St. Bertin, by several writers, in part by St. Prudence, bishop of Troyes, and perhaps by Hincmar.
A monk of Saint Gall, Anonymous.	The end of the ninth century.	... ...	Des faits et gestes de Charlemagne.
	Tenth Century.		
Remy, in Burgundy.	Died about 908.	Monk at St. Germain d'Auxerre.	1. Commentaries on the Bible; 2. Theological works; 3. Commentaries on the ancient grammarians and rhetoricians.

Name.	Date.	Condition in Life.	Works.
Reginon.	Died in 915.	Abbot of Prüm.	1. A chronology from the birth of Jesus Christ until the year 906; 2. A collection of canonical rules.
Abbon.	Died about 924.	Monk at Saint Germaindes Pres.	A poem on the siege of Paris by the Normans in 885.
Hucbald, in Flanders.	840—930.	Monk at Saint Amand.	1. Poems; among others, a poem in honour of the Bald, dedicated to Charles le Chauve, in which all the words begin with c; 2. Lives of the saints.
Saint Odon, in le Maine.	879—942.	Abbot of Cluny.	1. Theological writings; 2. The lives of the saints, especially that of Saint Gregory of Tours; 3. Poems.
John, of Italian origin.	About the middle of the tenth century.	Monk.	The life of Saint Odon, abbot of Cluny.
Frodoard, at Epernay.	894—966.	Canon at Reims.	1. Poems; 2. The history of the church of Reims; 3. A chronicle from 919 to 966.
Helperic.	About the end of the tenth century.	Schoolmaster of Grand Fel.	A treatise on computation or supputation of time as regards the ecclesiastical calendar.
John.	id.	Abbot of Saint Arnould at Metz.	Several lives of the saints; amongst others, that of John de Verdiere, abbot of Gorze, and the relation of his embassy in Spain to Abderrahman, caliph of Cordova.
Adson, in Transjuran Burgundy.	Died in 992.	Abbot of Montier en Der.	1. A treatise on the Antichrist, celebrated in the middle ages; 2. The lives of the saints.
Arnoult.	End of the tenth century.	Bishop of Orleans.	Letters entitled *de Cartilagine* (on the Cartilage), remarkable as an essay at anatomical studies. They are inedited
Gerbert, at Aurillac.	Died in 1003.	Pope, under the name of Silvester II.	1. Works on mathematics; 2. On philosophy; 3. On theology· 4. Poems; 5. Letters.

VII.

Chronological Table of the Councils and Canonical Legislation of Gaul, from the Fourth to the Tenth Century.[1]

Date.	Place.	Present.	Object of the Council, Rules, &c.
314	Arles.	33 bishops, 14 priests, 25 deacons, 8 clerks.	This council was convoked by Constantine, to pronounce on the subject of the Donatists; and of Cecilian, bishop of Carthage. *Rules.*—That each priest reside in the place in which he was ordained. That the faithful who become governors of provinces receive letters of communion, in order that the bishop of the place they inhabit may be able to watch, and excommunicate them, if they act contrary to the discipline. That the priests and deacons who quit the places assigned to them, shall be deposed. The council orders that Easter should be celebrated everywhere the same day; excommunicates those who carry arms in time of peace, usurious clerks, and calumniators; forbids deacons to celebrate the office; orders that absolution shall be received in the same place where excommunication was pronounced; forbids bishops to encroach reciprocally on their rights, and interdicts to the deacons of towns the power of doing anything without the consent of the priests.
340	Cologne.	14 Bishops, 10 envoys from Bishops.	Euphratus, bishop of Cologne, having denied the divinity of Jesus Christ, the faithful and clergy of Cologne denounce him as a heretic, and he is condemned and deposed.
353	Arles.	... ...	This council, at which the emperor Constantius assisted, and the Arians prevailed, deposed Paul, bishop of Trèves, who would not sign the condemnation of Saint Athanasius.
356	Beziers.	... ...	This council, convoked by Saturnin, bishop of Arles, and which decided nothing, banished Saint Hilary, bishop of Poictiers, to Phrygia.

[1] It will be at once seen that in this abstract I have only inserted the most important of the canons.

Date.	Place.	Present.	Object of the Council, Rules, &c.
359	In Gaul.	... ...	This council condemned the Arian formula adopted at Sirmium.
360	Paris.	... ...	This council condemned the Arian formula of Rimini; communicated this resolution to the bishops of the east, and excommunicated Saturnin, bishop of Arles.
374	Valence.	21 bishops.	*Rules.*—It is forbidden to confess a crime, whether true or false, in order to escape from holy orders. The council forbids the ordaining those who have been twice married, or who have married a widow. It excommunicates virgins consecrated to God if they marry; and those who, after their baptism, sacrifice to demons, or make use of pagan purifications.
383 Date uncertain.	Nîmes.		
385	Bordeaux.	... ...	This council was held at the request of Ithace against the Priscillianists. Instantius was deprived of his bishopric; Priscillian appealed to the emperor, who put him to death.
386	Trèves.[1]	... ...	This council declared Ithace absolved from the death of the Priscillianists. Saint Martin there communicated with him, for which he never forgave himself.
395	Turin	... ...	This council treated only of affairs of discipline, and the pretensions to primacy of the bishops of Marseilles, as well as the rivality of the bishops of Vienne and Arles. *Rules.* — That no bishop shall receive a clerk of another bishop and ordain him for himself. That no one who has been rejected shall be admitted to the communion. That those who have had children after their ordination, shall be excluded from the major orders.

[1] We have, as usual, preferred the date of Sirmond to that of Labbe, because the events of these two councils clearly prove, that that of Bordeaux must have taken place before that of Trèves. I can only conclude that Sulpicius Severus deceived himself, when he said that after the year 384 St. Martin was present at no council; or, which is very possible, it is an error of the copyist.

Fifth Century.

Date.	Place.	Present.	Object of the Council, Rules, &c.
429	In Gaul. Place uncertain.	... ..	This numerous council assembled in compliance with the wishes of the Bretons, who demanded from the bishops of Gaul succour against the heresy of Pelagius; the council sent them Saint Germain and Saint Loup.
439	Riez.	13 bishops, 1 bishop's envoy.	This council was held on the subject of the bishop of Embrun, who had been consecrated by two bishops only. Several canons of discipline were made at it. *Rules.*—That if two bishops only shall ordain a bishop, they shall, for the future, be excluded from all ordinations and councils. That when a bishop dies, the nearest bishop shall take charge of his diocese. That no person shall interfere with the consecration of a bishop without having been invited to do so by the metropolitan. That it be permitted to country priests to give the blessing, to consecrate virgins, to confirm neophytes, and that they conduct themselves as superiors to the priests, and inferiors to the bishops.[1] That a council be held twice a year.
441	Orange.	16 bishops, 1 priest for a bishop.	This council was engaged only on affairs of discipline. *Rules.*—That no one shall reduce to servitude those who belong to the church. That one council shall not be dissolved without indicating another, the rigour of the weather preventing the holding two councils a year. That the functions of an infirm bishop shall be fulfilled by another bishop, and not by priests. The council forbids repeating confirmation, delivering up those who take refuge in a church; forbids a bishop to communicate with him who has excommunicated another bishop, or to ordain deaconesses; orders that some of the graces of the church be

[1] This passage proves that chorepiscopi, or rural bishops, are meant; a class superior to priests, but inferior to the bishops.

Date.	Place.	Present.	Object of the Council, Rules, &c.
			granted to idiots, and that catechumens shall be present at the reading of the Gospel.
442	Vaison.	... ...	This council was occupied with affairs of discipline. *Rules.*—That those who retain the offerings of the dead shall be excommunicated. If a bishop does not acquiesce in his sentence, he can appeal to a synod.[1]
444	Vienne.	... ...	This council was presided over by Saint Hilary. Chelidonius, bishop of Besançon, was deposed for having married a widow. *Rules.*—That the priests shall receive the holy Chrism every year, at Easter, from the nearest bishop, and not at their own mere discretion.
About 452	Arles.[2]	44 bishops.	This council was held against the Novatians, the Photinians, or Paulinists, the Bonosians, the Arians, the Eutychians. Several canons of discipline were made at it. The council also was engaged with the *lapsi*, that is to say, those who had given way during the persecution. *Rules.*—That no one shall be consecrated bishop without a letter from the metropolitan, or from three provincial bishops. That in a contested election the metropolitan must vote with the majority. The ordination of a clerk out of his diocese, and without the approbation of his bishop, is null. A bishop who does not come to the council, or who quits it before the end, is excommunicated. A bishop is guilty of sacrilege who neglects to extirpate the custom of adoring fountains, trees, and stones. When there are priests present, deacons must not administer the body of Jesus Christ. Actors shall be excommunicated. That penance shall not be given to married people without their mutual consent. *C. d'O.* The causes of clerks must, under

[1] The judgments of the metropolitan are doubtless here referred to.

[2] We find among the canons of the council of Arles, twenty which belong, as it would appear, to that of Orange; they are distinguished by the titles C. d'O.

Date.	Place.	Present.	Object of the Council, Rules, &c.
			pain of excommunication, be brought before the bishop. *C. d'O.* If a bishop builds a church in the diocese of another bishop, which cannot be prevented without a crime, he must not think he has therefore the right of dedicating it; that is reserved for the bishop in whose diocese it stands; but he will have the privilege of placing what clerks he pleases therein. To avoid simony in the election of bishops, the bishops shall name three persons, among whom the clergy and the people shall choose. The council forbids the clerks to practise usury, to charge themselves with the conduct of other peoples' affairs, to have in their house, after they have passed the deaconship, other women than their grandmother, their mother, their daughter, their niece, or their wife, converted like themselves. The canons of the council of Orange give to priests the power of confirming a dying heretic, grant penance to the clerks, permit them to absolve dying persons without penance, on condition of their performing penance if they recover. They grant baptism to demoniacs, and those who have suddenly lost the use of speech, and excommunicate any person who, having lost his serfs, owing to their having taken refuge in a church, shall possess himself of the serfs of that church.
About 453	Angers.	8 bishops.	This council was held on the occasion of the consecration of Talasius, bishop of Angers. *Rules.*—That those who renounce the priesthood for the army shall be excommunicated. That monks who wander about without letters of leave shall be excommunicated. That a bishop shall not advance the clerk of another bishop.
455	Arles.	13 bishops.	This council assembled to terminate the quarrel existing between several bishops and Faust, abbot of Lerens.

Date.	Place.	Present.	Object of the Council, Rules, &c.
461	Tours.	8 bishops, 1 bishops' envoy.	This council was composed of bishops assembled for the feast of St. Martin. Several canons of discipline were made. *Rules.*—That a clerk shall not travel without letters from his bishop. That a clerk who has permission to marry, shall not marry a widow. If a clerk is guilty of drunkenness, he must be punished according to his order.
About 465	Vannes.	6 bishops.	This council was composed of bishops assembled for the purpose of the consecration of the bishop of Vannes. It discussed points of discipline. *Rules.*—That without the permission of his abbot, a monk shall not ask for a private cell. That each abbot shall have but one monastery. That, under pain of excommunication, no clerk shall practise divination by Saints' names, or the Holy Scriptures. The council forbids clerks to be present at Jewish wedding-feasts or entertainments; orders all who are in town to attend at matins; and prescribes for all the province (Brittany) one order of ceremonies and chant.
475	Arles.	30 bishops.	This council was held against the predestinarians.
About 475	Lyons.	... ...	This council was also held against the predestinarians. We are ignorant of what passed.

Sixth Century.

Date.	Place.	Present.	Object of the Council, Rules, &c.
506	Agde.	25 bishops, 8 priests, 2 deacons, representatives of their bishops.	This council was not occupied with dogma. All its canons, of which 24 out of 70 belong to the council of Epaone, are upon discipline. The twenty-four rules of the council of Epaone will be found in their place. Saint Cesaire presided at this council. Gratian adds canons taken from various authors; one against sorcerers, another against usurers; the first of all forbids to bishops and

Date.	Place.	Present.	Object of the Council, Rules, &c.
			priests the effusion of blood; there is another against quarrelsome persons, scandal-mongers, and calumniators. At the end of this council is a letter from Theodoric to the Roman senate, which appears to be the result of it, and in which priests are forbidden to sell the goods of the church. *Rules.*—If a bishop has pronounced an unjust, or too severe excommunication, and warned by the neighbouring bishops, he does not withdraw it, they must not refuse the communion to those who have been deprived of it. All that is given to a bishop becomes the property of the church. The council prescribes the tonsure of clerks, the fast of Lent, and the communion at the three great feasts. Freedmen are protected by the church. Every person must be present at mass every Sunday, and not to leave until the conclusion, under the penalty of being publicly reprimanded by the bishop. The bishop can dispose of the minor goods of the church, and of his vagrant serfs. The clerk who shall suppress or deliver up the titles of possession belonging to the church, shall be excommunicated, and condemned to pay out of his own property the damage which shall accrue thence to the church. Priests, deacons, and sub-deacons, are forbidden to be present at wedding feasts. A clerk guilty of drunkenness, shall, according to his order, be deprived of the communion during thirty days, or submitted to a corporal punishment, *corporali supplicio.* The council deprives of his priesthood the clerk who robs the church; orders that a young clerk shall not be preferred to an elder one; if, however, the latter cannot fulfil the duties of an archdeaconate, he shall have the title, and the bishop must choose some one to exercise the functions. This council fixes, at the age of forty years, the time when virgins take the veil, at twenty-five that of the deaconship, at thirty that of priesthood and episcopacy. It forbids conferring the monastic order

Date.	Place.	Present.	Object of the Council, Rules, &c.
			upon married men without the consent of their wives; it renews a canon of the council of Vaison, upon the care to be taken of exposed children. It forbids the celebration of great feasts out of the parish; to sell or to give the goods of the church; to build new monasteries without the permission of the bishop; to build monasteries for men near those of the women, and to ordain penitents. It commands the church to defend freedmen, and to distribute the salaries of priests according to their merits. It also regulates several rules of worship.
511	Orleans.	32 bishops.	This council was convoked by Clovis, on the advice of Saint Remy, whose signature, however, is not to be found. Many bishops were there from the kingdom of the Visigoths, which had just been conquered by Clovis. *Rules.*—This council made several canons upon the right of asylum, and prescribed that the criminal and serf who had taken refuge in the church, should not be delivered up until they had stipulated for their safety. That no secular person shall be ordained without an order from the king or the judge, and that the children and the grandchildren of clerks shall be under the authority of the bishop, instead of that of their parents. That no one shall be excommunicated for having, without proof, claimed anything belonging to the church; that the abbots shall be subject to the bishops, and the monks to the abbots. That no person shall celebrate Easter in the country. That the bishop, if not ill, must on Sunday attend the nearest church. That if, through humanity, the bishop has lent land to be cultivated, the length of time must not occasion any prescription. That no monk, instigated by ambition or vanity, shall, without the permission of his abbot, abandon his brethren to build a separate cell; that any professed monk who marries shall be expelled the ecclesiastical order.

Date.	Place.	Present.	Object of the Council, Rules, &c.
			The council also orders, that if a bishop has ordained a serf without the permission of his master, he must indemnify the latter for his loss, but the clerk will remain ordained; it forbids any one to marry the widow of a priest or deacon; places under the power of the bishops the real property given to the church, and secures to them a third part of the offerings; enjoins them to provide the poor and sick with clothes and nourishment, and regulates several articles of worship.
515	St. Maurice.	4 bishops, 8 counts.	This council was convoked by king Sigismond, converted to the Catholic faith, upon the subject of the foundation or restoration of the monastery of Saint Maurice, and the rules to be established therein.
516	Lyons.	... ...	It is known by a letter from Avitus, that this council was held, and that he assisted at it. Nothing else has come down to us concerning it.
517	Epaone, in the Viennese, now Jena, in Savoy	25 bishops.	There exist two circular letters by which Avitus and Viventiolus convoke to this council the bishops of their provinces: Avitus insists upon the importance of making a good choice of priests charged in times of sickness with signing for their bishop. Viventiolus declares that clerks are obliged to come to the council, while it is only permitted to the laity, that the people may know that which is regulated by the bishops. *Rules.*—That priests, bishops, and deacons, shall not possess sporting dogs or falcons. That an abbot shall not, without the authorization of the bishop, sell the goods of the abbey, neither shall he enfranchise its serfs, for it seems unjust that while the monks are obliged to work every day upon the land, their serfs should enjoy repose and liberty. That no bishop shall sell the goods of the church without the approbation of his metropolitan; he may only conclude useful exchanges. If an abbot, convicted of fault, is refractory, and will not receive a successor from

Date.	Place.	Present.	Object of the Council, Rules, &c.
			his bishop, the affair must be taken before the metropolitan. If any one has killed a serf, without the consent of the judge, he must expiate this effusion of blood by a penance of two years. The council imposes the same penance on those catholics who have fallen into heresy. That if a serf, guilty of atrocious crimes, seeks refuge in a church, he shall only be exempted from corporal punishment. The council declares null the donations or legacies made by priests and bishops of the goods of the church; it forbids priests to serve a church in another diocese, without the consent of their bishop; to be present at the feasts given by heretics; it permits the laity to accuse clerks; it forbids placing the relics of the saints in country oratories, unless there are priests in the neighbourhood to serve them; it forbids bishops and clerks to receive women after the vesper hour; orders all the provincial bishops to conform themselves to the order of offices established by the metropolitan. It forbids the young monks and clerks to enter the monasteries for women, unless they go to see a mother or a sister. It orders all the noble citizens to come at Easter and Christmas, to receive the bishop's blessing. We must add to the canons of the council of Epaone, several rules which belong to it, and which have been placed in the council of Agde of 506; these are their principal provisions: Bishops are allowed to dispose of their own goods, but not of those of the church; the council condemns to restitution out of their own property, those priests and deacons who have disposed of the property of the church, and declares null the enfranchisements that they have made. It forbids clerks to practise magic; it will not allow the ordination of factious, usurious, and vindictive clerks; it forbids the clerks that are not consecrated to enter the sacristy, and to touch the sacred utensils; and to the deacons to sit down in the presence of the priests.
517	Lyons.	11 bishops.	This council was held on the occasion of a

Date.	Place.	Present.	Object of the Council, Rules, &c.
			certain Stephen, who had married his sister-in-law. There are no canons that call for remark; they are a repetition of some already cited. Fraternal union among the bishops is recommended.
524	Arles.	14 bishops, 4 priests for their bishops.	This council was held and presided over by Saint Cesarius, on the occasion of the dedication of the cathedral of Saint Mary. *Rules.*—Although we ought to observe the ordinances of the ancient fathers, as to the longer duration of the conversion of the laity, before their ordination, yet as the number of churches augments, and the want of clerks is greater, it is ordered, without prejudice to the ancient rules, that no metropolitan bishop shall make a bishop from the laity; that the bishops shall not make a laic priest, or deacon, until a year of noviciate. That the bishop who has ordained a penitent or a bigamist, shall remain a year without saying mass.
527	Carpentras.	16 bishops.	This council was presided over by St. Cesarius; it has but one article. The fathers arranged to meet at Vaison the next year. *Rules.*—That what belongs to a church, shall be distributed to the clerks who serve it, and employed in reparations. That if a bishop has more expenses than money, and there are in his diocese parishes in the contrary situation, he can apply their surplus to his expenses, leaving them the sum necessary to the wants of their churches and clerks.
529	Orange.	14 bishops, 8 *viri illustres.*	This council was assembled for the dedication of the cathedral of Orange, built by the prefect Liber; but the true cause of its convocation by St. Cesarius, was a writing by Faust, bishop of Riez, "De gratiâ Dei quâ salvamur," which was suspected of semi-Pelagianism. The council fixed, in 25 canons, the doctrine of St. Augustin, but did not make it into discipline.
529	Valence.	... ...	This council was convoked by St. Cesarius (who could not preside) against the semi-Pelagians.

Date.	Place.	Present.	Object of the Council, Rules, &c.
529	Vaison.	12 bishops.	This council was presided over by St. Cesarius. *Rules.*—That, as is the salutary custom in Italy, the priests, when they have no wives, shall receive in their houses young lecturers, whom they shall instruct, and thus prepare for themselves worthy successors; and when these are of age, if by the fragility of the flesh, they wish for a wife, they are not to be prevented from marrying. That, the same as in Italy and the Eastern provinces, the *Kyrie eleison* and the *Sanctus, Sanctus,* shall be said every day at the mass. That the pope's name shall be recited in our churches. As, not only in the apostolic seat, but also in the East, Africa, and Italy, the malice of the heretics causes them to deny that the Son of God has always been equal with the Father, after *Gloria*, &c., *Sicut erat in principio,* has been added; and we order that the same shall be observed in all the churches. The council permits all the priests to preach, not only in the towns, but in all the provinces, and prescribes that when they cannot do it, a deacon shall read the homilies of the holy fathers.
533	Orleans.	26 bishops, 8 priests.	*Rules.*—That no bishop having received notice from his metropolitan, fail to come to the council or to the consecration of a co-bishop. That the metropolitans convoke each year the bishops to the provincial councils. That the bishops shall receive nothing for the ordinations. That no bishop shall refuse to attend the funeral of another bishop, and that he shall demand nothing for his trouble and expenses. That a bishop attending the funeral of a bishop, shall assemble the priests and entrust the goods of the church to persons worthy of confidence. That no person in a church shall sing, drink, or do anything unbecoming. That no one who is unlettered or ignorant

Date	Place.	Present.	Object of the Council, Rules, &c.
			of the form of baptism shall be ordained deacon or priest. On account of their frailty, women are excluded from the deaconship. Catholics who return to the worship of idols and eat flesh offered to idols, or animals killed by the bite of a beast, or suffocated, shall be excommunicated. That no priest shall live with secular persons without the permission of the bishops. The council condemns to degradation the deacon who shall marry in captivity, and the clerks who disdain to acquit themselves of their functions. It excommunicates abbots who resist bishops. It renews the ancient form for the consecration of the metropolitan, and orders that after being chosen by the provincial bishops, the clerks, and the people, he shall be consecrated by the provincial bishops. It forbids marriages between Christians and Jews.
535	Clermont.	Bishops.	The council was held the 11th year of his reign, by Theodebert, king of Austrasia, who was more favourable to the clergy than his father had been. *Rules.*—That no bishop shall dare to propose any affair to the council before those which regard the amendment of manners, the severity of the rule, and the saving of souls. That bishoprics shall be given according to merit, and not to those who merely ask for them. That the clerks shall not rise against the bishops by the help of the power of the laity. That those who demand from kings the property of the church, and by a horrible cupidity seize the goods of the poor, shall be excluded from the communion and the donation shall be null. That Jews shall not be constituted judges over Christian people. That if a bishop will not by canonical rigour prevent the priests and deacons from having commerce of any kind with women, he shall himself be excommunicated. The council forbids priests private orato-

Date.	Place.	Present.	Object of the Council, Rules, &c.
			tories to celebrate the great feasts away from the cathedral church. *Canons derived from different authors.*—That the priests shall inform the people where the inns are situated. The innkeepers must not refuse to lodge any traveller, and must not make him pay for anything more than the market price, or the affair must be taken before the priest, who will oblige them to sell with humanity There shall be no action against a bishop who has without interference possessed the diocese of another bishop during thirty years. (Some words are wanting here, but it is evident that the council recommends that in this case the limits of the dioceses shall not be confounded.) As regards priests who are accused of fornication, or any capital crime, and who have no colleagues to swear with them, as to their innocence, they must be judged by the canons. A bishop may, with the concurrence of the clerks, help his family with the church treasures.
538	Orleans.	19 bishops, 7 priests.	*Rules.*—If clerks placed under the patronage of any of the laity, shall makeit a pretence to disobey their bishop, and refuse to fulfil their functions, they must be separated from other clerks, and shall receive nothing from the church. It shall be in the power of the bishop to decide whether or not the clerks attached to a monastery or a church shall or shall not retain what they possessed before their ordination. If any clerks, as by the inspiration of the devil happened lately in several places, rebel against authority, unite in conspiracy, and take mutual oaths, or mutually subscribe an agreement to that purpose, nothing shall excuse such presumption, but the affair shall be taken before the synod. That no serf or labourer shall be admitted to ecclesiastical honours. That no one shall be present at divine service with warlike arms.

Date.	Place.	Present.	Object of the Council, Rules, &c.
			If a judge, knowing that a heretic has re-baptised a catholic, does not seize the heretic and send the affair before the king, for we have catholic kings, he shall be excommunicated during the space of a year, This council repeats the rules of the preceding, concerning the separation of priests from women; sub-deacons are included. We must repeat, says the council, what we know is not observed. It orders, also, as regards the newly converted Christians, on account of the novelty of their faith and conversion, that the forbidden marriages they have contracted previous shall not be broken. It renews, also, the anathemas against those who obtain or alienate the goods of the church. It excommunicates, for six months, the bishops who shall make an ordination contrary to the canons; for one year, him who in such a case has deceived the bishop, clerk, or witness. It expels from his order the clerk guilty of any capital crime. It directs them not to restore but to buy at a just price the Christian serfs who have sought in the church an asylum against their Jewish masters, who would impose on them anything contrary to their religion, or shall not have fulfilled the promises made when they were restored upon a former occasion. It refers clerks, who complain of the bishops, to the synodal judgment. It complains, that the people have been told that one may not travel, or cook, or clean houses or one's person on a Sunday; it declares these observances more Jewish than Christian, and holds permitted all that was allowed before; it excludes the cultivation of land, which would prevent the attending church. It forbids people to leave church before the end of mass. It interdicts, also, "for, by the grace of God, we have catholic kings," from Holy Saturday until Easter Monday, the Jews from mixing with the Christians in any place or on any occasion.
541	Orleans.	38 bishops, 11 priests,	The council was occupied with discipline. *Rules.*—The council orders the celebration

Date.	Place	Present.	Object of the Council, Rules, &c.
		1 abbot each for 1 bishop.	of Easter according to the usage of Rome, and decides that each time there is a doubt upon the epoch of a solemnity, the apostolical usage ought to be observed. That the parish priests receive the decrees of the canons, so that they or their people cannot excuse themselves on the plea of ignorance of what is necessary for their salvation. If a bishop, who has left none of his own property, has disposed of that of the church, it must return to the church; but if from the serfs of the church he has made a number of freedmen, they remain free, but they must not fall away from their allegiance to the church. If bishops quarrel among themselves for lands or other possessions, on being warned by the letters of their brothers, they must arrange between themselves or submit to arbitrators. Bishops, priests, and deacons, are exempt from the wardship of the administration, because it is just to retain for Christians what the law of the world did for the pagan priests. That the slaves of the priests and of the church must neither pillage nor make prisoners, for it is iniquitous that ecclesiastical discipline should be stained by the crimes of the servants of those who frequent the sacrament of redemption. Serfs who have fled to the church under pretext of marriage, and believing that thus they can marry, must be returned to their masters or parents; and the clerks must not protect such unions. If parishes are placed in the hands of powerful men, and the clerks, warned by the archdeacon of the city, neglect to acquit themselves of their duty towards the house of the Lord, they must be corrected according to ecclesiastical discipline. If Christians, slaves of the Jews, have fled from their masters and demand their liberty, we order that, as in the ancient laws, having given a just price they be set at liberty. If any one desires to have a chapel on his own premises, he must assign sufficient land for it and furnish it in with clerks, who will celebrate the offices in a proper manner.

Date.	Place.	Present.	Object of the Council, Rules, &c.
			The council orders also that the consecration of a bishop shall take place in the town which he is to govern; it forbids proprietors of chapels to receive strange clerks without the consent of the bishop of the place. It forbids heirs to take what has been left to the church; it also forbids any one to marry a girl without the consent of her parents. It excommunicates those proprietors of chapels who would hinder the clerks who serve them from acquitting themselves of what they owe to the divine service. It excludes from ordination those who descend from unemancipated serfs, and assures to the churches the return of all of which the bishops have given out the usufruct.
549	Orleans.	50 bishops, 21 priests, archdeacons or abbots, each representing a bishop.	This council condemned the errors of the Eutychians, the Nestorians, and, according to Baluze, of the Arians, whose heresy was reaching Orleans. *Rules.*—A serf shall not be ordained, even though he be free, against the will of his master. If it has been done, the serf must be returned to his master; but if he exacts from him services incompatible with the honour of the ecclesiastical order, then the bishop shall give two serfs to the master, and take the one who has been ordained.
549 or 550	Clermont.	10 bishops.	This council assembled a short time after that of Orleans. *Rules.*—As we have discovered that several people reduce again to servitude those, who, according to the custom of the country, have been set at liberty in the churches, we order that every one shall keep possession of the liberty he has received; and if this liberty is attacked, justice must be defended by the church. The prisoners must be visited every Sunday by the archdeacon, or some one proposed by the church, that all their wants may be attended to. The veil may not be given to virgins when the will of their parents, or their own, leads to the monastery, until three years' trial.

Date.	Place.	Present.	Object of the Council, Rules, &c.
			A bishop knowing that there are leperous persons on his territory, or in the town, must furnish them with all that is necessary. A master who has not kept the word he gave to this serf to induce him to leave the church, shall be excommunicated. If the serf refuse to leave the church upon the word of his master, he can employ force, that the church may not suffer from calumny, as if she withheld serfs. If a master is a pagan or a heretic, he must present Christians worthy of confidence to swear for him. No one may be permitted to obtain a bishopric with the help of presents, but, with the consent of the king, the pontiff elected by the clergy and the people must, as prescribed in the ancient rules, be consecrated by the metropolitan, or some one commissioned in his place, and the provincial bishops. No one shall be made bishop over those who refuse to have him, and (it would be a crime) the consent of the clergy and citizens must not be constrained by the oppression of persons in power; if it be so, the bishop who has been elected more by violence than by a legitimate election, shall be for ever deprived of the usurped pontifical honour. Excommunication may not be lightly pronounced. Priests may not at an unfitting time see even their near relations. Bishops may not ordain in a diocese vacant by the death of its bishop. No bishop must be placed above another, unless the latter has been guilty of some crime.
About 550	Toul.	... ...	This council was convoked by Theodebald, king of Austrasia. Nicet, bishop of Trèves, had excommunicated several Franks for incestuous marriages. This irritating them, they insulted the bishop. The issue of this council is not known; its epoch is not precise.

Date.	Place.	Present.	Object of the Council, Rules, &c.
550	Metz.	... ...	Saint Gall, bishop of Clermont, being dead, the bishops present at his funeral wished to consecrate as his successor Cato, who was elected by a great part of the people; but the archdeacon Cautin, coming to king Theodebald, acquainted him with the death of the archbishop, but concealed the rest. The king gave him the bishopric; and the bishops, then at Metz, consecrated him, and he was bishop in spite of his flock, by the violence that the king employed towards the deputies of Clermont.
554	Arles.	11 bishops, 8 priests, deacons, and archdeacons.	*Rules.*—No priest shall depose a deacon or subdeacon without the consent of his bishop. The clerk shall not waste the property which has been given him for his use by the bishop. If a young clerk does so, he must be corrected by the discipline of the church; if he is old, he must be looked upon as an assassin of the poor. The council also made several rules for keeping under the spiritual and temporal power of the bishop, the monasteries of men and women. It forbids abbots to travel without the permission of the bishop.
555	In Armorica, place uncertain.		This council excommunicated Maclou, bishop of Vannes, who, after the death of his brother, Chann, count of Brittany, quitted his bishop for the countship and a wife.
556	Paris.	27 bishops.	This council, convoked by Childebert, king of Paris, and presided over by Sapaudus, bishop of Arles, deposed and shut up in a monastery Saffaracus, bishop of Paris: Eusebius his successor.
557	Paris.	16 bishops.	This council was assembled to prevent by laws the dispersion of the goods of the churches, that the Frank kings gave to the first-comers. *Rules.*—Several laws against the detainers of church property, those who receive it from the kings, those who attack the personal property of the bishops, because the goods of the bishops are the property of the church. It forbids bishops to try to get possession of

Date.	Place.	Present.	Object of the Council, Rules, &c.
			another's goods, and orders, without prejudice to royal liberality, the restitution thereof to the legitimate proprietor. It forbids any one to carry off or to marry, under favour of the king, a girl or a widow without the consent of her parents. It annuls the ordination of a bishop named by the king against the will of the metropolitan and the provincial bishops, and the citizens; and as in several things ancient customs are neglected, the council renews and recommends the observance of the ancient laws. The council also orders the church and the priests to observe the will of the defunct as regards serfs left by will to keep the tombs.
563	Saintes.	... ...	This council elected Heraclius in the place of Emerius whom Clotaire had made bishop of Saintes, Clotaire being dead in the interval, but Charibert made them receive Emerius, and imposed fines on the bishops, amongst others, on Leontius, the metropolitan of Bordeaux, who had convoked and presided at the council.
567	Lyons.	8 bishops. 5 priests. 1 deacon.	This council was convoked by king Gontran, to judge Salone, bishop of Embrun, and Sagittaire, bishop of Gap, who were thorough brigands. They were deposed by the council; but they appealed to Pope John, and were by his order reinstated in their sees. *Rules.*—As to the ruin of their souls many have made captives by violence and treason, if they neglect to restore those they have taken captive, as the king orders, to the place where they have long lived in repose, they must be deprived of communion with the church. The council orders that discussions between bishops must be decided by the metropolitan, and that no bishop shall give communion to him who has excommunicated another bishop. That wills by which clerks, or other persons, have left anything to the church, shall always be valid, whatever fault may be in the form thereof. It forbids bishops to reclaim the liberalities of their predecessors.

Date.	Place.	Present.	Object of the Council, Rules, &c.
567	Tours.	7 bishops.	This council was assembled during the wars of the sons of Clotaire, and when the kings made use of the goods of the church to meet the expenses they incurred. Saint Radegonde wrote to the council to demand the confirmation of her rule. Her demand was granted. *Rules.*—This council, like many others, strongly recommends concord amongst the bishops. It orders that citizens and country priests shall nourish their poor, that they may not be obliged to go to other cities; it reiterates all prohibitions about women, and orders several precautions that suspicion may not fall upon the clerks. It forbids priests and monks to sleep together; it excommunicates the judge who shall refuse to separate a monk from the wife he has taken since his profession; it regulates the monk's fasts; it forbids several pagan superstitions; it renews all the menaces against those who, whilst our lords make war upon each other, invade or reclaim the goods of the church; and declares those judges and lords excommunicated who oppress the poor in spite of being warned by the bishop. The council orders that bishops only shall give letters of recommendation; that before sending away an abbot or an archpriest, they take counsel of all their priests and abbots, under penalty of being themselves excommunicated. It excommunicates priests who do not keep the rules of celibacy; prescribes that they shall help each other when one of them is insulted by indocile clerks. It forbids women to enter monasteries of men.
573	Paris.	21 bishops, 1 priest.	This council was assembled to decide the affair of Promotus, who had been consecrated bishop of Chateaudun, against all canonical rule. The council declared him deposed, according to the demand made by Pappolus, bishop of Chartres, administrator of the church of Chateaudun during the vacancy.
575	Lyons.		
577	Paris.	... ...	This council judged the affair of Pretextat.

Date.	Place	Present.	Object of the Council, Rules, &c.
578	Auxerre.	The bishop of Auxerre, 7 abbots, 34 priests, 3 deacons, all from the diocese of Auxerre.	This synod was held by Aunachaire, bishop of Auxerre; nothing was discussed but questions of discipline and ceremonies. *Rules.*—This synod forbids many pagan superstitions; it orders all priests to attend the synod in May, and the abbots to come to the council in November. It forbids repasts in churches, and allowing young girls and secular persons to sing there. No clerk shall summon any one, but he shall authorise his brother, or some other layman to do it. Every layman, who has despised the warnings of his arch-priest shall be excluded from the church so long as his disobedience shall last, and shall pay besides the fine that our glorious king has imposed. The synod forbids two masses to be said the same day on the same altar; to put a corpse upon a corpse; to receive the offering of those who have committed suicide; it also forbids clerks to hear or celebrate mass unless they be fasting; priests or deacons to assist at executions, or at sentences of death. No clerk shall summon another before the secular judge; priests may not sing or dance at feasts; abbots and monks may not be godfathers. It regulates the penance of an abbot who has not enforced the observance of the laws upon celibacy; his penance ought to take place in another monastery than that of which he is the head.
579	Châlons.	... ...	This council was convoked by Gontran to judge anew Sagittaire and Salone. They were condemned as guilty of high treason and being traitors to their country, the bishops having found that their other crimes could be expiated by canonical penance. The council consecrated a bishop for Maurienne, and subjected it to the bishop of Vienne.
579	Saintes.	... ...	The council recommended to the mercy of Heraclius the count Nantinuis, whom he had excommunicated, and who demanded absolution. The bishop granted it.

Date.	Place.	Present.	Object of the Council, Rules, &c.
580	Braines.	... ...	This council judged the affair of Gregory of Tours, accused by one Leudaste. The cause was gained by Leudaste.
581	Lyon.	... ...	This council reprimanded several bishops for negligence.
581	Macon.	21 bishops.	This council was convoked by Gontran. *Rules.*—No clerk shall wear silk or other secular vestments that do not become his profession. A judge who has without sufficient cause—that is to say, without a charge of manslaughter, theft, or craft, arrested a priest, shall be excommunicated. No Jew shall be made judge over Christians, nor shall they be permitted to receive taxes. The council forbids Christians to serve Jews, and gives to Christians, serfs of Jews, the power of redeeming their liberty. The council made a law upon the letters from bishops to other bishops concerning the redemption of captives, recommending that their authenticity be examined. It orders bishops to take care of the lepers found in the territory of their city, that they may not go to other cities.
583	Lyon.	8 bishops, 12 bishops, legates.	
584	Valence.	17 bishops.	The council confirmed the donations that Gontran, his wife and daughter, had made to churches.
585	Macon.	43 bishops, 15 envoys, 16 bishops without sees	The council convoked by Gontran, was composed of all the bishops under him, amongst whom several had been deprived of their sees by the Goths. He then wrote to all the bishops and judges of his kingdom to make them execute the decrees of the council. It was in this council that took place the celebrated discussion, of which it has so often been said, the question was whether women had a soul. The fact is, that a bishop insisted that woman ought not to be called *homo*; but he submitted to these two reasons,

Date.	Place.	Present.	Object of the Council, Rules, &c.
			that the Scripture says that God created man, male and female; and that Jesus Christ, son of a woman, is called the Son of Man.
			Rules.—The council orders that Sunday shall be more exactly observed; that every Christian shall present offerings; that the tithes shall be paid regularly, and that no baptisms shall be celebrated except in the time prescribed, unless it is a matter of necessity.
			One of the canons commences thus:—It behoves us to bring to their first state all those things of the holy church that we know are degenerated by the lapse of time.
			That no priest being intoxicated, or having broken his fast, dare to celebrate the sacrifice.
			The council made a law for protecting freedmen before the church, and charged their bishops to plead their cause. It also regulates, that if any powerful person has a quarrel with a bishop, the affair must be carried before the metropolitan, and no violence employed against the bishop; it orders the same to be observed as to priests and deacons.
			It forbids judges to decide about widows and orphans, without having informed the bishop, their natural protector, or, in his absence, one of his priests, and to decide all in deliberating with them.
			It forbids bishops to have their houses protected by dogs, as being contrary to hospitality. It forbids one corpse to be put in the sepulchre of another without the permission of those to whom it belongs. It regulates all the marks of honour that a layman ought to render to a clerk in meeting him, and the manner in which the clerk ought to respond.
			The council forbids clerks to assist at the trial of criminals.
			It orders that all demands be judged according to the laws and canons, " for treading under foot the laws and rules, those who are near the king, and are inflated by the power of the world, usurp the goods of others, and without judicial action or proof, not only deprive the poor of their fields, but eject them from their dwellings."

Date.	Place.	Present.	Object of the Council, Rules, &c.
587	Andelot.	... ...	This assemblage of bishops and nobles counselled and confirmed the peace between Gontran and Childebert.
588	Clermont.	... ...	This council was held by Sulpice, bishop of Bourges, with his suffragans, about certain parishes, which the bishops of Cahors and Rhodez were disputing; the latter gained the cause.
588	Place uncertain.	... ...	This council was occupied with several crimes, amongst others, with the murder of Pretextat, archbishop of Rouen.
589	Sourcy.	... ...	This council ordered that the entry of the town be granted to Drontegisile, bishop of Soissons.
589	Poitiers.	... ...	This assembly excommunicated Chrodielde and the nuns of the monastery of Saint Radegonde.
589	Châlons.	The bishops who were with Gontran.	This assembly confirmed the excommunication pronounced by the council of Poitiers.
589 590	Narbonne.	7 bishops.	This council was convoked by Recared, king of the Visigoths. *Rules.*—The council forbids clerks to wear purple vestments; to stop upon public places; to mix in the conversations which are held there; and to meet in councils or plots, under the patronage of the laity, which had been already forbidden by the council of Nicea (of Chalcedonia, according to Labbe.) It orders abbots not to inflict upon the guilty imprisoned in the monasteries any other penance than that imposed by the bishops. The council forbids certain pagan superstitions, and condemns the guilty, if they are freemen, to penance; if they are slaves, to the rod. It orders clerks to be subordinate to their superiors; forbids those who are at the altar to quit it during the celebration of mass; it forbids, under penalty of a fine, the Jews interring their dead with chants.

Date.	Place.	Present.	Object of the Council, Rules, &c.
590	On the confines of Auvergne, of Gerardin and Rouergue.		This council judged the affair of Tetradia, divorced from Didier, and first wife of Euladius, who claimed the property she had taken in flying to rejoin Didier.
590	Poitiers.	6 bishops.	This council judged the quarrel between Chrodielde and the abbess of the monastery of Poitiers.
590	Metz.	... ...	Gilles, bishop of Reims, was deposed in this council for the crime of high treason. Chrodielde and Basine were received into grace.
591	Nanterre.	... ...	The little king, Clotaire II., was baptized in this assembly.
594	Châlons.	... ...	This council regulated the manner in which the offices should be said in the monastery of Saint Marcel.
			Seventh Century.
	Châlons.	... ...	Queen Brunehault, in this council, deposed Saint Didier, bishop of Vienne.
615	Paris.	... ...	This council was convoked by Clotaire II. *Rules.*—No bishop shall choose a coadjutor for himself. No judge shall arrest a clerk without the knowledge of a bishop. The council forbids any one to touch the goods of a deceased ecclesiastic until his will is made known. It forbids bishops and all who have power, whether clergy or secular, to seize the goods or rights of a bishop. It forbids bishops and archdeacons to take possession of what has been left by a priest or an abbot, and to despoil the church under pretext of the good of the church. It forbids Jews to demand from princes any authority over Christians, and orders that he who has obtained it shall be baptized with all his family

Date.	Place.	Present.	Object of the Council, Rules, &c.
A little after the preceding.	Place uncertain.		*Rules.*—The council forbids making a layman archpriest, unless it be because the merit of his person has made the bishops judge it necessary for the consolation of the church, and the defence of the parishioners. If freedmen have sold themselves, when they are able to give the sum for which they sold themselves, they ought to receive their liberty; if amongst such persons, the husband has a free wife, or the wife a free husband, their children shall be free. The council forbids celebrating in the monasteries, unless by the permission of the bishops, baptisms and masses for the dead, or interring the laity there. It forbids depriving without reason, archpriests and the archdeacons.
625	Reims.	41 bishops.	There are after this council synodal statutes of the church of Reims, but they are thought to be of much later date; they contain nothing of importance. *Rules.*—The council renews the laws against the conspiracy of priests, and the snares they hold out for their bishops. It orders bishops to seek out and convert the heretics that may be found in Gaul. It orders that those whose lives shall be saved by their seeking refuge in the churches shall promise before being set at liberty to accomplish the canonical penance. If a Christian is forced to sell his slaves, he may not sell them to any but Christians, under pain of excommunication. If Jews wish to make their Christian slaves adopt their persuasion, or make them suffer cruel torments, they shall return into the power of the fisc. The council forbids receiving the accusation of persons who are not free, and reducing freedmen to servitude; it forbids, as did almost all the preceding councils, to regard as a bishop him who is not a native of the place, and who has not been chosen by the will of all the people, with the consent of the provincial bishops; it forbids bishops to break the sacred vases unless it is for the redemption of captives.
627	Mâcon.	... ...	Agrestius, monk of Luxeuil, rigorously at-

Date.	Place.	Present.	Object of the Council, Rules, &c.
			tacked the rule of Saint Columban; the abbot Eustache defended it; and the council sanctioned it.
628	Clichy.	Bishops and nobles, convoked by Clotaire.	The council of Clichy was occupied with public peace and ecclesiastical discipline.
633	Clichy.	16 bishops, king Dagobert and some noble laymen.	This council treated of fugitives and the asylum of the church of Saint Denis.
638	Paris.	9 bishops, king Dagobert, 3 noble laymen.	This council confirmed the privileges of the church of Saint Denis.
645	Orleans.	... ...	This council was assembled by Saint Eloy against a Greek who preached the heresy of the Monothelites. He was opposed by bishop Sauve, and driven from Gaul.
648	Bourges.	Provincial synod.	
650	Châlons.	38 bishops, 5 abbots, 1 archdeacon.	The council of Châlons deposed Agapius, and Bobon, bishops of Digne. *Rules.*—The council forbids consecrating at the same time two bishops for one town; confiding the property of parishes and the parishes themselves to laymen; selling slaves beyond the dominion of the king (Clovis II). It forbids judges to visit parishes and monasteries, which are under the jurisdiction of bishops, and to send before them clerks and abbots, to make them prepare lodgings. It forbids electing two abbots for one monastery, or one abbot to choose his successor, or abbots and monks to seek the protection of the nobles, and to go to the prince without the permission of the bishop; it complains that those nobles who have chapels shake the allegiance of their clerks to the jurisdiction of the ordinary. It forbids carrying arms in church, or attacking any one there to kill or wound him; it also forbids that women should sing indecent songs there.

Date.	Place.	Present.	Object of the Council, Rules, &c.
About 658	Nantes.	... ...	Nivard, bishop of Reims, consented in this assembly to the renovation of the monastery of Hautvilliers, near Marne.
664	Paris.	25 bishops.	These bishops confirmed the privileges granted to the church of Saint Denis by Landry, bishop of Paris. Labbe mentions this assembly but does not reckon it.
669	Clichy.	Bishops and nobles.	King Clovis in this assembly had the privileges of the church of Saint Denis committed to writing.
670	Autun.	... ...	This council, held by Saint Leger, was only occupied with monastic discipline, and prescribed nothing new on this subject. *Rules.*—Let the priest, or deacon, who does not know perfectly by heart the symbol of Saint Athanasius be condemned by his bishop. No layman shall be looked upon as catholic who does not go to communicate at Christmas, at Easter, and at Whitsuntide. No woman shall mount to the altar.
About 670	Sens.	34 bishops.	This council confirmed the privileges of the monastery of Saint Pierre-le-Vif.
679	Place uncertain.	... ...	This council condemned the Monothelites, and sent three legates to the pope, two bishops and one deacon.
685 or 684	In a royal palace.	... ...	Ebroin deposed in this council Saint Leger, and Lambert, bishop of Maestricht.
688	Id.	... ...	Saint Leger and Ebroin being dead, three bishops disputed for the body of Saint Leger; the council adjudged it to Ansoald, bishop of Poitiers.
692	Rouen.	16 bishops, 4 abbots, 1 legate, and many of the clergy.	This council granted several privileges to the monastery of Fontanelles, upon condition that it should not swerve from the rule of Saint Benedict.

Eighth Century.

Date.	Place.	Present.	Object of the Council, Rules, &c.
719	Maestricht.	... ...	Saint Willibrod and Saint Swithbert presided at this synod, which sent Saint Boniface and several other missionaries to preach the gospel to the Germans.
742	Germany.	Carloman, 7 bishops named, several others, and their priests, noble laymen.	Carloman convoked this council which was held at Augsburg or at Ratisbon; he had just arrived from Italy, and had received from pope Zachary the order to hold this council It is Carloman who speaks in these canons. *Rules.*—By the council of holy priests and my nobles, we institute bishops for the cities; we place Boniface at their head, and we order that synods shall be held every year. Priests are forbidden to carry arms, except those who are necessary in the armies to say mass, and to hear the confessions of sinners. Parish priests must submit to their bishops, and render them an account of their conduct every year. One must be cautious with strange and unknown bishops. Unknown priests and bishops may not be admitted to the holy mystery. The bishops, with the aid of the count (Gravio), must watch that the people do not fall into any pagan superstition. (Several dispositions follow regarding the conduct of the priests.)
743	Leptines.	... ...	This council was held by Pepin; it confirmed the decrees of the council of Germany. Pepin placed at the head of the bishops whom he had chosen, Abel, archbishop of Reims, and Adorbert, archbishop of Sens. Saint Boniface presided at this council; the object of it was to reform the clergy; the bishops, priests, and all the clerks promised to change their habits, and to conduct themselves according to the ancient canons; the monks received the rule of Saint Benedict; chastisements were denounced against those, male or female, who should be guilty of adultery. It is Pepin who speaks. At the end of this council are found several

Date.	Place.	Present.	Object of the Council, Rules, &c.
			pieces which appear to belong to it: the renunciation by the Saxons of the worship of Odin, in the German language; a list of the pagan superstitions of the Germans; an allocution on illicit marriages, one on morals, and one against the Jewish observance of the sabbath; also the canons given by Boniface; they contain nothing new. *Rules.*—We order that he who is in possession of a house, shall give a sol to the church or monastery. We order, as my father ordered before, that he who has practised any pagan superstition, be condemned to a fine of fifteen sous. Canons and statutes decreed by the synod held by Boniface, according to the order of the Roman pontiff and the prayer of the principal Franks and Gauls. These canons commence and finish by a profession of obedience to the pope, whom they engage to consult and obey in all things; they promise also to ask from him the Pallium. The metropolitan must hold a council every year; every bishop on his return from council must assemble his priests and his abbots and exhort them to observe its decrees; every bishop must visit his diocese every year; every priest must at Lent render a complete account of his conduct to his bishop. The metropolitans must watch the bishops and inquire about their zeal. If a bishop cannot correct his priests, he must carry the affair to the archbishops, as the Roman church has insisted upon my making a vow to indicate to her those priests whom I could never correct.
744	Soissons.	23 bishops, several clerks and laymen.	This council with the consent of the princes and the people, condemned the heresy of Adalbert; it made several canons of no interest; it is signed by Pepin and Radbod.
745	Germany.	... ...	This council deposed on the demand of Saint Boniface, the bishop of Mayence, who had killed some one in war. Carloman, who had convoked this council by the advice of Boniface, and his brother Pepin, gave to Boniface the bishopric of Mayence, which was made metropolitan of Germany.

Date.	Place.	Present.	Object of the Council, Rules, &c.
748	Duren.	... ...	This council was convoked by Pepin to occupy itself with the repair of churches and the affairs of the poor, widows and orphans, to whom it was urgent that justice should be rendered.
752	Vermerie.	... ...	This council was held in the presence of Pepin. *Rules.*—The council forbids giving a woman the veil against her will, and in this case declares her at liberty; the priest who has done it is disgraced. A freeman who has married a wife, believing her to be free, can marry again upon learning that she is not; and so for a woman, unless her husband has sold himself through poverty, and she has consented to it, and the price of the sale has kept her. He who knows that the woman he marries is a serf must keep her. A serf who has a concubine who is a serf, can quit her and receive another from the hands of his master; but he would do better to keep her. If a man is obliged to fly, and his wife refuse to accompany him, he can marry again after he has done penance. If a freed serf has commerce with a woman who is a serf, must marry her if the master give his consent; if not, so long as she lives he may not have another wife. He who permits his wife to take the veil cannot marry again.
752	Metz.	... ...	This council was held under king Pepin; all its dispositions bear the mark of civil authority. *Rules*—The count must force the priests to attend the synod. No one shall, under any pretext, stop the pilgrims who are travelling to Rome. A livre may not contain more than 22 sous, of which one must be for the coiner. Franchises must be preserved. This council confiscates the goods of those who make forbidden marriages, and condemns to pecuniary and corporal punishment those who aid or tolerate them.

Date.	Place.	Present.	Object of the Council, Rules, &c.
755	Verne.	Nearly all the bishops of Gaul.	The council was held by the order and in the presence of king Pepin. *Rules.*—There must be bishops in every town. All must obey the bishops whom we have constituted metropolitans, from this time until we can do it more canonically. There shall be every year two synods, one in the calends of March, in the presence of the king, and in whatsoever place he please; the other in October, and in the place that the bishops shall have chosen in March. All the ecclesiastics that have been so directed by the metropolitans shall come to the second synod. The bishop shall have the power of correcting his clergy and the monks. Those men who say they have been tonsured for the love of God, and who live on their property, and according to their fancy, shall be shut up in a monastery, or shall lead a canonical life under the direction of the bishop. If a monastery has fallen into the hands of laymen, so that the bishop cannot amend it, and the monks wish for the salvation of their souls to leave it, and to enter another, they must be permitted to do so. Bishops who have no diocese must not exercise any function in the diocese of other bishops. As the people have been persuaded that they may not on Sunday go on horseback, on oxen, or in carriages, or travel or prepare their nourishment, or cleanse themselves or their houses, (and as this is more Jewish than Christian,) we have decided that Sunday may be kept as it has been hitherto. We think that we ought to abstain from cultivating the land, that we may have more facility to come to church; if any one does work that is interdicted, his chastisement does not belong to the laity, but to the priests. All laymen, whether noble or not, must be married publicly. No church may remain more than three months without a bishop. Royal monasteries must render account

Date.	Place.	Present.	Object of the Council, Rules, &c.
			of their income to the king; those of the episcopacy, to the bishop.
756	Leptines.	... ...	This council was held by king Pepin, who endeavoured to procure the restitution of church property: not being able to succeed, they imposed a rent of twelve deniers on the farms on this property, and they ordered a levy of ninths and tenths with the same view.
757	Compiegne.	20 bishops, 14 ecclesiastics.	This council was held by king Pepin in the general assembly of the people. *Rules.*—All the canons of this council regard marriage; they permit the wife of a leper to marry another man, if she has the consent of her husband; and the man who has married in a fief to which he has followed his lord, after the death of this lord, if he is despoiled of the fief which he received, and has left the wife he received at the same time, and married again in his own country, is permitted to regard this second wife as legitimate.
758	Compiegne.	... ...	This assembly, which perhaps ought not to be counted here, was that in which Tassilon, duke of Bavaria, swore fidelity to Pepin.
759	Germany.	... ...	Guarin and Ruithard, employed by the fisc, condemned to prison for disorderly conduct, Othmar, abbot of Saint Gall, whose only crime appears to be that he had complained and still complained of their exactions.
761	Wolwich.	... ...	Pepin held this assembly in Auvergne; they disputed against heresies on the Trinity. Pepin made many donations to the neighbouring churches.
763	Nevers.	... ...	Pepin held this assembly; it has left nothing regarding the church.
764	Worms.		
765	Attigny.	27 bishops, 17 abbots.	Nothing remains of this assembly except the methods taken by its members to assure themselves a great number of masses and prayers after their death.

Date.	Place.	Present.	Object of the Council, Rules, &c.
766	Orleans.		
767	Gentilly.		In this assembly, held, like the preceding, by Pepin, there was a discussion between the Greeks and the Romans touching the Trinity and the procession of the Holy Ghost and images.
767	Bourges.		
768	Saint Denis.		
770	Worms.		
771	Valenciennes.		
772	Worms.		
773	In Bavaria.	5 bishops, 13 abbots.	
773	Geneva.		
775	Duren.		
776	Worms.	... ...	Many Saxons were baptized in this assembly.
777	Paderborn.	... ...	In this one also.
779	Duren.	... ...	These rules bear the title of capitularies, but they are nevertheless canons of the ecclesiastical assemblies held by Charlemagne. *Rules.*—Bishops who are not ordained must be so without delay. Churches cannot give asylum to men condemned to death. There are many other dispositions, but they relate more to public police, than to ecclesiastical discipline.
780	Near Lippe.	... ...	This council was occupied with the erection of episcopal sees in Saxony, and the construction of several churches.
782	Near Lippe, or at Cologne.		
785	Paderborn.	... ...	Witikind was baptized.
786	Paderborn.	... ...	They occupied themselves with the affairs of the church of Saxony.
786	Worms.		
787	Worms.		
788	Ingelheim.		

Date.	Place.	Present.	Object of the Council, Rules, &c.
788	Narbonne.	29 bishops, Didier, the pope's legate; 3 envoys from bishops and one chancellor.	This council treated of the heresy of Felix, bishop of Urgel, and the limits of the diocese of Narbonne. Under the date of 789, there is a collection of capitularies, given by Charlemagne upon ecclesiastical discipline; the council of Soissons calls them synodals; they are in a great part taken from Eastern canons and the decrees of the popes. Charlemagne held that year an assembly at Aix la Chapelle.
790	Worms.		
792	Ratisbon.	... ...	This council condemned Felix, bishop of Urgel, who said Jesus Christ was the adopted son of God.
794	Francfort.	The bishops of Gaul, Germany, and Italy, 2 legates from the pope.	This council condemned for the third time, Felix and Elpaud, archbishop of Toledo, who held the same opinion as Felix. The council rejected with anathema the doctrine of the council of Constantinople upon the worship of images, regarding it as idolatrous. *Rule.*—The council ordered a maximum price for the sale of goods, and ordered the new money to be received. It forbids avaricious cellarers to be chosen in monasteries. Abbots may not blind or mutilate their monks; ecclesiastics and monks may not drink in an alehouse; clerks of the king's chapel may not communicate with clerks who are rebellious to their bishop. Bishops may not absent themselves from their diocese more than three weeks. Bishops may not be ignorant of the canons and the rules; they may not invoke new saints; the sacred woods must be destroyed.
797	Aix-la-Chapelle.	... ...	This council was occupied with the subject of the construction of the monastery of St. Paul at Rome.
799	Aix-la-Chapelle.	... ...	This council received the abjuration of Felix.
799	Ratisbon.	... ...	The date of this council is uncertain, amongst other things it treats of the chorbishops or country-bishops. Traces of it are only to be found in the capitularies of Charlemagne.
800	Tours.		

Date.	Place.	Present.	Object of the Council, Rules, &c.
	Place uncertain. Worms.	... ...	Nothing is left of these councils and their date; it is only known that they occupied themselves as to the manner in which the priests could purge themselves from the crimes of which they were accused.

Ninth Century.

Date.	Place.	Present.	Object of the Council, Rules, &c.
802	Aix la Chapelle.	... ...	This council was occupied with the reform of monastic and ecclesiastical discipline. All who were present swore fidelity to the emperor.
809	Aix la Chapelle.	... ...	This council treated of the question of the procession of the Holy Ghost which had been raised by John, a Jerusalem monk; he sent a legation to the pope to have his decision. The council was also occupied with discipline, but nothing was decided.
813	Arles.	... ...	These five councils of 813 were held by order of Charlemagne, for the reform of ecclesiastical discipline; much is repetition; the general intention was to oppose the ignorance, grossness, and violence that pervaded the clergy; all recommend to the priests and bishops retirement from the affairs of the world, goodness and study, and interdicts them avarice, &c. These dispositions so often repeated in several councils, announce the progress that the secular spirit was making every day in the clergy. There are also several questions upon tithes, the observation of the Sabbath, monastic discipline, and the stability of ecclesiastics. These councils recommend a great preparation for communion, and seem to desire that the laity should not communicate so often. *Rules.*—The council orders that the bishops shall carefully instruct the priests and the people regarding baptism and the mysteries of the faith. They must preach not only in the towns, but also in the parishes.

Date.	Place.	Present.	Object of the Council, Rules, &c.
			Bishops must protect the poor against oppression, and address themselves to the king to procure the cessation of it. It forbids the laity to receive money from the priests to recommend them to benefices.
813	Mayence.	30 bishops, 25 abbots.	*Rules.*—The council orders that powerful persons, counts, bishops, &c., may only buy the goods of the poor in public under pain of nullity. It prescribes rules for the canonical life of the clerks. It forbids holding assemblies for temporal affairs in the church. It recommends the priests teaching the people the Creed and the Lord's Prayer, at least, in the vulgar tongue, if they cannot learn them otherwise, and declares free the clerks and the monks tonsured against their will.
813	Reims.	... ...	*Rules.*—The council forbids a priest to pass from an inferior title to a superior one; monks may not attend secular pleadings; a town or monastery may not have more servants of God in it than it can well contain.
813	Tours.	... ...	*Rules.*—The council recommends bishops to read, and, if possible, to retain by heart the gospel and the epistles of Saint Paul; not to give way to excesses at table; not to amuse themselves with games of actors, and to exhort priests to fly them, and also the chase. It forbids priests to give the communion, indiscriminately, to all those who attend mass. It recommends all the faithful, rich or poor, to submit to the bishops
813	Châlons.	... ...	This council was occupied with the administration of penance, and it pronounces anathemas against those penitential works whose errors are certain, and the authors uncertain. Their appreciation of sins was very unequal. The council counts eight sins, from which it is difficult to keep; these are the deadly sins; and hatred is comprised therein. It is, without doubt, this which makes the eighth.

Date.	Place.	Present.	Object of the Council, Rules, &c.
			Rules.—The council forbids bishops to require a private oath from the priests they ordain. It forbids separating the serfs united in marriage; it condemns to penitence, but does not separate from their husbands those women who to gain this end have their children confirmed. Some think that we ought to confess our sins to God alone, others that we ought to confess them to the priests; both one and the other are useful in the church of God. The confession which is made to God purges from sin; that made to the priest teaches us how to purge ourselves of them, for God is the author and the distributor of health and salvation, and he accords much by the invisible effect of his power, and much by the action of the doctors. The council declares that confession ought to be entire.
814	Lyons.	... ...	This council named Agobard archbishop of Lyons, in the place of Leidrade, who had retired in a monastery at Soissons.
814	Noyon.	11 bishops, 8 abbots, 4 counts, several of the clergy.	This council, which was held by Wulfaire, archbishop of Reims, and his suffragans, terminated a dispute about boundaries between the bishops of Soissons and Noyon.
	Trèves.	... ...	The date of this council, held by Hetton, archbishop of Trèves, is uncertain.
816	Aix la Chapelle.	... ...	*Rules.*—This council, according to the order of Louis le Debonnaire, made two regulations, one for the canons in 145 articles; the other for the nuns in 28. Louis sent copies of it to each metropolitan, with the order to see them observed in their provinces. These two rules are extracted from the fathers and the councils, and contain nothing of any importance except the growing tendency to impose monastic life upon the clergy. This rule of the canons differs very slightly from that of a monastery. *Rules.*—This rule given to the nuns, as well as a multitude of canons at this epoch, shows the difficulty the bishops had to reduce them to the obedience they wished to impose

Date.	Place.	Present.	Object of the Council, Rules, &c.
			on them; the following dispositions recur continually: Abbesses must submit to the bishops; abbesses may not go out without the permission of the bishop; abbesses may not give the veil, nor take upon themselves any sacerdotal functions. We see, too, that they had a great difficulty in making them keep the cloister; for the councils frequently forbid their receiving men, monks, or priests, at forbidden hours, and without necessity.
817	Aix la Chapelle.	... ...	This council was composed of abbots and monks alone; they only treated of monastic discipline.
818	Aix-la-Chapelle.	... ...	This council condemned several bishops who had taken the part of his nephew Bernard against Louis le Debonnaire.
818	Vannes.		
819	Aix la Chapelle.		
820	Thionville	... ...	This council, held by the archbishops of Mayence, Cologne, Trèves, Reims, their suffragans, and the deputies of the other provinces of Gaul, pronounced ecclesiastical punishment and fines against those who should be found guilty towards clerks.
822	Attigny.	... ...	It was in this council that Louis le Debonnaire submitted to do penance.
823	Compiegne.	... ...	This council was occupied with ecclesiastical goods usurped by the laity. The legates of pope Paschal were there.
824	Paris.	... ...	This council was occupied about the worship of idols. The authors of the collection regard as forged the acts which bear its name, but have no knowledge of the real acts. The council was held on the occasion of two legates being sent on the same question to the pope by the emperor of the east. The council also sent its acts by two legates to the pope. *Rules.*—The canons of this council are contained in three books. In the first, in

Date.	Place.	Present.	Object of the Council, Rules, &c.
			thirty-four articles, the council established the distinction of the two powers, and placed that of the priests much above that of the kings. It announces to the clergy the necessity of correcting themselves; it insists upon the right administration of baptism, and the necessity of well explaining the meaning of it to the people; it declares against simony, against the avarice of the bishops, which it endeavours to check, by renewing the ancient dispositions as to the goods of the church; it also makes several rules which apply to manners. It demands that two councils be held every year in each province, and that the priests, deacons, and all those who are aggrieved attend them. The council assimilate the chor-bishops to the seventy disciples of Jesus Christ, and complain that they wish to assume the functions of a bishop. The council orders bishops to watch the schools with care, and to summon the scholars to the provincial council. It interdicts commerce, and the occupations of a farmer to the priests and monks, and enjoins exact residence to the bishops and priests. It forbids bishops who are not in want to take the fourth part of the offerings; it forbids priests to give the veil, and women to take it themselves; it complains bitterly that women serve at the altar, and even give to the people the body and blood of Jesus Christ. It forbids, unless in a case of absolute necessity, to say mass in houses and gardens; it forbids forcing the priests to do so—at any rate, it cannot be done without an altar consecrated by the bishop. It also forbids celebrating mass without having any one to respond. The second book of the council treats of the duties of kings. It is there declared that, "No king ought to think he holds his kingdom from his ancestors, but from God." The rest of the book treats of submission to the king, the duties of Christians, and the respect to be shown in churches, in thirteen articles. The third book is a letter from the bishops to the king, in which they give him an ac-

Date.	Place.	Present.	Object of the Council, Rules, &c.
			count of all that has passed in the council, and indicate to him the rules they wish particularly to be observed. Besides those we have mentioned, they added others. They demand that schools should be founded in three places in the empire, that the efforts of his father and his own should not perish by negligence. They demand that he send from the palace a crowd of priests and monks, who reside there in spite of their bishops. They complain against the custom of celebrating Service on holy days in the chapels of the palace. In short, they give the king several counsels, in which the tone is very different to the habits of respect the bishops had contracted with Charlemagne.
826	Ingelheim.	... ...	This council was occupied with the affairs of the church. Louis le Debonnaire received there the envoys from the pope, and from the Holy Land.
829	Paris.	... ...	Louis le Debonnaire convoked these councils of Paris, Mayence, Lyons, and Toulouse, which were held the same year, 829. He indicated the bishops who should compose it, the questions to be treated, and the capitularies they should adopt. Of these councils we have only that of Paris. It is probable that they much resembled each other.
829	Mayence.		
829	Lyon.		
829	Toulouse.		
829	Worms.	... ...	This council confirmed the resolutions of the four preceding ones.
830	Lyon.	7 bishops, 2 chorbishops, 13 abbots, priests, or deacons, 14 proxies.	The synod confirmed the donation that had been made to the monastery of Saint Pierre de Bezon by Alberic, bishop of Langres.
831	Nimeguen.	... ...	This assembly deposed Jesse, bishop of Amiens, who had taken part against Louis le Debonnaire.

Date.	Place.	Present.	Object of the Council, Rules, &c.
833	Worms.	26 bishops, 5 abbots.	Alderic, archbishop of Sens, permitted in this council, that the abbey of Saint Remy should be removed.
833	Compiegne.	... ...	This assembly deprived Louis le Debonnaire of the crown.
834	Saint Denis.	... ...	This assembly again admitted Louis to the communion and the empire.
834	Attigny.	... ...	This assembly was occupied with the bad state of the church. The bishops referred to lay judges the decision of a question of marriage, reserving for themselves the power of applying a penance, if it must take place.
835	Metz.	... ...	Louis complained in this council of Ebbon, archbishop of Reims, who had excommunicated him. Ebbon chose judges from amongst the bishops according to the African canons.
835	Thionville.	43 bishops.	Louis again received absolution in this council. Ebbon was condemned, and abdicated.
836	Aix la Chapelle.	... ...	This council was assembled by the order of Louis le Debonnaire, to deliberate upon three objects which form the matter of its three books: 1st, the lives of the bishops, twelve articles; 2nd, the doctrine of the bishops, twelve articles, and the doctrine and lives of the inferior orders of the clergy, sixteen articles; lastly, 3rd, the person of the king, his children, and his servants, twenty-five articles. The last articles of this book have, however, no direct connexion with its title, and are general dispositions. The council also addressed to Pepin, king of Aquitaine, a treatise, in three books, in which it confirmed, by the authority of the Scriptures, the things it had ordered. The first book has thirty-eight articles; the second, thirty one; the third, twenty-seven. They are all citations, narrations, and reflections, and contain no positive disposition. As to the canons, they are only the repetition of the preceding councils. The third book, that part which relates

Date.	Place.	Present.	Object of the Council, Rules, &c.
			to the king, and to several other points, is the copy, sometimes abridged, of the third book of the sixth council of Paris. *Rules.*—The council recommends to the priests to watch that the faithful who are confided to them be baptized and confirmed, know the Creed and the Lord's prayer, and how they ought to conduct themselves; and that they be corrected of their faults as they ought, and do not die without confession, sacerdotal prayers, and extreme unction. It recommends that there should not be in the monasteries for women dark places and corners, where they can offend God without being seen. It recommends that, where it is possible, every church have its priest, who will govern it himself, or under the conduct of a priest of superior grade. It forbids fasting, marrying, and pleading on Sunday. It recommends communion every Sunday.
836	Cremieu, in the Lyonnais.	... ...	Agobard, archbishop of Lyons, and Bernard, bishop of Vienne, had been deposed by the council of Thionville for having deposed Louis le Debonnaire. This council was assembled to judge them, but nothing could be decided, on account of their absence. They were at last restored to grace.
839	Châlons.	... ...	This assembly regulated the affairs of the church and the state. In 841, an assembly was held at Ingelheim, at which twenty bishops assisted, and several of the clergy; by the order of Lothaire, then emperor, it returned to Ebbon the see of Reims, from which he had been deposed.
841	Auxerre.	20 bishops, 4 abbots.	This assembly ordered a fast of three days on the occasion of the battle which had just taken place at Fontenay.
842	Bourges.	... ...	This council, held by the partisans of Charles le Chauve, approved the deposition of Ebbon.

Date.	Place.	Present.	Object of the Council, Rules, &c.
843	Toulouse.		Nothing remains of this assembly but the capitularies of Charles le Chauve. We can easily perceive that they were given at the solicitations of simple priests; they are only given while awaiting a general council. *Rules.*—The bishops must not take it ill if the priests lay claims before the king; they must not insist upon a too strong protestation from the priests; they must not demand it when they are not making the visit of their diocese, and they must only demand it once when they visit it twice; they must not divide the parishes to receive double; they must not constrain the priests to attend more than twice a-year at the councils.
843	Coulaine.	... ...	This assembly was held by Charles le Chauve; the capitularies which remain recommend the observance of the duties towards God and the royal power; they offer nothing curious.
844	Loiré, in Anjou.	... ...	The canons of this council are to the same effect as the preceding; it appears that they relate to the rebellion of Count Lambert.
844	Thionville.	... ...	This assembly was presided over by Droyon, bishop of Metz; it was held in the place called the Judgment Seat. The three sons of Louis le Debonnaire here made peace, and passed several capitularies, which had for their object to order the affairs of the church. *Rules.*—Bishops must be ordained for the vacant sees, and those who have lost theirs must take them again. The monasteries confided to the laity must be given in charge to religious persons, male or female. Ecclesiastical property must not be invaded.
844	Vern.	... ...	This council had nearly the same aim as the preceding one; it was presided over by Ebroin, bishop of Poitiers. *Rules.*—Send persons to chastise those who contemn the divine and human laws; let

Date.	Place.	Present.	Object of the Council, Rules, &c.
			religious men visit the monasteries, to inquire into the relaxation of discipline. Clerks and monks who have deserted must be returned to their churches and convents. Ecclesiastical goods must be returned; the churches must be provided with pastors. Those bishops who do not go to war, whether it be on account of the feebleness of their body, or by the indulgence of the king, must confide their men to one of the faithful, that the military service may not suffer by it. Kings and bishops may not reside long with the bishops; and they must not oppose themselves to the holding of the provincial councils. No novelty must be adopted in the explanation of the Scriptures. Bishops must have some one to instruct the country priests. Laymen must not employ the priests of the church in the care of their farms. The king may not take canons into his service without the consent of the bishops. Do not demand from the priests illicit tributes upon the tithes and the goods of the church.
845	Bauvais.	... ...	This council was held by Charles le Chauve and his bishops; it is for the same end as the two others.
845	Meaux	... ...	This council repeated and confirmed the canons of the preceding councils; it made a great many new ones, of which several repeated ancient dispositions; all are in the same spirit as the three preceding ones: ecclesiastical reform and the restitution of goods and immunitico.
846	Vannes.	... ...	Nomenoe, prince of Brittany, after having expelled several bishops, named others, augmented the number of sees, assembled the bishops on his side, and had himself crowned king.
846 or rather 847	Paris.	20 bishops, 5 abbots.	This council forbade Ebbon the diocese of Reims, until he submitted to his judgment about which the pope was occupied. They

Date.	Place.	Present.	Object of the Council, Rules, &c.
			terminated what they could not finish at the council of Meaux. *Rules.*—The prince must give to the bishops, powers signed with his seal, that when they need civil authority, they can so accomplish their divine ministry. Royal chapels must not be confided to laymen, but to ecclesiastics.
847	Mayence.	13 bishops, many of the clergy.	Raban, archbishop of Mayence, held this council with his suffragans and their clergy; the council was occupied with discipline, and reclaimed the rights and immunities of the church. It condemned a prophetess, named Thiota, who announced the end of the world, and denounced the ecclesiastical orders. *Rules.* — No penance shall be imposed on the dying, but they must be contented with their confession, and the alms and prayers of their friends, and they must give them the viatic, and pray for them; if they get well, they must submit to the penance. The council grants Christian interment and the prayers of the church to criminals executing, after they have confessed.
848	Mayence.	... ...	This council condemned the monk Gottschalk, who maintained the doctrine of predestination; Raban presided at the council; Gottschalk was sent to Hincmar, archbishop of Reims.
848	Lyon.	... ...	This council was occupied with the affair of a priest, named Goldegaire; it offers nothing interesting.
848	Limoges.	... ...	This council grants the demand of the canons of the church of Saint Martin, who desired to be made monks. The bishop of Limoges consented with reluctance.
849	Chartres.	... ...	Charles, brother of Pepin, demanded and received the tonsure in this council.
		... ...	
849	Kiersy.	16 bishops, 3 abbots, several of the clergy.	This council condemned Gottschalk again, had him beaten with rods, and put in prison.

Date.	Place.	Present.	Object of the Council, Rules, &c.
849	Paris, according to some, Tours.	22 bishops.	This council was held at the invitation of Lantraun, archbishop of Tours, on the subject of Nomenoe, and addressed him a letter of reproach, in which it menaced him with excommunication.
850	Moret.		
851	Soissons.	... ...	Pepin, king of Aquitaine, was in this council deposed and tonsured.
852	Mayence.		
852	Sens, date uncertain.	13 bishops, 2 abbots.	This council confirmed the privileges of the monastery of Saint Remy.
853	Sens.	... ...	This council refused to consecrate bishop of Chartres, Burchard, recommended by Charles le Chauve, but who was unworthy of it.
853	Soissons.	27 bishops, 6 abbots, several of the clergy.	This council admitted Burchard to the episcopacy; it was occupied in supplying the wants of several churches; on points of general discipline, and ordinations made by Ebbon, predecessor of Hincmar, at Reims; they were annulled. Charles le Chauve consulted the council upon the instructions that he should give to his envoys; they were approved. *Rules.*—Instructions of Charles le Chauve. Our envoys must take care, how the lords take it ill, when the bishops or their servants strike their serfs with their rods, to correct them; they must know that then they will be submitted to our ban and to a rigorous chastisement. Our faithful must know that we have declared to the synod, that what we should grant of the goods of the church to an unreasonable demand, were it to a bishop or to an abbot, will not avail; they must then take care not to make such demands.
853	Kiersy	... ...	This council made four canons against Gottschalk, and excommunicated again a nobleman, named Fulcre, who had left his wife to espouse another.
853	Verncric.	22 bishops.	This council looked to the affairs of many churches.

Date.	Place.	Present.	Object of the Council, Rules, &c.
855	Valence.	18 bishops and many of the clergy.	This council made many canons about predestination, and about particular interests and objects of discipline. It was favourable to Gottschalk. *Rules.*—That the bishops take care not to ordain persons unworthy of the ministry. The council blamed the custom of taking the oath, in judicial proceedings, because it necessarily led to perjury. It blamed also the judgment by battle, and refused to those who were slain Christian burial. It recommended the erection of schools of science, divine, humane, and for church singing, seeing that the long interruption of study, ignorance of the faith, and the neglect of all sciences, had invaded many of the churches of God. That there is nothing reprehensible in the priests' service towards the bishops.
857	Kiersy.	.. ...	This council was held for ecclesiastical reform, and convoked by Charles le Chauve.
857	Mayence.	.. ...	This council discussed questions concerning ecclesiastical law.
858	Kiersy.	The archbishop of Rouen and his suffragans, the suffragans of Reims.	This council addressed to Louis le Germanique, who was invading the states of Charles le Chauve, a letter of advice and reproach.
858	Soissons.	... ...	This council was held by order of Louis le Germanique, who had entered Gaul, sword in hand.
859	Metz.	6 bishops, 3 archbishops.	This council occupied itself with the quarrels of Louis and Charles.
859	Langres.	2 archbishops, many bishops.	*Rules.* — This council made 16 canons, which were confirmed at the council of Toul or Savonieres, and which are only found there. The six first confirmed the canons of the council of Valence in favour of Gottschalk. The twelfth canon recommended that each congregation have a superior of its order.

Date	Place.	Present.	Object of the Council, Rules, &c.
859	Langres.	8 bishops.	
859	Toul.	The bishops of twelve provinces.	This council occupied itself with the peace between Louis, and Charles; with the complaints of Charles against many bishops; with the Breton bishops, and points of discipline.
860	Aix la Chapelle.	... ...	These two councils were held for the divorce of Lothaire and Teutberge, at a month apart: they pronounced the divorce.
860	Aix la Chapelle.	7 bishops.	
860	Coblentz.	2 abbots, 10 bishops, and many of the laity.	This council occupied itself with the peace between the kings; they here made a treaty.
860	Toul ou Savonieres.	40 bishops from 14 provinces.	This council made some canons about discipline.
860	Toul ou Tusey.	... ...	This council occupied itself about the affair of Ingeltrude, wife of count Boson, who had quitted her.
861	Soissons.	... ...	Hincmar excommunicated in this provincial synod, Rothade, bishop of Soissons.
862	Sens.	... ...	It is not known precisely where this council was held, which deposed Heriman, bishop of Nevers.
862	Aix la-Chapelle:	8 bishops.	This council permitted Lothaire the second to espouse another wife than Teutberge.
862	Sablonières.	... ...	This council occupied itself with the accusation brought against Lothaire II., protecting Ingeltrude and Judith, the daughter of Charles le Chauve, who, without his consent, had espoused the count Baudouin.
862	Pitres.	37 bishops, 11 abbots, many ecclesiastics.	This council confirmed the privileges of many monasteries, and took many measures to re-establish the order in the state and church.
862	Soissons.	... ...	This council occupied itself about the affair of Judith.
862	Soissons.	... ...	This council occupied itself about the affair of Rothade, who, in the council of Pitres, had appealed to the pope; he was deposed.

Date.	Place.	Present.	Object of the Council, Rules, &c.
863	Senlis.	... ...	According to Pagi, this council is the same as the preceding.
863	Metz.	... ...	This council, composed of bishops of the kingdom of Lothaire, approved his divorce; the pope annulled the judgment, and excommunicated the bishops.
863	Place uncertain in Aquitaine.	... ...	This council excommunicated Etienne, count of Auvergne; it was held by order of pope Nicholas, who had some legates here.
863	Vermerie.	... ...	This council occupied itself about the abbey of Saint Calais, which the bishop of Mans claimed as under his jurisdiction; it pronounced in favour of the abbey.
866	Soissons.	35 bishops.	This council was held by order of Pope Nicholas, who, after having ordained that it should restore to Rothade his bishopric, wished to do the same for Wulfade and the clerks ordained by Ebbon, since his deposition by Hincmar: it did as he desired.
866	Troyes.	20 bishops of 6 provinces.	Hincmar was attacked in this council by some bishops who wished to please the king; however, he finished by prevailing, and made it give an account to the pope of all that had passed, as he had ordered. Pope Adrian wrote to this council that it should consecrate no other bishops than such as should be named by the emperor; the bishops refused.
868	Place uncertain.	Bishops of Gaul and Bourgoyne.	This council was occupied about discipline.
868	Worms.		
869	Vermeriæ.	29 bishops.	Hincmar, bishop of Laon, and nephew of Hincmar, archbishop of Reims, accused before this council, by Charles le Chauve, and by his uncle, of having made some unjust excommunications, failed in his oaths to the king, and unjustly deprived some clerks of their benefices; he appealed to the pope.
869	Metz.	... ...	This council gave to Charles le Chauve the

Date.	Place.	Present.	Object of the Council, Rules, &c.
			kingdom of his nephew Lothaire, who had died in Italy.
860	Pitres.	12 bishops.	
870	Attigny.	Bishops of 10 provinces.	Hincmar, bishop of Laon, again accused, again appealed to the pope.
870	Cologne.		This council treated of discipline.
871	Douzy-les-Prés.	22 bishops, 8 envoys of bishops, 8 ecclesiastics.	This council deposed the bishop of Laon.
873	Châlons.	5 bishops, 1 rural bishop, many of the clergy.	This council was occupied with a discussion between two churches of Châlons.
873	Cologne.	11 bishops, 5 priests, 1 deacon.	This council confirmed the privileges accorded to the prebendaries of the cathedral of Cologne.
873	Senlis.	Bishops of two provinces.	This council, convoked by Charles le Chauve, degraded from the order of deacon, his son, Carloman.
874	Douzy-les-Prés.		This council was occupied with forbidden marriages, and the invasion of church property.
875	Châlons.	46 bishops.	This council confirmed the privileges of the monastery of Tournus.
876	Pontion.	2 legates, 5 bishops, 3 abbots.	This council was held a little after the coronation of Charles le Chauve, as emperor, it confirmed the acts of the council which he had held at Pavia, just before. *Capitularies of the council of Pontion.*—That the holy Roman church be honoured and revered by all, as the mother of all churches, and that no one dare to act unjustly against her right and power, and that she have power, and fitting strength to show towards the universal church a pastoral solicitude, and to invoke for all, by her holy prayers, the Author of all things. And that respect be paid by all towards the lord John, our spiritual father, sovereign pontiff, and universal pope; that all receive, with great veneration, the things that, ac-

Date.	Place.	Present.	Object of the Council, Rules, &c.
			cording to his sacred ministry, he has decided in his apostolic authority, and that we render to him, in all things, the obedience which is his due. That the imperial dignity be respected by all, and that no one disobey with impunity that which the emperor shall ordain, by letters or by messages. *The Capitularies enact:* That the bishops lead, with their clerks, a canonical life; that they treat the counts and vassals of the king as sons, and that these shall honour them as fathers; that the bishops shall have the authority of the missi dominici; that the bishops and the counts, in their circuits, shall not lodge at the houses of the poor, unless invited.
878	In Neustria.	... ...	This council, presided over by Hincmar, received the complaints of the emperor Louis III. against the devastations that had been committed in his states by Hugues, the son of Lothaire II., and Waldrade; the council menaced Hugues with excommunication.
878	Troyes.	Pope John, and 29 bishops.	This council excommunicated, by command of pope John, Lambert, duke of Spoleto, Adalbert, Formoso, bishop of Porto, and their partizans. It heard the complaint of Hincmar, bishop of Laon; confirmed many privileges, and made many canons. It excommunicated also those who invaded the property of the churches. The pope here crowned Louis le Begue.
879	Mantaille in the Viennoise.	29 bishops.	This council, composed of bishops and grandees of the kingdom of Arles, gave to Boson the title of king.
881	Fimes.	... ...	This council was held in the church of St. Macre, in a place now named Fimes, and which is between the diocese of Reims and Soissons; the council occupied itself with discipline and ecclesiastical reforms.
883	Toulouse.	The bishops of Septimania and Aquitaine.	The account of this council is found in the life of Saint Theodard, archbishop of Narbonne; being curious as a picture of manners, we give an extract, while agreeing

Date.	Place.	Present.	Object of the Council, Rules, &c.
			with father Labbe, that its authenticity is doubtful: "The Jews of Toulouse complained to king Carloman of the injuries that they suffered from the bishop and people of this town, who, three times a year, beat and maltreated one of them; the affair was referred to a council of bishops of Septimania and Aquitaine; the discussion was opened there; the Jews complaining of the injustice of the treatment they suffered, the Christians calling it a just chastisement. "Then Theodard, who was very young, with the permission of the bishop of Toulouse, spoke, and produced two acts, one of Charlemagne, the other of Louis le Debonnaire, which established that the Jews of Toulouse, having called Abderrahman to France, Charles had only allowed them their lives, upon the condition that, on Christmas-day, Good Friday, and Ascension-day, one of them should receive before the door of the church a beating from the hand of a notable, and make an offering of three pounds of wax. "The bishops having heard these things, and being consulted by the duke, cried out, 'Far be it from us to oppose anything to this just and equitable decision of the king.' "The discussion between Theodard and the Jews continued and warmed. The Jews pronounced against Jesus Christ such blasphemies, that the duke, furious, menaced them with the last extremities; then they threw themselves at the feet of the bishop, entreating him to obtain their pardon from the duke, in such a manner, that, remaining subject to the torture the emperor had decreed for them, they might live in peace and safety. "The duke consented, after some resistance, but adding the following condition, suggested by Theodard; that the Jew who was to be scourged, before being struck, should declare, in a loud voice, before all the assembly: 'It is just that the heads of the Jews should be submitted to the blows of the Christians; because they would not submit to Jesus of Nazareth, Lord of lords, and King of kings.' If the Jew

Date.	Place.	Present.	Object of the Council, Rules, &c.
			refused this, then he should be struck seven times, that it might be accomplished which was written in their law: *I will punish you sevenfold, lifting up myself against you.* "The bishops approved of this, the duke added it, and the king confirmed it."
886	Châlons.	9 bishops and a chancellor.	This council confirmed the privileges of many churches.
886	Near Port Nimes.	19 bishops.	Theodard, archbishop of Narbonne, held this council against Selva, a Spanish clerk, who had ordained himself archbishop of Tarragona contrary to the canons, and had ordained, in spite of Theodard, Eumiza to be bishop of Gerona; they were both deposed, and their episcopal vestments torn off them; they had the rings taken from their fingers, and their pastoral staffs broken over their heads.
886	Cologne.	5 bishops, 4 abbots, some clerks, and some of the laity.	This council made many canons against those who took possession of church property, those who oppressed the poor, and those who contracted forbidden marriages.
888	Saint-Maurice.	Bishops and grandees.	This council elected for king of Transjuran Burgundy, and crowned Rodolph, the son of Conrad the Second.
888	Mayence.	The archbishop of Mayence, of Cologne, of Trèves, and their suffragans.	This council was held the first year of the reign of Arnold, with the object of reforming the discipline, and repairing the disorders occasioned by the invasions of the Normans. *Rules.*—The council forbids that for the future the priests should have any women in their house, even their own sister, on account of the disorders resulting therefrom. It forbids that a clerk of an inferior order should accuse a clerk of an order superior to his own; it regulates how many witnesses should be required for judgment: for a bishop, 72; a priest-cardinal, 40; a deacon-cardinal, of Rome, 26; a sub-deacon, an acolyte, 7. That the witnesses should be men of good repute, having wife and children. This canon is taken from the council of Rome.

Date.	Place.	Present.	Object of the Council, Rules, &c.
			That the witnesses should be at least fourteen years of age.
888	Metz.	4 bishops of Belgium, 1 abbot, clerks, laity.	This council ordered a fast of three days and solemn prayers, to obtain peace and the retreat of the Normans. *Rules.*—That no lord shall receive anything of the tithes of his church, and that the priest who serves the church shall take them wholly for the divine office. That a priest shall have only one church; unless his own have been joined from all antiquity to a chapel which may not be separated from it.
889	Saint Jangoul.	4 bishops, abbots, 6 counts.	This assembly (*placitum*) was occupied by the order of the queen Ermengarde, widow of Boson, with a complaint of the monks of Guiny against a certain Bernard, who had seized some of their property
890	Valence.	Bishops and grandees of the kingdom of Arles.	This council made Louis, son of Boson, king.
890	Worms.	The archbishop of Reims, his suffragans, the archbishops of Cologne and Hamburg, many neighbouring bishops.	This council occupied itself with the quarrel of the archbishops of Cologne and Hamburg, who were disputing for the church of Bremen. It was held by order of the pope Formosus.
891	Mehun-sur-Loire.	16 bishops.	This council decided, that no one should be elected abbot of St. Pierre de Sens but by the brethren.
892	Vienne.	The bishops of the kingdom of Arles, 2 legates.	*Rules.* — Let laymen who have killed, mutilated, maimed, dishonoured a priest, do penance, and seek to amend themselves. That no one possess himself fraudulently

Date.	Place.	Present.	Object of the Council, Rules, &c.
			of the alms of a dying or sick bishop or priest. That laymen neither give or dispose of churches without the consent of the bishops on which they are dependent, and that they exact no tribute, under form of gift, of priests, at their entry upon churches; that they extort from them nothing by violence.
893	Reims.	... ...	Foulques, archbishop of Reims, crowned in this council Chailes le Simple, competitor of Eudes.
894	Châlons.	4 bishops.	This council admits to the proof of the communion a priest accused of having poisoned the bishop of Autun.
895	Tribur.	22 bishops.	This council, composed almost entirely of German bishops, occupied itself with ecclesiastical reform, by order of king Arnould. *Rules.*—That the Wehrgeld, given for the death of a priest, be divided into three parts—one for the church, the other for his bishop, the third for his parents. It is a sacrilege, calling for penance, to enter a church with a sword unsheathed. If a bishop in his progress has fixed for the canonical assembly the same day that the count, wittingly or unwittingly, has fixed upon for holding his court, let all, including the count himself, leave the court to attend the bishop's assembly; but if the bishop in his own town and the count have named the same day for their respective assembly, let him who first named the day have the preference, always saving the dignity and power of the bishop. Any priest who, even under compulsion, has committed homicide, shall be deposed. When necessity requires it, persons may be buried out of the parish appertaining to the cathedral church; in such cases, let the parish be selected in which the person has paid tithe. It is a frightful thing, and hereby interdicted, to claim any money for the ground in which a person is buried. That none of the laity be buried in the churches. That in a quarrel between a lay-

Date.	Place.	Present.	Object of the Council, Rules, &c.
			man and a priest, the layman be interrogated by oath, the priest by the communion, because the priest ought not to swear. In memory of the blessed Peter the Apostle, we honour the holy apostolical seat of Rome, in such manner that this church, mother of the sacerdotal dignity, is for us the mistress of ecclesiastical right. If, then, which may God prevent, some priest working against our ministry, being accused to us of having brought a forged letter from the apostolic seat, or anything that could not thence, that it may be in the power of the bishop to keep him in prison until, by letters or message, he has called upon his apostolic sublimity to explain, by a worthy legate, the rules of the Roman law, and that which we ought to do to conform to it. If a church is the property of many coheritors, let them agree among themselves, that the service of God shall not suffer; but if, in place of this, they do not agree in the choice of a priest, and that quarrels happen between themselves, or between the priests, let the bishop take the relic from the church, shut and seal the door with his seal, in order that they may not celebrate any office until they shall have provided themselves with a priest worthy to take care of the holy place, and procure the salvation of the people of God. The count is not allowed to force any penitent to plead. That whoever has committed adultery with a woman, cannot marry her. If a husband, dishonoured by his wife, wishes to kill her, and she flies to the bishop, he should endeavour to dissuade the husband from his project, and if he does not succeed, he ought not to deliver her up to be killed, but to put her carefully in a place chosen by herself, where she can live safely. If persons who live in adultery make to themselves mutual donations, let it serve for their child, but they shall have nothing in common when they separate. The council makes many other canons re-

Date.	Place.	Present.	Object of the Council, Rules, &c.
			garding illegal marriages, and penitential canons.
Uncertain date.	Nantes.	... ...	This council occupied itself with discipline, We are ignorant of its date; its third and tenth canons are transcribed from the seventh book of the capitularies collected by Benedict Diacre. Sirmond does not think it impossible that the canons belong to the grand council held at Nantes in 658, which Frodoard mentions. We have left them in the place that Labbe assigned to them. *Rules.*—That the priests before celebrating mass, Sundays and fête days, interrogate the people if there is any one from another parish, in spite of his own priest; send him from the mass, and oblige him to go to his own parish: if he finds persons engaged in rancorous quarrels, let him reconcile them. The council excepts from the obligation of attending mass in their parish those who are travelling, or pleading. That the priests be aware that the tithes and offerings are the revenue of the poor and strangers, and that they are not given to them, but only confided to them, and for them to render an ac count thereof to God. The council orders that before making an ordination, the bishop assemble the priests and prudent men, versed in the law of God, and question them on the life, the birth, the country, the age, and education of those who are to be ordained, the place where they have been instructed, if they are learned, if they know the law of the Lord, above all, if they are of the catholic faith. The council occupies itself afterwards with confraternities, confines them to objects which relate to salvation, to offerings, to keeping in repair the church lights, and the monthly prayers, the alms, the funerals, and other pious objects. It recommends, when meetings are necessary, and that a repast follows, it should be modest and frugal, and that all should be orderly. Priests and the laity met in these confraternities. The council complain of women speaking of public affairs.

Date.	Place.	Present.	Object of the Council, Rules, &c.
			at public assemblies, unless with the permission of their bishop, and for their affairs, or commanded by him. The council recommend to the bishops and priests, to strive to abolish the pagan superstitions.
897	Port, in the Nimois.	4 bishops; 8 ecclesiastics.	This council ordered the bishop of Maguelonne to restore to the church of St. John the Baptist the domains that he had awarded to the church of St. Andrew.
		Tenth Century.	
900	Reims.	12 bishops.	This council excommunicated the murderers of the archbishop Foulques.
906	Barcelona.	8 bishops.	Although this council took place in Spain, we give it here because it was composed of suffragans from Narbonne; discussed the rights of this metropolis, and that the following one, upon the same affair, was held in France, and that, at this epoch, the count Vico of Barcelona was a fief of France. This council agitated the question whether the church of Osona, at present, belonged to Narbonne.
907	Saint Tiberi, in the diocese of Agde.	10 bishops.	This council freed the church of Osona from all dependence and service towards the church of Narbonne: Aurnste, archbishop of Narbonne, agreed to it.
909	Jonquieres, diocese of Maguelonne.	11 bishops.	This council gave absolution and benediction to count Suniaire and all his family.
909	Troli, in the Soissonnais.	12 bishops.	This council occupied itself with ecclesiastical reform; it cited frequently the capitularies and decrees of the popes; it finished its session by a profession of its faith, upon advices from Rome that the Greek heresy, regarding the procession of the Holy Spirit, was still alive in the East. *Rules.*—This council complained of the state of the monastic orders; a great number of monasteries have been destroyed by the pagans; in the monasteries of men or

Date.	Place.	Present.	Object of the Council, Rules, &c.
			women dwell lay abbots, with their wives, their children, their soldiers, and their dogs; and if one presents the rules to them, they reply, as Isaiah, " I know not how to read." The council extends to all products the obligation to pay tithe. Some, perhaps, may say, I am not a labourer, I have neither land or flocks for which I can give tithe; let every one know, be he a military man, a merchant, or artisan, that the source from whence he draws his living comes from God, and to him he ought to give tithe. The council attributes to the non-payment of tithes, the devastations of pagans and bad seasons. The council prohibits, according to the capitularies, secret marriages, from which result many disorders, which give birth to the blind, the lame, the deformed, &c.; it is necessary that the priest who performs the marriage interrogate the parties, to ascertain if the woman is a relation of her future husband, or spouse of another, or adulteress. The council requires the oath of seven witnesses to convict a priest of having lived with a woman; if these fail, he can justify himself by his sole oath. The council renews a canon of the council of Valencia, in Spain, which forbids the parents of a bishop dying without a will to take possession of his property before the ordination of his successor, or the consent of the metropolitan, for fear that they possess themselves at the same time of things belonging to the church.
911	Fontaine Couverte, near Narbonne.	... ...	This council occupied itself with a quarrel between the bishops of Urgel and of Pallarie, on a question of boundary.
912	Tours.	The archbishop of Tours and his suffragans.	This council decided that the festival of the translation of the remains of St. Martin should be celebrated. One finds at this epoch, the canons of Gautier, archbishop of Sens: Constitutiones ex concilio Galteri, archiepiscopi Senonensi;

Date.	Place.	Present.	Object of the Council, Rules, &c.
			this appears to indicate that he held a council, but we have no other indications; these canons of discipline are not important.
915	Châlons.	7 bishops.	This council occupied itself with discipline, and received restitution of the goods of the church, which had been usurped by Rodolph, Count of Macon, alarmed with a menace of excommunication.
921	Troli.	... ...	This council gave absolution to Count Erlebald, who had died excommunicated.
922	Coblentz.	8 bishops; many clergy.	This council, at which Charles le Simple and Henry L'Oiseleur were present, made many canons of discipline. *Rules.*—If the laity have chapels, it is against law and reason that they receive tithes and nourish with it their dogs and their mistresses; it is better that the priests should receive it. It is asked, what ought to be done with one who has seduced and sold a Christian; we are of opinion he is guilty of homicide. Let a layman who wishes to give away his property know that he cannot give away the tithes of the church where it is situated; if he does so, the act will be null, and he will be himself under the censure of the church.
923	Place not known, in the Remois.	The archbishop of Reims, and his suffragans.	This council imposed a penance on those who were at the battle of Soissons, between Charles le Simple and king Robert.
924	... ...	Bishops; many counts.	Etienne, bishop of Cambray, received at this council satisfaction from Count Isaac; he gave him absolution.
926	Charlieu.	3 bishops.	This synod restored to the monastery of Charlieu, ten churches which had been taken from it.
927	Troli.	6 bishops.	This council, convoked by order of Count Heribert, whose son aged five years had been elected archbishop of Reims, was held in despite of king Raoul, and admitted to penance

Date.	Place.	Present.	Object of the Council, Rules, &c.
			count Herlnin, who had remarried during the life of his wife.
927	Duisberg.	... ...	This council excommunicated those who had blinded Bruno, bishop of Metz.
932	Erfurt.	13 bishops; many clergy.	This council prohibits calling a Law Court seven days before Christmas, fifteen before Easter, seven before Saint John, in order that all have the facility of going to church to pray. It prohibits imposing extraordinary fasts.
933	Chateau-Thierry.	... ...	This council consecrated the bishop of Beauvais.
935	Fismes.	7 bishops.	This council anathematised those who usurped the goods of the church.
941	Soissons.	The suffragans of the diocese of Reims.	This council decided in favour of Hugues, son of Heribert, against Hartaud, who pretended also to the archbishopric of Reims; the bishops went to Reims and consecrated him there.
942 or 943	Bonn.	22 bishops.	We are ignorant of the positive date of this council, or if two were held consecutively; there is nothing remaining of them.
943	Binden in Germany.	... ...	There is no account of this council.
944	Trenorch, or Tourneux.	7 bishops; many clergy.	Convoked by order of Duke Gilbert; this council decided, that the relics which had been transported from the monastery of Trenorch to that of St. Porcien in Auvergne, should be returned.
947	At Fontaine, diocese of Elne, in Roussillon.	... ...	This council deposed, by order of Pope Agapetus, and restored immediately the bishops of Gerona and Urgel; it granted to the bishop of Elne the highest rank, after the archbishop of Narbonne. (The see of Elne has been since transferred to Perpignan.)
[illegible]	Verdun.	8 bishops; many abbots.	This council adjudged to Artaud the see of Reims.

Lightning Source UK Ltd.
Milton Keynes UK
UKHW011842281118
333023UK00011B/835/P